WHEN MADNESS COMES HOME

WHEN MADNESS COMES HOME

*Help and Hope for the Children, Siblings,
and Partners of the Mentally Ill*

Victoria Secunda

HYPERION
New York

Library of Congress Cataloging-in-Publication Data

Secunda, Victoria.
    When madness comes home : help and hope for the families
of the mentally ill / by Victoria Secunda.—
1st ed.
      p.   cm.
    Includes bibliographical references and index.
    ISBN 0-7868-6171-1
    1. Mentally ill—Family relationships. 2. Adjustment (Psychology)
3. Family psychotherapy. I. Title.
RC455.4.F3S42 1997
362.2'0422—dc20 96-28612
                 CIP

Paperback ISBN: 0-7868-8326-X

Designed by Paul Chevannes

FIRST PAPERBACK EDITION

10 9 8 7 6 5 4 3 2 1

For Deborah

CONTENTS

ACKNOWLEDGMENTS

It would have been impossible to write this book without the extraordinary kindness and generosity of many people.

To the siblings, offspring, parents, partners, and consumers (as many people with mental illness prefer to be called) who courageously recounted their experiences in lengthy interviews, I am grateful beyond measure. I found these people, who cover the socioeconomic spectrum, through three sources: an ad I placed in the *Pennysaver*, a publication of classified advertisements in the New York metropolitan area; friends and colleagues who introduced me to interview subjects; and the National Alliance for the Mentally Ill, which graciously ran a notice about my project in its newsletter, *The Advocate*. I can never repay these men and women for their candor, insights, and most of all, their trust. In order to protect their privacy, I have changed all names and identifying characteristics.

I am also deeply indebted to the following researchers, clinicians, and other authorities who gave me interviews and, often, sent me their writings:

Abby Ambinder, Ed.D., family counselor, Aging and Dementia Research Center, department of psychiatry, New York University School of Medicine; Lawrence Balter, Ph.D., professor, department of applied psychology, New York University; Joyce C. Burland, Ph.D., psychologist; Rex Dickens, Siblings and Adult Children Council, NAMI; Kenneth O. Doyle, Ph.D., psychologist, financial planner, and professor, University of Minnesota School of Journalism and Mass Communication; David Elkind, Ph.D., professor of child study, Tufts University; L. Erlenmeyer-Kimling, Ph.D., professor, departments of psychiatry and genetics and development, Columbia University College of Physicians and Surgeons, and acting chief, department of medical genetics, New York State Psychiatric Institute; Jane S. Ferber, M.D., director of the Family Training Center and associate director of psychiatric residency training, Creedmoor Psychiatric Center and assistant clinical professor of psychiatry, Columbia University College of Physicians and Surgeons; Laurie Flynn, executive director, National Alliance for the Mentally Ill; Frederick J. Frese, III, Ph.D., director of psychology, Western Reserve Psychiatric Hospital; Rose Marie Friedrich, R.N., M.A., college of nursing, the University of Iowa; Charles R. Goldman, M.D., professor and director of public psychiatry training program, department of neuropsychiatry and behavioral science, University of South Carolina; Gary Goldsmith, cofounder and past president, National Depressive and Manic Depressive Association; Judy S. Itzkowitz, Ph.D., cofounder, Sibling Information Network; Louise J. Kaplan, Ph.D., psychologist and psychoanalyst; Ronald C. Kessler, Ph.D., professor, department of health care policy, Harvard Medical School; Clarice J. Kestenbaum, M.D., clinical professor of psychiatry and director of training, division of child and adolescent psychiatry, Columbia University College of Physicians and Surgeons; Karen Gail Lewis, Ed.D., A.C.S.W., faculty member, Johns Hopkins University, and family therapist; Sonya Lively, R.N., M.A., college of nursing, University of Iowa; Trudy L. Mason, public relations consultant and New York State Democratic Committeewoman; Donald J. Meyer, director, Sibling Support Project; Demitri Papolos, M.D., assistant professor of psychiatry and codirector, program in behavioral genetics, Albert Einstein College of Medicine/Montefiore Medical Center; Carla Perez, M.D., psychiatrist; David C. Rowe, Ph.D., professor of family studies, University of Arizona; Arnold J. Sameroff, Ph.D., professor of psychology, University of Michigan Center for Human Growth and Development; Jill Bolte Taylor, Ph.D., codirector, Harvard Psychiatry Brain Collection; E. Fuller Torrey, M.D., psychiatrist and guest researcher, National Institute for Mental Health Neuroscience Center at St. Elizabeth's Hospital; and Gerri Zatlow, director and founder, Siblings for Significant Change.

For sending me material about their work, I am indebted to E. Mavis Hetherington, Ph.D., professor of psychology, University of Virginia; Mary Klevjord Rothbart, Ph.D., professor, department of psychology, University of Oregon; and C. Rick Snyder, Ph.D., professor and director, doctoral and postdoctoral clinical psychology programs, University of Kansas. Catherine Johnson, Ph.D., Bruce Sobol, M.D., and Jan Yager, Ph.D., also sent me invaluable material. In addition, I am grateful for the unflagging cooperation of the staff of the Ridgefield Public Library in Connecticut.

For providing leads and sending literature, thanks to Rose M. Armstrong, National Depressive and Manic-Depressive Association; Farrell Fitch, NAMI; Doug Fizel, American Psychological Association; Lee Herring, American Psychological Society; Kara S. Hugglestone, American Association for Marriage and Family Therapy; J. Scott Punk, National Mental Health Association; Diane Swanbrow, University of Michigan; Marilyn Weeks, National Institute of Mental Health; and Melissa Wajnert, NAMI.

Dennis P. Gehr, president of Dennis and Company, a consumer survey research organization in Stamford, Connecticut, crunched the numbers and made sense of my survey data with professionalism and good cheer.

For reading the entire manuscript, providing invaluable comments and criticisms, and advising me through crises large and small, I give special thanks to Dr. Demitri Papolos, Janice Papolos, and Janet H. Gardner.

I am particularly blessed to have Elaine Markson as my literary agent. Through the years, Elaine has given me wise counsel, unstinting support, and friendship. No author ever had a more fervent, able advocate.

Robert Miller, publisher of Hyperion, who acquired this and my previous two books, and Brian DeFiore, editor-in-chief, have been constant sources of encouragement and understanding. Jennifer Barth edited this book with a keen eye and uncommon sensitivity. Lisa Jenner Hudson was the quintessence of efficiency and morale-boosting.

For much-needed hand-holding and guidance during the four years it took to research and write this book, I am grateful to Barbara Coats, Charles and Peggy Cook, Erik and Linda Rodgers Emory, Valerie and Hank Enders, Gloria Hochman, Mary Alice Kellogg, Herb and Shirley

Mitgang, Marlin Potash, Susan Reid, Nancy Rubin, Ann McGovern Scheiner, Eugene Secunda, Ada and Philip Quigg, and David and Jane Bryant Quinn.

As I thundered toward my deadline, Jennifer Wallace helped to nail down wayward footnotes.

To the members of my family who supported me in this undertaking, my gratitude and admiration. Special appreciation goes to my daughter, Jennifer Morrison Heller, whose art, extraordinary insights, and, above all, friendship, fill my cup.

My greatest thanks are reserved for my husband, Shel Secunda, who lovingly abided with and anchored me throughout this project. He took care of hearth and home with uncomplaining patience. He read every word of my manuscript, summoning the bravery to tell me when I had committed literary carnage. He has always sustained me and championed my work. For these and other gifts, I will be forever in his debt.

—VICTORIA SECUNDA, Ridgefield, CT, 1996

PREFACE
FAULT LINES: MY SISTER, MYSELF

There is a photograph in my album taken on a glorious summer afternoon in the 1980s. It's a typical family snapshot—middle-aged brothers and sisters and spouses and their kids frozen in a moment of congenial reunion. Arms are linked, or rest easily on shoulders or encircle waists; fingers are tightly laced; faces are grinning in collective affection on the sun-washed deck of my sister Deborah's* suburban house. In the center of the photo is Deborah, her face plump with mirth, laughing at a now forgotten witticism—some nimble verbal pratfall of the type that has always been prized in my family, particularly by my brainy sister, who could be counted upon for an appreciative guffaw.

I gaze at the picture today and think of another sun-drenched summer day at Deborah's house a dozen years earlier. That morning her husband had called me—a rare, and therefore possibly urgent, event. In a taut voice, he had said, "Deborah is having a breakdown. She has to be admitted to the hospital, and they're expecting her. She knows she needs to go, but she won't get into the car with me—she's convinced I'm going to kill her. Can you come over and take her? I'll follow right behind you."

I raced from my house to Deborah's, forty-five miles away, and found her dependable, devoted husband pacing in the front yard, frantically beckoning me to go immediately into the house. Deborah jerked open the door to admit me, then slammed and bolted it shut. "Don't worry," she whispered, "he can't get in."

I looked at my sister and saw a stranger. Her usually soft brown eyes had deepened into a darker hue; her formerly rounded and yielding body had become razor thin, her necked roped with veins. Exhaustion

---

*not her real name

xiii

had sapped her skin of color. She hadn't eaten or slept in days, not daring to close her eyes, in perpetual motion, on constant agitated alert to the bizarre possibility that she could at any moment be murdered by her life's partner. And now she was darting from room to room, feverishly locking windows, trying to keep her "killer" at bay.

Her raw terror engulfed me. I knew that she could, in a split second, look at me and "see" another predator—her sister as assassin. Deborah's paranoia fueled my own, our mutual dread fired in very different cauldrons. She feared she'd be attacked by her husband; I feared I'd be attacked by her.

As she ricocheted through the house I followed in her wake and, when she wasn't looking, quietly unlocked each window, unbolted each door. I slipped into the kitchen to remove sharp knives from their tidy drawers and hide them in the oven. I planned an exit route in case she suddenly turned on me.

It was unthinkable. I was preparing an escape from my own big sister who, when I was a child, had patiently taught me how to tie my shoelaces and jump rope double Dutch and play hopscotch and balance a book on my head. My sister, whom I had watched, awed, as she preened for her high school senior prom, and who later, when she was away at college, had invited me to visit because I missed her so. My sister who, after my own college graduation, had let me languish on her couch for six weeks as I lamented my impending adulthood.

The same sister stood before me now, a wild thing, her contorted imaginings coming from a place I did not know, could not reach. It wasn't really Deborah. I couldn't grasp it, couldn't bear it. She was an alien. A desperate, dangerous imposter. My gentle sister was gone and a terrifying stand-in had taken her place.

Feigning composure, I coaxed Deborah out of the house and into my car, which I'd hastily parked in the driveway. Her husband was seated in his car, the motor running, out by the curb. "See? He's too far away to get you," I said, trying to reassure her that it was safe, she was safe from him, she was safe with me.

I buckled Deborah into the seat belt, backed down onto the street and, with my brother-in-law trailing far behind so she couldn't see him, led our tiny caravan to the hospital, a half hour—an eternity—away.

I made mindless small talk with my not-sister, trying to distract her, to keep her concentration out there, not in here, not on me, not on us, but on a neutral zone of inanities. She responded with a cascade of nonsensical words, a soliloquy of disconnection. She announced every bumper sticker, every street sign, every house number, every billboard that slid into her view, a nonstop jumble that drummed an odd cadence to this melancholy journey.

Gripping the steering wheel, I tried to soothe her by softly repeating the disjointed words that burst out of her like buckshot, reframing them into a calming incantation. And all the while I furtively glanced into my rearview mirror to make sure her husband was still following us—he was separated from us by a truck, continuing to keep a discreet distance—and prayed that Deborah wouldn't suddenly punch open the door at a stop light and run.

When at last we reached the hospital parking lot, my brother-in-law waiting a half block away, I took Deborah's arm and eased her out of the car and into the dizzying summer heat. Hand in hand we walked up the marble hospital steps and were embraced by the cool, hushed semidarkness of the lobby, where a nurse stood by a desk with forms Deborah was to fill out.

Suddenly Deborah recoiled, pushing backward against me in a rush of panicky awareness of where she was and what she was here to do: Commit herself to a mental ward. A psychic lockup.

"It's okay," I crooned, "it's going to be fine, I'll stay with you as long as you like," at the same time gently prodding her stiffened body in the direction of the papers, inching her toward her ticket in and my visa out. A sour mixture of deliverance and remorse rose in my throat. I wondered if I was doing the right thing. My heart breaking, I felt I was betraying her utterly.

Her lips formed an angry line as she picked up a pen and then stood motionless, staring at the papers, her hand paralyzed in midair. "Just sign," I pleaded, stroking her arm. "These people will help you. You can get some rest here and no one will hurt you. It's only temporary. You'll be out soon—six weeks, tops. *Sign.*"

At last she lowered her trembling hand and slowly filled in her name on the damning document, one painful letter at a time, like a first-grader practicing the alphabet. I breathed a sigh of guilty relief. She was in. Someone else could take over. Someone who knew how to repair broken minds. Someone who could bring my sister back.

Two days later, the drugs had washed the demons from her body, replacing them with an eerie serenity, and I was allowed to visit her. We sat opposite one another at a table in the dining room of the ward shared by other patients and their visitors.

I had seen Deborah like this before. Well, not exactly like this. The other times, she was already in the hospital—another one, a former estate, its guests mostly rich kids—groggily docile from her medications. Or she was at home and off her meds, translating for me the coded messages that were being beamed at her through the television set, outraged that she was being "talked about" by news commentators. "Hear that?" she'd say. "Did you hear what they said?" I wanted to say yes, but of course I hadn't heard anything of the kind. I said nothing because I didn't know what else to do.

Yet never during any of those earlier episodes and hospitalizations, which began when she was in her early thirties, had I felt *imperiled*. Usually they were triggered by her decision to forgo the despised drugs, which made her feel lousy. She'd start to unravel. Her mind would cave in. She'd try to kill herself—swallowing shampoo, cutting her wrists, overdosing on pills. Once she was back on her medications, she'd return to her prestigious job, pick up her active life, and things would be normal again.

This time was different. This time, she was not only deranged, but dangerous, scaring me out of my wits. This time, she was in the cheerless ward of a hospital that had all the amenities of a bus station. This time, I wasn't sure she'd recover. And this time, I was—or so it felt—my sister's executioner.

Now there was no avoiding the terrible truth of my sister's condition. I knew—I took it all the way in—once and for all: My sister, my genetic and generational partner, could lose her mind. Schizophrenia, manic-depression, chronic depression with paranoid features, take your pick, over the years she'd worn all those labels, and I hadn't really understood what they meant. None of them had sunk in. Until now. My sister had broken apart, and if it could happen to her, that meant it could happen to me. If not to me, perhaps—horrible, please, no—to my seven-year-old daughter.

It is impossible to exaggerate the feeling of calamity, the firestorm of colliding emotions, that I experienced with this awful awareness. I wanted to be anywhere but here. All around me were inmates young and old in rumpled bathrobes, shuffling along the bare corridors, or sitting, mute and slack-jawed, staring at nothing. I felt lost and frightened and helpless and stupid, a traveler in another country where I did not know the language or laws or landmarks.

Something inside me snapped as the reality of my sister's madness and its implications took up permanent residence both in my disbelieving mind and in my relationship to her. Mental illness became, that day, the invisible, uninvited third party in what had previously been a sibship of two. And with this phantom presence, my calculus of our family and my sense of safety in the world collapsed.

As Deborah lit one of an endless stream of cigarettes, I poured us each a cup of coffee and surveyed her expressionless face, trying to gauge who or what was behind it. Expelling a cloud of smoke, she fixed me with an even gaze and quietly said:

"Do you think I'm crazy?"

"Oh, God," I blurted, laughing giddily and raking my hair with my fingers, the way parents do when a child asks an important question and they stall for time, trying to formulate an important answer, grasping for just the right words. Her question stunned me. It was the first time she had ever asked my opinion of her, had ever invited me to pass judgment. I felt that everything between us rode on my response.

"Sometimes," I carefully replied. "Not all the time. But sometimes."

The truth. But not too much in this, the most honest, unguarded moment we'd ever had with one another. I did not want to bruise what had over the years gradually become an increasingly tentative bond. I wanted to say something that might knit us together in unconditional love and acceptance. Something that might heal our connection. Here. In a psych ward.

As I watched her mulling over my words in her medicated mind, I ached with questions:

Why her, and not me? We both had had an inordinate amount of distress and confusion in our childhoods, enough to undermine anyone's sanity. For one thing, my mother and father, between them, had been married a total of seven times, producing from their various unions five children and the attendant unwieldiness of divided loyalties. In addition, my parents were alcoholics. Their drinking tended to unleash in my mother a torrent of harsh criticism and in my father an incestuous bent. As the primary target of both, I always figured that I would be the child who cracked up. It was the perfect recipe for madness.

Was the fact that I had not broken down been because Deborah and I simply experienced our childhoods differently? She was, after all, several years older. And although we shared the same mother and grew up in the same house, we had different fathers. So we are half sisters. (For the record, both my parents and her father are deceased.)

Moreover, Deborah and I were born temperamental opposites. She was introverted and exasperatingly private, sharing no secrets, revealing no weaknesses; I was wildly extroverted and needy, seldom having an unexpressed thought, currying favor and spilling my guts with a gusto that made her wince. Where she was restrained and passive, I was eager and curious; where she was placid understatement, I was impulsive bombast.

Surely the cause of her illness was more than just stylistic differences. Did she perhaps have different fault lines—separate pressures and traumas in childhood—from mine? As the eldest child still living at home, Deborah had borne the brunt of my parents' storms, becoming their calm center. She was the steadying force, the prematurely dependable diplomat, the stoic peacemaker. She was surrogate parent to her siblings and to our mother during my parents' divorce, defending her to us even as she hid the liquor bottles. "You're exaggerating," Deborah would say whenever I complained about my mother or father.

If my sister had troubles of her own, or felt as shaky as I did, she gave no clue. By the time she hit her teens, she spent less and less time at home, growing up and away from me, freed at last from baby-sitting and troubleshooting, weary, no doubt, of the weight of being the perfect, loyal, responsible child. She was out the door to high school, to the library, on dates, to her friends' houses, her father's place on weekends, to college, and finally, marriage. Gone, her inner world hidden; sweet, but distant. Inscrutable. The last person on this earth, I would have thought, ever to crash.

Might her illness, then, be biochemical? I fervently wanted to blame our mother for Deborah's mental meltdown, but obviously I couldn't; I was, arguably, "normal," a veteran of centuries of therapy but still standing, living evidence that childhood environment doesn't explain everything.

Maybe genetics could. Our maternal grandfather had as a young man been shipped to Europe for a "rest cure" every now and again to recover from what we later decided was depression. His black moods echoed in each of his grandchildren. Deborah might have received a surfeit of rogue genes that shoved her into the psychological abyss, leaving the rest of us clinging just short of it.

Another possible explanation for her illness was that her siblings had made things worse for her, piling on more stress than we knew or she could bear. Had I—this was my mother's theory—led the pack by somehow saying or doing things over the years which damaged her irreparably?

Or was her illness in fact her *sanctuary*—my theory—the price of her family peacemaking, the sonic boom of her childhood? A socially acceptable, blame-free, walled retreat where no one could make demands upon her or harm her or judge her? Did madness provide for her a place to withdraw to and be let alone when the world became too much for her?

All these theories and ponderings congealed into one overarching question: *Could her illness have been prevented*, or at least diminished, if we'd had loving, wise parents capable of providing us with stability and love and encouragement?

I was unable to get answers from her that day at the hospital. With the sole exception of asking me what I thought about her mental state, she never followed up with another question or invitation to talk about it. The subject, as with so many sensitive subjects having to do with the past, was closed.

Although she recovered fully from that terrible episode—it was, interestingly, the last time she was in the hospital, and after it, she thrived—the line between us had been indelibly drawn by her illness and my recognition of it. I was not about to cross it again; I did not want to do anything to upset her now painfully apparent fragility. If I had to *know* why she had mental illness, I was on my own; I would have to ask someone else.

Such questions are the genesis of this book. Unlike my sister, I have never been able to let well enough alone. The insatiable journalist in me has always craved more facts, explanation, interpretation, meaning, resolution.

In writing *When You and Your Mother Can't Be Friends*, I was trying to understand how it is that some mothers and daughters, the closest of kin, could be anathema to one another. And in writing *Women and Their Fathers*, I wanted to find out what it's like to have a loving, dependable father who never leaves and never takes unfair advantage.

With this book, I wanted to know how that most common, confounding, and terrifying of ailments—mental illness—affects family ties and each member's sense of self. I needed to try to untangle the thorny connections between cause and effect, to find out where family harmony—or mayhem—ends and madness begins, and the impact of one on the other. I had to discover why one of my siblings cracked open and the rest of us were still more or less intact.

Most of all I wanted to find out what had happened to Deborah, not least because my other siblings and I—and our children—might also be at risk of breaking down. We would need to take measures to recognize mental illness, and have some sense of how to manage it. Perhaps my research would be useful to other siblings and children of the mentally ill and help them to feel less alone, less perplexed, and less frightened.

I knew, going into this project, that Deborah would want no part of it. At the same time, I could not, as an ethical matter, write the book without at least telling her about it, and also about my desire to discuss her briefly and anonymously in a preface. She was, after all, its inspiration.

In short, I needed her approval in order to proceed. And so, during one of our annual birthday lunches together, I discussed the project and its title with her. To say that I was skittish about broaching the subject does not begin to describe my anxiety about her reaction, not so much because of her illness but because I still, and forever, wanted her goodwill.

With pounding heart and feathery voice, I began, "Remember that time years ago when you asked me if I thought you were crazy? I've had a lot of time to think about it. Now I think that all of us in the family have a touch of madness. I'm trying to find out why you have a diagnosable medical condition that can be treated with drugs, and I get to be just plain neurotic, a lifer in therapy. It could easily have gone the other way."

Deborah listened intently—she was always the family intellectual— as I went on to say that while her illness and our relationship motivated me to write the book, neither she nor I would be its focus. Primarily it would be about how other siblings, as well as children and partners, have dealt with mental illness in their families, and what the effects have been on their connections to one another and on their separate identities.

Finally I put it to her: "Would any of this be a problem for you?"

She thought about it for a long while. And then, to her everlasting credit and to my immense surprise and relief—I nearly wept—she replied that it would not, providing I protected her and her family's privacy. (I have kept my end of the bargain by excluding all identifying characteristics.)

This was among my sister's more courageous moments. Perhaps because she had endured so much, both as a child and as an adult, she was beyond caring what other people might think. Maybe she wryly chalked it up to another of her kid sister's unseemly and altogether too personally revealing literary displays—yet another example of my inability to resist the spotlight. Quite possibly, she was stronger than I gave her credit for. I do know that she considered the subject of families of the mentally ill to be important. In any case, she raised not a single objection.

The result is this book, which for me has been the bridge back to my sister. Through my research, I have arrived at a better understanding and admiration of her. I've been able to accept her as she is and to recognize her need *not* to know, not to rouse the past.

Most of all, I have reached a deeper appreciation for who each of us is: one who from time to time retreats into an alien, unreachable world, cocooned from certain too harsh realities, the other unable to leave them alone.

With love, I dedicate this book to Deborah.

INTRODUCTION

Expert Witnesses: The Unique Authority and Traumas of Family Members

Telling someone that there's mental illness in your family, and watching the reaction, is not for the fainthearted. Such a revelation is bound to make almost any listener a bit uneasy.

First they blink, momentarily stunned as they try to absorb this unsettling disclosure, quickly scanning the landscape of memory to find a parallel kinship, some similar family lore to contribute to the subject, if only to be polite.

Lacking a corresponding connection, they then scout the wider horizon for common ground. Maybe they once had a classmate who cracked up and was sent away, never to be heard from again. Perhaps they've encountered the homeless mentally ill on their way to work, stepping over or around the disheveled human forms that slumber on subway grates or slump, muttering, in doorways.

More often, the uninitiated glean their information from lurid tele-

1

vision bulletins: "Man escapes hospital for the criminally insane, shoots five—film at eleven." Or from graphic newspaper headlines: "Nude Woman Found Wandering on Interstate, Says She's God."

Unless they've had firsthand, day-to-day experience with mental illness, it's a conversation killer to say that you are a veteran of such devastation. Most people don't really *get it*. Why should they? In general, the scant knowledge they do have is, at best, grotesquely distorted, at worst, just plain inaccurate.

Mental illness isn't something you can actually see or touch—it's an invisible disability. Victims of brain disorders *look* normal, at least physically—no wheelchairs, hearing aids, or white canes betray their inner torment. The only thing visible about mental illness is its symptoms—particularly alarming when untreated—which to many people aren't a manifestation of "illness" at all but, instead, indicate a lack of will, a defective moral compass, or a dearth of family values.

Compounding the problem is that unlike cancer, alcoholism, and AIDS—all of which have come out of the closet and into the public ken—mental illness is the last taboo, shrouded in stigma and fear; it costs people their jobs, their credibility, and, in some cultures, their chances of ever getting married.

And so, when you come clean about your mentally disturbed relative, most people, with fidgety, fumbling puzzlement, will say, "How awful. I'm so sorry. But thank God you're okay, right?" and drift on to another subject.

Unless, of course, the person you tell *does* know from dreadful experience what you're talking about. Then, in hushed tones, he or she very likely will wearily sigh, "Me too. I almost never tell anyone, though. Most people can't handle it. It's so hard to explain, I've stopped trying. What a relief it is to talk to someone who understands."

The terrible irony of all this is that mental illness has, in fact, touched the lives of the majority of people. To begin with, over five million American adults have a severe form of mental illness such as manic-depression and schizophrenia. When you add other mental afflictions such as anxiety disorder and substance abuse disorder (addiction often occurs as a result of self-medicating undiagnosed mental illness), the numbers climb: An estimated ten percent of the population suffers some disability from mental illness in any given year. As to lifetime prevalence—meaning, how many times in your life you are likely to have a bout of it—studies show that *half* of all Americans have had at least one episode of a serious, diagnosable psychiatric disorder.

The result is that the total number of people *directly affected* by mental illness is astronomical. Taking the most conservative statistical approach, if 26 million Americans (10 percent) currently have some kind of incapacitating mental disorder, and if each of those citizens has two parents, one sibling, and one child, that means that over *100 million Americans have mental illness in their immediate families.* And that's without counting extended kin and partners.

With such numbers, you'd think that everyone would know the ten warning signs of mental illness, and that there would be universally available treatment and unlimited research dollars to find a cure. Instead, mental illness is hushed up, seldom recognized, and usually untreated, subject to wild stereotypes, fearful speculation, and denial.

Most people don't want to talk about mental illness. They can't fathom that something you can't see or touch can cause you to lose control of your mind, the very core of your selfhood—can make you do or say things that are the stuff of horror novels.

"BUT, THANK GOD, YOU'RE OKAY, RIGHT?"

As hard as it is to explain mental illness, it's even harder to describe what it's like to live with someone who has it, because you may not altogether be able to explain it even to yourself. For when mental illness comes home, so too does stigma, and with it, disbelief, misinformation, and frequently, chaos—especially, and uniquely, for the children and siblings of its most severely afflicted victims.

Of all the terrible consequences of madness, among the most anguishing is what happens to younger family members who bear repeated, traumatic witness to it. They are the least likely to be identified, or to identify themselves, as in serious turmoil and in crucial need of help. If and when they are considered, it's generally in terms of how they can be useful to *others*—specifically, their mentally ill relative.

In the best of circumstances, the last thing these young people want to do is cause their parents one more ounce of trouble. Most parents, as they watch their finances, energies, and dreams evaporate, are stretched to the breaking point in trying to get help for the ill relative. In the worst of circumstances, either the afflicted person refuses treatment or the family itself cannot acknowledge that there's anything wrong.

Either way, the ripple effects on the identities of these young witnesses can be devastating, accumulating one injury at a time. These effects begin like a tiny, almost imperceptible crack in a window, which slowly and ineluctibly produces other cracks, steadily dividing and subdividing until they become a fragile mosaic of wounds. The structure is still whole—but only barely.

IDENTIFYING THE PROBLEM: RIPPLE EFFECTS

Imagine what it's like to be a child whose profoundly depressed mother does not respond at all to a simple "Look what I did in school today," or who suddenly switches moods, talking nonstop nonsense for thirty-six hours, and then disappears for months because she has to be hospitalized.

Imagine what it's like to be told by your father, before he goes to work each day, to keep an eye on your potentially suicidal mother when you get home from school—but he is so preoccupied that he never really explains what is going on, never asks how *you* are doing, and neither does anyone else.

Imagine what it's like to have your mother, who has schizophrenia but won't take her pills, suddenly come thundering into your room to scream at you for sassing her, when in reality it's the voices in her head that are taunting her.

Imagine what it's like to be teased at the bus stop by kids who shout, "You live in a booby hatch," or to have friends who aren't allowed to play at your house because your otherwise gentle and loving father, during a relapse, was once carried, raving, into a police car.

Imagine that your psychopathic brother sexually molested you for years, but you never told your parents because they'd already been through so much with him—being lied to and bullied and unable to persuade him to see a psychiatrist and feeling like utter failures—that it would destroy them.

Imagine having your beloved brother one day make captain of the debating team and the next day, out of the blue, beat you up and trash your room because, he says, the CIA is inserting thoughts into his brain; and after that day your parents don't do anything to stop it from happening again because he'll "outgrow it" or he's "fallen in with a bad crowd."

Imagine having an older sister, who is getting her doctorate in graduate school, steal your parents' credit cards during a visit home and spend thousands of dollars because, you later discover, she's in an uncontrollable manic state; the upshot is that your college tuition is gone and there's no way to get it back. But you mustn't hold it against her because she is, after all, "sick."

Sleeper Effects. Now imagine that you are an adult, and you must tell the man or woman you've fallen in love with that you cannot move out of town because you must help look after your mentally ill parent since there's no decent, affordable place where he or she can be cared for. And, by the way, this thing may be genetic, so you're not sure you ought to have children.

Imagine that your manic-depressive sister has gone off her medication and keeps showing up on your doorstep, threatening to kidnap your kids, or writing to all your neighbors saying that *you* are the family lunatic and ought to be put away; the police can't help because she hasn't really *done* anything yet, and anyhow, she says there's nothing wrong with her and the law's on her side because she's got rights.

Imagine what it's like to know that your schizophrenic brother, whom you are closer to than anyone else in the family, is at his worst when he stops answering the phone—that's when he's thinking about killing himself—and you live in another state and you can't get your parents, who live only thirty miles from your brother, to break into his house because "He's just manipulating us again." Only your guess is that this time, it's for real.

Imagine that your parents, who are getting on in years, are in the process of rewriting their wills, and they've asked you to be your ill sibling's conservator. This job may entail receiving as many as forty phone calls a day from the sibling at your office or home; doling out the sibling's inheritance because otherwise it would be blown in a week; hiring detectives because the sibling has disappeared and could be living on the street or lying in the morgue; visiting the sibling in jail because he or she has burned down someone's house. The responsibility provokes a heated debate with your other siblings because you'd much rather they shared this burden and they would much rather not have any part of it.

Imagine what it's like to have your wife inform you that she's had it with your constantly dropping everything and dashing over to your parents' house at all hours because of yet another family crisis. *This* is your family now; your children need you and you've got to choose—your kids or your relatives—and if you choose wrong, she's leaving.

Imagine what it's like to be truly angry about something, and then, *wham*, to clamp a lid on it. Extreme expressions of feelings could cause someone to respond with even *stronger* feelings and maybe assault you; and then the person could be taken away or even commit suicide because you couldn't keep your damn mouth shut. Moreover, if you act anything but "normal" at all times, someone might think you are "crazy" too and lock you up in a mental hospital against your will. So you don't ever allow strong feelings to surface. You close off all emotions, all excess, sealing yourself up in a tomb of numbness.

Finally, imagine yourself daring to suggest that you are a candidate for all manner of stress-induced physical and psychological difficulties. You may have the genetic risk of getting one or another form of mental illness because it's hanging from several branches of your family tree. Or you may be seriously depressed, or have a bleeding ulcer, because your ill relative keeps finding new ways to try to commit suicide. Yet you are dismissed by relatives or by a mental health professional as being "not really sick" but merely among the worried (*very worried*) well, and what have you got to complain about, at least you're not insane.

If most people imagined or knew such things—all true stories that siblings and children of the mentally ill have told me—they'd have a better idea of what it means to say, "I have mental illness in my family." And they'd also realize that in all likelihood you are anything but "okay."

Siblings and children of the mentally ill are the invisible casualties of an invisible illness. Seldom are they studied or written about by researchers, or helped for themselves alone. The lay literature is top-heavy with books about the problems of parents of the mentally ill. To the extent that the needs of offspring and siblings are also addressed, generally it's in the context of their usefulness as adjuncts to the family-as-treatment team.

Within that context, there is much good news. Mental illness is eminently treatable. Most of its victims are not incapacitated *all the time*. When properly diagnosed and medicated, they are generally able to hold down jobs and participate fully in their families and in society. Moreover, researchers are tantalizingly close to cracking the elusive biogenetic and biochemical codes of mental illness. In the last decade, gigantic advances have been made in the diagnosis, treatment, and understanding of its causes and effects.

The bad news is that all this hard work is slowly but surely being impeded. Because of governmental budget cuts, rigid insurance restrictions, and the closing of many mental health facilities, the numbers of mentally ill people who receive no treatment and have no place to go are skyrocketing.

Siblings and offspring are caught in the fallout. As their parents die, they are being called upon to assume responsibility for their afflicted relatives' care. This is a burden they may be altogether unwilling to take on—depending, among other things, on how the illness was handled early on, the sturdiness of their current family ties, and the depths of their own wounds.

The purpose of this book is to examine what it's like to grow up with or live with someone who has or develops mental illness, and to provide validation, information, help, and hope for its *other* victims, the siblings, children, and partners.

The goal is not to point a censuring finger at the parents of the mentally ill who, for the most part, are already reeling from being blamed for what is primarily a biochemical or genetic vulnerability, and from being buffeted by assorted health care and justice system bureaucracies. It is all these parents can do to hang on to their marriages, jobs, friendships, and the esteem of their other children, and one would not wish to add to their burden.

Nor is the goal to provide a treatise on brain disorders—thousands of books, dating back to the ancients, have explored this riveting subject—although the illnesses will, of course, be discussed.

Rather, the goal is to shine a light of understanding upon those members of the family who, it will be argued, are in many ways as irrevocably changed by mental illness and the stigma surrounding it as are the afflicted themselves, and in as much need of attention, comfort, and guidance. In helping them, we indirectly help their parents and the mentally ill as well.

The best way to fight stigma is knowledge. And so, the ultimate purpose of this book is to raise public awareness *by bearing witness to the witnesses themselves.* The book will describe the experiences of siblings and offspring, and their unique knowledge of the myths and facts of mental illness. It will cover what they wish could have been done differently and what they have gained from their experience. It will explore their often ambivalent attachments to one or more family members. In particular, this book will chronicle the harrowing price that these witnesses have paid for being normal.

This book is not about the sick. It is about and for the arguably well, the uneasy, uncertain, and fragile survivors.

I interviewed seventy-five siblings and offspring of the mentally ill, all but one (a teenager) between twenty-three and seventy-four years of age and spanning the socioeconomic spectrum. In order to gain a wider perspective on their stories, I also interviewed a dozen parents of mentally ill offspring, fifteen spouses or live-in partners, and fifteen "consumers," as people with brain disorders often prefer to be called. All the consumers have been hospitalized at least once, and are faithfully adhering to their treatment plans. Some are totally disabled and receive government disability benefits; others function superbly in the professions, the arts, and the mental health system; several are married and have children.

In some cases, whole families volunteered for study, allowing me to observe the impact of mental illness from the perspective of each member, including the consumer, and its effects on their relationships to one another. In other instances, I talked to pairs of siblings—one a consumer, the other not. In still other cases I interviewed consumers with their partners or spouses.

I also read countless books and studies; talked to leading researchers, clinicians, policy makers, legal scholars, prison officials, and financial planners; interviewed directors of support networks for siblings of people with special needs. Finally, I attended the national convention of NAMI—the National Alliance for the Mentally Ill—at which many of the nation's most distinguished scientists shared their latest findings with families of the psychiatrically impaired, who comprise NAMI's membership.

From these interviews, and over a period of three years of research, I was able to gain insights and knowledge that were unavailable to me when my sister became sick over thirty years ago, and which are still unknown by most people whether or not they have an afflicted relative.

In talking to siblings and offspring of the mentally ill, certain themes and key issues emerged, among them:

Fear of Breaking Down. The most pervasive legacy that looms over the lives of the siblings and offspring is the possibility that they, too, will become mentally unhinged. "Anniversary reactions" punctuate their calendars—five, or twenty-five, years from now, I'll be the same age my relative was when he or she got sick. Family members constantly monitor themselves for signs of madness: If I have a fantasy, might it really be a hallucination? If I lose my temper, will I ever be able to stop? Am I a psychological time bomb?

Arrested Development. Age is a crucial variable in how the siblings and children are affected by mental illness. Madness truncates the maturing process by freezing the relationship with the ill relative at the moment illness strikes. For example, if a brother or sister suddenly develops schizophrenia, normal sibling rivalry grinds to a halt; but so, too, does healthy competition which spurs growth. Similarly, if a mother becomes chronically depressed, the development of a child's separate identity stalls, since the starting point of healthy attachment either ruptures or was incomplete to begin with.

A Skewed Sense of What's "Normal." Siblings and children often lose the sense of where they end and the ill relative begins; boundaries wither because what is reflected back to a child by the ill relative often makes no sense. You cry, they laugh. You tell a harmless joke, they think you're plotting against them. Moreover, the line between what's acceptable behavior and what isn't becomes blurred. For example, animosity in someone else's family could be an infrequent and punishable offense. However, because it is a symptom of many mental illnesses, hostility may be habitual and unchecked in yours. This distorted sense of "normal" can later infect intimate relationships; irritability, even verbal abuse, raises no red flags.

Deferred Dreams. Many siblings told me that they took scant pleasure in their successes as they grew up because their talents stood in such heartbreaking contrast to a sick sibling's struggles. Often, their parents urged them to keep their achievements hidden so as not to make the afflicted sibling feel discouraged. In addition, siblings and children frequently were unable to go to their college of choice, or had to quit school, because the family's savings had been spent on psychiatric treatment, or because they were needed at home. Consequently, many of them postponed, and sometimes actively sabotaged, their dreams.

Fear of Failure. Other junior family members felt that they had to take up the banner of the fallen relative by being perfect, getting straight As in school and becoming high achievers in adulthood—in a sense, succeeding for two. Many of them, unable to measure how much is enough, rise to every challenge and opportunity, and are vulnerable to burnout or breakdown.

Guilt. One way in which children make sense of tragedy is to feel that they caused it. Had they done something differently—something *more*—disaster could have been averted. Long after they are grown, siblings and offspring are often suffused with guilt: Am I bad because I survived? Will I drive my partner, or my kids, crazy? Do I have any right to be happy?

The Grief That Never Ends. Mental illness is a kind of living death. A psychotic episode can obliterate, or utterly alter, the ill person's personality. At such times the person seems uncanny—both there and not there, alive in body but dead in spirit, or animated by frightening, unseen forces. In addition, diagnoses and treatments are slippery, shifting constantly. A medication will work, like magic, for a time and then suddenly lose its effect. Such personality death creates a grief that has no true resolution—it is instead a permanent, painful ''maybe.''

Dual Identities. Many respondents said that they had always led double lives—one inside the family, another outside—each compromising the other. In early life they often tried to disappear at home, rocking no familial boats, but at school attempted to be ''normal.'' When they were grown, they endeavored to be like other adults, embarking on careers and starting families of their own. But they knew that at any time the phone could ring and they would be recruited to deal with the latest crisis. They felt suspended between two worlds: their carefully constructed separate lives, and the illness that beckoned them back home.

Difficulty with Intimacy. Most siblings and offspring, later in life, have trouble allowing themselves to become close to friends, lovers, even therapists. Trust comes hard, since while growing up, things were seldom what they seemed to be; everything could be fine in the morning and demolished by noon. Intimacy has already been so risky— and defenses against pain so solidly crafted—that healthy attachment may not be among their skills.

Fear of Having Children. This issue is second in weight only to becoming ill oneself. Over *half* of my sample do not have children. They are afraid either of passing on a "bad" gene, or behaving toward their children as their ill relative behaved toward them.

Setting Limits. Many family members are all but literally held hostage by mental illness. They are unable to turn away afflicted kin who invade their lives and sometimes threaten to kill themselves if they aren't allowed to do whatever they want—such as move in, yell and scream, borrow money, or destroy property.

Isolation and Loss. Siblings and offspring lose more than just a "normal" family. Extended family frequently retreat, leaving dollops of uninformed opinion and judgment in their wake—insisting, for instance, that the "crazy" relative, who might be in full remission, be excluded from weddings and holiday gatherings. Young family members must grow up quickly, and often alone, becoming champions of their ill relative and uncomplaining copers.

Unfinished Family Business. The greatest predictor of whether or not mental illness will unite or divide a family is the tenor of their relationships before the disorder surfaced. For some siblings and offspring, mental illness was the least of their difficulties—it had been preceded by years of family estrangements or abusiveness. Mental illness simply compounded an already bad situation.

Searching for Meaning. Painful ethical and moral questions bedevil nearly everyone I interviewed. Why my brother and not me? Does biology explain everything, and if so, what of prevention? Are dysfunctional parents off the hook? Alternatively, are loving parents being punished by an uncaring God? What are surviving children to do with their anger and sorrow? Are they automatically *obliged* to take over when their parents are gone? As for partners and spouses—especially where children are involved—whose needs should come first? Are the moral imperatives of romantic choice the same as those of biological kinship? And what of the mentally ill themselves? Are they not human beings first, capable of being reached, touched, inspired, believed in—entitled to the respect of being held accountable? Most important, can any good come out of all this?

Patterns of Reaction. Depending, among other things, on their temperaments, age, family socioeconomic status, and the severity of the illness, siblings and children fall into certain general behavioral categories and family roles. These roles, which sometimes are exchanged or overlap, include:

• *The Custodian,* who cannot stop giving, continually being called upon during crises large and small;

• *The Bystander,* who either tries to stay out of sight or feels torn by the ability to see everyone's side;

• *The Adversary,* who loudly takes issue with parental decisions, or bickers constantly with siblings, or is in chronic trouble at school or elsewhere.

FINDING SOLUTIONS

As bleak as all this may seem, there is a great deal that siblings and offspring can do about their dilemmas. This book will help them sift through their experiences and arrange them in manageable portions; they can then begin the process of healing. Most survivors already have the skills to help everyone else in the family. Now they can use those skills to empower themselves.

• They can identify the difference between family estrangements that fester beneath the illness and those that are a result of it;

• They can find the words to repair or build bridges to their family members, or to renegotiate family ties;

• They can learn how to say no to the mentally ill relative, and also to other members of the family;

• They can become aware of differing "set points" for involvement in the illness, and build on them—they can help in a way that is best, at the time, for them;

• They can deal with the varying seasons of mourning, adaptation, acceptance, and eventual readjustment;

- They can evaluate what can be fixed, and relinquish what cannot;
- They can decide when, why, where, with whom, and how to speak up about their own experience;
- They can establish networks of support, including workshops for very young siblings and offspring, and for spouses and partners;
- They can find out where to go for professional help for themselves.

But the greatest hope for junior family members can be found in simply listening to the testimony of other survivors, and then coming out of the closet, as it were, to make mental illness real and knowable rather than a sinister secret.

No one knows more about the subtle workings of mental illness than the siblings and offspring who have lived with it. To be sure, such specialists as psychiatrists and neuroanatomists—to say nothing of police officers, lawyers, and judges—know a lot *about* an afflicted family member. But generally, they know only the diseased part. Most of these authorities, however compassionate and heroic their efforts to treat and to cure, get to escape at the end of the day by going home.

Not so the junior family members, who are seldom off duty and never off guard. Their job is not to unlock the mysteries of molecules and synapses, but, rather, to contain their consequences, and to try to stay connected to the gifts and talents of the people behind the illness.

In talking to these siblings and offspring, I have been impressed more than anything by the ways in which, often from very early childhood, they have grown stronger at the breaking points. These witnesses have much to teach us.

It is to them that this book is addressed, to give them a sense of entitlement, to encourage their belief in themselves, and especially to help them recognize and bind up their own wounds. For only by putting themselves *first* will they at last be able to embrace and fully inhabit their own lives and dreams.

The process begins in the past: looking back at what happens when madness comes home.

PART ONE

BREAKING POINTS:
Hostages of Mental Illness

CHAPTER I

Shattered Families:
When Lightning Strikes

This was not the son we brought up. This was a madman.

—Roberta, 50

Spring is Roberta's favorite time of year. In the dreary final weeks of winter, before she leaves for her teaching job each morning, she peers down expectantly at the patch of barren earth by her front door, looking for signs of life. It's a game she likes to play, watching for tender green shoots that soon will poke up as if by magic, daffodils she herself put in years ago, her miniature field of dreams.

Gardening has been Roberta's passion ever since her three kids were in high school and no longer needed so much of her attention. But in recent years her flower beds have been a tangle of neglect. She hasn't puttered in the soil outside her Connecticut colonial since one particularly fine Saturday in June of 1991. There simply hasn't been time.

That day, she and her husband, John, an accountant, had spent the afternoon preparing for the seasonal shift outdoors—hauling home geraniums from the nursery, dusting off flowerpots, setting out lawn chairs. By sundown, aching exquisitely and in no mood to cook, the couple went out for an early supper, came home, and in seconds fell asleep.

What happened next is every parent's worst fear: "We got the proverbial call in the middle of the night," says Roberta. At 2:00 A.M., the phone rang and John picked it up. Some guy on the other end, claiming to be with the Seattle police, was saying that their twenty-six-year-old son, Matt, was in custody, charged with armed robbery and kidnapping.

"This is a joke, right? Do you realize what time it is?" John blurted groggily, rubbing the sleep from his eyes. His son lives in Portland, he babbled, Matt couldn't have done anything like that, he has a good job, he's a college graduate, he's got an IQ of 140, he's a former Boy Scout, he's a sweet kid who wouldn't hurt a flea. There must be some mistake.

But it wasn't a mistake. For six months, their painfully shy son hadn't been working at all. He was broke and about to be thrown out of his apartment, his utilities already shut off for nonpayment. The "good job" was one of hundreds of lies he'd been telling them because he had trouble concentrating on anything but the weird fantasies that kept piercing his mind.

As Matt later explained it, he kept ruminating about what it would be like to be *really bad*, just once. Like a gangster in the movies. If only he could make a big score and become a writer—his lifelong dream—maybe his parents, who had often been on his case for "laziness," would be proud of him.

His head buzzing with delusions of fame and danger, Matt drove north to Seattle. There, at gunpoint, he held up the cashiers of three small shops. The kidnapping rap was for handcuffing them—"restraint," it's called. He was caught on a fluke. Some cops spotted him making a wrong turn, and when they pulled him over, they noticed his gun on the seat beside him. And now he was looking at a twenty-five-year stretch behind bars.

Getting nailed was a relief, he told me when I flew out to interview him in prison, because at last he could stop pretending. In fact, he said, being locked up was the *best* thing that could have happened. It was the only way he ever would have faced the fact that he had a serious mental illness—"manic-depression," the prison shrink concluded—and he wasn't just the underachieving "family fuckup," trailing a lackluster third behind his brilliant older sisters. Now he had nothing but time to let it all sink in: the enormity of his crimes, the pain he had caused his family, the years of deceit and terror and struggles every day not to let it show, which led to the horrifying night when madness finally brought him down.

Incarceration may have been Matt's salvation, but for his family, it was the gateway to hell. By the time I met his parents in 1993, his bad debts, his lawyers' fees, trips to Seattle to try to get him transferred to a prison psych yard, huge phone bills, and assorted other expenses had cost them over $100,000 and had ended any hope of their ever retiring.

In the two years since his arrest, they hadn't been able to visit their daughters, who live in the Midwest, even missing the birth of their first grandchild. Their evenings revolved around the hours Matt was allowed to call home. Their days were eaten up by battling the legal system, trying to slash through prison red tape, attempting to understand dense psychiatric texts, and praying that their son wouldn't be raped or stabbed, that he could hold on for three more years, when he'd be up for parole and they might get him home and in treatment.

And always they wondered: Why didn't we see this coming early on? Why were we so hard on him? As an ex-con, how will he ever get a decent job? And how will we ever be able to make it up to our daughters, not being there for *them*?

CHAIN REACTION

When mental illness strikes the families of its victims, it's like lightning. Usually it hits the highest point in the family hierarchy first: the parents. That's because disorders of the brain often show up relatively early in life, which puts the parents in charge of finding and paying for appropriate treatment and providing care.

In the case of schizophrenia, for example, the age of onset typically is late adolescence or the early twenties, although there have been reported cases as young as five. Manic-depression can also show up early (although later onsets are common), perhaps in a slightly different developmental form, and can result in suicide attempts as young as age five.

And like lightning, mental illness seems to strike without warning, which makes it difficult to forecast with scientific precision. Psychiatric disorders lurk deep within the victim's brain, waiting for the body to mature and for a buildup of stress to trigger them.

Still, usually, there are warning signs—mood swings, crying jags, apathy, changes in appetite or sleep patterns, attention deficits, rage, hypersensitivity, bizarre thoughts. The trouble is, these are all boilerplate quirks of many teenagers, of many women right after childbirth or during menopause, and of many men in midlife crises.

That's what's so tricky about mental illness. The warning signs can *look* like just plain life. Families are often unaware that a brain disorder is unfolding right in front of them. Until, that is, the symptoms start to make the person act in ways that are completely out of character, such as thinking they're being spied on or hearing things that aren't there, as if possessed by supernatural forces.

Laurie Flynn found out about such things in a massive twist of irony: She had just taken the job of executive director of the National Alliance for the Mentally Ill in 1984 when she herself "lived the NAMI experience," as she puts it. Laurie knew relatively little about brain disorders; she had landed the post primarily because of her considerable motivational and lobbying skills.

The mother of twelve children (seven of them adopted), the child least likely ever to have anything wrong with her mind, or so Laurie thought, was her firstborn daughter, Shannon, then eighteen.

She was the golden girl. You only wanted all your daughters to do this well. She was valedictorian of her class, a National Merit scholar, star of the school play. True, she'd been spending a lot of time in her room, but we just figured she was a little anxious, writing college applications and separating from the family—all within the range of normal.

One day Shannon collapsed in tears in the girls' room at school, but everyone thought it was just stress. Then one night two weeks later, when Laurie came home from work, Shannon was gone and no one knew where she was. For hours, Laurie was on the phone calling the police and all of Shannon's friends, and driving around the neighborhood looking for her. "They were the longest hours of my life," Laurie recalls.

Fifteen miles away, a security guard at an apartment complex noticed Shannon sitting alone in the lobby, and discovered that the Maryland police had a bulletin out for her. By the time Laurie got there, Shannon was catatonic. "It was like she'd left her body—there was nothing behind the eyes. This perfect child had dropped straight down, and had to be hospitalized. And suddenly, I had an understanding of NAMI I would never have had any other way." Laurie continues:

Someone I loved was extraordinarily not right, and I had no idea why or what I could do. I was guilt-ridden that there was something I could have done, didn't see, and terrified that this brilliant, lovely girl's future had blown up, terrified that she'd never get out of the hospital, terrified that the minute she did get out, she'd kill herself. I mean, it was *dreadful*.

Laurie was fortunate because she had access to many of the nation's leading scientists and psychiatric experts. Her daughter, diagnosed and successfully treated for schizoaffective disorder (which, together with other major mental illnesses, will be defined later in this chapter) has since finished college, works full-time, and lives on her own.

In the very long meanwhile, however, Laurie's younger kids worried that they might say something to set Shannon off, or become mentally ill themselves. If "Miss Straight-A-Perfect" could get sick, "Miss B-Student-Not-Perfect" could be next. Plus, it seemed to them that someone had to be really sick to get any attention in the family. Says Laurie:

All of life revolved around "Is Shannon okay?" Your week ran on a very tight schedule. I got up, took a good look at the other kids so I wouldn't think they were crazy, went to work, came home, made a fast dinner, ran to the hospital, came home, went to bed. And I did it all over again the next day. On weekends, we really noticed the person who wasn't there. Everyone in the family would be kind of hanging around, either talking obsessively about Shannon, or not talking about her, because somebody might cry.

The Second Tier. In other cases, mental illness may not appear until later in life. Then it's not always the parents who first become aware of it. Sometimes, it's the victim's children.

Cathy, forty, was an uncommonly intuitive eleven-year-old when she witnessed her mother's first breakdown—as it happens, while her father, a successful attorney, was out of town on business. At five o'clock one morning, her mother, then thirty-seven, shook her awake and said, "You kids have to get up and get dressed quickly. We're going to get into Daddy's van and drive up to the lake. Our neighbor is going to kill your little sister, and we have to get away."

Says Cathy:

I knew instantly that the problem was with my mom. Our neighbors were wonderful people. And her plan was just so irrational—my dad's van had a stick shift and she didn't know how to drive it. She *hated* that van. So I knew she was in pretty bad shape. I tried to calm her down. I told her we could come up with a better plan and that we shouldn't go anywhere until it got light. She was willing to let me take over, thank God. I called my uncle and he came and got us. Later we reached my dad, and he came home and took her to the hospital. They said she had late-onset schizophrenia. We were in shock. No one had ever seen her like this.

David, twenty-nine, was the first member of his family to notice that his father, then sixty, was "acting peculiarly." His dad had always had a moody side, but after he and David's mother divorced three years earlier, he began to withdraw from the world. He took early retirement from his civil service job in Chicago, and wouldn't visit David and his wife, not even after the birth of their son. He had an endless list of limp excuses. He had a "head cold." Or he had to "run errands." Whenever

David called him, his dad would talk about events that had never occurred. And then he stopped answering the phone altogether.

Now David was feeling not simply wounded, but scared. He decided to go over to his father's apartment to suggest that he see a
therapist. When he got there, his father, who had become alarmingly
thin, refused to get professional help. He claimed that everything was
fine, he just had a lot on his mind. Says David:

> At that point I just burst into tears. I said, "Dad, you've been pushing
> me away for months, you don't want any part of my life, you haven't
> even met my son, you're emaciated. Can't you see there's something
> wrong?" My father's voice cracked and he said, "Please, David, no
> doctors." As I left, he picked up the telephone and pointed it at the
> TV, thinking it was the remote. That afternoon, I called a psychiatrist.

The following morning, David and his cousin went over to his
father's place and literally forced him out the door and into a cab. At
David's insistence, his father signed himself into the psychiatric unit
of a nearby hospital and was put on antidepressants. Within two
months, he was recovered and stabilized on medications. He had been
doing silent battle with major depression for thirty years and might
have died, a de facto suicide, had his son not forced the issue.

Born in a Storm. For still other family members, mental illness
doesn't suddenly descend on their lives like a bolt from the blue.
Instead, they are born into it. They spend their childhoods seldom
experiencing anything *but* a relative's mental illness, even if it's not
identified as such. This is particularly true of those children whose
families cannot accept the reality that mental illness has moved in.

Fran, now forty-two, came into the world during the onset of her
mother's severe and chronic manic-depression. Fran never knew her
mother either as mentally healthy or even in remission. Her much
older brother was grown and in the army when she came along, and
it was just Fran and her parents, living a hardscrabble existence on a
small farm in rural Vermont. Fran recalls:

Dad and I simply had to handle it. Mom's first hospitalization in a private facility took all the money, so she would have to be really far gone for him to bring her to the state mental institution. He didn't believe in taking medications, so most of the time she was either catatonic or talking constantly to relatives who were dead. During the day, I'd go to school and my dad would sit with her; when I got home, he'd go out and do chores and I'd stay with her. I don't think she was ever fully aware that I was even in the room. And of course, my dad, being a tight-lipped sort, never talked about it. It's hard for me to describe my feelings about those years—I don't remember feeling anything.

AN ELUSIVE ILLNESS: SOME PRELIMINARY CAVEATS

As these case histories illustrate, mental illness comes in all shapes and degrees of severity, at all ages and in all socio-economic levels. Indeed, some of its victims are historical and artistic legends. Abraham Lincoln, Virginia Woolf, Leo Tolstoy, John Keats, Isaac Newton, Anne Sexton, and Winston Churchill all suffered from disorders such as manic-depression.

In order to understand what it's like to be the child or sibling of such people, famous or otherwise, it's useful to know exactly what mental illness is and is not. But before we plunge into the technical psychiatric thickets—which few but the most committed readers will find riveting, because it's so *complicated*—it's important to cut a preliminary path of caveats.

Stigma. From the outset, the subject is fraught with peril, because the moment the label of mental illness is applied, its primary side effect and complication—stigmatization—sets in.

For the genuinely afflicted person, mental illness presents a devastating catch-22: If you *don't* have a diagnosis, you can't get the right treatment, and then you run the risk of trying to hold yourself together with a cobweb of sanity as a mental hurricane bears down.

Yet if you *are* diagnosed and then treated for mental illness—

which, by the way, has a higher treatment success rate (60 to 80 percent) than heart disease (41 to 52 percent)—you run the risk of becoming a kind of leper, earmarked as contagiously defective.

Diagnostic labels, William James observed a century ago, become "clubs to knock a man down with. Call a man a cad and you have settled his social status. Call him a degenerate, and you've grouped him with the most loathsome specimens of the human race, in spite of the fact that he may be one of its most precious members."

On this score, little has changed. The moment word gets out about your diagnosis, people begin to see you in a wholly new light, as though you were a grenade with the safety pin removed. Current and future employers may fear that you'll go berserk and commit a violent or embarrassing act during business hours; the people closest to you may pull back, thinking you'll explode at the slightest verbal jostle.

Which goes a long way toward explaining why only 20 to 40 percent of Americans with psychiatric disorders get treatment. As Kate Millet writes in *The Loony-Bin Trip*:

> . . . when you come right down to it, whether you were even crazy or not, guilty or innocent, manic or sane as a bedbug—you've been jailed for madness and that doesn't go away. It hangs around in everybody's eyes; it's in the talk you don't hear and in the tones you do. And the shame doesn't go away.

"*Deviance*" and Other Misnomers. Being labeled "mentally ill" has other perils. Let us suppose, for example, that you are a teenager who isn't mentally ill at all but are *considered* to be because you're just different or simply profoundly unhappy.

What we're talking about here is the notion of *deviance*—being sufficiently unlike your peers that people begin to think you're sick in the head and thus congenitally damaged goods. The reality may be that you're perfectly normal. Maybe you're a late bloomer, or slightly eccentric, or a creative sort, living mostly in your mind. Or maybe you're reacting to traumatic events in your childhood by feeling despair, or flunking out of school, or picking fights, or using drugs for solace or escape.

Such young people may have nothing physically wrong—such as faulty genes or inherent biochemical abnormalities—with them. All the same, they could end up being sent to a psychiatric facility by their parents, whether well-meaning or just fed up.

In her disturbing book, *And They Call It Help: The Psychiatric Policing of America's Children*, Louise Armstrong reports that two thirds of the children in private, for-profit psychiatric hospitals were placed there not for severe mental illness but for being social misfits, poor students, or the family problem child. "It is a long way," Armstrong writes, "from a *diagnosable* disturbance to the kind of hellish childhood that produces chronic emotional anguish and perhaps behavior that disturbs society. . . ."

Social control is but one element of the misuse of the term "mental illness." Actual misdiagnosis, where the "illness" stems from the context itself, is another. In these instances, the "deviant" person may be reacting normally to abnormal circumstances.

Psychiatrist Judith Lewis Herman forcefully makes the distinction between inherent pathology and normal adaptive coping in her book *Trauma and Recovery*, in which she describes the psychological damage done to misdiagnosed victims of rape, domestic violence, and other atrocities. When people are held captive by prolonged and inescapable verbal or physical brutality, their brain chemistry automatically prepares them for survival by putting them in perpetual crisis readiness.

This kind of constant vigilance can wreak havoc on the brain and take on a psychological life of its own long after the trauma or captivity have ceased, resulting in lingering survival behaviors—such as numbing or tuning out—that are similar to severe mental illness. "When and if a breakdown occurs," Herman writes, "it can take symptomatic forms that mimic virtually every category of psychiatric disorder. Survivors fear that they are going insane or that they will have to die." (Herman's theoretical paradigm will figure prominently in this book; siblings and offspring are also often held in "captivity" by the actions of their disturbed kin.)

The majority of these survivors are not insane; rather, they are victims of what Herman calls "complex post-traumatic stress disorder." They may be mentally and emotionally anguished, even fragmented and dysfunctional and in desperate need of counseling. Yet often they are mislabeled as schizophrenic or manic-depressive, for example, as though they were flawed to begin with—instead of being seen as admirable for their adaptive mental strengths.

Which is why, as Nancy C. Andreasen, M.D., Ph.D., of the University of Iowa, notes in her book *The Broken Brain,* many researchers avoid the term "disease," which implies a medical model, and prefer the term "disorder," which implies other causes, such as trauma, of mental distress.

Other thorny psychological assumptions can be culturally-driven, further blurring the already fuzzy line between "normal" and "abnormal." For example, in the United States, being sensitive, unaggressive, and easily moved to tears are considered to be normal attributes of women. Thus, the clinically depressed woman who weeps at the drop of a hat and describes her innermost feelings and fears might be seen as merely premenstrual rather than someone in serious need of professional help.

At the same time, physical aggression, risk-taking, even brutality, are considered to be "normal" attributes of men, some of whom pay for their macho behavior in jails. Yet among all prisoners—most of whom, it must be remembered, will one day be released—an estimated one in fourteen is severely mentally ill.

Then there's the matter of people who are truly mentally ill but are thought simply to be undisciplined social parasites. I am speaking, of course, of the homeless, an estimated third of whom have serious brain disorders but cannot get treatment now that they have been "deinstitutionalized"—that is, evicted from psychiatric hospitals and other facilities which increasingly are shutting down.

There's also the matter of being truly mentally ill but receiving *the wrong diagnosis.* Many people are diagnosed and treated for afflictions they don't have—to the detriment of disorders they *do* have—in part because arriving at a proper diagnosis is so difficult. Many disorders have similar symptoms, such as psychosis, which does not mean that the people who suffer from them have the same illness.

Thus, you might have manic-depression but be treated for schizophrenia, which among other things entails the danger of having no relief from your symptoms. As Harrison G. Pope, Jr., and Joseph F. Lipinski, Jr., M.D., point out in their article "Diagnosis in Schizophrenia and Manic-Depressive Illness," lithium helps the majority of people with manic-depression, but people with schizophrenia rarely respond to the drug. Symptoms are not enough to achieve a correct diagnosis; other factors, such as family history and pre-illness functioning, must also be taken into account.

On the other hand, someone might be termed "mentally ill" when he or she is anything but. For instance, in certain quarters, unathletic boys with gentle, artistic dispositions cause all manner of brow-furrowing among parents who assume that such are the characteristics of homosexuality and hence, of psychological pathology. These boys may or may not be gay. The point is that neither sexual orientation nor poetic personalities are symptoms of *mental illness*.

One more clarification is in order: Some medical conditions produce symptoms that *look* like mental illness but that aren't. These diseases include brain tumor, viral encephalitis, temporal lobe epilepsy, cerebral syphilis, multiple sclerosis, Huntington's Disease, AIDS, stroke, thyroid disease, and autism. A medical workup is necessary to rule out such diseases.

Finally, the point must be made that mental illness and wickedness are not synonymous. In recent years, the so-called "Twinkie defense" has been used in courts of law in an attempt to excuse, by virtue of alleged temporary or total insanity, a host of hideous crimes that are the deeds of people who may be morally bankrupt but are seldom mentally diseased. Most abusive parents, political assassins, and spouse batterers do not have diagnosable brain disorders.

For these and other reasons—the most significant of which is to provide a picture of what family members are up against—it is crucial to know the definition of true mental illness. What follows, then, is a crash course in psychiatric disorders, the severest of which afflict the parents and siblings of the people we will meet throughout this book. First we will define the illnesses, then describe how they are treated professionally, and finally, discuss what causes them.

A TRUE DIAGNOSIS: THE ILLNESSES

The most important book on the subject is the *Diagnostic and Statistical Manual of Mental Disorders*, the fourth edition of which was published in 1994 by the American Psychiatric Association. Nearly 900 pages long and the product of the work of 1,000 mental health professionals (as well as extensive field-testing and debate), *DSM-IV* classifies mental disorders and their symptoms as standardized guidelines for the diagnosis, treatment, and study of people with mental illness.

Taking into account considerable overlap of symptoms—and cautiously adding that each classification is far from homogeneous—*DSM-IV* defines "mental disorder" as

> a clinically significant behavioral or psychological syndrome or pattern that occurs in an individual and that is associated with present distress (e.g., a painful symptom) or disability (i.e., impairment in one or more important areas of functioning) or with a significantly increased risk of suffering death, pain, disability, or an important loss of freedom. . . . Whatever its original cause, it must currently be considered a manifestation of a behavioral, psychological, or biological dysfunction in the individual.

Mental illnesses, which in the aggregate affect men and women in equal numbers, have been divided into four general categories, for survey purposes, by Ronald C. Kessler, Ph.D. and his colleagues at the University of Michigan Institute for Social Research. Using Dr. Kessler's categories and statistical findings, as well as *DSM-IV* diagnoses and other sources, here is a brief rundown of the symptoms of major mental disorders and the percentages of Americans who have them. (Note: These symptoms must persist from two weeks to six months, depending on the condition, to qualify as mental illness. For further reading on brain disorders, see Bibliography.)

Affective Disorders. These affect 20 percent of Americans and include major depression and manic-depressive illness, as well as cyclothymia and dysthymia, milder forms of depression. According to Dr. Demitri F. Papolos, M.D., and Janice Papolos in their book *Over-*

coming Depression, such illnesses are considered abnormalities of mood and energy. The emotional highs are called "mania," which can make you feel as though you could live forever without sleep; or that you are the smartest, strongest person alive; or that you can't get enough sex; or that you can do whatever you want with no sense of tomorrow. Mania can cause its victims to be unusually talkative, or to go on lavish spending sprees, or to get involved in fights.

The emotional lows are called "depression," which can make you feel as if you're on the bottom of the ocean where all colors, light, and hope are leeched away (15 percent of people with major depression commit suicide). William Styron, in his book, *Darkness Visible: A Memoir of Madness*, variously describes depression as a "veritable howling tempest in the brain," "an immense and aching solitude," and an "unfocused dread."

People who experience both emotional "poles"—the highs and the lows—have "bipolar illness." According to Kay Redfield Jamison, Ph.D., professor of psychiatry at the Johns Hopkins University School of Medicine and herself diagnosed with manic-depression, this disorder is not a "dementing illness." Most of its sufferers never become chronically insane.

Anxiety Disorders. These include phobia, panic disorder, obsessive-compulsive disorder, and post-traumatic stress disorder and affect 25 percent of Americans. Anyone who's ever broken into a sweat and felt dizziness or chest pains upon entering an airplane (phobia), or who runs back to the house exactly five times to check the stove every time he or she goes out (obsessive-compulsiveness) knows what it feels like to have such disorders.

In evolutionary terms, one would not wish to be entirely anxiety-free. As Edward O. Wilson notes in *On Human Nature*, "[B]etter to crawl away from a cliff, nauseated by fear, than to walk its edge absent-mindedly." But for those too richly endowed with it, anxiety can be crippling. Victims of these disorders, explains Dr. Andreasen, have a surfeit of the "fight or flight" response, which can be chronic and can be triggered by situations that are inherently tame, such as public speaking or even leaving their own homes.

Substance Abuse Disorders. These include alcohol and drug abuse and dependence and affect nearly 27 percent of the population. They are called "diseases" in part because of a possible biogenetically based addictive personality.

Of greater importance is the fact that these disorders frequently occur in tandem with other mental illnesses. Dr. Kessler reports that roughly half of American substance abusers *also* have disorders such as manic-depression, and vice versa. But when asked which came first, the addiction or the brain disorder, *84 percent* of these "dually diagnosed" people say that the symptoms of mental illness preceded their addictions. It is likely that they began using drugs and alcohol to suppress the "howling tempest" of madness and to avoid the stigma of a diagnosis. Studies show that most addicts would rather be called "junkies" than "crazy."

Other Disorders. These include "nonaffective psychosis" (a "summary category," as Dr. Kessler and his colleagues call it, made up of such illnesses as schizophrenia and schizoaffective disorder) and antisocial personality disorder.

Schizophrenia, the most catastrophic mental illness, is said to be an abnormality of thinking because it affects cognitive functioning; it can damage a person's capacity for insight and judgment. This and other forms of nonaffective psychosis are suffered by 0.7 percent of the American population, which may not sound like a lot until you realize that that's *2 million* people.

The symptoms of schizophrenia include inappropriate emotional responses or no emotional response; terrifying visual and auditory hallucinations (which also occur in affective disorders); and believing that some outside force, such as the FBI, is inserting sinister ideas into one's head, or that strangers can read one's mind; 10 to 13 percent of schizophrenics commit suicide.

If you've ever seen a homeless person looking at you and talking gibberish, or swathed in layers of wool in mid-August, or accusing you of saying things about the person when you haven't spoken a word, or quietly muttering to him- or herself, the person may have schizophrenia. But not all people diagnosed with this illness are equally impaired; some are "high functioning," meaning they hold jobs and respond well to their medications.

Then there's schizoaffective disorder, an illness falling somewhere between schizophrenia and the affective disorders, with varying symptoms of each. Some psychiatrists think it's a subtype of schizophrenia; others think it's a subtype of the affective disorders. People with this diagnosis also vary widely in their functioning. For instance, the diagnosis was given to a man I interviewed who graduated at the top of his class at college, looks like an ad for Brooks Brothers, quotes Chaucer, composes gorgeous songs, has dozens of friends, holds a prestigious job, and made me laugh so hard I had to go to the ladies' room. And all the while he was seeing Dante's *Inferno* flickering over my head, a symptom which, along with several others, he mutes with medications, psychotherapy, and sheer determination.

As to antisocial personality disorder—also called "psychopathy" and "sociopathy"—it affects 3.5 percent of Americans. It is described in *DSM-IV* as "a pervasive pattern of disregard for, and violation of, the rights of others that begins in childhood or adolescence and continues into adulthood." For a more vivid "definition," read any newspaper story about bullies who kill for carfare, or who slam infants against walls—stories that almost always contain this punchline: "The suspect showed no emotion." Whether or not this behavior is a *disease*, however, is a matter of some controversy. The majority of sociopaths are male, poor, and live in urban settings. Many people would consider the "disorder" to be more indicative of a defect in character than in the brain.

As this synopsis of disorders suggests, the diagnosis of mental illness is a very slippery slope. Scientific knowledge expands continuously as new discoveries are made. Not every professional is equally seasoned. Age and experience produce changes in brain chemistry, just as mental illnesses do. Some people have but a single episode of illness, while others recurrently break down. Some consumers are more motivated and responsible than others.

Thus, it is not surprising that diagnoses frequently shift. Schizophrenia, for instance, is overdiagnosed in the young; it and other mental illnesses are underdiagnosed in the old. In addition, an estimated

56 percent of Americans diagnosed with one brain disorder also have two or more others.

For all these reasons, it is *imperative* that an extremely careful assessment be made by one or more well-trained, empathic psychiatric or psychological professionals before an accurate diagnosis can be reached.

THE TREATMENTS

As difficult as these illnesses are to diagnose, as frustrating for many consumers are the treatments, which bring their own set of discomforts. But without them, life for many of the mentally ill and their families can resemble, as one parent put it, "being on a roller coaster blindfolded."

The single greatest terror for these families is "noncompliance"— that is, not taking one's medications—because of the turbulent and menacing behavior that untreated mental illness can unleash, particularly if substance abuse is involved. Among paranoid schizophrenics, for instance, the threat of violence is very real. When unmedicated, these consumers *believe* the voices in their heads that tell them they are in mortal danger. Medical students on shifts in psychiatric wards are warned never to allow such a consumer to block a doorway, thereby trapping the doctor.

Of all people with schizophrenia, an estimated 12.7 percent are violent. But so are 11.7 percent of people with major depression, and 11 percent of those with mania or bipolar disorder. (It should be noted, however, that most violent acts are not committed by the mentally ill.) The families of such consumers often deal with violence on a daily basis. According to a 1986 survey of NAMI families, 38 percent reported that their afflicted relative had been violent or destructive at home, usually when not taking their medications.

Yet often these families cannot get their blatantly deranged kin into a psychiatric facility, in part because of the burgeoning patients' rights movement. According to E. Fuller Torrey, M.D., in his book, *Surviving Schizophrenia: A Manual for Families, Consumers and Providers,* half of all schizophrenics are untreated, a major reason being "changes in laws making involuntary hospitalization and treatment more difficult to effect for individuals who have no insight into their need for treatment. Sadly misguided civil rights lawyers and 'patient advocates' regularly defend individuals' right to be psychotic. . . ."

Drug Therapies. Even when a consumer *is* "compliant," however, the pharmacological rainbow of medicines may be of only partial help. In general, these drugs dull the "positive" symptoms (as they are called) of mental illness, such as hallucinations or paranoia, but may have little effect on the "negative" symptoms, such as poor social skills and indifference to personal hygiene. While some of the newer antipsychotic drugs help with negative symptoms, tolerance for any given drug may vary widely.

Even as they help, medications can also inflict harm. Ask consumers themselves and many will report that refusing to take their medications is not simply a matter of denial of their illness, although that may be part of it. Rather, noncompliance can be a function of these drugs causing the consumer to wonder what fresh hell this is. As one man with schizophrenia put it, "I'd rather be crazy than feel like cement."

The side effects of these drugs run from minor to excrutiating. Some are merely annoying, such as sluggishness. Others are worrisome, such as reduced sex drive, diarrhea, and weight gain. Still others are terrifying and embarrassing, such as tremors and uncontrollable muscular contortions in the face and body. And some are potentially lethal. They cause a sharp drop in white blood cell counts and damage the immune system, brain, or internal organs. For this reason, they should be monitored by a weekly blood draw.

Then there's the matter of cost. Drug treatment alone—not counting hospitalization and doctors' fees—can cost tens of thousands of dollars a year. Moreover, in this era of managed care, more and more health insurance companies are putting lower lifetime caps on mental health benefits. For example, a policy that provides $1 million in total coverage for physical illnesses will generally allow only $50,000 for mental illness, an amount that can be wiped out in the early years of severe brain disorders. (In September 1996, the first federal parity legislation requiring insurance companies to offer comparable coverage for physical and mental illnesses became law.)

Regardless of who pays for it, and despite the side effects, countless consumers nevertheless do extremely well on their medications. Proper medication is lifesaving, and enables people to lead full and productive lives, but not before as many as ten years of trial and error have savaged the morale, endurance, and finances of consumers and their families. Finding the right dosages and combinations of drugs can be an agony. Lithium, and several anticonvulsants, for instance, are wonder drugs for millions of people with manic-depression. But the drugs may take several weeks to kick in. For some people, alas, they may not kick in at all.

The most discouraging word in the lexicon of health care is "refractory"—meaning the drugs are just not working. The courage of mentally ill people who year after year, relapse after relapse, continue in their quest for effective treatment and a modicum of peace is awesome. Key to their perseverance is the support of family or friends who won't let them give up.

Other Medical Treatments. When drug treatment does not work, other treatments are attempted. For refractory consumers suffering from depression, for example, electroconvulsive therapy (ECT), or "shock" treatment, can be a "miracle cure" and has the highest success rate of all treatments for severe depression. Administered under anesthesia, a small electrical current produces a brain seizure which, for some reason, seems to jump-start healthy chemical functioning in the brain. ECT causes minimal, and almost always temporary, muscular stiffness and memory loss. Unfortunately, relapse occurs for half of these consumers, who often receive multiple treatments and are maintained, if possible, on drug or other therapies.

A more benign, and possibly revolutionary, experimental procedure is being studied by NIMH researchers, but it is not available to the general public. Called "Repeated Transcranial Magnetic Stimulation" or RTMS, it can be used instead of ECT. According to Dr. Robert M. Post, RTMS "does what ECT does without producing a seizure. You put a magnet over the brain and stimulate it with low frequencies. There is no anesthesia, and no memory loss.'' Like ECT, however, RTMS also requires reapplication, and may not work for everyone.

The Psychotherapies. The least intrusive treatments are the "talking" therapies such as counseling, group therapy, cognitive-behavioral and interpersonal therapies, vocational rehabilitation, and psychoeducation (for further discussion of these therapies, see chapters 8 and 13).

After a long period of disfavor in parts of the scientific community, talking therapies have recently enjoyed a comeback. The advantages are that they offer ongoing human contact in a structured, caring, professional relationship. They also increase compliance with taking medications. In addition, recent studies suggest that these therapies can be as effective as drugs in treating even the most severe forms of depressive illness, for example, and in some cases may be preferable to drugs.

The downside is that talking therapies get lower insurance reimbursement rates than do drugs, the theory being that pills work more quickly. But drugs alone are not, with rare exceptions, enough to make life for the mentally ill—who, in many cases, have lost years of their lives to the limbo of illness and hospitalization—altogether worth living. Says Dr. Clarice J. Kestenbaum, director of training in the division of child and adolescent psychiatry at Columbia University's College of Physicians and Surgeons:

> A pill can't give you insight. Although it can help you control your behavior, it can't teach you social skills. It is important for mentally ill people to combine medication and psychotherapy in order to get better.

THE CAUSES

We come to the root causes of mental illness. Nearly everybody—consumers and family members alike—asks the same questions: How could this happen? What caused it? Are all schizophrenics, or manic-depressives, or obsessive-compulsives alike? How do you explain the person with a specific diagnosis who is a world-famous achiever and on everyone's A-list, while another person with exactly the same diagnosis seldom has a sane moment, can't hold a job, is a pain to be around, and is unable to function on his or her own?

The answers to these questions are as varied as the illnesses themselves. The professional consensus is that these disorders are biologically based vulnerabilities that can be triggered or induced in a variety of ways by such environmental stressors as financial or marital troubles. But within this loosely knit, general rubric, there are many loopholes.

The literature on mental illness teeters on the high theoretical wire between two opposing viewpoints. One favors biological causes—the "nature" camp. The other favors environmental causes—the "nurture" camp. While very few researchers would argue categorically that brain disorders are entirely either nature or nurture in origin, the level of dissonance between these camps makes family members and consumers groan in frustration.

The debate begins with a chicken-egg conundrum. Mental illness can be caused either by tainted genes passed on from previous generations or by faulty brain chemistry, such as misfiring neurotransmitters (chemical substances that carry messages from one nerve to another). Or it can be caused by a weakened immune system, or a virus, or a fetal injury.

But studies have shown that extreme environmental stress can also cause corrosive changes in previously normal brain chemistry, which can lead to mental illness. And faulty genes themselves don't tell you much, because you also may have characteristics that modify their expression, such as charm or intelligence, which compensate for the flawed genes. Plus, psychotherapy can *also* create changes, of the healing variety, in brain chemistry.

Put in more user-friendly terms, for every psychobiological rule there's an exception. For example, some kids from abusive, drug-addicted, inner-city families, whose pedigrees are peppered with mental illness, become, against all odds, role models of heroic sanity. Yet Matt, described at the beginning of this chapter, was raised in a loving, solid, middle-class family, was given every advantage, and *still*, against all odds, became mentally ill. (For a detailed discussion of risk factors and outcomes, see chapter 9.)

Since a gene or chemical has not yet been identified as being *absolutely and in all cases* a cause of mental illness—which would help to determine exactly what role nature and what role nurture plays in these disorders—researchers and clinicians will continue to choose theoretical sides, drawn one way or the other by suggestive evidence and competing methodologies.

In the "nature" camp we find the devotees of pure science who, armed with data from recent advances in DNA research, twin and adoption studies, and laboratory animal experiments, argue that mental illness is overwhelmingly a matter of biology. Among these theorists is E. Fuller Torrey, M.D., a tireless researcher and NAMI advocate, who says:

> I would assert very strongly that there is not an ounce of evidence that families cause either schizophrenia or the affective disorders, any more than they are the cause of Parkinson's disease or Alzheimer's. Families do play a role in determining the severity and course of illness, and how well the person will do. But I don't think it's a very large role.

The scientists who argue that virtually no single biological feature or trait is independent of environmental shaping are in the "nurture" camp. Arnold J. Sameroff, Ph.D., of the University of Michigan Center for Human Growth and Development, an equally indefatigable and esteemed researcher, has conducted longitudinal studies of schizophrenic mothers and their children, with particular attention to context. He believes that environment plays a crucial role in the development of mental illness:

> If you ask the question, "Are children of schizophrenics a risk group?" the answer is yes. If you ask, "Is it because their mothers are schizophrenic?" the answer is not clear. The bottom line is that if a schizophrenic mother is divorced, has very little education, has six kids, no

money, and a lot of stressful life events, there is a very high probability that her children will have problems. If a schizophrenic mother has none of these other stressors, then it's unlikely that her kids would have problems.

To add one more bit of confusion to the nurture/nature debate, it is possible to carry a gene for severe mental illness yet never actually become mentally ill yourself, or if you do, to have a very mild form of it. On this point, psychologist David Elkind, Ph.D., professor of child study at Tufts University and author of *Ties That Stress*, offers an interesting analogy:

> Let's say you have a predisposition for asthma. If you grew up in Arizona, you might never develop it, whereas if you grew up in Cape Cod, you probably would. The same could be true of a predisposition for depression. If you grew up in a well put-together family, you might never develop it. But if you grew up in a family where there's a great deal of conflict and anger, then the predisposition for depression might manifest itself.

For all these competing theories, most clinicians, who are in the trenches of actual diagnosing and treatment, fall somewhere near the center of the theoretical continuum and view mental illness as some combination of nurture and nature, some mix of biochemistry and experience, some blend of genetic and environmental luck.

This brings us back to the families of the mentally ill, who ultimately are left to sort all this out for themselves.

DEALING WITH WHAT IS:
LIVING WITH MENTAL ILLNESS

In his book, *Brothers and Keepers*, John Edgar Wideman could well be speaking for these families when he writes,

> You never know exactly when something begins. The more you delve and backtrack and think, the more clear it becomes that nothing has a

discrete, independent history; people and events take shape not in orderly, chronological sequence but in relation to other forces and events, tangled skeins of necessity and interdependence and chance that after all could have produced only one result: what is.

Family members are often held hostage by the day-to-day reality of disorders that continue to confound the best scientific minds. Depending upon where they stand in the family hierarchy when lightning strikes, each member will bring to and take from the experience something different.

For parents, few torments equal that of being informed that their child—the flesh of their flesh, the repository of their love and hopes—has a chronic and incurable mental illness. But at least many of them can look back on their preparenting years and remember a time when their family problems seemed less insurmountable.

In many ways, it's worse for the children and siblings of the mentally ill, and not simply because they may one day inherit the responsibility for their afflicted kin. Rather, it's because their evolving identities and dreams for the future are intertwined both with the abnormal and with the anguish of family reactions for a much longer portion of their lives.

These younger people must deal with *what is and what will be*. They must try to stay out of a storm not of their genetic or environmental making, yet they are unable to avoid its destructive path. Some, as we shall see in the next chapter, are in jeopardy from the very moment of their births.

CHAPTER 2

When a Parent Is Mentally Ill

When I was little, I always knew my mom wasn't like other people. But I was never actually scared of her until one day when I was around five. I had skinned my knee playing, and I ran into the kitchen, looking for her to give me a hug. She was going on and on about how the neighbors were poisoning our food and spying on us. And for the first time, it occurred to me that this was not a safe place to be. So I just turned around and left. I walked outside, crossed the street, and sat under this big tree. And I remember thinking, This tree is a better home than the one I have—I'm really scared to be in the house, but I don't have anywhere else to go. Isn't there anybody who can help?

—Martha, 41

No one ever told Martha when she was growing up that there was something wrong with her mother—not in so many words, anyway. Once in a while her dad would wistfully muse, "You know, your mom really was wonderful before this thing got hold of her."

But no one ever gave the "thing"—which began shortly after Martha's birth—a name. Or explained why her mom would suddenly start screaming that radio waves were being sent into her head. Or why she was so critical, never giving kisses or caresses. Or why she was never hospitalized. The one time Martha's father tried to have her committed, her mother bolted from the car en route, *begging* him not to make her go to such a terrible place. He took her back home.

Thus, the house itself became an asylum. Whenever Martha's mom would unravel, it was a sign to everyone in the family to get lost. Martha would go down the block to find someone to play with or to sit under

41

her tree. Her older sister would spend the night at a friend's house, and her dad, when he wasn't at work, would go fishing. After a few hours, or weeks, the storm in her mother's mind would blow over. But it would always come back, an open secret that no one mentioned.

It was the unspoken family rule: This is not something we are going to discuss. Every time Martha raised the subject with her dad, he'd just cloud up and turn his head away. Her sister, who had spent her early years knowing her mother as loving and cheerful, didn't want to hear or talk about it. So most of the time Martha tried to pretend nothing was happening.

It wasn't until she became an adult, right after the birth of her own child, that she was able to give her mother's problem a name. Martha decided to visit her mother's doctor because she remembered being told that the "thing" had started with childbirth and she was afraid she'd start unraveling, too.

"You are aware," said the doctor in gently reassuring tones, as though to jog Martha's unwilling memory, "that your mom has schizophrenia. But I don't think you're likely to get it."

Says Martha:

I nearly fell off the chair. As soon as he said that word—*schizophrenia*—I realized how much terror I'd lived with all those years and how angry I was. My first thought was, Okay, give me someone to blame this on. My mom's parents were terrific, so I couldn't blame them. My dad was a real nice guy, so I couldn't blame him. And I never really blamed my mother, even though she never admitted she was sick. So there was no one to blame. But I couldn't help wondering: Where was everybody when I needed them? Why didn't my dad deal with it, talk about it, insist she get help? Why did we have to live that way?

LITTLE MURDERS

To be the child of a mentally ill parent is to have one's identity tethered to an unpredictable phantom force. Life becomes a series of good-byes—an inexorable weave of differing and changing realities.

The moment the parent leaves the real world and enters the world of madness, the child must enter that world as well because of his or her utter dependency on the parent. But unlike the parent, the child has *not* lost touch with reality, and cannot escape it; rather, the child absorbs it with punishing acuity.

Psychiatrist Jane S. Ferber, M.D., has spent thirty years treating the mentally ill and their families, serving in such positions as director of the Family Training Center at the Creedmoor Psychiatric Center; director of the Acute Day Hospital at the Bronx Psychiatric Center; and at a community mental health facility in affluent Westchester County. In those years she has worked on crisis teams and in private practice, seeing every conceivable permutation of the impact of a parent's madness on his or her children. Says Dr. Ferber:

> To have a severely ill parent is really to live in a nightmare world you can't get away from because your parents are the people you look up to and on whom you pattern yourself. They're the ones who are supposed to set limits, model some form of healthy interpersonal behavior, and help you understand what reality is. But when the parent is psychotic, everything becomes completely distorted. Children are easily overwhelmed by strange and powerful emotions, and with these patients, you have nothing but strange and powerful emotions. There's either tremendous withdrawal or tremendous agitation, sexual abuse, violence, and strangeness—the patient thinks angels are in the room having a sexual orgy, that kind of thing. And since little kids think they're the cause of everything, they really try to bend themselves round these very sick parents, contorting themselves to fit in with these very, very crazy people. These children feel enormous helplessness, always trying to please, to make the parent get better. Yet they are terribly neglected—you see little kids sitting all day in dirty diapers, not being fed. Some of these kids, when they grow up, tell me, "It's better to have no mother than a crazy mother."

The children of such parents, says Dr. Ferber, spend their lives trying to undo the damage of these early experiences, attempting to learn what "normal" is—as though it were a second language. Indeed, virtually all the adult offspring I interviewed said approximately the same thing: "For me, weirdness was routine. I had to be taught that the whole world isn't insane."

Mixed Messages. According to London psychiatrist Michael Rutter, the three most anguishing experiences of life are the loss of a meaningful relationship; events that are uncontrollable; and events with lingering consequences. All three coalesce when one's parent, upon whom life itself depends, becomes mentally ill. Of these experiences, it is loss that is perhaps the most devastating.

The concept of brain disorder as "loss"—in the same vein as physical death—at first seems perplexing because the afflicted person is still alive. But what is lost is the parent's dependable awareness, protectiveness, and ability to respond in ways that are predictable, comforting, and above all, *mutual*. The order of things gets turned upside down; where the parent was supposed to be a safe harbor, now he or she is marooned by bewildering forces that strand and can endanger the child as well.

Children of the mentally ill have unique disadvantages. Schizophrenic mothers, for example, have difficulty in responding emotionally to their offspring. These mothers are often unable to provide structure and stability because they themselves are so disorganized in their thinking. Mothers with affective disorders can also find the demands of child-rearing overwhelming; their tolerance for stress can be nonexistent, and the normal needs of a child can catapault them into despair or fury. Depressed mothers tend to experience more friction with their children and judge them more negatively than do other people who know the children. These mothers seem to "see" problems in their kids that may not exist.

But does this mean that their children are automatically doomed to lives of regret and sorrow, their identities a psychological shambles? Why is it that some kids seem to view their early deprivations as challenges, while others collapse under their weight? The answers to these questions depend on a number of interconnecting variables, among them:

• the child's age when the parent becomes mentally ill;
• the child's psychological defenses;

- the child's innate temperament;
- the family context;
- the availability of a well parent or caregiver;
- the willingness of the ill parent to get treatment.

THE CHILD'S AGE

In her book, *No Voice Is Ever Wholly Lost*, psychologist Louise J. Kaplan, Ph.D., describes mental illness as "psychological death," which can be more excrutiating to a child than a parent's physical death. Says Dr. Kaplan:

When someone dies, you eventually say, "They're gone and they're never coming back." But when someone is suffering from severe mental illness, they're in an altered state of consciousness. A person is unrecognizable and frightening because they're beyond the border between being dead and being alive. They look human. They look like the person you used to know. But the forces that animate them are something you don't know. It feels mechanical, out of the realm of human experience.

When a parent, due to a brain disorder, is incapable of participating fully in a nurturing relationship—that is, both reading and sending appropriate messages—the child is denied an essential component of human growth, says Dr. Kaplan: a nourishing emotional conversation, or "dialogue," in which one learns how to survive in the world. The absence of such a dialogue can leave the child dangling, with no firm foundation in which to put down roots—particularly if the illness occurs at the very beginning of the child's life.

Loss In Early Childhood. When the parent-child dialogue is "derailed" early on, the loss to the child is searing, especially if the mother, generally the primary and more emotionally fluent caregiver, is sick, rather than the father.

Children are at their most teachable in very early childhood because they depend on others for survival. Thus they watch the mother intently, picking up her every cue. And to the best of their abilities, they'll try to please her by matching her mood. Infants as young as two days old can imitate smiles or frowns, and in a group can even distinguish the sounds of their mothers' voices. This exquisite ability to engage peaks between two and six months—a period described by one researcher as "perhaps the most exclusively social . . . of life."

If the mother is mentally ill, says Dr. Kaplan, she is experienced by the infant as "uncanny." The mother is both there and not there, alive in body but dead in spirit, or animated by unseen demons, reflecting back to the child not warmth or welcome but, rather, emotional deadness or diabolical harshness.

Infants react to a mother's emotional distance, or fearsome intrusiveness, with a flurry of inviting or aversive activity. They try to incite the mother's better, healthier self by protesting—crying, or clinging, or screaming with rage. Given enough maternal uncanniness, the infant eventually quits trying. The child withdraws the invitation and expects to receive nothing back or anticipates only emotional mayhem.

Thus infants may in time respond to their ill mothers with their own psychological near death, preferring to feel nothing than to be aware of the *lack of reciprocity*—the dearth of an echoing, reassuring response. That way, writes Dr. Kaplan, "There will be no disappointment or hurt. . . ."

A child can feel the same sense of loss when the father, rather than the mother, is mentally ill—especially if the child is a little older and is already acquainted with the father's pre-illness warmth and involvement.

Rachel, twenty-five, clearly recalls the New Hampshire autumn afternoon soon after her third birthday when she and her five-year-old brother, Mark, sat in a pile of leaves and watched an invisible monster slip into their beloved father's body. She says:

My parents were planting some bushes, and suddenly my father got this crazy look in his eyes. He picked up a pitchfork and went after my mom, screaming "Die, devil, die!" She grabbed my brother and me and ran next door to call the police. My father spent the next three months in a psych hospital being treated for schizophrenia.

When he was released, Rachel's father seemed to have been restored to his usual jovial self. But soon he stopped taking his medications. Over the winter months, other terrifying moments, relieved only by her father's deathlike trances, composed the dynamics of Rachel's life. Sometimes he would lie on the couch for hours, staring silently out the window at dripping icicles. Other times he'd be a blur of bizarre activity, suddenly snatching up a pair of candlesticks, forming a cross with them, and holding them in front of Rachel's mom to "kill" her.

By spring, he had begun threatening the family with knives. So one morning, Rachel's mother took her and her brother out to the car, and with only the clothes they were wearing, drove all the way to the Pacific Ocean, as far from New Hampshire as she could possibly get. She later married a rock-steady, loving man who, says Rachel, "saved our lives and gave us the world." Although Rachel occasionally sees her biological father, who is an outpatient at a community mental health facility, it is her stepfather whom she calls Dad.

Nevertheless, the memories of those early years are etched into Rachel's identity. As she recounts the long ago escape from her father, she begins to sob.

The thing is, he's a genius, like Einstein. And he's a fantastic musician. He loves to play the guitar. I remember him carrying me on his shoulders, and the two of us looking at bubbles in the windowpanes. I remember him reading to me and being very kind. What's been hardest is I'm afraid to be alone with him—he scares me—yet I remember him as such a gentle, wonderful man. I feel so guilty. I mean, he's got no one.

Rachel's ambivalent feelings about her father reverberate in her shaky sense of self. She worries constantly about the integrity of her own sanity. "It's almost a physical thing," she says. "I have to pat myself all over and check myself to see if I'm still in my body." She is everyone's emotional first-aid kit, with little time for herself. And she's terrified of getting any professional help, even though she knows she needs it, because it might, like the opening of Pandora's box, unleash the same demons that undid her father.

Instead she is a patchwork quilt of fretful coping. She binges and then vomits. Or she peers at her reflection in the mirror, tracking the pattern of tiny wrinkles that are beginning to score her face, seeing them as so many little fractures. "A lot of times I feel like I'm coming apart," she says. "I'm trying so hard just to keep myself together, to *not* break down, and it's starting to show in my face."

As Rachel's story illustrates, the loss of a parent to mental illness is often more than symbolic. Children of the mentally ill are much more likely to experience a separation from their parents—either because of divorce or death—by age eighteen than are the children of normal parents.

Whether symbolic or physical, however, these separations can set into motion a process of unending grief. Key to this mourning is the chronicity of abandonments—they happen over and over, in tandem with the tides of the parent's illness—the cycles of psychological death and rebirth. Indeed, in young parents, these illnesses are often extremely severe, thus exposing the small child to repeated psychotic episodes and parental absences.

Loss in Middle Childhood. The same sense of unending mourning can occur with older children as well. Children who are beyond toddlerhood when their parents become ill have a longer history, obviously, of their parent's mental health. Memories of the pre-illness connection stand in startling contrast to the parent's psychological decay. Because of the child's greater maturity and cognitive abilities, the sudden change can feel as though they've been hit by a sledgehammer.

By any yardstick, Liza, sixty, had a perfect childhood. The daughter of a doting and wealthy father, a professor of philosophy, and an extraordinarily elegant and affectionate mother, she and her younger brother grew up feeling privileged and cherished. Says Liza:

> My early memories of my family are really wonderful. I remember my mother brushing her hair before going out to a party and looking very beautiful. She and my father were madly in love. She had a luminous personality and great warmth—I adored her. Everyone did.

Liza's perfect life shattered when she was eleven. Within a period of six months, her mother toppled from gracious benevolence to howling madness—"totally crazed," says Liza, by the most acute case of manic-depression her doctors had ever seen.

There must be a stronger word than "crazed" for what Liza's mother became. Everything about her turned into grotesque deformity, a rapid dissolve from Jekyll to Hyde. When putting on lipstick, she would extend the boundaries of her lips up her cheeks, making her mouth a fire-red gape. She'd wreathe herself in a frenzy of mismatched scarves and jewelry. Her hair would be a cantilever of knots. Most terrifying were the noises—she'd lock herself in the bathroom and utter unintelligible, gutteral sounds.

She seemed to be charged with superhuman strength. In a last-ditch effort to stave off hospitalization, Liza's father hired a psychiatric nurse to look after her mother. It proved to be a grave miscalculation. She pushed the nurse down a flight of stairs. That night her mother was put into an institution.

A month later she returned from the hospital with a bag full of pills. As long as she took them, her doctors said, she'd be capable of staying home in the care of the family's servants. But the pills gradually lost their sway, and Liza's mother sank into a psychosis from which she would never emerge.

Liza pauses in her narrative to take a gulp of air in preparation for a description of her mother's final descent into madness. In an almost inaudible voice, and with palpable difficulty, Liza continues:

> I remember very vividly the last day she lived at home. She went berserk at the breakfast table with my father. He was trying to calm

her down, and suddenly they were locked in a terrible physical battle. I knew this was just horrible. Horrible. Horrible. My little brother was hustled out of the room by a maid. But I had to go to school. So I went out into the hall to get the elevator, and stood streaming with tears, because there was nobody who could come comfort me. I can still see the mosaic on the floor by the elevator, and hear the cater-wauling that was going on in the apartment. Somehow, I managed to pull myself together and get through the schoolday.

When I came home, my mother was gone, and my father told me that she was too sick ever to leave the hospital. The doctors had said that she would either kill somebody or kill herself, and that she had to have a lobotomy. The operation didn't make her a vegetable, but it didn't cure her either. I visited her in that hospital for the next thirty years. She died there.

Liza presses a handkerchief to her eyes and heaves a sigh. Then she adds, "You know, for me the major thing wasn't even her illness. The major thing was losing her to the illness."

Rising to her feet, Liza suggests that we take a break from her awful chronicle and have a cup of tea. I ask her how she managed to cope with the loss of her mother, and the losses that were to come— her brother also became mentally ill.

With that, she releases a guffaw. "I had a gift then, as I do now," she says, scooting into the kitchen, "of not paying attention if things look too horrible. One learns pretty quickly to take the bizarre as normal. I am an *expert* at papering things over."

THE CHILD'S PSYCHOLOGICAL DEFENSES

Over the course of her life, Liza has proven to be extraordinarily resilient. But, as she is the first to admit, she had a head start by having wonderful parents and economic security to begin with. More-over, unlike most of the offspring and siblings we will meet through-out this book, she was spared the day-to-day anxiety of living with mental illness after her mother was institutionalized. Even so, Liza had to learn ''pretty quickly'' how to defend herself against disappointment.

According to John Bowlby, author of *Attachment and Loss*, the earlier the separation from one's parents, the more ingrained will be a child's confusion and anxiety, and the more ''pathological'' the subsequent mourning. Children who are primed early in life for emotional abandonment will react strongly every time they sense anything remotely like it, protecting themselves as they move through the years with increasingly intricate layers of psychological armor.

Mechanisms of Defense. Children of the mentally ill choose from an array of forks in the developmental road, in accordance with their psychological makeup, the behavioral lessons they have learned along the way (such as family vows of silence and secrecy), and—as we shall see in a moment—their dispositions.

Some children, says Bowlby, become extremely *self-involved.* They blame themselves for their loss and/or frantically try to redress it.

Others *displace* their anger and grief to avoid reexperiencing the original loss. One way of doing this is to corral their painful feelings into emotional bullpens, where the original loss takes a less noxious form. Phobias, Bowlby believes, are a convenient place to stash awareness of loss. Better to stay out of elevators, for example, because of irrational fears than consciously relive a parent's psychological death.

Another way of reducing the pain is by putting the loss out of one's awareness, as Liza did. In this regard, Bowlby makes an important point: *Denial* can be not so much a blatant disregard for what *is* as a feverish attempt *not to reexperience what was.*

These children have thoroughly digested their losses. Future losses can be smelled from afar, and an automatic, protective emotional numbness kicks in. Bowlby calls this emotional detachment *defensive exclusion*, which peaks in the first three years of life but which can be mobilized at any age.

Defensive diversions work in other ways as well, says Bowlby. Some children will *disavow*, or become distant from the person who inspires anxious feelings of loss.

Still other children don't disavow. Rather, they go through elaborate psychological maneuvers to keep the healthy aspects of the parent alive while tuning out the sick parts. This process is called *splitting*. Some children divide up their good and bad feelings for their ill parents. In viewing their parents as convalescent ideals (think Elizabeth Barrett Browning), or abiding wretched parental neglect or cruelty in the name of diagnosis ("she can't help it; she's sick"), they attempt to quarantine their own "disloyal" feelings of anger.

In the most hideous cases of prolonged torture and abuse at the hands of the most severely disturbed parents (here I draw on the work of Frank Putnam, M.D., head of the unit on dissociative disorders at NIMH), some children will divide *themselves* up into *multiple personalities*, defending against their own psychological death by delegating their agonies to as many as 100 "alters" which each carry a morsel of manageable pain. According to Dr. Putnam, multiple personality disorder is not considered true, inherent madness. Rather it is a trauma-induced, ingenious solution to inescapable torment.

In all these ways, a parent's psychological death can find its fragmented reflection in the child's defenses.

Legacies of Defense. Efforts by children to protect themselves psychologically, says Bowlby, fall into three patterns of emotional transaction with others: "anxious and ambivalent" attachments; "compulsive caregiving"; and avoidance of all "affectional ties."

As we shall see in part three of this book, these patterns will have loud repercussions in the private and occupational lives of the offspring of the mentally ill, as well as in their ties to their original families. The defenses built early in life are difficult to dislodge, not simply because they are so ingrained, but because they once worked so well.

TEMPERAMENT

Bowlby and his disciples are not without critics. Many developmental psychologists and personality researchers argue that it isn't a parent's mental illness per se which defines these children. Rather, it is the way they *perceive* traumatic events: The "lens" is their own innate temperaments which, scientific evidence suggests, tend to be hard-wired in the genes.

According to these researchers, a child's responsiveness to pain or loss is more closely related to biology than psychology. Some children are simply more inherently sensitive or assertive than others, and their future lives reflect their dispositions as much as their parents' mental health or lack of it.

In other words, children themselves bring something to the parent-child party, which has everything to do with how they *experience* it. Any parent of more than one child will attest to the fact that no two children are identical. Even identical twins aren't always identical: Studies show that they often differ enormously in temperament, as well as in other attributes.

Developmental psychologist Mary K. Rothbart, Ph.D., and her colleagues at the University of Oregon define temperament as biologically based differences, contoured by age and experience, in emotionality or "reactivity," and in the tendency to be curious about, or to avoid, the unfamiliar, known as "self-regulation."

According to this school of thought, children aren't simply passive lumps of uniform clay who are shaped into cookie-cutter forms by the family environment. It's the other way around: Children shape their environments as much as they are shaped by them.

Consider Mark, thirty, referred to earlier in this chapter. You will recall that his younger sister, Rachel, is an extremely sensitive, volatile, and articulate young woman who with only the slightest encouragement hemorrhages with emotion about her schizophrenic father—and about nearly everyone else, too.

Mark, a professional musician, shares with Rachel their ill father, but here the family resemblance ends. Where Rachel is by nature a live wire, it would take an exploding bomb to capture Mark's attention. He gives new meaning to the term "laid back." These differences in the siblings' temperaments are mirrored in their recollections of their father. Indeed, when each describes him, you'd think they were talking about two different people.

Mark perceived his father in a more benign light than his sister did—so much so that after their parents divorced, Mark went back to live with him for a year when he was ten. Says Mark:

> Most of what I remember about my dad is positive. I loved making music with him. And he always had interesting hobbies. He had a million tools—I didn't know how they worked, but they were fun to play with. True, he had the TV blaring twenty-four hours a day, and his meds made him sound like he was stoned. But I think I had a really good childhood with my dad. It was a shocker when my mom took us away from him because I was never afraid of him. The only reason I didn't stay was because I spent so much time taking care of him. I had to have my own life. But I really miss him. If I had the bucks, I'd build a house big enough for him to live with me.

Thus the reality of a parent's mental illness may mean different things to different children within the same family, tailored according to their temperaments. As Drs. Judy Dunn and Robert Plomin, professors of human development at Penn State, point out in their book, *Separate Lives: Why Siblings Are So Different*, "Children's perceptions of events are . . . probably more important in relation to their development than are the 'actual' events themselves."

Resilience and Optimism. That some children are sturdier, or more resilient, than others depends in large measure on how they explain to themselves their parent's mental illness, which some researchers call "explanatory style." In their book, *The Resilient Self: How Survivors of Troubled Families Rise Above Adversity*, psychiatrist Steven J. Wolin, M.D., and psychologist Sybil Wolin, Ph.D., observe that 90 percent of the children of schizophrenic parents do not themselves become schizophrenic. The apparent immunity of these children is that they *interpret* their circumstances in self-protective ways.

Resilient children, say the authors, share certain abilities, such as insight, independence, initiative, creativity, the ability to form outside attachments, morality, and a sense of humor. These survival skills tend to cluster according to personality type. Some are the attributes of sociable children, while others are the skills of intuitive types. But whether shy or effusive, these children do not internalize their afflicted parents' psychological wounds. They manage to keep them at a safe distance.

Genetic Timetables. To a large degree, these perceptions are governed by children's genetic unfolding over time. All the genes one inherits are present at birth, but many of them turn on or off, at different ages. The most obvious examples of this are puberty and menopause, when hormones switch on and off.

Another example is intelligence: Children's cognitive skills become greater as they grow up because of the timetables of certain genes. According to Dr. Plomin, the percentage of turned-on genes governing cognitive abilities increases with age: approximately 20 percent in infancy, 40 percent in childhood, and 50 percent in adolescence. (Thus, Martha, mentioned at the beginning of this chapter, wasn't aware that the house she grew up in was not just different, but "unsafe," until she was five—her ability to comprehend was by then better developed.)

While the *timing* of certain genes may be similar, the ways in which they are *expressed* may vary considerably. For example, how and what children are able to learn cognitively is filtered through their temperamental makeup. Some kids are challenged by demanding teachers; highly sensitive kids are terrified of them. It's easy to figure out which kind of child will learn more of the material being taught.

Niche-Picking. University of Virginia psychology professor Sandra Scarr, Ph.D., could easily be talking about Rachel and Mark when she writes, "[E]nvironments children receive are at least in part the result of their own personal characteristics, such as interests, talents, and personality."

An intriguing concept in this regard is what Dr. Scarr calls "niche-picking," wherein children—even infants—find their place in the environmental scheme of things and build on it. Put simply, children inspire certain behaviors in their parents by themselves being delightful or irritating, eager or passive.

Thus, since Mark and his father have similar temperaments and gifts, it is entirely possible that Mark simply brought out the best his father had to give. Whereas Mark's sister, Rachel, who is much more similar to her emotional mom, may have sparked her father's over-reactions to stress.

Goodness of "Fit." Which brings up another piece of the temper-ament puzzle: the innate personalities of the mentally ill *also* differ. One of the biggest surprises in recent research is that mental illness does *not* affect basic temperament. Interestingly, temperament may also play a role in what form mental illness takes. According to per-sonality researchers, psychopaths tend to be extroverts, while people with anxiety disorders tend to be introverts.

If a child's temperament is radically different from the parent's, a clash of perceptions is inevitable. Drs. Alexander Thomas and Stella Chess, pioneers in personality research, call this phenomenon "good-ness of fit." For example, if a manic-depressive mother tends to be gentle and loving between episodes of illness, and if her child is passive and easy to please, the "fit" between mother and child will be relatively good. If, on the other hand, the same mother also has a child who is a tan-trum-throwing insomniac, the "fit" will be poor, to neither's benefit.

Studies regarding the outcomes of children of depressed mothers bear this out. An easygoing child who is relatively impervious to outside stim-ulation will be less likely to react to a mentally ill mother with distress, hence reducing the chance of drawing the mother's irritable fire.

Hence, genes play a large role in the relationship between mentally ill parent and child. Says psychologist David C. Rowe, Ph.D., profes-sor of family studies at the University of Arizona and author of *The Limits of Family Influence: Genes, Experience, and Behavior*:

> Mental illness blends against the background of character traits. That's why not all people who are depressed are exactly the same, and not all people who are manic are exactly the same. It's like some alcoholics are aggressive drunks, and some are happy drunks.

Misattunements. Dr. Rowe concedes that genes don't operate in a vacuum. Eventually, given enough ruptures and painful experience, the hardiest child will reach the saturation point. A parent's prolonged psychotic state can push youngsters to their temperamental limits. Parents with severe mental illness often are unable to be emotionally attuned with a child, as we saw earlier. In that instance, the child may experience a kind of emotional short-circuit, triggered by a pileup of "misattunements." Dr. Jerome Kagan of Harvard calls this "the threshold function." In his book, *The Nature of the Child*, he writes, "[U]p to a point, quality of experience is of minimal importance for [a child's] future. But once that threshold is crossed, the consequences are more serious."

Which is where the family environment of children of the mentally ill comes in.

THE FAMILY CONTEXT

Any discussion of the impact of mental illness on children must include the context within which the illness blooms or fades. Temperament may be inborn, but it isn't static—children display their temperamental repertoire in response to how they are treated.

Most researchers agree that the basic child-rearing environment—which, after all, is imposed rather than chosen—has much to do with whether or not an inborn talent is given the opportunity to express itself in the first place. The environment also determines the extent to which the extremes of a child's temperament are evoked or reinforced. A child's efforts to adapt to a parent's mental illness can stretch the child's innate coping mechanisms to the breaking point—*especially if the context in which the child is developing is chaotic.*

One of the most compelling investigations of the environmental context of children of the mentally ill was a three-year study conducted by Dr. Constance Hammen and her colleagues at UCLA. Called the UCLA Family Stress Project, she wanted to examine the outcomes of the children of women suffering from depressive disorders from the point of view of psychosocial variables rather than purely genetic ones. (Dr. Hammen excluded fathers from her study, since women, as has been mentioned, tend to be more central to the lives of their children.)

One reason Dr. Hammen selected depressive illness is that most studies historically have focused on schizophrenia. Yet affective disorders are far more common, and can be as damaging to the children of its victims—in some cases *more* harmful—as other mental disorders.

Dr. Hammen's target sample consisted of thirty mothers with either chronic depression—which she calls "unipolar"—or manic-depression. Most of these mothers were in their thirties and were either divorced or separated (mentally ill people have higher divorce rates than the general population). Their children were between the ages of eight and sixteen when the study began.

What made Dr. Hammen's study groundbreaking was not so much that she included control groups—matched for the ages of the mothers and the children—in her study, but, rather, the contents of these control groups. One group, unsurprisingly, consisted of normal mothers and their children.

It was the *other* group that was particularly intriguing. This group consisted of mothers who had severe, chronic, recurrent, and debilitating medical disorders with early onsets (diabetes and rheumatoid arthritis) that required professional attention and occasional hospitalizations—just as depressive disorders do. The sample was selected to compare the effects on children of a parent's disruptive *medical* versus *mental* illness.

Of all the children, those who fared worst, whether they were girls or boys, were those whose mothers had depressive illness, in particular unipolar mothers who tended to respond to their children with criticism, irritability, or simply by ignoring them. But it wasn't mental illness *in and of itself* that made these women inadequate mothers.

Perhaps Dr. Hammen's most important finding was that unhappy or poorly adjusted children were *also* found among psychiatrically normal mothers who were chronically crushed by poverty or the lack of social supports. These mothers had similar difficulty in relating well to their children. Put another way, depressed mothers in remission whose lives were not otherwise too troubled often functioned *better* than "normal" mothers who were demoralized by huge life stresses.

The bottom line of Dr. Hammen's study—based on 1,000 interviews of all the mothers and their children, as well as reports from teachers and therapists—was this: Children who tended to be doing poorly in school or who showed signs of unhappiness or even of mental illness shared similar risk factors, *regardless of whether or not their mothers were mentally ill.* The risk factors were chronic stress, maternal depressed mood, and family disruption.

Thus it is not *a diagnosis of mental disorder per se* that bodes poorly for children of the mentally ill, a conclusion with enormous social, political, and health care implications. As Dr. Hammen puts it, "A major logical error is committed repeatedly when offspring outcomes (or other characteristics) are attributed to the parental diagnostic status itself. . . ." The "error" is in ignoring the other ingredients of the environmental context that complicate, and are complicated by, the diagnosis.

I have gone on at some length about Dr. Hammen's study for this reason: In my interviews of the adult offspring of the mentally ill, it was brought home to me again and again that the illness was often the least informative aspect of their family experience. The lives of these children were made immeasurably worse by the paucity of ameliorating help and comfort from other members of the immediate and extended family, and by the stunning lack of professional intervention for the children themselves.

My own comparatively informal study simply corroborates Dr. Hammen's findings, which cannot be overstated in their significance. Several other well-funded, scientific studies have shown that the severity of illness is intimately linked with environmental stress, and that environmental stress is not good either for the mentally ill or for their children. Dr. Hammen's study makes this melancholy point with uncommon clarity and eloquence.

THE AVAILABILITY OF A WELL PARENT OR OTHER CAREGIVER

Another crucial variable in how children are affected by a parent's mental illness is the accessibility of a well parent or other caregiver, such as a grandparent or full-time housekeeper, to offset its ravages. While the subject of partners of the mentally ill will be explored in great detail in chapter 4, it is important to mention it here.

A significant finding in Dr. Hammen's study was the role of fathers. The children most at risk for mental, academic, and social problems in her study either had a mentally ill father living at home *or* had a healthy father who disappeared.

In my own study, the worst-case scenarios were either when a well parent abandoned the family (nearly half, or 48 percent, of these marriages ended in divorce, compared to a 30 percent divorce rate of parents of ill children) or was present but emotionally unavailable to the children.

Shirley, fifty-four, has blocked out a lot about her mother's bipolar illness. But two aspects of her childhood remain vibrant in her memories: The first is that after her mother became sick, her bitter and angry father became increasingly withdrawn from her. The second is that she had an overwhelming sense of loneliness and hopelessness— despite having an older brother—which took years of therapy to undo. Says Shirley:

> When you lose one parent to illness, you lose the second parent, too, because the well parent is so focused on the illness rather than on the children. And the children are so busy just trying to survive that they aren't really much help to each other. I really feel as if I grew up as an orphan.

THE WILLINGNESS OF THE ILL PARENT TO GET TREATMENT

The capacity of ill parents themselves to get help for their impairments is the final variable determining how children weather their parents' mental storms.

Justin, thirty-three, also felt orphaned by his mother's mental illness, in this case schizoaffective disorder. Justin's childhood was haunted by his mother's almost constant paranoia and verbal cruelty.

He felt abandoned by his father, who dealt with his wife's illness by spending as much time traveling on business as possible (his parents eventually divorced). Justin was the primary target of his mother's furies, from which he vowed to escape as soon as he was of legal age to do so.

Alas, Justin's "escape" is far from complete. To this day, his mother's rages and paranoia have not dimmed—indeed, they literally trail Justin everywhere. His mother, who is independently wealthy, does not believe there's anything wrong with her. And because she cannot be institutionalized against her will unless she is actually in the act of doing something dangerous or life-threatening, she has made Justin's life a living hell.

Goaded by the delusion that her son cannot survive without her, Justin's mother stalks him. She keeps filing missing persons reports to locate him. She frequently calls the police to say that her son is being beaten up by his friends. Justin has been forced to keep moving from state to state to try to find a measure of peace from his mother's madness.

Wherever he goes, Justin always gets an unlisted phone number. And somehow, his mother always finds him. He has gotten orders of protection against his mother, but she always violates them. Thus Justin has become an expert at living on the lam, as though he himself were a criminal. Says Justin:

I can't get away from her—she always ends up on my doorstep. Once she even rented an apartment in the same building. And her story is always the same: "You're my baby. You need me to tell you what to do." When I tell her to leave me alone, she says, "Oh, you don't mean that." I called the police hundreds of times, and they wouldn't do anything. Once, she tried to have me kidnapped—she hired some private detectives to "rescue" me from my girlfriend. I was so desperate that I finally persuaded a homicide detective to investigate my case, and my mother was committed to an institution. But in the state where I live, they have to let you out after a certain amount of time. So now she's on the loose again, and I don't know when she's going to show up next. I don't wish her harm—but I don't want anything to do with her. The upshot is that her freedom is protected. Mine isn't.

Unlike many of the offspring of the mentally ill I interviewed, Justin does not feel a sense of ambivalent, bittersweet loss. Rather, he feels that there is no place on this earth where he can find sanctuary from the unbalanced, untreated woman who gave him life.

WHEN THE PAST IS, AND ISN'T, PROLOGUE

In all these ways, the child of a mentally ill parent can feel forsaken, an emotional and sociocultural afterthought—*unless* the child has a close, stable relationship with at least one caring person. As we shall see in chapter 6, a well parent or other relative, a friend, a supportive teacher, a concerned neighbor, or a loving godparent can provide the consistency and respite that these children desperately need. These tender mentors can make all the difference in how the children of the mentally ill ultimately turn out, and whether they can learn to trust anyone but themselves.

But these mentors cannot do it alone. Children of the mentally ill need more than emotional sustenance. They also need mental health and legal systems that are responsive to their needs and to the needs of their families.

The hope for these children rests on the ability of well members of the family, *in partnership with outside resources*, to both contain the damage of a severe brain disturbance and to prevent the conditions that might evoke it in the next generation.

All too often these outside supports are absent. Children of the mentally ill are often forced to grow not so much *up* as *around* their relatives' afflictions, rather like a tree that curves around a boulder.

This is true not only for such offspring but for the siblings of the mentally ill as well.

CHAPTER 3

When a Sibling Is Mentally Ill

Who should have looked out for whom? I think that's the question. Until I was fourteen, my older brother always looked after me. But once he cracked up, it didn't follow the pattern. Did that mean that I was supposed to look after him? Or that I had no right to be mad at him? Not only was he not looking after me, neither were my parents, because he took all their attention. The payoff is that I have a handy kind of resourcefulness. But sometimes I wish I didn't have to be so resourceful. I feel like the Marlon Brando character in On the Waterfront—*my brother should have taken care of me.*

—Luke, 34

Whenever Luke talks about his older brother, Hank, he speaks of their relationship in almost mythic terms, likening it to the Kennedy brothers, with himself in the Bobby Kennedy role, taking up the cudgel of the fallen leader.

When they were growing up, Hank was his kid brother's hero, his pacer, his inspiration. Where Hank was tall and athletic, Luke was a scrapper. Where Hank was polished and glib, Luke was his eager impersonator. Where Hank was the glamourous focus of everyone's attention, Luke was his adoring acolyte, warmed by his brother's reflected glory.

"I measured myself against everything he did," Luke recalls. "Hank was always the trailblazer, and I was the tenacious one, trying to compete with him and his friends and be as tough as they were so they'd let me hang out with them. And to a large degree, I succeeded.''

But when Luke's brother mentally crashed and burned two decades ago—shot down at eighteen by schizophrenia—Luke was forced to come out from his brother's comforting shadow, reluctantly catapulted into the lead. Until Hank got sick, he had been Luke's scout, clearing the path for his little brother, showing him the way, covering for him when he screwed up. Now Luke was the front-runner, forging ahead alone, without his landmarks. Surpassing his brother meant forfeiting his closest comrade and champion. It was as though the sun had gone out.

Hank's schizophrenia threw the family constellation out of orbit, and the illness itself became its black hole. All his parents' time, energy, and finances were devoured by the disorder and its fallout. Over a period of three years, Hank dropped out of college, assaulted Luke and his father, tried to kill his mother, and was arrested for various public disturbances. Finally, his harried parents, fearing for their lives and Luke's safety, had no choice but to commit their first-born to a locked psychiatric facility.

The toll on them was so great that Luke's highest priority was never to do anything that might cause them any worry. That meant being ''perfect.'' He buried his own needs and desires lest he, too, be swept away by the same uncontrollable forces that had consumed his brother.

''I became very measured in my responses,'' he says. ''It's not easy for me to get angry, because I don't know if I'll be able to stop. I might go crazy, like my brother. I'm not sure where the emotional borders are. So you learn to detach, to not be upset by anything. The price is a kind of self-annihilation.''

Since Hank's very great fall, Luke has spent the bulk of his life and professional career—he is a playwright—creating other mythic heroes in whose protective shadow he can find sanctuary, and against whose glorious deeds he can measure himself. And while he takes a certain pride in having come through with no visible scars, he can't help wondering what might have been if Hank hadn't gotten sick. After all these years, he still misses the big brother he used to look up to.

''I talked to him on the phone the other day,'' says Luke wistfully.

"He said, 'You know, it wasn't so long ago that I was older than you.' I said, 'Hank, you still are.' But I knew what he meant. Because the time will come when it's up to me to take care of him. And that's not the way it was supposed to be."

A LEAGUE OF ONE'S OWN: THE SIBLING PARTNERSHIP

As we saw in the last chapter, losing a parent to mental illness often means being deprived of two parents. But losing a sibling to a brain disorder can mean being stripped of *three* key family members: the mother and father—whose stamina is drained by the illness (or by papering it over)—and the afflicted sibling as well.

Since mental illness generally does not strike until after siblings have spent their formative years growing up together, to well siblings it can feel like being utterly betrayed by one of their own—a trusted teammate, a confidant, an ally. To understand what it means to lose a sibling to mental illness, it's important to understand what it means to have a sibling in the first place.

The Sibling Connection. Prior to the 1980s, the sibling relationship was considered by many psychological theorists to be a "secondary bond," an adjunct to the parent-child relationship. But recent research suggests that siblings can have as great an influence on each other as their parents, and sometimes an even greater one. Parents are the yardsticks for children's rank in the family hierarchy, marking the division between children and adults. The sibling connection, however, is the yardstick for how children *rate*, and especially how they define themselves.

Just *having* a sibling dramatically contours the family into which one is born. Obviously, for firstborns and only children, parents are their sole reference points. As soon as siblings enter the picture, the reference points multiply, and the child's identity begins to grow in comparison to, and in relationship with, his or her brothers and sisters. This changing cast of influential characters is one of the many reasons why each child—depending, as we saw in the last chapter, on temperament—experiences the family differently from the others.

Siblings are each other's first and most enduring partners in life. For one thing, they are of the same generation. They are partners in *time*, with an indefinite future of mutual influence ahead of them. For another, they are partners in *development*, closer to one another in evolutionary steps than to the senior generation.

Siblings are also partners in *distribution*, vying for the same parental "goods"—who has a bigger allowance, later curfew, larger piece of pie. And they are partners in *intimacy*, for the relationship is a dress rehearsal for friendships and romantic ties later on. Siblings often share their rooms, their toys, and their innermost secrets, the ones they wouldn't think of telling a grown-up.

This intimacy allows siblings to "practice" love, hate, and the art of gentle, or not so gentle, persuasion in a relatively safe arena— relative, that is, to taking on their parents, whose greater power is not to be trifled with.

The "Parental Vacuum." Of course, a great deal of what happens between siblings is mediated by parents, who must walk the thin line between too much involvement in the relationship and too little.

In *The Sibling Bond*, psychologists Stephen P. Bank, Ph.D., and Michael D. Kahn, Ph.D., argue that the *intensity* of that bond depends on the degree to which there is a "parental vacuum." If parents are loving and available, encouraging each of their children's unique abilities rather than insisting that they adhere to a rigid norm, siblings can sort out their separate identities and their relationship with minimal bloodshed.

In their study of intensely loyal siblings who have experienced a variety of life stressors, Drs. Bank and Kahn found that these siblings shared certain commonalities, including closeness in age, and at least one parent who set an example of love and caring and who did not play the siblings off against each other.

When siblings feel equally valued, they do not have to scuffle over uneven parental regard. Their parents keep a weather eye on the sibling attachment, stepping in only when one sibling clearly is being cruel to another, teaching the value of justice and negotiation. This partial parental vacuum allows siblings to learn to decipher their own and each other's feelings and moods, likes and dislikes. In this case, the sibling tie does not become a knot—rather, it settles into a kind of loose accommodation.

But when parents are absent or emotionally unavailable—when they create an all but complete parental vacuum, especially in large families—siblings loom larger in importance. They become each other's last resort, for good or ill. In some cases, siblings become so mutually dependent that they are in danger of losing their separate identities. In other cases, rivalry sends them scurrying into separate corners, and each keeps scrupulous tabs on who gets more, or less, of anything.

At a certain level, however, it doesn't matter what parents do. Siblings will always keep score. It's how they begin to measure *themselves*.

Social Comparison. According to Judy Dunn, Ph.D., and Robert Plomin, Ph.D., in their book, *Separate Lives: Why Siblings Are So Different*, this scrutiny of self and other, which researchers call "social comparison," starts in infancy and is a key component in the formation of one's identity.

Siblings are keenly aware of each other's varying talents, levels of self-confidence, and personalities. Indeed, this very awareness often results in the recognition that a sibling is "off"—that is, showing symptoms of mental illness—even before a parent does. Says Gary Goldsmith, cofounder and past president of the National Depressive and Manic-Depressive Association, "Siblings are often the eyes and ears of the family. They pick up on the warning signs."

And because of this penchant for comparison, siblings are exquisitely sensitive to parental favoritism, which can be showered either on the child who is in some way flawed, in need of special treatment, or on the child who shines, a source of parental pride. The surprise here is that being favored does *not* increase a child's self-esteem. As one group of researchers put it, "Being *singled out* is the potential risk factor. If *both* children are harshly treated, then *neither* is at risk."

Natural Enemies/Natural Allies. While parents may be duty-bound at least to attempt setting an exemplary, evenhanded example of behavior, siblings are not so constrained. Because they know each other so well, they can provoke one another with breathtaking ease. But they can also serve as each other's reality check: If, for instance, a parent is abusive, or does something that is out of character, siblings can confirm for one another that such behavior is wrong or odd.

Thus while siblings may be natural enemies, carving out their individual niches and jockeying for parental favoritism, they are also natural allies joined by blood, shared history, and common environmental ground. No matter how bitterly they may quarrel, or how rough their justice, when confronted by a common enemy they will frequently be as one in loyalty.

To determine how attached siblings feel toward one another—compared to how close they feel to their parents—Victor G. Cicirelli of Purdue University studied 100 college women. The overwhelming majority of respondents felt closer to their favorite sibling than to either parent, and indicated that they were more likely to share similar views with, feel understood by, and be relaxed with a cherished sibling.

Within these sibships themselves, of course, there were patterns of affinity. Laterborns felt closer than earlier borns, possibly because first- and secondborns identify more strongly with parents, having had greater access to them. And siblings who were close in age felt more attached to each other than to a sibling who was either much older or younger. In this study, gender did not prove to be a significant factor in sibling preference.

Other studies, however, show that gender does play a role in the sibling buddy system. Interestingly, some researchers have found that opposite sex siblings are often *closer* and have less conflict than same sex siblings. Because their "individuality" is a gender given, they don't have to work so hard to be unique.

Withal, siblings in general tend to retain a kind of "us" versus "them" attitude. In a study of 40 pairs of same sex and opposite sex adolescent and preadolescent siblings and their mothers (fathers weren't included), psychologist Sandra A. Graham-Bermann of the University of Michigan found that siblings consider themselves to be more alike than their mothers do. While each child's individuality may increase with age as they select and expand on their separate niches,

Dr. Graham-Bermann concludes that no matter what the age, siblings still maintain this perception.

According to another study, siblings who are bosom buddies do not feel close because of "family obligation." The only siblings who feel "obliged" are those who *aren't* close. This has obvious implications for parents who apply pressure on their children to be nicer to, or take care of, each other.

Identification: The "Mortar" of Sibling Ties. If there is one word to sum up the special intimacy of sibling partnerships, say Drs. Bank and Kahn, it is "identification": seeing oneself in the other. It's simply easier to relate to a family member of your own approximate age and rank—which is why siblings react so strongly to each other's high or low opinion. Studies show that children are more likely to pay attention to a sibling's criticism than to a parent's, even though they may hate hearing it.

It is precisely because of this identification that the loss of a sibling to mental illness is uniquely traumatic. An afflicted parent represents a picture of what one could become in the far distant future. But a mentally ill sibling, in whom one sees oneself, represents an image of what one is in danger of becoming *now*.

THE SIBLING VACUUM:
LOSING A SIBLING TO MENTAL ILLNESS

When a brother or sister develops a severe brain disorder, the family hierarchy goes through a kind of earthquake. To begin with, the "parental vacuum" enlarges as mothers and fathers do what they are supposed to do, which is to take care of the sickest child first. Their ability to contain the damage of the illness and at the same time remain alert to the needs of their well children—no small feat—makes all the difference in how the well children cope.

Yet even a parent's most herculean efforts will not spare well children the inevitable grief, and pileup of losses, that a sibling's madness spawns. For then there is not just a parental vacuum, but a *sibling vacuum* as well, as we saw with Luke at the beginning of this chapter.

When a sibling becomes mentally ill, he or she takes on a new, and fluctuating, persona, like a radio signal that keeps fading in and out. The sibling still looks the same, and sometimes even acts the same, but is fundamentally altered—sometimes psychologically "there," sometimes "not there," depending on the severity of the symptoms and the responses to medication.

When this happens, normal sibling rivalry and individuation, resentments and idealizations, are moot, and the well sibling is stranded in a limbo of confusion. It is as if all the rules suddenly changed in the middle of the contest. One cannot enter a healthy competition when one's afflicted brother or sister can barely get out of the gate. It wouldn't be fair. The relationship as it was—the familiar and predictable rhythms of reciprocity—in many ways withers, and with it a part of the well sibling's identity.

"Parents sometimes embrace the myth that their handicapped child is the only needy one," writes psychology professor Milton Seligman, Ph.D. "In some families the non-handicapped sibling is the most needy."

Of course, all siblings do not experience a sibling's mental illness in exactly the same way. Like the loss of a parent to mental illness, the impact of a sibling's instability also depends on certain interconnected variables, including:

• the severity and chronicity (i.e., frequency of episodes) of the illness;
• the age of the well sibling when illness strikes;
• the degree of pre-illness sibling closeness;
• the emotional family climate;
• the availability of outside support.

THE SEVERITY AND CHRONICITY
OF THE ILLNESS

While mental illness tends to incubate for as many as twenty years before it erupts, most of the siblings I interviewed could look back at their childhood years with the advantage of hindsight and say, "It began way back when we were kids. My sibling was always 'different.' "

Gail, forty-six, remembers her big sister Meredith, fifty, who was diagnosed with schizophrenia in her twenties, as always having been timid and childlike. Says Gail:

> Even though she was the eldest, she was always easily frightened, and always followed everyone's rules. Things that didn't bother anyone else bothered her. She was scared of shadows on the wall. I'd hold her hand walking down the street so she wouldn't be afraid. To this day, I do that. I protect her. There is a silver lining here: Her illness made me strong. Unlike my sister, I don't do *anything* on command.

To witness the childhood unfolding of mental illness is to see it at its worst. The earlier the onset, the more chronic and disturbing it is, particularly if it is not identified or treated. The trouble is, it's hard to parse out how much of a child's distressing behavior is simply quirky and how much is *sick*—and if it is "sick," *which* illness it is.

Early Signs of Schizophrenia. Judith L. Rapaport, M.D., director of the child psychiatry branch of NIMH, and her colleagues have recently been studying early onset schizophrenia, focusing on a core group of thirty-two children who clearly had the disorder by age twelve. "Even when they were small toddlers," she says, "these children had a lot of learning and developmental unevenness, and around the age of eight began having brief psychotic symptoms, such as hallucinations." Unfortunately, she adds, such early forms of schizophrenia are frequently misdiagnosed as autism or some other disorder.

According to Dr. E. Fuller Torrey and his colleagues, an estimated 25 to 40 percent of people with schizophrenia had a number of difficulties early on. These consumers were slow to talk and to read, were emotionally withdrawn, and had limited social skills and few friends. Their difficulties played out against the backdrop of their temperaments. Some were shy, easily frightened, dependent, and gentle. Others were unusually aggressive.

Early Signs of Affective Disorders. The same pattern of early difficulties is often true of people with affective disorders as well. In a survey of people with bipolar illness, nearly 60 percent reported that they'd had symptoms in childhood and adolescence. In fact, says Dr. Demitri Papolos, the younger the onset of bipolar disorder, the more severe the symptoms. When it shows up in adolescence, it *looks* like schizophrenia—complete with delusions and hallucinations—and, says Dr. Papolos, is misdiagnosed 90 percent of the time.

Dr. Rappaport believes that these early versions of affective disorders are probably "more malignant" forms of them. "Children with severe depression," she says, "particularly boys under age twelve, can hear voices that are accusing them of being dirty or smelly. Yet their families are being told that these children have schizophrenia."

What makes mental illness in children particularly alarming is the possibility of self-destruction. According to NIMH, most people who kill themselves have either diagnosable mental illness or substance abuse disorder. Suicide is the third leading cause of death among teenagers. Thus countless surviving siblings are acquainted with the harrowing loss of one of their own, and with feelings of guilt that they couldn't prevent it.

THE AGE OF THE WELL SIBLING WHEN ILLNESS STRIKES

The response of well siblings to these disorders depends in large measure upon their age when the illness manifests itself—and, in particular, on *what they are told about it*. Unless children are informed and educated about mental illness, they will root around for their own explanations for a sibling's peculiar behavior, a far more bruising experience than being told the truth.

One researcher has found that siblings of the mentally disabled often draw their own distorted conclusions and experience a variety of specific fears. They often feel that they caused it. They wonder if they'll "catch" it. They are dismayed about what to say to people about it. They worry about what will happen to the sibling. They feel guilty about their own feelings of anger.

And, of course, the younger they are, the more these fears will haunt them.

Effects in Early Childhood. For very young children, a sibling's symptoms can be particularly wounding because the normal boundaries between self and other—which are only just forming—are punctured again and again by the ill sibling's abnormal behavior.

Sidney, fifty, recalls every detail of the night his older sister, at age fourteen, had her first breakdown. She woke up screaming that there were snakes in her bed, and Sidney, then nine years old, padded out to the hall to find out what the commotion was. There he found his sister pounding their mother on the head with her fists. Sidney's mother, a widow, broke free of her daughter's grip and ran to the phone to call the police, who arrived in minutes. As they carried his raving sister out the door—she was taken to a hospital, where she was diagnosed as having bipolar disorder—Sidney, still barefoot, was dispatched by his mother next door to stay with a neighbor. Of those early years growing up with his sister, he says:

> For a long time, no one really explained what was wrong with her. All I knew was she was always vicious to me. Once she caught me in her room looking at her books, and she beat the hell out of me. If I got a new toy, she'd tear it apart. She would constantly tell me I was disgusting. The one time I had a tantrum about how mean she was, my mother screamed, "If I have two crazy children, I'll kill myself!" So from that day on, I was a perfect son. I don't think I ever consciously did anything to give my mother a moment's pain—I adored her. But I've never gotten over my sister's cruelty. To this day, when people ask if I have siblings, I'm always tempted to say, "I'm an only child."

Many young siblings, in their confusion, try to put as much emotional distance between themselves and the disturbed sibling as possible, creating a psychological moat to ward off the invasions of a brother's or sister's madness. These well siblings live in perpetual uncertainty, terrified that if they themselves do or think anything out of the ordinary, they will lose their minds, or be sent away from the family—just as their hospitalized siblings have been.

The identities of well siblings in the world outside are no less tenuous. Young children are mortified if they appear to be in any way "different" from their peers. If they are seen in public with the sibling when he or she acts "weird," they frequently are engulfed by enormous shame—guilt by sibling association.

Don Meyer, director of the Sibling Support Project at Children's Hospital and Medical Center in Seattle, who gives educational and peer support programs (called "Sibshops") for school-age brothers and sisters of chronically ill children, is an authority on the singular difficulties of siblings of the mentally ill. He says:

> Invisible disabilities can be especially poignant for siblings, because there is the expectation of normalcy. Mentally ill kids look normal. Siblings are more likely to be embarrassed by siblings with invisible disabilities because people might think you have what they have; if your brother acts goofy, it must mean that you're goofy, too. Kids get stared at when their mentally ill sibling acts strangely in public— whereas the sibling of a child, say, with cerebral palsy gets cut some slack.

Onset in Adolescence or Early Adulthood. When mental illness appears later in well siblings' lives, they often identify less with the ill sibling and more with their parents. Part of this parent identification occurs because these offspring have already begun moving out into the adult world, going to college, embarking on careers and marriage, having children, and becoming their parents' social peers.

The need to prop up their beleaguered parents—fueled by the parallel need for a safe family harbor to which they can periodically return—can eclipse empathy for a fallen sibling. In these cases, parents and offspring often reverse roles. While the parent is trying to help and protect the ill child, the other children are trying to help and protect the parents *from* that child.

Recall Matt, described at the beginning of chapter 1, who went to jail at the age of twenty-six after committing three robberies while in a psychotic state. Matt's illness didn't erupt until he was old enough to be on his own, beyond his parents' legal ability to force him into treatment. His behavior made his older sisters, Louise, twenty-seven, and Debby, twenty-nine, furious. Says Louise:

> He deceived us. He kept telling me he was doing well, getting a good job and all that, only later to find out he was lying. He borrowed money from me and never paid me back. He may be mentally ill, but don't ask me to trust him any farther than I can throw him. I don't have any pity. He's a con artist.

Louise's sister, Debby, is also distressed by her brother's illness, but for different reasons. She is torn apart by loyalty to her parents, and by sympathy for her brother's psychological torment. The result of her ambivalence is that she feels she's losing emotional ground. Says Debby:

> I was the only kid I knew growing up who didn't give her parents any trouble. And now I feel I have to keep that up—I don't want my folks to have any more problems than they already have. So when I'm really miserable, I tell my problems to my sister instead because I know I'm not destroying her by unloading. If my parents see me unhappy, they get really worried, which makes me *more* unhappy. I always thought my parents were so tough, and I've been surprised by how hard my brother's illness hit them. So I definitely don't want to burden them. But protecting my folks forces me not to deal with my own problems.

THE DEGREE OF PRE-ILLNESS SIBLING CLOSENESS

According to Drs. Bank and Kahn, sibling bonds tend to cluster in three categories of intimacy:

• *Close identification*, in which there is a sense of being identical or extremely similar. These siblings often idealize, and are blindly loyal, to one another;

• *Partial identification*, in which siblings either savor each other's differences and are able to learn from them, or feel hostile toward one another, but not so much so that they break off all contact;

• *Distant identification*, wherein siblings either actively reject each other, striving to be as unalike as possible, or "de-identify" with one another, vowing seldom, or never, to meet again.

These patterns of identification prior to an illness have everything to do with how the well sibling will respond when a brother or sister breaks down. Says family therapist Karen Gail Lewis, Ed.D., coauthor of *Siblings in Therapy: Life Span and Clinical Issues*, "A sibling's reaction is directly related to the relationship before the illness."

Consider the following examples of unrelated women who were sexually abused by their mentally ill brothers, and how very differently the women were affected by the abuse.

Inga, thirty-four, grew up in a house where brutality was routine. When her alcoholic father was on a tear, he'd line up all four kids and, one by one, lash them with a belt—always silencing them with the warning, "If you tell your mother, you'll get it worse next time." For her part, Inga's mother would make excuses for her husband because she, too, was battered by him.

Each of Inga's siblings reacted to their father's bullying in a variety of ways—by running away, or hiding in their rooms, for example. But the reactions of Inga's older brother Ralph were particularly ominous. Ralph took his frustrations out on Inga by intimidating and sexually molesting her. But he never mistreated Inga's younger sister, who harbors more sympathy for him.

By the age of twelve, the degree of Ralph's cruelty and disruptiveness had reached critical mass, and even his parents had to admit that there was something wrong with him. He was hospitalized repeatedly for schizophrenia. But his mental fragility summons in Inga no trace of mercy. Clearly a sibling who is "distantly identified" with her brother, she says:

> I hate my brother's guts—he was basically rotten to me from day one. I've already told my parents that when they die, there's no chance in hell I'm going to take responsibility for him. I've done my time. I can't afford to let him anywhere near me.

Compare this case to that of Paula, twenty-seven, and her brother, Fred, thirty. Although Paula was never beaten up by her older brother, her *mother* was, becoming her son's punching bag in her efforts to protect her children from him. But when she wasn't looking, Fred would grab Paula's genitals or breasts, threatening to rape her.

Paula didn't tell her parents because, she says, "they were going through hell," and she didn't want to add to their already staggering burden. But the primary reason Paula kept her secret was that of the three siblings, she and Fred were always the closest.

Paula falls into the category of "close identification" with her brother. When she was little and had a cold, Fred would keep her company by playing dolls or cutouts with her. Paula worshipped him and so, for a time, did everyone else. He was the most popular kid in school, always getting As, a star athlete.

Around the time of his fourteenth birthday, he began to disintegrate. He failed every subject in school. He started using street drugs and was increasingly violent at home. In those years, Paula got her share of her brother's furies. For instance, if she didn't give him a sip of her soda, he'd cuff her. Eventually, he was hospitalized for schizophrenia, and spent the next four years in and out of assorted institutions, spelled by months at home where, inevitably, he'd resume his violent ways.

Still, Paula was then, and is now, Fred's devoted defender. She can never forget how kind her big brother was to her when she was a child, and feels that it is her responsibility to stay emotionally connected to him, since no one else in the family can any longer bear to (although he's always included in family gatherings). Says Paula:

I know he's mean. But he's also too crazy to grasp anything. Maybe I just got used to his abuse, but my take is that anything he does wrong, it's not his fault because it isn't him. Fred hasn't had a coherent thought since he was fourteen. I mean, he thinks he killed Hitler. This is a person who will sit up all night crying like a three-year-old, saying, "I love you" and clinging to you. I would never turn my back on him. My parents and I already decided that when they die, I will be his conservator. I told them that whatever they were planning to leave to me, they should give to Fred—he'll need it.

For each of these women, the past sibling relationship was prologue to their post-diagnosis connection. But as they themselves acknowledge, their very different feelings about their brothers are tinged by the family values with which they were raised—in Inga's case, an eat-or-be-eaten attitude; in Paula's, the importance of family loyalty.

EMOTIONAL FAMILY CLIMATE

Whether chaotic or loyal, however, no family can remain unscathed by a relative's psychological death. Even in the best of circumstances, a parental vacuum is all but inevitable when mothers and fathers are distracted by a child's mental illness. The disorder itself becomes a kind of toxic presence even when the afflicted child isn't around.

Greta, thirty-nine, was at first relieved when her sister was hospitalized for bipolar disorder. For a change, Greta, then twelve, would get her parents' undivided attention. But soon she realized that even with her sister out of the house, nothing had changed. Says Greta:

> At the dinner table, we'd sit there not knowing if, God forbid, my sister would call, begging to be brought home. Every time the phone rang, my mother would jump to pick it up and Daddy would race upstairs to get on the extension. If it wasn't my sister calling, they'd come back to the table. If it was my sister, they'd stay on the phone forever. And I'd sort of watch this performance, night after night. I discovered very quickly that it didn't matter if my sister was there or wasn't there. The whole focus was still on her.

When a sibling's mental state is in ruins, the sibling mini-hierarchy shifts. The ill child is treated by parents as younger than he or she is, and the healthy sibling as older, charged with greater responsibilities. Most well siblings will try to rise to the occasion.

Whatever their feelings for an ill brother or sister, siblings often find that the most important thing in life is to make sure *their parents are okay*. After all, their survival depends on their parents' well-being, especially if the children are not yet adults.

It is not so much guilt or empathy that drives these siblings to be super good, or to seem super calm. Rather, it is fear that if they do anything to cause their parents to falter, the whole family might collapse. As we shall see in chapter 6, in these situations well siblings contort themselves into roles to help restore some sense of balance, however frail, within the family.

Siblings of the mentally ill are given a number of bewildering messages by their overwrought parents. They learn to suppress their own intense feelings, particularly of anger, which might be construed by the parents as a sign that these children, too, are going to pieces. Siblings often learn that *any* outbursts will be met with parental disapproval. They can no longer be themselves. Says Dr. Clarice J. Kestenbaum:

> Siblings of the mentally ill have their childhoods taken away from them. They feel that they can't be bad, act up, be naughty, be like a kid, because they don't want to be a double disappointment to their parents. And then they may become very depressed.

Such emotional paralysis was the family leitmotif when Hillary, forty, a psychotherapist, was growing up. She adored her brother Tim, forty-four, when they were kids, largely because he stood in such colorful, if demonic, contrast to their conservative, rather prim parents. Says Hillary:

> Tim was the biggest influence of my childhood. He was an enthralling presence—all the excitement would begin when he was around. He'd beguile you and then terrify you. He'd put you in the clothes dryer and count how many times you'd go around. Or he'd say, "Let's play cowboys and Indians," then tie you to a tree, hold a hatchet to your throat, and walk away, leaving you there for hours.

If Hillary's parents were aware of this sadistic tendency in their firstborn, she does not remember any discussion of it at the time. What she does remember is that when Tim was fifteen, he started flunking, drinking heavily, and getting arrested by the police for minor crimes. Her parents' solution was to send him to a rigidly authoritarian summer camp where, they hoped, he might be muscled into self-control. He was soon invited to leave.

Back home, he developed a taste for cocaine and even more remarkable cruelty, on one occasion flushing a kitten down the toilet. In town, he was known as a hothead, famous for beating up his girlfriend of the moment. At eighteen, Tim simply ran away, and with rare exceptions hasn't been seen since.

His parents never considered that he had a brain disorder (Hillary thinks he's a textbook psychopath). The shame of it would have been too great.

Through those years of growing up without her brother, in ways it was as if he'd never left. Everything Hillary or her siblings did was filtered through their parents' anxiety that one of them would turn out to be a family disgrace. Tim was the norm against which they were judged: If you behaved, you were "not Tim." Says Hillary:

Any mild rebellion looked to my parents like more kerosine on the family fire. You could see the horror in my mother's face if I did anything that seemed to her slightly out of line—she' say, "You know who you remind me of when you do that." So it was in the air, this *thing*, and it had a pervasive, depressing effect. I gave up any outward sign of seeming different. There was this tension that something terrible was about to happen, and that you might be the cause of it. You were all in this little boat and any rocking could cause the whole thing to splinter and fall apart, and you'd all drown, because it was all too much for my parents to bear. They were done in by a terrible sense of failure; it just poisoned everything. It took me a long time to recover.

•

THE AVAILABILITY OF OUTSIDE SUPPORTS

It is because parents of mentally ill children are so overwhelmed and frightened that outside family supports are crucial to the well siblings' emotional well-being. Yet the specific concerns of brothers and sisters are seldom considered by mental health practitioners and policy makers.

Says Don Meyer of the Sibling Support Project:

All siblings worry enormously about being as ill as their brother or sister. Little kids need to know that they didn't cause it, and that they can't catch it. Grade school kids need to know how to explain the illness to themselves as well as to others, who will surely ask. Teenagers need to know what the parents' plans are—adolescents frequently get the message that they have to foresake their futures for their ill siblings. And adult siblings remind me of nothing so much as parents of newly diagnosed kids. They're thrust into the wacky world of agencies and programs and regulations and acronyms, and often are clueless because nobody's reaching out to them. There's a lot of lip service in the professional field to the notion of "family support." But usually that means working only with the ill child and his parents.

Of all the difficulties siblings of the mentally ill face, perhaps none is as imponderable and damaging as their invisibility to the very professionals whose job it is to notice and respond to their confusion and despair.

In my sample of forty-three brothers and sisters of the mentally ill, only three were ever directly approached by a health care worker during family visits to their hospitalized siblings. One of these exceptions is Celia, thirty-six, who says that the attention she did get—when she was twenty-four—was too little, too late. She recalls:

My sister was in the same mental institution on and off for ten years. One time when I was visiting her, I couldn't get her to talk to me. She was catatonic. So I left her room, walked down by the nurses' station, and I just broke down crying. I said, "I'm sorry, she won't say anything and I'm just so discouraged.'' The nurse looked at me and said, ''You should go to the group therapy session.'' I said, ''What group?'' She said, ''The support group for family members.'' I said, ''Is this something new?'' She said, ''Oh no—we've always had them.'' Here I had been going to this hospital for years. They knew who I was—my sister had been in there dozens of times. And they were just getting around to telling me there was help for people like me. No one in the hospital had ever said, ''You are being badly affected by your sister's illness.''

The result of this professional neglect is that virtually all the siblings I interviewed have an abiding distrust of the mental health system. That over 75 percent of them in later life got therapy for themselves *anyhow* is a tribute to their triumphant hope over bitter experience. Perhaps only in adulthood was it safe for them to go back into psychologically troubled waters. At least this time, it could be on their own terms.

Until they finally get around to asking for help—*if* they ever ask—these siblings tend to wander in the emotional wilderness, suspended between the twin imperatives of their families' crises and their own misshapen identities.

THE LEGACIES OF A SIBLING'S MENTAL ILLNESS

Because of the power of the sibling partnership, brothers and sisters of the mentally ill inherit certain enduring legacies (which will be explored in detail in part three of this book), chief among them feelings of entrapment and unending grief.

A sibling's illness is virtually inescapable. These emotionally fragile kin will continue to be their well siblings' generational partners into adulthood and old age, even if they do not see each other very often. Since a sibling is the only contemporary family witness to one's childhood, the loss of his or her ability to remember it accurately, and to grow emotionally in tandem with a well sibling, is a kind of living death.

As one woman, now in her thirties and with a husband and children of her own, told me:

> We all worry that every time the phone rings it will be more bad news. The whole world stops and you get sucked up by the illness. The desire to be able to fix it all is very strong. Perhaps if I do this or that, it will all work out. I won't have to watch everything I say. I can be happy without feeling guilty that my brother will never experience happiness. And I won't feel the sadness of watching helplessly as my parents struggle to make sense of it. Every decision, every thought, is tied to the illness. It's like wearing a leash.

This despair and helplessness is true not only of the siblings—and, as we have seen, the parents and children—of the mentally ill. It is true for the *partners* of the mentally ill as well, who have their own unique set of problems. They are not related to their partners by blood. Therefore, their choices can be even thornier—a war between self-preservation and moral obligation, with no clear ground rules.

CHAPTER 4

When a Partner Is Mentally Ill

Maybe someday somebody's going to figure out that the real victims here are not just the people who get sick, but the families, too. There must be some way to help families when a member gets out of control. Maybe if we could have gotten the right kind of help from the doctors and the legal system when my wife got sick, my kids and I wouldn't have had to suffer like this—our lives were sacrificed.

—Charles, 51

Last May, Charles and his wife, Alma, celebrated their twenty-fifth wedding anniversary. Actually, "celebrate" would be overstating it. The couple spent the evening the way they always do, sitting in the living room, with Alma watching television and Charles doing paperwork he brings home each night from his job at an insurance brokerage firm. No matter what the business crisis or backlog, Charles never works late at the office. Every evening at precisely five-thirty, he walks in the front door of his split-level home in Minneapolis. Because if for any reason he's delayed, Alma is on the phone, frantically looking for him.

To call theirs a "marriage" in the conventional sense of the word would be a stretch. They haven't had sex in years. They have no social life. They never go to the movies or away on holiday. Their kids rarely visit. The phone never rings.

Of course, it wasn't always like this. Way back in high school, Charles and Alma were wildly in love, their future bright with promise. He was an ambitious young man on his way to an Ivy League college and she—shy but brilliant and full of fun—was about to enter the state university. As soon as they got their degrees, they were married.

Three years later, Alma gave birth to twin sons, and Charles was over the moon with happiness. But then one night when he came home from work, he found his wife in tears. "I'm a terrible person," Alma sobbed. "The babies have been fussing all day, and I keep thinking about drowning them." Charles replied, "You're not a terrible person, but we really need to talk to someone about this." The psychiatrist they consulted said Alma had acute depression, and put her on antidepressants.

And so began Charles's twenty-year pilgrimage into the mental health maze, and the gradual dismantling of his dreams. In the beginning, Alma's illness seemed manageable. Every so often, she'd be swallowed up by despair, her psychiatrist would change her medications, and her bleak mood would lift. Six years into the illness, however, Alma sank into a twelve-month depression that pills didn't budge. Says Charles:

> She'd sit in a chair all day and not move. Absolutely catatonic. The kids and I did everything—cooking, washing, ironing, cleaning. I felt very protective of her. She was just so pitiful. I kept thinking, Well, this will go away. Instead, it got worse.

When Alma emerged from her long psychological sleep, something new had been added to her emotional repertoire: mania. Gone was the shyness; in its place was a whirlwind of angry self-absorption. Indeed, it was the mania that nearly did Charles in. Alma abruptly decided that she didn't need pills or her doctor anymore. She began having extramarital affairs, bragging about them to Charles and laughing at him for being "weak." She started spending lavish amounts of money on herself, on one occasion ordering 200 pairs of sandals.

Charles, whose business was thriving, managed to cover the bills, but he couldn't put a stop to Alma's extravagance. Her name was on the mortgage to their house, so she could acquire credit cards with impunity. Nor could he get Alma's doctors to give him much guidance. "They'd just prescribe more pills," he says bitterly, "and send you on your way—good-bye and go to hell."

Little by little, the family's world shrank. In restaurants, she'd overturn plates of food, so the couple stopped eating out. At home, she tyrannized her children. She pressed them into constant domestic service and berated them if their work fell short of her impossible standards, never allowing them to have play dates. During the night she'd be on the prowl, creating tomorrow's mess by knocking lamps off tables and throwing dishes.

"You couldn't set limits on her," says Charles. "Every time I tried, there'd be hell to pay. To keep the peace, we humored her. She ruled the roost." In an attempt to give his kids a breather, on weekends he'd take Alma on walks, and in the summer, the boys went away to camp. But he couldn't monitor Alma all the time. He had to earn a living to bankroll her illness and spending habits which, together, have cost him $250,000 so far.

The part that really makes Charles tremble in the telling is that it was nearly impossible to get Alma involuntarily hospitalized, no matter how deluded or destructive her behavior. Says Charles:

> It was always the same runaround. I'd call the police or local mental health facility, and I usually got nowhere, because she wasn't "a danger to herself or others." One time I was so desperate, I went to the town judge and said, "Either you give me the commitment papers, or you'll be in the hospital yourself, because I'm going to kick your teeth in." I got the papers, but it took the stuffing out of me.

Ever since his kids went off to college, they've seldom come back. Charles never puts any pressure on them, since he feels so guilty about what they went through when they were growing up. "I've always told them, 'Go live your life,' " he says.

While the peaks and valleys of Alma's illness have eased somewhat in recent years—she resumed taking her medications, and most of the time she's in a pharmacological fog—life for Charles is an uneasy peace.

Of all the extraordinary aspects of this chronicle, perhaps the most remarkable is that Charles has stuck it out. Few people would have blamed him if he had simply plucked up his kids and decamped—indeed, the boys used to beg him to do just that. When I asked him why he had not, Charles replied, "She always said she'd kill herself if I left. Anyhow, the way I was raised, you don't pass the buck. You take care of your own."

THE DANCER OR THE DANCE

Falling in love with a person who has, or who develops, mental illness is like starting in the middle of someone else's story. With no mutual prologue to draw upon, one is guided only by one's own experience and hopes—the belief that this will be the happily-ever-after part of life. In some cases, the illness may not yet have put in an appearance. In others, the vulnerable person is already in treatment, the symptoms apparently well in hand.

But until you actually live with someone who has a brain disorder, it's virtually impossible to anticipate the encumbrances that often accompany it. Partners of the mentally ill quickly find out what most parents, siblings, and offspring already know: how difficult it is to distinguish between the person and the illness.

The difference for partners, as opposed to kin, is that they must be not only caregiver, but lover, too. They may also be called upon to serve as both mother and father to their children, as well as primary, if not sole, breadwinner, depending upon the cadences of the partner's illness.

People with affective disorders, for instance, often have trouble sustaining their marital roles and communicating well with their partners. They can be extremely needy and exacting, requiring constant reassurance, or they can be totally unresponsive. People with schizophrenia can be even more withdrawn and unresponsive, and in any case require a lot of elbow room and quiet.

The trick for well partners is to figure out when such behaviors are "the illness talking," as mental health professionals put it, and when they are the result of honest-to-God crankiness or manipulation that cries out for limit-setting. It's hard to keep giving and caring for someone if there is little in return, or if what ricochets back is angry or demanding. Many well partners, their patience wearing thin, find themselves withdrawing emotionally or becoming short-tempered themselves, which can shatter the ill partner's piecemeal self-confidence—which, in turn, invites an avalanche of symptoms.

It is this coercive cycle of bruised feelings and angry response that can lead straight to relapse. For example, when family members are critical or are emotionally overinvolved, people with bipolar illness relapse 94 percent of the time, as compared to a relapse rate of 17 percent when families are more even-tempered and calm. High relapse rates also dot the medical charts of people with schizophrenia whose families are volatile.

The result is that partners of the mentally ill often feel they *cannot be themselves*. They must try to apply the brakes on their own emotions, adoping a brittle veneer of cheerfulness, because if they do not, the consequences could be grave. It's like living with a time bomb. Mentally disturbed partners don't just react—they overreact, so much so that they might be launched into the psychological netherworld, if not oblivion. And for many of their partners, the strain can become unbearable.

Painful Bargains. Having a mentally ill lover or spouse frequently presents the well partner with a menu of unsatisfying choices, particularly when children are involved. On the one hand, the fragile partner may have no other source of emotional or financial support, and might be destroyed if the relationship were to end. On the other hand, there is the stability of one's children, as well as one's own mental health, to be considered.

Complicating matters is that the moral thermostat of obligation is set lower for partners than for parents, siblings, or offspring, who are bound by blood and the ancient traditions of loyalty. Partners are connected by choice, and that which is chosen can be unchosen. After all, the well partner has a theoretical bailout position: returning the ill person to his or her family of origin.

The irony is that people with mental illness tend to fare *better* with partners, with whom they frequently have a more intimate and confiding connection, than with kin. According to psychiatry professor Silvano Arieti, M.D., partners and spouses are less likely to treat their vulnerable mates as if they were helpless children, whereas parents may consciously or unconsciously encourage filial dependence. A partner, who has a greater investment in the ill person's adult participation, simply expects more and has less incentive to remain in the relationship if the afflicted person doesn't at least *try* to function. The ill partner is highly motivated to cooperate.

But while the ill partner may fare better, the well partner may fare worse. For one thing, there is the loss of companionship, to say nothing of a social life if the afflicted partner is in a psychotic episode or cannot withstand the stimulation of lively conversation and activity. For another, the couple's sex life may dwindle. Some medications blunt the senses and dull sexual ardor. The ill person's shaky self-esteem and awareness of winnowing options may have an equally cooling effect on desire.

Then, too, partners of the mentally ill may feel a guilty sense of complicity—that they somehow caused the illness, or made it worse. As Kayla F. Bernheim, Ph.D., and Anthony F. Lehman, M.D., point out in their book, *Working with Families of the Mentally Ill*, spouses who are informed about the illness prior to marriage are less given to such remorse. But they may feel that they betrayed their children by knowingly bringing them into a family with so many built-in psychological complexities.

Partners of the mentally ill suffer other deprivations, such as reduction of income. People with chronic brain disorders, especially if they are untreated, often cannot hold a job due to scattered concentration or absenteeism. In a survey of people with bipolar disorder, for instance, nearly a third had been fired, and 46 percent had to stop working outside the home when their illness was not properly managed. Consequently, the partners and progeny of the mentally ill are often swept into a downward financial spiral.

Spouses and lovers also run the risk of physical and emotional burnout. An estimated 40 percent of well partners of depressed people, for example, are themselves so overburdened that they are candidates for professional help. Female partners are likelier than males to tilt into overload because of their multiple roles. When husbands are mentally ill, family and household routines may hardly lose a beat, because the wife, even if she works full-time, tries to maintain the domestic tempo. In contrast, when wives are ill, husbands, who are less seasoned in domesticity, tend to summon outside help—which is not to say that they, too, are not stretched thin.

Bittersweet Partings. All of this wreaks havoc on romantic commitment. In the survey of people with bipolar disorder just mentioned, nearly 60 percent reported that their relationships and marriages had either failed or were sorely tested when the illness was not under control; and even when it was under control, 32 percent experienced romantic losses. In another study, depressed patients were nine times more likely to be divorced than the general population.

Stanley, forty-six, is a veteran of such partings. By the time he got married at the age of twenty-four, he had developed too great a fondness for alcohol. Booze helped to dilute the harrowing sense of desolation that had repeatedly ambushed him since adolescence. Even after the birth of his son, he was unable to curb his drinking. And although his alcoholism didn't interfere with his work—he is a novelist—he started blacking out at night. His doctor said that if he didn't dry out, he'd die.

Sobriety seemed to him a more killing fate—it flushed out the demons that lurked beneath his liquid safety net. "It felt like the ground opened up and I was falling into the center of the earth," he recalls of his first breakdown. Every winter for four years in a row, he had to sign himself into a psychiatric facility to have his depression eliminated by shock treatments. He also began psychotherapy with a compassionate psychiatrist who helped him to reel in his furies. He hasn't had a drink, or relapse, in twenty years.

But his romantic track record is littered with loss. Stanley's illness cost him his marriage, a casualty of his drinking, hospitalizations, and his lingering insecurities. The few romantic liaisons he's had since his divorce have all fizzled. Of his fitful lovelife, Stanley says ruefully:

> Whenever I get close to a woman, I'm terrified of being rejected. So I get depressed again. When that happens, I get very, very defensive. That's frightening to women, and they pull away—they can't handle it. I can understand that. It's a lot to ask of anyone.

Alicia, fifty-six, has also had her share of romantic failure, but in her case, she was the well spouse who left. There was little incentive to stay. Her husband, who had severe bipolar illness, was either dangerously psychotic, threatening to kill the family, or lying on the couch staring at the TV. Or he was in the hospital. Alicia had more than just her own safety to worry about. She also had to consider the well-being of her two small children. Says Alicia:

> He resisted getting any kind of help. He'd say, "I don't need it. I'm not sick," even though he used to see angels flying over our bed. If I had wanted to devote my life to just trying to keep him out of the hospital, I'd probably still be living with him. But I had two kids to protect. I used to feel guilty for leaving him. Now I feel even *guiltier* for having married him in the first place. If I hadn't left, we'd all be in much worse shape. We might have died.

As these examples illustrate, mental illness can gradually erode the romantic bond. The question, then, for partners of the mentally ill is not so much "Why don't you leave?"—the majority of spouses and lovers do—as it is "Why do you stay?"

Part of the answer is that for many of these faithful partners, there are rewarding trade-offs. But, according to my interviews and research, these trade-offs depend heavily on one or more of the following factors:

- the nature of the relationship prior to illness;
- the capacity of the ill partner to resume his or her pre-illness role;

• the ability of the ill partner to "own," or take responsibility for, his or her illness;

• the family history of the well partner.

THE NATURE OF THE RELATIONSHIP PRIOR TO ILLNESS

For the first ten years of their relationship, Arnold, forty-four, an attorney, and his lover, Steve, thirty-nine, a high school teacher, were exceptionally happy. Both were extremely well-liked by their colleagues and friends; they traveled all over the world; they shared a passion for opera and literature. Life was perfect.

And then one sultry afternoon five summers ago, Arnold got a puzzling long-distance call at his Boston office from Steve, who was in Albuquerque at a teachers' convention. Arnold recalls:

> Steve is an enthusiastic guy, but this time he sounded wired. He told me I was to close my practice at once because he had just put a down payment on a house and wanted us to move there immediately. I said we'd talk about it when he got back. The next day I got a call from the manager of Steve's hotel, who said that Steve was holed up in his room, howling that the CIA was after him.

Fortunately, Steve himself recognized that something was dreadfully wrong with him. With the help of his colleagues, he got on a plane back to Boston.

What was "wrong," the doctors said, was late-onset schizophrenia. Steve signed himself into a psychiatric hospital, where he stayed for eight months. After he was discharged, he was able to resume his teaching job and the couple's active social life. But within a year, the medication he was taking stopped being effective and he gradually deteriorated. No longer able to work, he had to go on full disability benefits. Since then, he has been bounced from one drug treatment to another, with only fair results. All that's left of his former self is an enduring sweetness, a kind of childlike innocence, along with what

Arnold calls an "elegant memory"—he never forgets a face or a name.

Early into the illness Arnold was determined to make Steve well. But as time went by, he realized that his partner would never fully recover, and that Steve's present condition was irreversible. Although Steve is seldom totally psychotic, he's nowhere near completely lucid. He's convinced, for instance, that the FBI is tailing him.

In the last five years, most of the couple's friends have dropped them. Arnold is on twenty-four-hour-a-day call, because sometimes Steve gets lost walking around Boston and he has to go find him. Arnold has had to turn down clients because he can't accept cases that require out-of-town business trips. The strain of taking care of Steve has begun to catch up with Arnold. His blood pressure has skyrocketed, and recently he started psychotherapy to try to reduce his stress levels.

When asked to choose one word to sum up his life today, the word Arnold selects is "trapped." He continues:

> I wouldn't wish this on my worst enemy for the simple reason that this is not a terminal illness; it's permanent. Steve depends on me. I'm terrified of the enormous responsibility of just keeping him alive, which I know is not my legal responsibility. But I believe it's my moral responsibility. If the tables were turned, he'd do the same for me.

Arnold may feel snared, but he would never consider leaving Steve, who earned his devotion over the years prior to the illness. And Steve is just functional enough that many of the qualities that enamoured Arnold in the first place are still intact. To leave someone so kind, and who poses no threat, is for Arnold unthinkable.

As this vignette illustrates, love may not make up for all the losses that mental illness exacts, but it helps, especially among couples who have had a long history of true friendship, tenderness, and mutual caregiving. For them, the fact that a partner is sick is almost beside the point.

For other couples, however, love is not enough. There has to be a good deal more to keep them together.

THE CAPACITY OF THE ILL PARTNER TO RESUME A PRE-ILLNESS ROLE

Another important component of romantic commitment is how mentally ill partners functioned before the disorder set in, and whether or not they are able to resume their former roles once their symptoms abate.

Researchers at the Clarke Institute of Psychiatry in Toronto report that the best outcomes for people suffering from schizophrenia, for example, are those who, prior to the illness, were sociable, had friends and hobbies, enjoyed a measure of achievement at school or at work, and were able to perform sexually. They tend to be able to return to their former roles.

Of course, not all mentally ill people are able to resume *all* their former roles. Many can continue working, but some cannot. Yet even totally disabled casualties of brain disorders are often capable of resuming their *domestic* roles—as parent, partner, and friend. As long as an afflicted partner is able on some level to provide vital, cherished reciprocity in the relationship, there is a much greater likelihood that a couple will stay together.

It must be remembered that mental illness damages only part of the brain's utility—IQ, for example, is not affected. With certain psychologically impaired people, it's virtually impossible for friends and co-workers to detect their disorder because they are able to compensate deftly for their vulnerabilities. And while life post-diagnosis may not be exactly a breeze for them, through sheer determination the majority are able to pick up most of the pieces of their former selves and press on.

Such a person is Fred Frese, Ph.D., director of psychology at Western Reserve Psychiatric Hospital in Ohio, who gives new meaning to the word "charismatic." Indeed, at the annual convention of the National Alliance for the Mentally Ill in 1995, one of the hottest tickets was a standing-room-only seminar at which he was a featured speaker. Dr. Frese is such a gifted and hilariously funny performer that he is invited all over the country to give talks to crowds of "CNPs"—or "Chronically Normal Persons," as he calls them—about mental illness.

Dr. Frese is an expert on paranoid schizophrenia because he has it himself. The disorder was diagnosed prior to his getting his doctorate in psychology in the 1970s. Because of his intelligence and warmth, he disguises his symptoms with singular grace. In fact, it is those very traits that caused his wife to fall in love with him twenty years ago and to raise four children with him.

Fred Frese is vigilant about his symptoms, constantly monitoring his need for medication. He carries a spare bottle of pills in the glove compartment of his car in case of emergencies. He has fashioned a number of tactics to "cover" for his illness, humor being chief among them. Still, he lives with a perpetual sensitivity to criticism—one of his symptoms—which feels to him like being hit with a sledgehammer. To make sure his symptoms stay in check, he carries in his wallet a little card—to be proffered if someone seems close to stirring them up—which reads:

I need to tell you that I am a person suffering from schizophrenia. When I am berated, belittled, insulted or otherwise treated in an oppressive manner, I tend to become emotionally ill. Could I ask you to restate your concern in a manner that tends not to disable me. Thank you for your consideration.

Although Dr. Frese has his limitations—before he gives a speech, or attends a convention, he increases his medications—he is nevertheless a hardworking and highly esteemed professional. Having experienced his own hell in assorted back wards of mental institutions, few people are as qualified as he is to help others in their struggle with mental illness, and to be a role model for them.

"There have been so many individuals with manic-depression and schizophrenia who have made contributions to society," he says. "We have specific deficits, and by using other parts of our brains, we are able to make up for those deficits. Having a brain disorder doesn't mean we can't contribute."

Researchers cite this very ability to return to what they call "premorbid functioning"—a Lazarusesque term for "your old self"—as being instrumental in couples staying together regardless of the specific psychiatric diagnosis, and in keeping the ill partner out of the hospital. In these cases, a mate's mental illness may not be as great an encumbrance to the well partner as outsiders might think. Dr. Arieti has observed that the "subjective burden" of a family member's mental illness may be a lot less than researchers, who are less intimately involved, may realize in their "objectivity."

The Eyes of Beholders. Of crucial importance in this regard is the way unimpaired partners *perceive* their mates' mental illness—that is, whether it's seen as a sign of sudden, no-fault disability, or a red flag of innate laziness and flawed character. Dr. John Richters of NIMH and psychologist Sheldon Weintraub, Ph.D., of the Stony Brook High Risk Project in New York, call this perception of illness "the symptom controllability hypothesis."

According to their theory, people who function well before the onset of mental illness tend to break down with a bang—that is, with "positive" symptoms such as hallucinations. Because such symptoms are so out of character, they are perceived as unintentional signs of true illness. And since "positive" symptoms are eminently treatable, these victims of mental illness are often restored to their former roles.

The same cannot be said of people with "negative symptoms," such as apathy or indifference to hygiene, say the researchers. For these people, the illness begins gradually, and the symptoms are therefore perceived as being part of the person's character—hence controllable and a matter of choice. It is negative symptoms that erode romantic partnerships, because they are construed as volitional. So, too, are symptoms of poor impulse control, such as alcoholism.

In their studies, Drs. Richters and Weintraub have found that spouses derive much more marital satisfaction if the mentally ill person's behavior is seen to have a *medical*, rather than simply *characterological*, explanation. Therefore, disturbed conduct can more easily be tolerated. By blaming the behavior on the illness, and not on the person, the well partner is able to make certain allowances for the afflicted partner, who is then encouraged to do his or her best to improve and take charge of the illness.

THE ABILITY OF THE ILL PERSON TO "OWN" HIS OR HER ILLNESS

Which brings us to another factor, indeed, *the key factor* in the weathering of a partner's mental illness: the "ownership" by the afflicted partner of his or her disorder—that is, whether or not the ill partner can recognize and get treatment for the illness, and be held accountable for its potential destructiveness. As Dr. Nancy C. Andreasen has written:

> Of course the mentally ill have responsibilities. While a person suffering from depression or schizophrenia may not be able to help the fact that he has the illness, it benefits neither him nor society to treat him as if he is a helpless and irresponsible cripple.

Helen, thirty-four, and Glen, thirty-six, have experienced both sides of this issue: what happens when a partner does, and does not, take responsibility for his illness. The couple have been married for twenty years. Well, *altogether* twenty years. For a three-year stretch right around the halfway mark they were divorced because Glen was dangerously psychotic and unwilling to accept his doctors' diagnosis: He had schizoaffective disorder. "Love was not enough to keep us together at that point," Helen says as Glen nods in agreement. "He was very intimidating."

Until he became sick, Glen was a congenial, slightly overweight truck driver who couldn't wait to return to his wife and five-year-old daughter, Maria, at the end of the workday. But suddenly, over a three-week period in the 1980s, he lost thirty pounds and was unable to sleep at night. Says Glen:

> I was supercharged. I was the bull in any corral who wouldn't hesitate to face any man, any time. It was like I was the leader and everyone was my follower. Then I hit bottom, and the illness started to snowball. The thing about mental illness is that it affects the brain, the center of

being. And when you have a brain injury, you don't have another organ available to assess the situation.

At Helen's insistence, Glen signed himself into a mental hospital. From that point on, it was clear that he was too sick to work. But the problem was not so much the illness as it was his refusal to recognize its existence. Glen stopped taking his medications and began using street drugs. He either ignored his wife and daughter or was verbally abusive to them. Helen asked him for a divorce, which Glen says was the best thing that could have happened. Losing his family forced him to acknowledge the price of his denial. He again signed himself into a hospital and spent a year there.

When he was discharged, Glen was a changed man, willing to abide by Helen's terms of reconciliation. She wanted full power of attorney so she could hospitalize him if he was unable to hospitalize himself. She informed him that while help would always be available, he alone was accountable for his behavior. Glen agreed to both terms, and the couple remarried. "If it weren't for Helen's strengths, there wouldn't be a marriage," says Glen. "I give her immense credit."

Helen realized the stakes of staying, particularly the potential risk to their daughter. She promised Maria that she would never be put in harm's way: If Glen started to become psychotic, he understood he'd have to be hospitalized.

All of these ground rules and agreements had their severest test two years ago, when Glen had the most terrifying episode of his life. He had been secretly collecting guns, and one morning he announced that he didn't want to live anymore, and that if Helen and Maria didn't leave, no one in the family would be alive by sundown.

Glen barricaded himself into the house and said he'd shoot anyone who tried to take him out. Helen and Maria ran next door to call the police—in minutes, the house was surrounded by squad cars. An extraordinarily calm and well-trained police officer was able to persuade Glen to come outdoors, unarmed, to get into an unmarked car—to lessen the family's embarrassment—and to go directly to the hospital.

What traumatized Helen most about this experience was not that her husband was as dangerous as a person can get. Rather, it was how close he came to being killed, either by his own hand, or by a hail of bullets if he'd actually opened fire on the police, who would have had no choice but to fire back.

Helen is certain that, under her loving watch—she is her husband's reality check—there will be no repetition of Glen's last episode. As time goes on, in all likelihood her gamble will continue to pay off. Many mental illnesses lessen their sting as the afflicted person ages. Longitudinal studies demonstrate that functioning gradually improves, at least in terms of the most alarming symptoms. For example, by the time people with schizophrenia reach their forties, many are able to resume their social and working lives.

With her eyes on that particular prize, Helen works only part-time, at night, when Maria, now fifteen, is home, so that Glen's moods are always monitored. The arrangement is fine with Maria, who says she likes having her dad around, even if he's sometimes irritable, because she gets to spend more time with him than any of her friends do with their fathers. Glen helps Maria with her homework and tries to attend all her soccer matches.

Over the years, Maria has become an astute student of human behavior, reading everything she can about mental illness and talking candidly with her parents about it. Her father's disorder and his openness about it have made her unusually mature and wise. She plans to put her firsthand knowledge to use by becoming a psychologist when she grows up.

For Glen's part, he is able, most of the time, to be a caring father and husband. Neither he nor his illness are concealed from the close-knit community in which the family lives. "I'm not hidden away," he jokes. Their circle of friends is, if anything, wider than it was before he got sick. When he's up to it, Glen and his family go on picnics or to the movies. And in between, he sleeps a lot, a consequence of the many drugs he must take to stay in this world.

None of this would be possible if Glen were not willing to hold himself responsible for his actions. He says:

I believe that it's all up to me to find help and to exert some self-control so I can have as constructive and happy and creative a life as

I'm still able to. And I'm much more open-minded than I used to be. This illness has really humbled me.

Helen believes that her husband's illness has brought the couple closer than they have ever been, the payoff for all their struggles. Says Helen:

I love my husband. The meds make him not want sex very often, but in its place we have the most intense friendship, something we didn't have before. I would hate to say that I wish men could have a mental illness so they could feel and have compassion for others, but that's what happened to Glen. We were lucky. Even though there's mental illness in this house, we are not a dysfunctional family.

THE FAMILY HISTORY OF THE WELL PARTNER

When Helen uses the phrase "dysfunctional family," she speaks from experience: She grew up in one. The family she has today is far better than the family she left behind when she got married, and she is determined not to lose it.

In such situations, the remembrance of things past, good and bad, and the compensations of increased sensitivity and newfound strengths often motivate well partners to stay in the relationship.

But sometimes, well partners stay for reasons that can be harmful not only to themselves but also to their partners and children. Indeed, the lens through which the well partner views the relationship can, in ways, be nearly as distorted as the thinking of the mentally ill partner. As we shall see in greater detail in chapter 10, the judgment of these "normal" partners can be blurred by unfinished emotional business from their own family histories.

Charles, mentioned at the beginning of this chapter, is a case in point. His father died when he was a child, and he remembers as though it were yesterday the anguish and shame he felt when teased by schoolmates for being a fatherless "mama's boy."

Whenever he thought about leaving Alma during the early years, all he could "see" was his own torment back when he was a kid. He didn't want to put his sons through the pain of growing up in a single-parent household. The fact that his sons were put through something far worse did not register until much, much later. They have each spent years in therapy, undoing the damage of their mother's rages which, had he left—or been able to have his wife committed—they would have been spared. Says Charles:

My wife has never made any effort to help herself. My advice to any young parent in that situation is, *run*. You've got kids to consider. It's not worth it to save one life if you have to destroy everyone else's.

In fairness, Charles didn't do as much as he might have to help himself, either. Like many partners of the mentally ill, he was unwilling to get therapy either for himself or for his children. "That's my fault," he says. "I just don't ask for help. Nothing makes me feel worse than being pitied."

When well partners have not resolved their own troubled childhoods—or when they are constrained by stigma from getting outside support for themselves and their families—they are often unable to protect their children from the ravages of a partner's illness. In such circumstances, their children may never thank them for their romantic fidelity, as we shall see in chapter 7.

SORTING IT OUT: TO STAY OR NOT TO STAY

Virtually all of the partners of the mentally ill I interviewed have had to construct parallel lives to find a sense of emotional gratification and respite from the strain of caregiving. Some have joined church groups, or devoted more time to their careers, or become advocates for the mentally ill.

To the extent that these men and women are studied by researchers and helped by clinicians at all, the focus almost always is on the sick partner rather than on the overburdened partner. Ultimately, most of these partners get lost in the emotional and sociological shuffle, left to soldier on alone. While they are often doing their utmost to prevent a partner's relapse, they themselves are frequently dangerously close to collapse.

Why must such weighty decisions and moral dilemmas, with which spouses and lovers wrestle daily, exist in a vacuum? Is there not some way to help them with their ambivalences, some guidance in choosing to stay or not to stay, some community of validation for their decisions either way?

The answer is yes. And no. As we shall see in chapter 8, there is a growing number of pioneering family education programs designed to help reduce the damage of mental illness and teach family members how to perceive, and react to, a relative's mental affliction.

This said, perhaps the greatest damage sustained by partners of the mentally ill is their own invisibility and isolation. These partners discover that advocates for themselves alone—as opposed to training in caregiving—are in short supply. As rare as support groups are for siblings and offspring of the mentally ill, support groups specifically for partners and spouses are even rarer.

But they do exist. In some communities, groups are beginning to form to help spouses and partners solve their quandaries and weigh the costs and benefits of staying in the relationship or leaving it (see chapter 13 and Appendix). In the sanctuary of a group of peers who share one's experience, it's possible to examine the deeply personal, and often humiliating, issues that friends, neighbors, and even one's children may have difficulty digesting.

Dorothy, whose husband of fifteen years has bipolar disorder, runs such a group in a Chicago suburb. In her experience, spouses and partners face similar problems. Says Dorothy:

> The most important issue for the well partner is that you sometimes lose yourself. You lose your self-respect because you become a savior, focusing solely on someone else. Sometimes that can lead to martyrdom and the subtle undermining of the ill person's recovery. You become isolated because your partner doesn't respond the way normal people do and often doesn't want you to have friends or other relationships.

You just learn that many of your needs are not going to be met, and you have to find ways to get some respite and ego repair. So the biggest question partners struggle with is, Should I leave? Because they're exhausted and see no escape. But to leave means that your partner might be on the street. I always recommend a support group to offer guidelines in making the decision with decency. We've helped people both ways—either in staying or in leaving. But I also recommend therapy to help you focus on just you, and to help you clarify what the choices are. In the long run, though, no one can make the decision for you. There's no right answer.

The urgent need to sort through such troubling issues might be obviated, or at least diminished, if there were more assistance from outside these relationships to help contain the damage and encourage the benefits within them. The more the mental health, judicial, and legal systems understand and formulate policies to help the partners of the mentally ill, the less likely it is that these attachments will end, or will end with such grief and so many painful loose ends.

Certainly the mentally ill need all the champions they can get. But surely those fighting in the trenches on their behalf need as much assistance.

These partners deserve enormous credit for their moral commitment to their mates which, as noted earlier, is one based upon choice rather than blood. Because of the intimate nature of their attachments, and because of their responsibility for their partners as well as their children, it is the partners of the mentally ill who often bear the biggest burden of all.

PART TWO

REFERENCE POINTS:
The Prism of
Mental Illness

CHAPTER 5

Altered Lives: Living With Mental Illness

I always knew there was something wrong with my mother, way before she had her first crack-up. I remember not ever trusting her or feeling safe with her—I was terrified that I'd do something to set her off. So I tried to be very, very good. And I kept wishing that someone would notice that I needed help. I had this great longing to crack up myself so that I could be taken care of for a while. I mean, my mother was a dangerous lady.

—Michael, 45

Living with someone who has mental illness is like having an invisible, deadly virus in your midst. It's not that disorders of the brain are infectious. What's "catching" is the feeling of emotional free fall, a sense that no matter what you do, you can't escape the feverish uncertainties of madness. The contagious part is the fear.

To be the child or sibling of someone who has severe and chronic mental illness is to be exposed repeatedly to behavior that can be so unruly, and so unfathomable, that sometimes you feel as though you're going to pieces yourself. Suddenly, nothing makes sense. All the familiar cues and connections—the patterns of intimacy and conflict, the reliability of *sameness*—are erased, replaced by an eerie unpredictability.

As we have seen, how a family responds to mental illness depends on its pre-illness stability as a unit, and on the innate immunities or vulnerabilities of each member. No matter how the family responds, however, everyone in it is forever changed, *especially* the children. Mental illness becomes the prism through which they view themselves, one another, and their future attachments. It can be the organizing principle of their lives.

Up to now, we've examined what brain disorders look like—their symptoms, possible causes, various treatments, assorted severities, and differing contexts and family pairings. But unless you've actually lived with an afflicted relative, it's hard to get a handle on what it *feels* like to coexist with the reality of mental illness all the time, every day.

The best way to understand the impact of mental illness on offspring and siblings is to take up residence with someone who has it. So let us "move in," if you will, with one family and find out from each of the children what happened when their relative—in this instance, their mother—became sick; how the illness changed their relationships; and the ways it shaped their identities. In this way it is possible to get a more complete picture of life with the mentally ill. The operative word here is "complete." Accuracy, as we shall see, depends on who's doing the talking.

Before we settle in with this family, an introductory caveat. Of course, no two families are identical in terms of age, socioeconomic status, and specific psychiatric malady. The importance of what follows, then, is not so much the facts of this particular case history, which are unique. Rather, the significance of this story is that it illustrates the range of emotions that mental illness evokes, which are extremely common.

RASHOMON: VARIATIONS ON A THEME

You've already met one member of the Schwartz family, Michael, at the beginning of this chapter. He and his older sister, Jessica, fifty-two, grew up in a small town in Arizona. Their father, a housepainter who worked six days a week, was just barely able to pay the rent and put food on the table. What he lacked in material wealth, however, he more than made up for in his generosity of spirit.

When his children speak of him, it is with a sense of reverent awe. He was utterly devoted to his family. He never had an unkind word to say about anyone. He always tried to make each of his children feel cherished. Above all, he never complained about the desolation of having a mentally ill wife. Rather, he was relentlessly understanding of her. Alas, the strain of his responsibilities caused his heart to give out when his children were twenty-five and seventeen.

Looking back, Michael and Jessica wonder how their father was able to bear his burden with such grace, for they sensed from the beginning that there was something strange, even lethal, about their mother. She had no friends. She never sat with the family during mealtimes—she'd stay in the kitchen, picking at her food. She constantly provoked arguments with her husband and children, particularly her daughter. And when she was *really* angry, she'd throw things. Like skillets. And irons. And knives.

Despite this hostile behavior, which her children describe in nearly identical terms, their feelings *about* her are remarkably different.

Jessica's Story. Until she was eight, Jessica was an only child, in the constant company of her mother. These were the years prior to her mother's first breakdown, during which her psychological furies were smoldering but had not yet burst into flames. Had Jessica known about such things as "affective disorders" she might have recognized in her mother's excitability a catalog of symptoms. She was impossible to please. She had a violent temper. She was incapable of expressing affection. She was a social isolate. And she had trouble sleeping.

In short, she had all the earmarks of manic-depression. A diagnosis wouldn't have excused the din of her endless criticisms and demands and her inability to curb them. But it might have given them a more objectively palatable, and less subjectively ravaging, explanation.

As far as Jessica knew, all mothers say things like, "Children are no pleasure"; insist that it's a daughter's duty to take care of her mother and younger sibling; and roam restlessly from room to room at all hours of the night. Says Jessica:

I never thought of her as sick. If this is all you've ever known, you think it's normal. I felt I was put upon this earth just to be a surrogate parent to my mother and my brother, but not to be a child myself. My mother was very manipulative, and I was very easily manipulated. I was petrified of her. She would tell me my father was a monster. She would never let me feel loved. I was always trying to get a kind word from her, to have her say I was a good daughter, and that she could *never* do.

If it weren't for her father, Jessica says, she doesn't think she could have survived those years. "He saved me," she says. "He was my anchor. He'd say, 'You make my life worthwhile.'" But she was unable to tell him her problems with her mother. She felt that he was so overtaxed by trying to eke out a living and appease his volatile wife that she didn't want to make things worse for him. Because he had to work such long hours, their brief moments together could not compensate Jessica for the emptiness she felt inside.

And so at the age of twenty-one, to get out from under, she got married. But her escape was only partial. Because she had been so thoroughly indoctrinated in loyal service to her family, and was so unskilled at claiming her own separate identity, she kept being snapped back home as though tethered to it by a bungee cord.

I took all my fears with me into my marriage—the fear of loss, of abandonment, of everything. I was like a person ripped in half, and it caused tremendous problems with my husband. I couldn't foresake my parents, and he resented my always running over there to take care of things which, in hindsight, I can't really blame him for. It got to the point that I didn't dare call them because I was afraid he'd get upset. I'd go down the street to use a pay phone. When we had our first daughter, he said, "Now you have three children—your mother, your brother, and the baby." As for my mother, she could not accept my child because she felt I was lost to her as a support. She told me the baby was so homely she couldn't bear to look at her.

After her father's death, Jessica's mother's illness worsened and the demands mounted. Now Jessica was in charge of making decisions about her mother's medical care, spending increasing amounts of time visiting her in the hospital, and stopping off at her parents' house to look in on her brother.

Michael, then in his early teens, began to rankle at his sister's dominance—he wanted to be treated as an adult. The siblings began squabbling about what was best for their mother, disagreeing on courses of treatment or which doctor to consult.

It is perhaps the friction with her brother that troubles Jessica most. "I don't think he ever realized the position I was in," she says, sighing. "I think he has very bitter feelings toward me, because I was more substitute parent than sister. It just destroyed our relationship. We never really got to know each other."

When Jessica's mother suddenly died two years ago at the age of eighty, the reference point of Jessica's life was extinguished, the purpose and momentum of her self-sacrifice abruptly snatched away. Recently she began therapy to pick up the strands of her divided loyalties, which braid into a single theme: her own lack of identity, and the feeling that all her ministerings to her mother and brother were for nothing. She is only beginning to recognize the ways in which her mother's illness picked her clean, leaving her to wonder what, if anything, is left of herself at this late date. Says Jessica:

It wasn't so much that I wanted everyone to heap praise upon me for being so virtuous, although that would have been nice. The biggest horror for me has been to realize my own complicity in being taken advantage of. How did I *allow* it? How could I permit myself to be treated this way by everyone? How could I not ask for anything for myself? But you see, when you grow up the way I did, you feel you're not a person. You don't have any rights. You are not entitled to have a life.

Michael's Story. In contrast to his sister, Michael sees his mother as a tragic figure and himself as heir to a treasure trove of interesting stories. "I know that sounds flip," he says. "Believe me, it cost me dearly." Still, his mother's illness did not destroy him. He credits his sister for his ability to retain a somewhat bemused detachment about their sad family history, and for making it possible for him to draw upon what he calls his "inner core of strength." (This was news to Jessica when I repeated to her, with Michael's permission, what he said.)

As he is the first to admit, the family Michael grew up in was very different from the family that shaped his sister. For one thing, Jessica did much of the caretaking spadework, sparing him the full brunt of his mother's symptoms until he was a teenager. For another, he was clearly his mother's favorite child, possibly because he was a boy and hence not a rival for gender turf. All in all, he recognizes that his mother was simply harder on his sister than on him, which did little to encourage sibling solidarity.

Still, Michael had his own bumpy filial ride. By the time he was fourteen, when his sister fled into marriage, it was his turn to be surrogate parent. In ways, caretaking had more alarming components for him than for Jessica, who was not around full-time to watch her mother's eventual psychological meltdown. Michael was very nearly his mother's only lifeline, at least until his father came home at the end of the day, and his mother knew it. Says Michael:

> My mother was overpowered by the anxiety that something would happen to me. I was counted upon to be there with her. If I was late, she would wander out of the house in a daze, looking for me, sometimes showing up at school, which was enormously embarrassing. People used to think she was my grandmother. She was a tired, prematurely aged, manifestly nervous woman. But she wasn't too bad until her crack-up.

Her "crack-up" occurred when he was fifteen. One day when he returned from school, he found his father and the family doctor in the living room, trying to calm his mother, who was lying naked on the couch, screaming that she wanted some guy who lived down the street to "fuck" her. Michael's father and the doctor covered her with a blanket and took her to a psychiatric hospital, where she was given shock treatments. "Back then, it was a devastating procedure," Mi-

chael says. "For a couple of days afterward, she looked like Jell-O—
her face would be kind of rubbery."

This breakdown was swiftly followed by others. Over the next four
years, she gradually began spending more time in the hospital than
out until, finally, she didn't come home at all. She was permanently
institutionalized. The fact that his father died during one of these crises, Michael believes, cannot have been a coincidence.

It was in the hospital that Michael's sympathy for his mother deepened, perhaps because by now she had become emotionally declawed,
rendered harmlessly pathetic. When he visited her, she either wouldn't
know who he was or wouldn't respond. She simply sat and gazed into
space. Still, he continued faithfully to visit her at least once a week.
When asked how he could keep it up with little or nothing in return,
he releases a small chuckle and replies:

> I actually thought I could help her. And you always hope. I certainly
> knew that she wasn't going to be a mother after so many years, and
> that she hadn't been much of a mother to begin with. But I thought,
> Jesus, you never know. Nobody's book is ever finished. Maybe there's
> a chance.

Amazingly, his hopes were realized. About twenty years into her
illness, it suddenly, and inexplicably, lifted. To his astonishment, the
woman who emerged from her long sleep was someone he'd never
known. She was lively and earthy, and had a "devilish" sense of
humor. She told elaborate, diverting anecdotes about her girlhood. She
laughed out loud, a sound he had never heard from her before. She
was, in fact, a lot like her son.

To realize that this interesting, bright, vibrant, kindred spirit had
been in there all along, behind the curtain of mental illness, gave him
a bittersweet glimpse of all that he had missed out on. "It was just a
shame," he says softly.

As sad as that realization was for Michael, so it was for his mother,
who spent the remainder of her life in a nursing home. Shortly before
she died, she said to him, "It all seems like a bad dream. I really wanted
to be able to love you, but I didn't know how. I'm sorry I wasn't a better

mother.'' Her reawakening gave both mother and son the closure for which he had patiently waited. Alas, his sister was not so fortunate. His mother was unable to extend the same olive branch to Jessica.

Double Exposure. Clearly Michael's portrait of his mother is more benevolent than his sister's. While it is true that he witnessed his mother at her very worst, from a clinical standpoint, that exposure was relatively brief. In any case, it was by then an unmistakable medical condition and hence, less threatening to him. By contrast, his sister had endured seventeen years of dutiful, thankless devotion to a mother who could give her little but scorn, and who, right to the end, could never tell Jessica that she loved her.

Because they experienced their mother's illness so differently—and because it was, in fact, a very different stage of the disorder as each came of age—the psychological wounds that brother and sister bear are vastly dissimilar.

For Jessica, the legacy is the lingering ache of having been robbed of her life. She says:

Regardless of how sick my mother was, I had a right to have my own needs. If somebody could have explained that to me—that I didn't have to feel guilty if I wanted anything for myself—that would have been the best present anybody could have given me.

For Michael, the legacy is different. Although he is happily married, he has never had children for fear of harming them, as though he himself were a carrier of some explosive pathology that might be detonated by parenthood. He also retains an abiding desire to be perceived as a very, very good boy. He says:

I have an endearing streak that sort of makes me gag. I have a hard time standing up for myself. I protect myself by being nice and giving in, and I always wonder if it's enough. Every day I look at my wife and I think, Will you still want to be with me tomorrow?

A WORLD APART: THE QUARANTINED FAMILY

When mental illness comes home, the family constellation is blind-sided. Drs. Stephen P. Bank and Michael D. Kahn, in writing about mentally ill children, put it this way: "Months and years go by, and members of the family slowly come to realize that the different child is not just different, not just difficult, but is deviant."

Parents must try to contain the damage of crazy behavior so that the family itself does not crumble. As for individual offspring, their differing dreams and identities are collapsed into one unifying mandate: Do not cause any further upset. The result of this imperative is that families may feel like collective oddities, mutually tainted by madness. Now the family itself becomes a kind of foreign body, inexorably "different" from other families. As E. James Anthony, M.D., writes:

> To some extent, the family is always sick along with its sick member—sometimes physically, sometimes psychologically, and often empathically.

To get a full understanding of how families function in the face of chronic illness, Dr. Anthony and his colleagues at Washington University School of Medicine in St. Louis conducted a study that was unique in its methodology. The scientists literally moved in for a week with spouses and children of people who had either schizophrenia, manic-depression, or tuberculosis. This extended, intimate examination of families in crisis enabled the researchers to gain rare insights into how families cope.

Among the researchers' findings was that family adjustment entailed an increasing tolerance for "deviancy," particularly in families that were disorganized before the illness set in. Because family members identified with one another so strongly, they began to take on some of the ill parents' characteristics, even exchanging symptoms. This was especially true of children, who did poorly in school and seemed to teachers as though "drugged," off in their own worlds.

What makes this study particularly intriguing is not so much that these children had emotional difficulties, which is not surprising. Rather, it is that since the families had become so inured to the ill person's disturbing actions, emotional "sickness" in the well family members *went unnoticed*—it wasn't perceived as out of the ordinary. The result was an outbreak of "small psychological epidemics." This tolerance for deviance was not garden-variety denial. It was *adaptation* to the abnormal, redefining bizarre behavior as normal.

Further blurring the boundaries between illness and health was that the children in this study tried to endear themselves to their ill parents by getting "sick." That is, they themselves became emotionally fragmented in a tragic effort to be on the same psychological wavelength as their impaired parent. Better a "sick" attachment than no attachment at all.

Dr. Anthony and his team noticed other patterns. For example, the social climate inside and outside the family began to shift. Families drew into their own inner circles and wandered away from outside relationships and activities. Within the family itself, members retracted further, becoming increasingly separate from one another.

The Redefined Family. In such circumstances, the family as it used to be is unmoored, adrift in a world of normals, which reinforces the family's punishing uniqueness. Here, the notion of social comparison is useful. Just as siblings compare themselves to one another in order to take their own measure, so, too, do families of the mentally ill compare themselves to other families.

And in the comparing, they find little common ground. Not for them the expectations and dreams of normal families over the life span. The stages of childhood, adulthood, old age, and the culturally valued traditions and ceremonies that celebrate them are subsumed by a single, endless, lonesome theme: *What will happen to the sick one?* Will he behave for this Christmas? Will she have hallucinations at that wedding? What can we count on? And who will take care of the sick one when, and if, we cannot?

HOLDING PATTERNS:
TAILORING FAMILY LIFE TO ILLNESS

This sense of social and emotional isolation is intensified by a cultural and political climate that, in the last twenty years, has become increasingly hardened to the plights of families of the mentally ill. With the advent of new generations of miracle drugs, legions of the mentally ill have been freed from psychoses and straitjackets. Because of governmental budget cuts and tougher insurance company restrictions, many psychiatric hospitals have shuttered their doors and closed up shop. The problems of the mentally ill have literally gone home.

An estimated 65 percent of discharged psychiatric patients return to their families to live, which puts families in the position of being the ill person's treatment team—with predictably varying results.

Ethnic Differences in Coping. To some degree, ethnicity plays a role in how families cope, according to sociology professor Allan V. Horwitz and nursing professor Susan C. Reinhard of Rutgers University. In their study of siblings and parents of white and black mentally ill patients, the investigators found that being black is protective in terms of the "burden" of mental illness in the family. Blacks are less likely than whites to perceive stigmatization with regard to mental illness. Hence, say the researchers, black parents may be more able to tolerate the symptoms of their mentally ill relatives.

Moreover, blacks, especially women, are much more likely than whites to take care of immediate and extended kin and to expect to be called upon to provide care rather than turn to outside resources. Since caregiving is a family value among blacks, siblings are more likely to offer help. This family support helps mentally ill blacks to function better.

In contrast, among whites, caregiving by parents of grown children is "less normative," the researchers report. Whites may have higher expectations than blacks that their adult children will be achievers and live independently, and may be more disappointed when their children cannot live up to those expectations. Thus, the subjective burden of caring for the mentally ill is heavier for whites than for blacks.

Recovery Rates and Coping. Regardless of ethnicity, however, the sad reality is that many mentally ill people—despite the finest outpatient medical attention, the most luxurious domestic surroundings, and the greatest possible family love and support—simply do not recover, or recover only somewhat. An estimated 15 to 20 percent of people with depression never get better. People with bipolar disorder tend to become more impaired with age, and the intervals between episodes of illness shrink.

With regard to schizophrenia, the good news is that an estimated one third eventually recover spontaneously. Alas, the remainder do less well as the years roll by. According to one investigator, by the ten-year, post-onset mark, 25 percent are completely recovered; 25 percent are greatly improved and are relatively self-sufficient; 25 percent are better but need a great deal of support; and 15 percent do not get better, requiring hospitalization, but not necessarily receiving it. The remaining 10 percent are dead, often by their own hands.

Since most people with mental illness are not so sick that they must be hospitalized, and because well-run halfway houses are prohibitively expensive, family life must be tailored to keep the ill person home, his or her symptoms in check. It is an enormous task.

To begin with, victims of brain disorders are often acutely sensitive to stress, such as noise, activity, even lively conversation. The most severely afflicted victims are vulnerable to periodic emotional shutdown just to close off all stimulation. It is a way of protecting themselves from further mental chaos. It's not necessarily that they feel nothing; sometimes, they feel *everything*, all at once. It's like going out into the sun after having your pupils dilated by an eye doctor. Even a little light is excrutiating, and you simply cannot keep your eyes open. As Dr. Nancy C. Andreasen explains in her book, *The Broken Brain:*

> Some neurons may in a sense become "overheated" and send or receive too many chemical messages. Short circuits may occur. . . . Mental illness is truly a nervous breakdown . . . that occurs when the nerves of the brain have an injury so severe that their own internal healing capacities cannot repair it.

The Therapeutic Family. To make such sensitivity to stress manageable, families must rearrange the emotional furniture of day-to-day life so that the sick member does not stumble into situations that might trip off a new bout of symptoms.

The best interests of the ill person, however, are not necessarily the best interests of everyone else. The family climate can become a kind of hothouse, with careful temperature (read emotional) control, just to keep the most fragile person stable. This may cause other family members to wilt from exhaustion and emotional deprivation. The normal, spontaneous exchanges of enthusiasm or petulance or outrage or just plain old rage must be dimmed, replaced by an artificial calm. It is a nearly impossible therapeutic ideal.

For example, when communicating with a mentally ill relative, families are advised by professionals (to the extent that such guidance is offered) to tie themselves into knots of accommodation with the following do's and don'ts: Keep sentences short and simple. Stay calm. Don't force discussion. Don't get into arguments. Disregard certain behaviors. Limit requests. Be accepting. Do not threaten. Set limits where possible. Do not become hostile or shout. Be honest. Acknowledge the ill person's feelings. Accompany praise with smiles and other encouraging body language. And keep a positive attitude.

The opposite of such pacification by family members is known in the mental health field as "expressed emotion" (EE). This behavior, which tends to land the ill person back in the hospital, includes yelling, overreacting, overinvolvement, criticizing, ridiculing, and blaming. One study found that nine months after being discharged from the hospital, 58 percent of psychiatric patients who had gone home to high EE families relapsed, compared with only 16 percent of those from low EE families.

Relative Happiness. For families of the mentally ill, a "good day" becomes a poignant matter of relativity in ways that are unimaginable to the outside world. In the case of severe schizophrenia, if the ill person took a shower, made his bed, worked part-time, or quietly watched television all day and joined the family for dinner, that would be construed as a good day. Conversely, a bad day would be when the ill person heard voices, refused to bathe or brush his teeth, tore off his clothes because they bothered his skin, sat staring mutely at a wall, or decided he didn't need his medications anymore, ran off, and couldn't be found.

The constant tension of worrying about the ill person eventually begins to eat at well family members as their equanimity, patience, even their health are nibbled away.

THE TOLL OF DOING GOOD

When it comes to the emotional costs of these family burdens, studies show that they are heartbreakingly heterogeneous, crossing all ethnic and economic boundaries. A survey of 125 white and nonwhite families of the mentally ill found that they shared painful similarities. Their feelings of helplessness and entrapment were directly related to the severity of the sick members' illnesses. While 83 percent of the families wanted the relative to live at home, only 58 percent of the kin of the most seriously disturbed relatives felt this way. When the relative was highly symptomatic, 71 percent of families did not wish to include the person in social activities. In one study, the strain of coping with mental illness was devastating. Family members were either depressed, sleep deprived, hypertense, had heart attacks, or abused alcohol.

Siblings and offspring in my own sample suffered these ailments, too, and reported others such as eating disorders, drug abuse, anxiety attacks, post-traumatic stress disorder, chronic mourning, chronic fatigue syndrome, sexual dysfunction, emotional numbing, suicide attempts, nervous breakdowns, and strokes.

One possible explanation for this medical toll on family members is the ''interruption theory'' of stress. According to sociologist Peter J. Burke of Washington State University, interruption requires having to deal with the unexpected and to shift gears. Thus, it is a stressor. When actions or thought processes are repeatedly and severely interrupted, the body's arousal system is triggered, making the person anxious, hence, more alert—or, as Dr. Burke puts it, ''distressed.'' By any yardstick, living with the mentally ill entails repeated, severe interruptions, and the toll may be registered in various forms of distress-induced illness.

Part of the strain of living with mental illness is that one simply cannot monitor or control the ill person's behavior all the time, especially if he or she is over eighteen. As much as families may try to keep a relative's illness under wraps, there are times when their carefully guarded secret is unavoidably hauled into public view. I am especially speaking here of those ill family members who get into trouble with the law. According to a study of NAMI families, 40 percent of their ill relatives have been arrested at least once in the last five years.

Adding to family stress is that many parents are forced into Solomonic choices. For example, several family members confessed to me that sometimes, in desperation, they secretly slipped medications into the ill person's food because the person refused to comply voluntarily.

Other families faced the harrowing prospect of putting the ill person out on the street. Perhaps their small children were becoming traumatized. Or the parents could not get a hospital bed for the symptomatic relative. Or the relative was too disruptive to live in supervised housing. Or the relative denied being ill in the first place. Parents then had to decide whether or not the family's safety outweighed the needs of the ill person. As the brother of a thirty-year-old man with severe schizophrenia told me:

> When my brother stopped taking his meds, my parents considered threatening to turn him out, hoping to force him into compliance. But then they couldn't go through with it. The constant worry of having a paranoid, fearful child living on his own for the first time in his life was too much for them. They'd rather listen to his verbal abuse and put him in the hospital when he gets out of control physically. My parents aren't getting any younger—their will to live is driven by worry. Their sole reason to exist is my brother.

This brings up one last factor of family stress: stigmatization. Since most families of the mentally ill *are* and *feel* so set apart from others, they are frequently loath to share their dilemmas and problems with the outside world and, all too often, even among themselves. The burden, shame, and complexities of mental illness are simply not translatable to people who have not experienced it. Should their secret get out, families are then judged in the harshest possible light, even by their own extended families.

According to Gerri Zatlow, director of Siblings for Significant Change, a New York–based agency that offers guidance to brothers and sisters of America's 43 million physically and mentally disabled citizens, families of the chronically impaired are often shunned by their relatives. Says Ms. Zatlow, whose brother has autism:

> When he was diagnosed, my family and I were no longer invited to family functions as a group. Relatives would say, "Come for Thanksgiving. Maybe your brother can go somewhere else," and of course we refused the invitation. We spent years not being welcome in their houses.

Satellites of Illness. In their isolation, the lives of family members rotate around the sick person like so many moons, the orbit of their identities dictated by the gravitational pull of pathology. One study of family members' perceptions of their relationships with one another, and with a schizophrenic relative, found that mothers were too emotionally wrapped up in the sick member. Fathers were too emotionally distant from the sick member and from acceptance of the illness. And parents' marriages were strained by overdependency of wives on husbands, and by husbands' insensitivity about their wives' distress.

I observed similar patterns in my own sample. Depending upon their position in the family hierarchy, each person undergoes a kind of reshuffling of their identities.

Reactions of Fathers. Studies demonstrate that fathers in general tend to be "instrumental" in expressions of love. For example, fathers are more likely to show a child how to fix a broken toy than to sit down to discuss how the child *feels* about the fact that the toy is broken. But mental illness is something fathers can't repair, which is not to say that they don't try—in their own instrumental way. The majority of fathers I interviewed commented not so much on their feelings of loss and sorrow, but, rather, on the inadequacies of the mental health and legal systems, and their own efforts, and powerlessness, to change them.

This reluctance of fathers to delve into deep emotional issues, particularly with their progeny, was one of the findings of a study of families conducted by Alice S. Rossi, Ph.D., and Peter H. Rossi. In their book, *Of Human Bonding: Parent-Child Relations Across the Life Course*, the Rossis report that fathers tend to be conversational "topic avoiders." That is, they are not inclined to discuss personal problems with their offspring.

In my own sample, the complaint most frequently mentioned by siblings and offspring was that their fathers simply wouldn't talk to them about what was happening in the family. Either these fathers ignored the problem or they "externalized" it, as therapists put it. They found sources outside themselves upon which to pin blame—the "wrong crowd" or "street drugs" or the mental health system or their spouse. But they had trouble acknowledging their own or their children's feelings, and reckoning with their own possible contributions to family dissonance

Reactions of Mothers. Mothers tend to be "affective" in demonstrations of love, zeroing in on a child's emotional response to difficulties and attempting to make the child feel better about him- or herself. In the Rossi study, mothers reported greater intimacy with their children than fathers, a phenomenon I found in my sample as well.

Because of this intimacy, the mothers I interviewed often appeared to be nearly as emotionally broken as their mentally ill children. They felt demolished by their inability to love their children back into health. Many of these mothers were beside themselves—there is no other way to put it—with feelings of failure. As one woman, whose child was diagnosed fifteen years ago, expressed it:

My soul was just destroyed by my daughter's illness. It was more than just rupturing. It killed me. For many years I blamed myself and withdrew from everyone, because I couldn't bear the pain. I even fired God.

All the mothers I talked to described a sense of culpability, wondering if they had caused the illness by not taking proper care of themselves when they were pregnant, or by not being good-enough nurturers.

On this score, maternal self-blame has, alas, been encouraged by pockets of the therapeutic community, which has historically censured mothers—and notably spared fathers—for all their children's psychological difficulties. The term "schizophrenogenic mother"—mom as agent of a child's biochemical vulnerabilities—is an intractible, even though discredited, hypothesis.

Reactions of Siblings and Offspring. Junior family members tend to feel equally helpless, not just because they want to make their ill relative better, but because they worry about the emotional fragility of their well parents. Most siblings and offspring want nothing so much as for the problem of mental illness to go away so that the family can go back to some version of normal, and so that their parents can resume their protective, all-knowing family leadership. To that end, they bend themselves out of shape trying to prop up their mothers and fathers.

Karen Gail Lewis, Ed.D., coauthor of *Siblings in Therapy*, has seen all these reactions in her group therapy sessions with families of the mentally ill. Says Dr. Lewis:

> Families hurt a lot. Fathers are used to feeling inadequate, mothers are used to being blamed, children are used to feeling worried, and no one talks about it. These family members all feel helpless and out of control—that no matter what they do, they can't make it better. And they live with that for years and years.

Few people know as much about such dynamics—in particular, the impact of mental illness on siblings and children—as psychologist Joyce Burland, Ph.D., the author of and guiding force behind "The Journey of Hope Family Education Course." Dr. Burland's qualifications to teach families how to cope with mental illness extend beyond mere clinical and academic expertise. Both her sister and her daughter have schizophrenia. Says Dr. Burland:

When a child becomes mentally ill, parents go into an emergency care-taking mode that builds around the failure to thrive. It's what keeps the human race going. What happens to well children is they think, "My parents can't see me. I'm off their screen." They become very angry, and very envious. Sibs feel as though they're standing outside the circle. But so do the other family members—every position around the stricken member is impossible. There is no good place to be.

Reactions of the Mentally Ill. Finally, we come to the person in the middle of this "circle," the mentally ill center of the family's tiny universe, who may be acutely aware of the fissures within the family created by his or her illness.

Such a person is Chloe, forty-four, a vivacious, bright, witty woman who was diagnosed with paranoid schizophrenia twenty years ago. She rents a room in the frame house of a family able to tolerate her "nuttiness," as she puts it, since her aged and infirm parents are no longer able to handle it. Says Chloe:

I know I'm a pain. When I'm in relapse, I believe in Martians, and I don't talk in reality. I think everybody else is bonkers and I'm the only sane one. In my mind, it's like a playground—I think I'm extremely entertaining! Still, I hate being locked up in the hospital, so I'm good about my meds. But I'm always calling my sister, always bothering somebody. Sometimes I think that if my family really loved me, they would take me in and take care of me. I honestly feel that if my sister loved me, she'd just cater to me. But she'd really have to deny herself. Because this illness is twenty-four hours a day. If I were her, I wouldn't be able to cope with it. So yeah, I can understand why I can't live with my family. Mental illness is not like cancer. People with cancer don't talk off the wall and aren't pains in the ass.

FORKS IN THE FAMILY ROAD: MAKING SENSE OF ILLNESS

Like any ongoing trauma, mental illness takes all families to a philosophical divide. Some families view the illness as a terrible curse of fate and see themselves as doomed. Others view the illness as a window of opportunity, a chance to examine their strengths and weaknesses and to improve their relationships with one another.

Initially, families of the mentally ill often try to make sense of their loss and inadequacy by blaming each other, or by blaming themselves. "If only" becomes a kind of mantra: "If only" my spouse had paid more attention to our sick child, or "if only" I hadn't married the person in the first place. "If only" my well parent had taken better care of my sick parent, or "if only" I hadn't been such a handful for them. "If only" my sibling hadn't taken that first hit of cocaine, or "if only" I'd been nicer to him or her. "If only" my parents had been more understanding of me when I first started hearing voices and couldn't concentrate in school, or "if only" I hadn't been born. "If only" none of these things had happened, then everything in the family would be fine and we wouldn't be in such a mess.

Most modern theorists and researchers emphasize the futility of such blame, since severe mental illness, while it may be triggered by family chaos, is, they believe, essentially biological in origin. Still, to say to a family, "It's not your fault" can be a catch-22.

On the one hand, if mental illness is *altogether* biochemical, then parents are off the hook, enormously relieved not to be the villains of the piece. On the other hand, parents may be left with feelings of utter despair, the sense that there's absolutely nothing they can do to make things better.

Some theorists suggest that feelings of helplessness can be reduced by taking a measure of responsibility for disaster. As Dr. Julius Segal of NIMH, points out, "[A]ssuming blame in the face of misfortune . . . helps to satisfy our need to believe that we are in control of our own destiny."

I prefer the term "accountability," which is less loaded than the term "blame." Accountability can be extraordinarily beneficial. When family members hold themselves and one another responsible for their own behavior—including, up to a point, the ill person—family functioning improves. In accountability there is hope, the chance to lessen by one's own efforts the damage of catastrophe, as we shall see in chapters 8 and 12.

But accountability has its limits. Self-flagellation has a way of paralyzing people, which worsens any situation. The reality is that there is only so much one can do to make the mentally ill better, or whole. For some families, as we have seen, the best that can be achieved is damage control.

However, while it may not always be possible to escape from the herculean task of caring for the mentally ill, the experience can have a transforming effect on family members. When catastrophe strikes, it forces one to examine one's own values and priorities and, perhaps, to gain new insights.

Psychiatrist Frederic Flach, M.D., calls this phenomenon "the law of disruption and reintegration." According to Dr. Flach, human growth and survival are a function of experiencing stress and growing as a result of it. That is, only when people are *shaken up* do they branch out and find new ways to cope and to take productive risks. As he explains it in his book, *Resilience: Discovering a New Strength at Times of Stress*:

> I . . . see falling apart as a normal—in fact, necessary—response to significant changes within ourselves or in our environments. . . . [T]his process might well be nature's mandate, forcing us to forfeit obsolete perceptions. . . .

It's difficult to imagine a more shattering experience than living with chronic mental illness, or to envision a silver lining. As we shall see in the next three chapters, such experience can serve only to bring out one's worst.

Yet living with mental illness can also bring out one's best. In fact, for many of the siblings and offspring I interviewed, it was the worst that *led to* the best, even though they fervently wish they hadn't had to learn the hard way. While this transformation took many years, those who found meaning in their family ordeals had the best outcomes.

Conversely, those who did not emerge with new strengths but, rather, with wounds that still ran raw were not able to profit from their terrible life lessons. Instead, in tandem with their afflicted kin, they lived in perpetual emotional disarray.

The voyage toward transformation, or disintegration, begins at the same point of departure: a relative's mental illness. It is at this point that siblings and offspring are forced to lead double lives—one inside the family, the other in the world at large.

CHAPTER 6

Double Lives:
Roles Inside and Outside
the Family

It's hard for parents to find the right balance between sick children and the non-sick ones. But you've got to deal with the well kids, too. Children go through the same hurt and worry that parents do, only nobody notices. I was always getting into trouble at school, but as long as I was functioning at home, my parents couldn't be bothered with me. They figured since I was quiet when I was around them, I was okay, which was the most astounding assumption. How could I possibly be okay? We were living in a complete nuthouse. I was suffering terribly.

—Joan, 38

As far back as she can remember, Joan's older sister, Nellie, was always a kind of fragile, exotic creature who required very special handling. Whenever Nellie was upset or anxious, which was most of the time, she'd trot after her mother and say, "Do you love me?" If she didn't get constant reassurance, she'd scream at her mother or threaten to kill herself.

When, at seventeen, Nellie finally made good on all her suicide threats by actually swallowing a bottle of sleeping pills, it came as no surprise to Joan, then twelve. Still, the experience was devastating to her. "I remember my father slapping my sister, trying to wake her up," Joan recalls. "I just stood there, frozen. I thought she was dead."

Nellie was rushed to the hospital, where her stomach was pumped and she regained consciousness. A psychiatrist examined her and diagnosed her as manic-depressive. On his recommendation, she was sent to a psychiatric hospital for six months. After being discharged, her condition worsened. She became even more hysterical and suicidal. On one occasion, she tried to jump out of her upstairs bedroom window.

It wasn't so much her sister's illness, however, that troubled Joan, terrifying as that was. Rather, it was her parents' reaction to it. Her mother became increasingly wrapped up in Nellie, acquiescing to her many demands, and at the same time grew more and more disenchanted with her shy, younger daughter. To the extent that her mother even noticed Joan, it was only to find fault.

"No one put any limits on my sister," says Joan. "There were never any consequences or punishments for her behavior. Yet my mother was always yelling at me about something, like my hair, or my room. My mother kept telling me that I should give in to 'poor Nellie' because she was 'very emotional.' That seemed to be her name. 'Poor Nellie.' "

Joan's father had his own reaction to Nellie's behavior, chiefly an inability to accept that she was, in fact, mentally ill. Says Joan:

> My dad didn't believe in psychotherapy. He accused my mother of sending their daughter away so she wouldn't have to deal with her. They fought constantly about it at night in their bedroom, which was right next to mine. They thought I wasn't listening. Of course I was listening.

As Nellie's illness worsened, and as her parents became more embattled, Joan herself began to change. Outside the family she started spending more time with her friends, drinking or just hanging out, and her grades in school plummeted. At home, she developed a protective shell to harden herself against the chaos that swirled around her. *Someone* had to be coolheaded during the crises that kept pounding the family, a job that only Joan seemed able to perform.

Once, when her sister had to be readmitted to the hospital, her parents were too distraught even to pack Nellie's suitcase. So Joan did it. In the hospital waiting room Nellie and her parents, awash with tears, embraced, unable to part from one another. "I did not cry," says Joan. "I looked at the nurse and said, 'This isn't working. You must take her now.' "

Joan decided that if her storm-tossed family was going to go under, she wasn't about to go down with it. She'd have to prepare for the time when she could escape, and school seemed to be her ticket out. She began to pay more attention to her grades.

One night while her parents were at the movies, Joan was in her room studying for finals. Suddenly Nellie appeared in the doorway, again talking about ending her life. Joan turned to her and shouted, "I've got an exam in the morning! If you're going to kill yourself, just get it over with!" At that, Nellie went into the bathroom and cut her wrists. Joan, by now practiced in disaster management, calmly called the doctor, who arrived just as her parents came home.

Together they all went to the hospital, and Joan's parents took her with them into the emergency room to watch the doctors stitch her blood-drenched sister together. Joan recalls:

It was torture, but still I didn't cry, which my parents couldn't understand. They thought I didn't care. They kept forgetting that I had spent years steeling myself against this kind of thing. So the fact that I had no visible reaction didn't mean anything. On one level I felt bad for my sister. But on another level I was just pissed. I had become very bitter and sarcastic because nothing I did mattered much to them. All I was supposed to do was keep the peace and be strong. That was my role.

Although her sister eventually recovered and, by maintaining an outpatient treatment regimen, went on to lead a relatively normal life, Joan continued to be the dry-eyed family truth-teller. The price of that role lingers in her biting wit, the caustic overlay of her long untended vulnerabilities. Only recently has she begun to let down her guard and try to find herself in the tangle of her identities: the wise guy she presents to the outside world, the stoic she had to become in the family, and the shy, frightened child she had to abandon in order to survive.

TROUBLE IN THE RANKS: SHIFTING ROLES

As this case illustrates, mental illness can create new rifts within the family. Regardless of pre-illness cohesiveness, however, all families enter a falling-apart period, as each person attempts to adjust to the reality of a member's psychological instability.

Just as power in the family emanates from the top, so too does worry and upset. In their demoralized terror, many parents impart mixed messages to their well children.

In the case of siblings of the mentally ill, the parental message often is, Pare down your reactions so you won't incite an episode. Don't achieve too much, lest your brother or sister feel defeated and discouraged. But don't achieve too little, either, so it won't appear as if we are terrible parents. Be self-reliant when we can't be here, or when we *seem* not to be here. Above all, *Do not become a "problem child" yourself.*

In such circumstances, according to Stephen P. Bank, Ph.D., and Michael D. Kahn, Ph.D., in their book, *The Sibling Bond*, many children fall into roles that reflect their closeness either to their parents, or to an ill brother or sister. Children who identify strongly with their parents "de-identify" with the sick sibling. That is, they side with their parents, doing everything in their power to help them and to be as different as possible from the ill brother or sister. Conversely, children who identify strongly with an ill sibling may become enmeshed with that sibling, even swapping symptoms with him or her.

Most siblings, say the researchers, fall somewhere between these two extremes. Rather than feeling compelled to choose sides, they identify both with their parents *and* with the sick child, serving as go-betweens and trying to heal everyone's wounds. In my own sample, I found similar psychological patterns among siblings. For example, Joan, mentioned earlier, took on a neutral, albeit flinty, family role.

However, I also observed these patterns of identification in offspring of the mentally ill. To these children, the mixed parental message was similar: Do not expect too much of either parent, but do not abandon us. Expect more of yourself, so that the illness will be contained and we can keep this family afloat. Above all, do not disgrace us.

In addition, I found another, equally important trend. Most junior family members adopted roles not only within the family but also, *and in tandem with them*, roles outside the family. At times, it was as if they were two different people—one at home, the other at school or with friends.

These outside roles were a key variable in how younger family members eventually turned out. The extent to which mental illness created lasting wounds in offspring and siblings was directly related to their abilities to develop rewarding identities and relationships *apart from* the family.

Age was a factor in determining which of these separate arenas— home, and beyond home—had the greater influence. Prior to adolescence, family roles tended to hold sway over outside roles. The younger the child, the more limited his or her access to other forums. However, as children matured and embarked on their separate lives at school and elsewhere, outside roles and relationships caught up with family roles in importance. By the time they were adults, outside roles began to overshadow family roles.

Another important factor in the formation of an independent identity was the availability of outside supports, such as grandparents, coaches, or teachers. When children were able to find adult mentors, in time they overcame most of their earlier adversities. They were able to put more literal and emotional mileage between themselves and their mentally ill relatives and reach a balance between their own interests and those of their original families.

When children could not find loving mentors, however, their psychic wounds often accumulated and festered. In adulthood, many offspring either remained embroiled in the family at the expense of their separate lives or cut off all family ties, as we shall see in later chapters.

Let us examine how these family roles take shape, and how they set the stage for children's roles in the wider world.

FAMILY ROLES

Most children, at first, try to pitch in and help as best they can when a member of the family is mentally ill. But the tenor of that help takes different forms, depending on the family's configuration and each child's temperament.

Based on my interviews, children's family roles cluster into three broad categories, which I have termed *Custodian*, *Bystander*, and *Adversary*. Sometimes these roles are assigned by parents, particularly in small families, where the pool of human resources is scant. In large families, roles are less rigidly imposed; if one child can't perform a function, another probably can. These roles may overlap and can be exchanged as the family evolves over time.

The Custodian. One child is generally singled out for the "parental" role. As Drs. Bank and Kahn point out, the role is driven primarily by worry. The idea *behind* it is to keep mothers and fathers from collapsing. Thus Custodians are super-responsible, serving as baby-sitters, performing and delegating domestic chores to siblings (if any), monitoring parents' moods, and in general acting like little adults. This role usually is occupied by firstborn girls. When mothers are emotionally unavailable, younger siblings tend to turn to an eldest sister—the mini-mother—for help and attention. In families with only boys, one of them generally assumes the role of "emotional leadership."

The Custodian role is a mixed blessing. On the one hand, "parentified" children may be elevated in family rank and feel a heady sense of authority. On the other hand, they are often neglected and overburdened, pressed into dutiful service with limited skills. For example, they can be extremely bossy. Studies show that older siblings are likely to mete out even *more* punishments to younger siblings than parents. Where a parent might lecture or negotiate, a brother or sister will simply coerce.

In forcing a child to grow up so fast, the seeds of potential family rancor are planted. The resentment of younger siblings toward the

Custodian can be acute, particularly if the role was acquired early in their lives and the sibling relationship was never close. On this score, Drs. Kahn and Bank draw an important distinction between "caregiving" and "caretaking." Caregiving is mutual; one person gives to another, fully expecting the favor to be returned. Care*taking*, on the other hand, is a one-way street. It means that one person does all the giving and makes all the sacrifices.

Many of the Custodians I interviewed felt exploited, even betrayed, both by their well and ill family members. Resented or resentful, Custodians often become stronger as a result of their abilities to perform adult tasks, which makes them less vulnerable to future breakdown. The child in this role may be "a deprived person but a masterful sibling" write Drs. Bank and Kahn.

Other Custodians, however, simply burn out over time. This is especially true of only children, who may be in danger of becoming emotionally disturbed, like the ill parent. In a study of offspring of the mentally ill, Joanne L. Riebschleger, a social worker, and her colleagues found that beleaguered caretaking children often blame themselves when their ill parents don't improve. These children feel that but for their own "badness," their parents' illness would be in remission, or even cured.

For reasons that will be explained in a moment, being the Custodian does not guarantee that these children will continue to play the role into adulthood. For many, once is enough.

The Bystander. This role often goes to middle borns, since the "power" position may already be occupied by an older sibling. Bystanders tend to be emotionally detached from the family, taking a longer view. They simply expect less from the family for themselves.

There are three variations to this role. Some Bystanders try to be *invisible* in the family so that they don't trigger an ill relative's symptoms or attract anyone else's irritable attention. Others are artful *diplomats*, shuttling between parents and siblings in their efforts to please and loyally support everyone. Still others, like backseat drivers, are *moral overseers*, judging who is, or isn't, doing their part in family functioning, but not getting too involved with hands-on caregiving themselves.

This middle-of-the road role can have distinct advantages. Says psychiatrist Jane S. Ferber, M.D.:

> There's something about not being noticed in these families that's very helpful. You can escape by going outward to others, or inward into your own imagination. Some of these children escape by attracting other people to replace some of the deficits in the immediate family. Turning inward has the same effect. These kids often get involved in books and learning.

Still, the role has a high price—mainly, parental neglect. In dysfunctional or emotionally overwrought families, the cost can be excrutiating. Some Bystanders are the family *prey*, abused by mentally ill relatives or the most aggressive well ones. These children, in the interests of family peace, seldom speak up about their abuse, and often are undone by it. Their sense of self is repeatedly compromised, stranding them in an overwhelming feeling of aloneness.

The Adversary. Children who take on this role tend to be outspoken family mavericks. Unlike Bystanders, these children are anything but neutral—anger, after all, is a *connector*. Adversaries often get caught up in arguments with their parents and siblings as they fight for attention.

Some Adversaries are hotheaded troublemakers and act out their anger in violent ways, especially in chaotic families. Sibling abuse in such families is common, the residue of mounting isolation and frustration. Says Gerri Zatlow, director of Siblings for Significant Change, "You're not supposed to hit a disabled relative. So you beat the crap out of the well siblings instead."

According to Drs. Bank and Kahn, troublemaking kids (the researchers call these children "terrorists") can serve a useful purpose in the family. They act as "lightning rods" for family stress, which, paradoxically, promotes family solidarity. These children reduce family tension by *distracting* everyone with their behavior. As scapegoats, they give the family an unambiguous excuse to blow off collective steam.

The Adversary role is laced with other ironies. Some of these children later become intrepid advocates for the mentally ill. Others are the first to seek, or to receive, outside help. By getting into scuffles in school or with the law, professional attention is brought to bear upon the family.

But let us not romanticize this role. Some Adversaries, to their families' shame, end up in jail or as morally bankrupt.

Roles and Parental Favoritism. In families of the mentally ill, favoritism—at least in terms of time—is a given: The sick one gets all, or most, of the parental attention. Well children must stand in line and compete for whatever parental affection and time are left over.

As we saw in chapter 3, sibling rivalry is largely a function of parental favoritism, which in turn influences which of these roles children adopt or feel comfortable with. Custodians are often the parents' favorite, although as often they are simply the most capable child. Bystanders are frequently a parental favorite because they cause no trouble. Adversaries appear to be the family underdog, as much as anything because they themselves are not always likable. But sometimes, in acting out everyone else's anger, they are secretly admired, thus tacitly encouraged, a de facto favorite.

In the long run, however, parental favoritism is a no-win situation. The psychological literature is replete with evidence of how damaging it is to sibling relationships. In their book, *Separate Lives: Why Siblings Are So Different*, Drs. Judy Dunn and Robert Plomin report on a national study of adolescent siblings which showed that children's stability, or delinquency, was related to uneven parental treatment. Well-adjusted children—in comparision to their siblings—were those who were closest to the mother, had more responsibilities, and were given a greater say in parental decision making. Disfavored siblings were less well-adjusted, the variable being the *comparative* parental treatment. Another study found that anxious and unhappy children tend to have mothers who are more controlling and less affectionate with them than with their other children.

When a child has a brain disorder, that child automatically gets "special treatment," which can drive a wedge of ambivalence between brothers and sisters. Well siblings may be grateful to be normal and feel sincere compassion toward the ill sibling. Yet they may also feel paroxysms of jealousy.

When a parent has a brain disorder, the same envy often occurs among offspring. You can't expect a mentally ill parent to do what normal parents can do. With one parent more or less out of commission, and the other overwhelmed with worry and caretaking, children fight among themselves over who gets the lion's share of the parental attention that remains.

Regardless of who has the psychiatric disability, parents frequently hold their normal children to a much higher standard than the ill family member: We expect less of the afflicted relative because he or she is sick. We expect a lot more of you because you *aren't*. Many of the siblings and offspring I interviewed commented acidly on the unfairness of this double standard. Being normal meant that they, unlike the ill relative, were cut no slack. They had to be *perfect*.

Susan, now thirty-three, recalls that her younger sister Patty, who was diagnosed as a teenager with manic-depression, always "got away with murder." Says Susan:

> I was allowed to do nothing. I was expected to get straight As, be neat as a pin, and toe the line. Even when I was a senior in high school, I had to be home at ten o'clock at night, including weekends. Meantime Patty was in big trouble in school, stayed out until all hours drinking, looked like a complete freak, and behaved weirdly. My parents kept making excuses for her, saying, "Well, she can't help it. She's sick." One time Patty wanted to go camping with some chums, which I was never permitted to do. My parents said to her, "Great! It'll do you good." This is one of the reasons I didn't get along with her.

Favoritism works to no one's advantage, least of all the psychiatrically disturbed. If you are favored because of your uncomplaining normalcy, you know that you could easily fall *out* of favor. If you are favored *because of mental illness*, there may be little incentive to think of yourself as more than just a diagnosis, or to rise above your awful biochemical luck.

The Influence of Temperament. Another factor in family roles is the inherent temperament of each child. For example, some kids who adopt the Custodian role are forced into it—they have no choice but to become parentified. But the role may be totally alien to their inherent abilities and tendencies, and so they awkwardly go through the motions. Yet other kids take to the role easily. Either they are born leaders, or they simply like being emotionally involved and nurturing, and they feel a sense of accomplishment.

According to David C. Rowe, Ph.D., who reviewed behavior genetic studies of temperament, the most enduring temperamental qualities are the "Big Five," each of which represents a continuum of a given tendency, from positive to negative. What follows is Dr. Rowe's list of positive examples of the Big Five traits:

• *Extraversion*, which includes such characteristics as sociability, assertiveness, and adventurousness;

• *Agreeableness*, which is friendliness, kindness, and warmth;

• *Conscientiousness*, which is being organized, dependable, and "planful";

• *Emotional Stability*, which is defined as being even-tempered, unflappable, and not a worrier;

• *Intellectual Openness*, which means having insightfulness, curiosity, and being a problem-solver.

The cardinal question is whether these traits are a function of genetic endowment or of family or cultural training. To tease out the answer, countless studies of identical twins either raised together or raised from infancy in separate families have been conducted in the last twenty years. Since identical twins share 100 percent of the same genes, these studies clarify the nurture/nature debate, with "nature" as the odds-on winner.

For example, in the University of Minnesota Twin Study, investigators found that *regardless of family upbringing*, children's behaviors fall into three general patterns of interaction, which are determined primarily by genetic makeup:

• *Positive Emotionality*—active and pleasurable involvement with others;

• *Negative Emotionality*—frequent stressful, anxious, and angry involvement with others;

• *Constraint*—cautious, subdued, and deferential involvement with others.

To take another example, the Texas Adoption Project found that genetically related people tend to be alike *intellectually*, again, regardless of whether or not they grew up together.

The consensus of these twin studies is that family influences are less enduring over time than biological influences. Life-span developmental psychologists have found that temperament tends to override family experience as the child moves out into the world. This conclusion is of enormous significance in terms of how siblings and offspring of the mentally ill *ultimately* fare.

However, none of these researchers suggests that environment is unimportant. Organisms don't develop in a vacuum. Rather, each person, in keeping with his or her temperament, *reacts* to the environment in unique ways, which is why no two people respond identically to the same family experience.

Perhaps the best way to understand how temperament operates is the notion of "thinking twice," as Dr. Joop Hettema of the Netherlands cleverly puts it. For example, an extrovert who receives an invitation to a large party might readily accept without a second thought. But an introvert might "think twice" about such an invitation and accept it reluctantly because large groups tend to deplete people with this temperament.

Situations that allow you to "be yourself," says Dr. Hettema, are preferable to those that don't. Thus, the extrovert at the party will be found chatting happily with everyone, the last to go home. The introvert at the party will hug the wall for comfort, watch the clock, try hard to make small talk, and fish for an excuse to beat a hasty retreat.

As this example illustrates, temperament is a function of the individual *plus* the situation that induces or represses it. To take another example, an introvert would feel right at home in Japan, where group identity and modesty are culturally valued. In the United States, however, where independence and in-your-face friendliness are valued, introverts are often dispatched to the nearest

assertiveness training seminar. In other words, context has an enormous effect on the expression of temperament: *The more powerful
the situation, the more influence it will have on behavior.*

In families of the mentally ill, particularly when a disorder is not
under control, powerful, disturbing norms are exerted on children. For
instance, most of the offspring of the mentally ill I interviewed said
that their most important day-to-day goal growing up was simply to
stay quiet so they wouldn't trigger their disturbed parents' rage or
other symptoms. Even the most extroverted, opinionated children
knew when to keep their mouths shut. Strategies tailored to survive
in such families are needed, even if they are not those a child prefers.

Fitting In. To behave in ways that go against the grain of one's
temperament is called *adaptation*. People are nothing if not adaptive.
It's how the human race has survived. Indeed, it is this very responsiveness to the environment that determines how deeply a person will be affected by it, positively and negatively. The less the context suits one's
temperament, the more energy will be expended in adapting to it.

Joan, mentioned at the beginning of this chapter, again comes to
mind. She was inherently shy as a child, but she *became* assertive.
One reason her family role cost her emotionally was because it *didn't
come naturally.* She is by nature a loner. At the same time, the role
had at least one important benefit: She learned to stand up for herself.
She made herself heard.

It's when children *can't* be heard that the trouble starts. If, for
instance, the norms at home are excessively powerful and overwhelming, and the child has no chance of fitting in, the results can be
catastrophic. When children's adaptive efforts fail repeatedly, as they
inevitably do, for instance, in chaotic families, they will be driven to
the negative extremes of their temperaments. An out-of-control Adversary, who goes from arguing to punching out family members, is
an example.

Home is by no means the only place children try to fit in. As
situations—researchers call them "domains"—change, children adjust accordingly, within the limits of their temperaments. For instance,
one domain outside the home is school. Other domains are sporting

events, summer camp, church. Differing contexts will evoke various adaptive maneuvers and strengths as the child tries to fit in.

Thus experiences outside the family *also* have a significant influence on children. Powerful norms may dictate the child's behavior at home, but elsewhere the child's natural capacities will have a chance to be displayed and encouraged, fine-tuned or toned down. The child who might become emotionally numb at home because of the chaos there might be extraordinarily open to other domains where he or she feels more relaxed.

The distinction was poignantly made to me by the introverted daughter of a schizophrenic mother. "Funny," she mused, "I can't remember anything about what my mother was like before I was age eight. But I can tell you everything about nursery school."

To summarize the influences of temperament and family context, most personality researchers agree that highly stressful family environments modify the expression of innate temperament. But so, too, do domains outside the family in which children receive support and encouragement.

ROLES OUTSIDE THE FAMILY

Virtually all developmental psychologists agree that it is not stress per se that is so destructive to children as it is its *inescapability*. One way to escape is to find a separate identity and definition of self beyond home.

A key function of stress is that it forces one to assess one's options and strengths. Many of the people I interviewed were able to apply their own talents and abilities, some of them a consequence of family coping, to the task of finding a role outside their stricken families when they were growing up.

Putting some emotional distance between themselves and their ill relative's disturbing behavior was a vital part of survival. In eliciting the attention of loving mentors, and by finding a niche in which they could succeed away from the family, many siblings and offspring were able to reinvent themselves. As one man, whose brother has schizophrenia, put it:

I always wanted people to get to know me, but I didn't want them to know *that*—my brother's illness. Because if you told somebody, they'd say, "Oh, God, your poor brother." And I'd think, what am I, chopped liver? I mean, it was another reason not to be recognized.

An important component of distancing oneself from turmoil is a sense of control. When you feel you have options, you can tolerate huge amounts of stress. To prove the point, researchers took a group of college students into a laboratory and told them they would receive a series of harmless, low-voltage electric shocks. Half of the students were given a button and informed that once the shocks began, they could stop the shocks by pushing the button. The other students were not given a button. Those who knew they could stop the shocks experienced less distress, anxiety, and pain than those who didn't. This study demonstrated that if you feel you have no control, you are helpless. And if you are helpless, you simply feel more pain.

Martin E.P. Seligman, Ph.D., defines helplessness as "the state of affairs in which nothing you choose to do affects what happens to you." Contexts outside the family can provide arenas in which what you choose to do *does* affect what happens to you, and where you can find a role that is meaningful to you, leading to a sense of control and accomplishment.

Based on my interviews of siblings and offspring of the mentally ill, these outside roles cluster into three domains of achievement: imagination, school, and friendship.

Achievements of Imagination. Many of the people in my study sample remarked on their abilities to retreat into their own fantasy worlds, where reveries of rescue, or blame, even of vengeance, gave them comfort. For those who grew up in the most catastrophic circumstances and isolation, imagination often was their last, sanity-saving resort.

Fran, mentioned in chapter 1, recalls that the only escape she could find from her manic-depressive mother's nearly constant delusions was her own imagination. She says:

My greatest fear was that what happened to my mother would happen to me, and by God, nobody was going to put me in a psych hospital. I didn't have any friends because I was afraid that if people got to know me, they'd see the flaws in my character and lock me away. I buried all my emotions. My saving grace was walking in the hills near the farm where I grew up. The one place I could allow myself to have emotions was a big rock in the woods. I would go to that rock and try to get in touch with the anger and the pain. It reached the point that I invented a woman who, in my mind, would walk up the trail and sit beside me on the rock and talk to me. She'd put her arm around me and say, ''I care what's happening to you.'' I went to that rock every chance I got.

Other people I interviewed spoke of the importance of creative expression as a means of escape. Art was their sanctuary because it allowed these people to address their feelings indirectly. Confronting them directly was too risky, because powerful emotions felt too much like madness.

One woman, whose sibling has schizophrenia, was able to escape through dance. She says:

I felt very trapped in my family because whenever I'd ask my parents about my sister's illness, they'd say it was none of my business. I tried getting at my feelings by just letting my mind wander, but it was too scary. I thought I might never come back—I'd go crazy. So I asked my parents if I could take ballet lessons, and they gave me permission. Instead of looking at my feelings head on, I approached them sideways by moving to music. I'd hold in lots of feelings at home, but they'd come out in dance class. It was a way I could safely get at really deep, nonverbal emotions.

One way to think of the imagination is as wishful thinking. Psychologist Hazel Markus and her colleagues use the term ''possible selves.'' If you can imagine yourself in a better place, it is a temporary solution to your very real current distress. Shelley E. Taylor, Ph.D., psychology professor at UCLA, variously calls such imaginings ''positive illusions'' and ''creative self-deceptions.'' Imagination allows you to distort your own reality in ways that can be emotionally sustaining.

Achievements in School. For people who did not have the temperament for dreamy respite—or were afraid of what it might unleash—achievement in school, through study or sports, served them well. One woman told me that since her mother, who has schizophrenia, was also a sculptor, the daughter was afraid of all artistic endeavors, even though she herself was creatively gifted. Says the daughter:

Creativity requires a certain suspension of rational thought, a willingness to be led by the heart into unknown territory. I wanted to do *anything* to avoid having to probe and root out the things that made me unique. Far better to try to seem normal, and hope it would stick.

For such people, doing well scholastically or on the playing field satisfied their sometimes desperate need for a sense of control. At least in school they could get measurable, predictable results in a structured setting; the only variable was effort.

For years, Jarred, twenty-five, now a graduate student, and his parents lived under the seige of his older brother's acute schizoaffective disorder (until the invention of a drug that caused it to vanish as if by magic). In those early years, his father, a television correspondent, was frequently on the road, and Jarred had to be "the man of the house."

Part of the problem was the difficulty his parents encountered in getting his brother hospitalized. For one thing, his brother was adept at hiding his symptoms in front of doctors and police officers. For another, state law made it almost impossible to commit someone involuntarily.

Thus, says Jarred, the family lived in a "reign of terror." On one occasion, his brother attacked their mother with a butcher knife and seriously injured her because he thought she was possessed by evil spirits. So, at the age of fourteen, Jarred became his mother's bodyguard. Says Jarred:

My brother's sleep cycles were completely off. He'd walk around the house in the middle of the night screaming and pounding on walls and doing crazy, raving things. When my dad was out of town, I'd stand watch while my mom slept, then grab a couple of hours of sleep when she woke up. From the age of fourteen until I went to college, I lived in fear not so much for myself but for my mother. I even took a martial arts course so I could protect her better.

Were it not for school, says Jarred, he never could have endured those years. Except for two close friends, he told no one outside the family about his brother's mental illness. It wasn't so much that he was ashamed of what was happening at home, he says, as it was his need to have a completely separate identity at school. His role at home was defined by madness. At school, he could define his role for himself. Says Jarred:

I loved going to school, because it was my escape. I always got high marks, and everyone liked me. It was a sane world for the day. It made me feel I was making my own decisions. But part of it was that I wanted to cram in as much knowledge as possible, in case I became mentally ill myself. I haven't aged out of the vulnerable period when people develop schizophrenia. So I felt, and still feel, a sense of urgency.

For Daphne, who grew up in as chaotic a family as one can imagine (as we shall see in the next chapter), school was her salvation. She says:

I had some terrific teachers who took an interest in me. I put my money on academia, on scholarship. I mean, that was my drug. Schoolwork and reading, figuring things out in my head, was my life. Margaret Mead was my role model. I used to think her best years were her last years. It gave me hope.

Such intellectual pursuits are enormously beneficial coping strategies for reasons quite apart from the elation of scholastic achievement. According to Peter J. Burke, Ph.D., who studies the relationship between stress and thinking processes, the formation of identity is affected by feedback. When you can't "read," or be "read by," other people, your identity is compromised. Living with someone who has mental illness can mean that you frequently bump up against unfathomable feedback.

To be able to find a context in which feedback is normal and comprehensible, in which you can develop *another* identity, is crucial for siblings and offspring of the mentally ill. Dr. Burke notes that having an outside identity can reduce stress because it can strengthen a *coherent* sense of self.

Thus, achievements of the mind, whether by going to graduate school, or learning the mysteries of automobile engines, or mastering the intricacies of basketball can offset and even replace the feelings of helplessness that occur when living with madness.

Achievements of Friendship. The third important domain of achievement for junior family members is the capacity to form attachments to people outside the family. Friendship is the kinship of choice. It can be the salvation of siblings and offspring of the mentally ill. Certain children have unique talents of the heart, sometimes called "emotional intelligence." They are able to trust *someone* beyond the family, to unburden themselves and to reveal their most embarrassing secrets and fears. In some cases, baring one's soul can be lifesaving.

Norma, twenty-nine, whose mother has severe manic-depression, was the Custodian in her family when she was a child, a role she continued to play until ten years ago. Her father, who couldn't cope with her mother's mental illness, would rush out the door each morning, leaving behind a "to-do" list for Norma. The strain of having to care for her mother, her siblings, and the household was so great that by the time she was nineteen, she had an ulcer and was spitting up blood.

One day, while driving on a highway, it occurred to her that by flooring the accelerator and veering off a bridge, her troubles would be over. But then, she recalls:

This voice in my head said, "Go to Elaine," my best friend. I went over to her house and told her the whole story of what was going on at home. She said, "You've got two choices: You can either tell your

father to get on the stick and deal with your mother, or you can leave.''
I said, ''I can't leave.'' She said, ''Yes, you can. We'll do it together.''
She literally dragged me out of the house and helped me find an apartment. When I moved out, I was finally able to sleep at night. I could
concentrate on making myself well. I had a best friend to watch over
me—she was my guardian angel. From then on, I got stronger, and my
health came back.

Countless research investigations have documented the importance
of friendship to mental and physical health. In a study of children of
psychotic mothers, for instance, the subjects all reported that ''significant others,'' whether family friends or coaches, were vitally important to their survival. Friendship was a ''safe zone'' in which these
children could feel accepted and be themselves.

So, interestingly, is an attachment to animals. One researcher found
that children who talked to pets about their feelings and experiences
were better able to make friends with people. The more these children
confided in their pets and felt welcomed by them, the more empathetic
the children were to their friends.

Whether in human or nonhuman form, loving acceptance by others
helps siblings and offspring of the mentally ill to believe in themselves
and in their futures.

DIVIDED LIVES

In all these ways, junior family members forge their separate roles
inside and outside the family. The influences of each echo in their
adult relationships, occupational choices, and family ties.

For some of these family members, however, there are alarming
splits in their identities. It is as if they have to choose between two
worlds: the world of home, and the world outside. To the extent
that such all-or-nothing choices are necessary, their emotional well-
being in each world is endangered. These young people are suspended somewhere between the realities of both, finding little
comfort in either.

The need to keep their separate worlds so sharply divided is seldom simply a consequence of their own poor decision making. Rather, it is the result of having been isolated in families that could neither cope nor get help for themselves. In such families, junior family members were at their wits' end, with devastating consequences.

CHAPTER 7

When Families Can't Cope

What was the worst thing about my childhood? Boy, ten years ago I could have told you. Now I'm not sure. I'd love to say it was my dad's alcoholism, or my mom's mental illness, or their divorce, or all the times we moved, or my being everyone's caretaker, or my brother's drug addiction. But at this point, I don't think anything was really worse or better than anything else. It was all just sort of different. I guess the "dysfunctional family" model works best. The bottom line is, it wasn't safe to be close to anybody. That's why I bailed out.

—Vera, 29

When Vera talks about her childhood, she takes pride in the fact that the self-confident, fair-minded person telling the story today is not the "the bitchy, whiny person I used to be who did nothing but complain about her terrible life." Indeed, she is a veritable catalog of the benefits of therapy, self-help groups, and long, prayer-filled, dark nights of the soul.

That she emerged from her childhood with a shred of hope, let alone the capacities for evenhandedness and renewal, is remarkable. Because her family was a sinking ship. "I had no one," she says.

Every night, when Vera's father, a real estate agent, came home from work, he'd break out a six-pack of beer, sullenly eat dinner, then pass out in front of the TV. Her mother, if she wasn't in the hospital being treated for severe manic-depression, would be off her medications, drifting in and out of hostile lucidity. Vera's older brother would go into town to do drugs. Vera would do the dishes, then retreat to her room.

And, of course, no one in the family wanted to talk about any of it. It was as though the house were in flames and nobody shouted "Fire!" Well, some people did, particularly her mother's parents, but their observations weren't very helpful. Says Vera:

> All my brother and I ever heard from our grandparents was, "You're making your mother crazy. Don't do anything to upset her." We always walked on eggshells. My dad wouldn't deal with anything—he'd just get mad if we were noisy. My mom didn't think there was anything wrong with her. My brother kept ordering me around, and was becoming a thug.

In an attempt to extricate herself from the family quagmire, at age twenty Vera moved in with her boyfriend and his elderly, arthritic mother. Vera was right back where she started—taking care of people—and within six months, she herself had a nervous breakdown. She was constantly in tears and couldn't drag herself out of bed. She recalls:

> Nothing in my life was clicking. I'd walked into another screwed-up situation that I couldn't make better, just like the one I grew up in. And then one night it hit me. I thought, What the hell is *wrong* with me? For the first time, I started to focus on my own problems instead of everyone else's. I realized that there was no way I could stay involved in all these sick relationships and get better. So I "divorced" them all.

Since then, she's gotten a good job with a public relations firm. She met and married a loving man who's her biggest booster. And she keeps her family at arm's length. She seldom sees her father, who has remarried. Whenever her mother calls, Vera asks her if she's taking her medications. If she isn't—which is most of the time—Vera ends the conversation by saying, "I can't talk to you when you're abusive or incoherent," and hangs up. She's told her brother, who still lives at home, that she's no longer in the troubleshooting business and that if there's a crisis with their mom, it's his turn to mop up.

Vera is an example of a child forced into being the family Custodian who gave up the job in adulthood when it began to erode her own sanity. It wasn't just because her mother was mentally disturbed and refused treatment that she cut off all family ties. Rather, it's because *nobody* in her family had anything to give. Vera had no alternative but to run for her life.

Still, she wishes it had never come to this, having to draw so hard a line. "Sometimes, I actually miss them," she says wistfully. "There are days when I can love my family with all my heart. But only from a distance. I can't do it up close because it's too dangerous. You can't go into that family unless all your armor is on. It just takes away your soul."

WORST-CASE SCENARIOS

Some families simply cannot cope with mental illness. There are those who would argue that these families *will* not cope and that there's a choice in the matter. Whether they will not or cannot, however, the result for children is the same: Their families, divided against themselves, collapse.

Of course, not all families of the mentally ill become emotionally splintered. Hardship often brings families closer together. It depends on the nature of the trouble—specifically, whether it stems from the parents' own behavior or from some other source.

According to Alice S. Rossi, Ph.D., and Peter H. Rossi, who have studied how family relationships evolve over time, the kinds of troubles that unite families are "nonemotional" in origin. That is, they are beyond parents' control—for example, being laid off from work or physical illness. As long as the parents are reasonably stable and their marriages reasonably solid, families are not destroyed by such setbacks. Rather, they pull together as a team and cope.

In contrast, say the Rossis, parents' "emotional troubles" divide families because they can be traced to the parents' *controllable* behavior. For instance, alcoholism and abusiveness tend to tear families apart. When parents are unable to manage their own feelings and conflicts or take responsibility for their own actions, they lose their ability to provide protective family leadership. Their children are then left to their own bewildered or destructive devices, to fend for themselves. It is such parental behavior, rather than mental illness itself, that leads to poor family coping, as the case histories in this chapter will illustrate.

When Biology Isn't Destiny. While much of the recent research on mental illness has focused on genes and biochemistry, many investigators argue that environment plays as big a role as biology. Dr. Ronald C. Kessler of Harvard University department of health care policy, for example, who has conducted twin research, is convinced that biology is not necessarily destiny. He says:

> There are no genes that in and of themselves seem to guarantee a psychiatric disorder. We know this because when you look at identical twins who have all their genes in common, if one twin has a disorder, the other twin does not necessarily have the disorder as well. So the environment clearly is very important. Genes create a differential sensitivity to environmental experiences. But biology doesn't control why there's so much murder in the America, or why so many people get divorced.

If ever a case could be made for the importance of "nurture" in the development and severity of mental illness, dysfunctional families provide graphic evidence. One of the difficulties of *proving* it, however, is that such families seldom volunteer for careful scientific studies. Even when they do participate, they often drop out, especially in longitudinal studies that follow individual families over many years. It is a notorious frustration for investigators to lose track of study subjects. Most studies and surveys, says Dr. Kessler, do not include the homeless or people in jails or single occupancy transient hotels.

Thus, in order to get a full understanding of the relationship between mental illness and family dysfunction, most researchers must rely instead on household populations or retrospective studies of people who have already lived through traumatic childhoods and who in either case are *willing to talk.*

Some studies that track families while mental illness is occurring in them turn to such organizations as the National Alliance for the Mentally Ill for a database of cooperative subjects. But the NAMI membership of 140,000 is comprised primarily of white, middle and upper-middle class, well-educated, and highly motivated parents who are eager to share their experiences with investigators for the greater good of their ill relatives. As a result, their problems and coping strategies are not applicable to all families. Says Dr. Joyce C. Burland:

> When you talk about the NAMI population, you're talking about caring families who are devastated by the trauma of having serious brain disorders decimate the lives of beloved family members. You're not talking about people who physically and sexually abuse their kids. I don't even see these people in my private practice of helping clients and their families cope with serious psychiatric illnesses. Families that are disorganized— where the father is beating up the kids or the daughter has a dissociative disorder because of sexual abuse—don't join advocacy organizations for obvious reasons. In fact, really disorganized families rarely seek support groups or therapy. There's too much chaos and denial going on.

The majority of young family members I interviewed who grew up in dysfunctional families are not NAMI members. Alas, many of them never heard of the organization. To the extent that their families ever even came in contact with the mental health system, generally it was because they were forced into it. Either an ill child was arrested by the police or the parents themselves had no choice but to hospitalize an uncontrollable, psychotic relative.

In these families, disorders of the brain were the least of their calamities. It was the parents' inability to *do something* about their myriad problems, and in particular to talk about them, that caused children to feel emotionally demolished.

"Difficult Families." Families like Vera's, described at the beginning of this chapter, are often referred to by mental health practioners

as "difficult." In their book, *Working with Families of the Mentally Ill*, Drs. Kayla F. Bernheim and Anthony F. Lehman categorize such families according to pattern of difficulty. The authors describe these families variously as "disengaged" (meaning wishing no responsibility for the ill relative), "hostile," "multiple patient," "high denial," and "dependent on the patient's illness" (that is, benefitting emotionally or financially). Many of these families eventually come around and make an effort to work with clinicians on behalf of their disturbed relatives. But others, say the authors, cannot be reached.

From "Difficult" to "Chaotic." When discussing families that can't cope, it's important to draw a distinction between "difficult" and "chaotic."

At times, all families of the mentally ill are difficult, as the unwelcome reality of a relative's persistent psychological impairment slowly sinks in. Resisting awareness is part of the grieving process that follows the psychological "death" of a family member. Thus, these families may be socially isolated, or in various stages of denial, or eager to keep the illness secret. In well-functioning families, however, sooner or later one or both parents "get it": They grasp the fact that a member has a serious problem that goes way beyond "different," and they mobilize themselves to get some outside assistance.

In chaotic families, however, outside assistance is the last thing parents are after simply because it *does* involve outsiders. These parents want no part of self- or any other kind of help or insight or inspection. In some cases, it's because they abuse alcohol and want their addiction, and their unpredictable or violent behavior, to remain undetected. Says Charles R. Goldman, M.D., director of public psychiatry training at the University of South Carolina School of Medicine, "Families with addictions tend to wall themselves off from the rest of the world and present a very false front."

However, according to the siblings and offspring I interviewed who grew up in chaotic families, while such addictions always made every problem worse, they were not the *main* problem. Rather, addictions and mental illness itself appeared to be the *effects* of long-standing, preexisting family strife. In these families, the wonder is not that at least one member of the family had a serious emotional or psychiatric disorder; the wonder is that they *all* didn't. In two of the most horrifying cases, every family member did, in fact, develop psychiatric symptoms.

Countless studies have found that the accumulation of emotional problems, and of parental abusiveness or neglect, are cataclysmic to children. Repeated early traumatization can overwhelm children's innate coping abilities, as though their emotional gears had been stripped. Personality researchers Alexander Thomas, M.D., and Stella Chess, M.D., have studied the damage done when environmental expectations persistently exceed children's abilities to meet them. "[B]ehavior disorders can develop with any temperamental pattern," they write. And Dr. Jerome Kagan and his colleagues at Harvard University department of psychology have found that children who are not innately fearful can become so as a consequence of chronic abuse.

Whether rich or poor, highly or poorly educated, white or black, drunk or sober, chaotic families have certain similarities, which cluster into three interacting patterns of dysfunction:
  • extreme social isolation;
  • pathological parental denial;
  • life-threatening secrecy.

EXTREME SOCIAL ISOLATION:
BY ANY OTHER NAME, "CAPTIVITY"

One of the hallmarks of chaotic families is that they try to be invisible to the outside world. They tend to keep to themselves, avoiding contact with neighbors and discouraging visitors. Theirs is a dreadful privacy. They want to insure their freedom to be emotionally lawless, beyond the reach of accountability. The most important variable in how long they and their problems can remain hidden is money.

Golden Gates. The most horrifying stories I heard were not necessarily those of families living on the razor's edge of poverty, racial oppression, and lucklessness. Rather, they were epics of privileged concealment.

One story stands out because it is the stuff of Greek tragedy: a high-born, wealthy family that had a very great fall. Back in the sixties, this family—let's call them the Smiths—was frequently photographed for the society pages of newspapers and magazines. The family consisted of a well-known and influential father, an attorney; a socially prominent, beautiful mother; a son, Paul, and two younger daughters, Daphne and Sylvia. Over a period of twenty years, all five family members would one by one succumb, like so many dominoes, to various forms of mental illness, from mild to severe.

It's hard to say exactly when the Smiths' troubles began. Daphne—now thirty-six, and herself a therapist—thinks it was when her mother, who was extremely vain, was in a waterskiing accident and her lovely face was mangled. Plastic surgery restored her health, but not her beauty. Losing her looks caused her to become angry and bitter, particularly toward Daphne, then ten, who was her father's favorite. The mother stopped going out in public, even for outpatient medical treatment, because she was afraid of being photographed. So her doctors came to her. Not a psychiatrist, however; she refused to get any kind of psychological treatment, even though, says Daphne, she was becoming more and more irritable, earmarks of an affective disorder.

The Smiths' social life evaporated as the parents withdrew from the world, shielded from it by their considerable wealth. Little by little their magnificent mansion fell into disrepair as gardeners and servants quit or were dismissed. The crumbling house was a metaphor for the turmoil that churned within it. Says Daphne:

My mother went through her kids like Medea. She constantly criticized and humiliated us, and complained about us to my father. He took whatever she said as gospel and was totally blind to her destructiveness.

Daphne's father made no effort to quell his wife's harshness, possibly, Daphne thinks, because his own sister committed suicide when he was a child and he was afraid of losing his wife as well. Instead, he began drinking heavily, and became physically abusive, particularly toward his son. By age twelve, Paul, who had always been volatile, began hitting back. His mother never put any limits on Paul's angry outbursts, not even when he began beating up Daphne. Sylvia was not beaten by her brother because she was his adoring slave. But she became increasingly fearful and anxious, and seldom went anywhere without him.

As time went by, the family continued to spin out of control. Paul began using street drugs, and at age twenty-five moved to a mountain retreat in the Southwest where he became a hermit, collecting guns and growing more and more paranoid. Sylvia, who had always been dependent on him and was by then having chronic panic attacks, joined him when she was eighteen. Daphne's father, too drunk to function, had to give up his law practice, and at the age of fifty-seven died of a heart attack. Daphne's mother died five years later, of cancer.

In all those years, the parents never sought any psychological help or support for themselves, nor for their children.

Standing in the rubble of this family is Daphne, who, unlike her siblings, managed to get professional attention for herself when she was in her twenties, indirectly because of her brutal brother. Paul had assaulted her, smashing her head against a radiator, and she drove to the hospital to have her injuries treated. A physician in the emergency room instantly recognized that she was depressed and brought in a psychiatrist to examine her. Daphne was diagnosed with cyclothymia, a milder version of bipolar disorder, was put on antidepressants, and began psychotherapy. Soon after that she went to graduate school and got her doctorate in psychology.

When I ask her to describe the legacy of her extraordinary childhood, she replies:

> Where do I start! My parents could never accept that anything was wrong with them. My brother is nuts—I'm terrified of him. If he comes anywhere near me, I'll have him arrested. My sister I've given up on. I guess basically I'm a stupid optimist. My therapist called me a "suicide-resistant depressive," which is funny, because I was *obsessed* as a kid with killing myself. I was lucky in that my teachers in school took an interest in me. And I've learned there are some questions you can't answer. You accept them but you don't dwell on them, because otherwise you'll go crazy, too. And that's the thing I'm most afraid of.

That's why I became a therapist—to try to prevent happening to other people what happened to my family.

The greatest tragedy of this family is not just the many terrible things that happened to it. Rather, it is that many of them were preventable. Psychiatry professor Jane S. Ferber, M.D., has treated many adult children of such gilded isolation. Says Dr. Ferber:

Some wealthy families are riddled with alcoholism, sexual abuse, or physical abuse, but nobody in the outside world ever notices. These parents are able to cover it over. People in the lower and working classes can't hide as well. They're much more under the scrutiny of public agencies and community officials.

Picket Fences. You don't have to be rich, however, to want to conceal family chaos from public view. Several siblings and offspring raised in middle-class chaotic families told me that their parents were more concerned about keeping up appearances than about their children's emotional well-being. Unlike Daphne, however, many of these young family members have never been able to extricate themselves from the damage of family isolation. Indeed, in adulthood, they continue to be ensnared by it.

Maggie, thirty-four, whose younger brother has schizophrenia, says that the hardest part of her childhood was the loneliness. "Outside we looked like the perfect family," she sighs. "Inside, we were all dying."

Maggie's synagogue-going parents lived a double life. They seemed to be solid citizens in public, but in private they were at loggerheads. Her father was an angry drunk, and her mother was an argumentative perfectionist. They loathed and continally baited each other. Maggie is convinced that her vulnerable brother was simply the most wounded casualty of their parents' mutual enmity and public face-saving. She says:

The only way my brother and I could shut out the noise and the fighting and screaming was to run to our rooms. I really think my brother had to enter the world of psychosis to escape. My mother never sought anyone's advice. She kept her problems with her husband to herself. She didn't even tell the family rabbi. Then, when my brother became ill, they were ashamed of him. For the first five years of his illness, they wouldn't get him treatment, even though he was getting more and more psychotic and destructive.

Finally, her brother became so violent that his parents placed him in a private psychiatric institution. But soon, their insurance money ran out. Since then they have made little effort to get actively involved with the community mental health system in order to obtain outpatient treatment and rehabilitation for their son. They won't go into marriage counseling or family therapy. They manage their son's illness by hospitalizing him on an emergency basis only.

Life at their house is a nightmare, in part because medications don't alleviate his symptoms, and in part because the mother is constantly on her son's back, criticizing him, which triggers his violent episodes. When he is psychotic, he punches holes in walls, yanks doors off their hinges, defecates and urinates on the floor, tears off his clothes, and walks around naked.

Maggie keeps pleading with her parents to settle their differences and do more for their son, but her entreaties are met with a wall of anger and hostile inertia. She feels stuck—unwilling to abandon her brother and unable to have a life of her own. Says Maggie:

Years ago, I moved to another state, but within three months my mother called me and said she needed me to be at home. Naturally, I came back. I wish I had stayed away, because once I returned, I got sucked in. I'm my brother's only advocate. My parents are constantly threatening to throw him out. He wants to come live with me, and if he weren't so sick, I'd let him. I don't see any light at the end of the tunnel. I feel like I'm just sitting on my wings, you know? I'm a classic underachiever. I didn't finish college. I've never gotten very far in my career. I've never married or had kids. I've missed my whole life, and I don't know what to do about it.

Captives of Isolation. Mental health practitioners refer to such family withdrawal as "social isolation." In chaotic families, a more fitting term would be what Dr. Judith Lewis Herman calls "captivity." These three women—Vera, Daphne, and Maggie—represent points on the continuum of family imprisonment. They were all held hostage by their dysfunctional families, rather like prisoners of war. Even though they could periodically "escape" by going to school, each day they had to return to the chaotic captivity of home.

In these cases, their outside roles were merely a temporary shell which each night was shattered by emotional or physical abuse and neglect. And while two of these three women managed to escape by cutting off their families, in ways all three are still in captivity, as their lingering ambivalences reveal.

PATHOLOGICAL PARENTAL DENIAL

Running through chaotic families is a river of "denial," a wimp of a word when one considers the havoc it can wreak. As noted earlier, under ordinary circumstances the reluctance to accept that a family member has mental illness is a normal part of mourning. Denial is a way of buffering oneself against the shock of too rapid awareness, like easing into frigid water rather than jumping in headlong. In some ways, denial can even be productive, a way of making sense of the incomprehensible.

According to Dr. Jerome Kagan in his book, *The Nature of the Child*, American parents tend to have a "template" of what their ideal child would be like. If a child deviates from that template, parents draw on one of four possible explanations. The first is biological—the child was "born" that way. The second is that the child is going through a "phase." The third is that the parents themselves have done something to cause the child's deviance. The fourth, and least common, explanation is that the child has "malevolent intention." It is this last "explanation" that runs riot in chaotic families, and which is so ravaging to children. Writes Dr. Kagan:

Generally, parents who are secure about their own qualities tend to be accepting of the child's deviations. Parents who are threatened by their own personal failures are likely to interpret extreme disobedience as a reflection of the child's willful hostility.

In chaotic families, parental denial is not just defensive, not just protective, but *malignant*. It cuts in every direction, like a sword. It isn't simply mental illness that is disavowed—so is everything else that goes wrong.

In my research, denial in chaotic families took two forms. One was disavowal of illness. The other was undermining of health.

Denial of Illness. Parents in this category adamantly refused to admit that there was anything psychologically wrong with an ill child because to do so meant that their own parenting behavior might be called into question. According to Dr. David Elkind, professor of child study at Tufts University, denial of illness is a vicious cycle that often begins with parents' own destructive behavior rather than with the illness itself. Says Dr. Elkind:

Some parents have a hard time accepting their role in the illness. They say, "Why are you blaming me? It's the kid who's doing bad things, not me." It gets externalized, because by the time the illness begins, parents don't see the connection to their own behaviors early on. Usually, the person doing the most denying is the person who has contributed to the child's negative behavior. These are the parents you want most to reach. But they are very reluctant to accept any kind of therapeutic intervention, because they inculcated this kind of behavior in the child in the first place.

A variation of denial of illness is what mental health professionals call *normalizing*. In a study of fourteen adult siblings of schizophrenics, Laina M. Gerace, Ph.D., R.N., professor of psychiatric nursing, and her colleagues at the University of Illnois found that some parents interpreted the ill child's disturbing behavior as "spoiled" or "sensitive." In one case, an ill child was not taken for treatment for fifteen years because the parents were able to find a more "normal" explanation for the child's abnormal behavior and deterioration.

Denial of illness seemed to be rampant in the most dysfunctional families in the Gerace study, and was directly related to the impact of mental illness on siblings. The more chaotic the families, the more devastating the impact and the likelier the siblings were to disengage from the families. But it was not illness alone that caused such protective distancing. Rather it was destructive parental behavior such as alcoholism, abusiveness, and combativeness.

Denial works differently when a spouse disavows the other spouse's mental illness. According to my interviews, in this case denial served to keep marriages together, for good or ill. This pattern of denial was particularly true of insecure women who had never worked outside the home and who had no family to fall back upon. However, husbands did their share of denying, too, especially those who were emotionally dependent on their wives and who could not face the prospect of being single fathers. In these situations spouses minimized, or justified, their partners' pathological behavior, with excruciating consequences to their children.

All of the offspring I interviewed who grew up in these circumstances told me that they *begged* the well parent to leave the ill parent, almost always to no avail. As one woman whose father had paranoid schizophrenia told me:

> My mother always said she'd leave my dad, but she never did, not until years later. She placated him. She made excuses for him, even when he was emotionally abusive to me. She'd say, "He doesn't mean it." If I complained, she'd scream, "Why are you telling me this?" I'm still mad at her because she didn't protect me from him.

Undermining of Health. Instead of ignoring mental illness, some parents seem to be obsessed by it, and may sabotage the mentally ill family member's recovery. This pattern is referred to by theorists as the "secondary gain" of illness. Undermining of health can have a variety of goals. One goal is to give the insecure parent an admirable role. For example, mothers who grew up in traditional families and who never had careers may feel a sense of importance in caring for an utterly dependent ill child.

Says psychiatrist Clarice J. Kestenbaum, M.D., of Columbia University's College of Physicians and Surgeons:

> Some parents unconsciously fight a child's getting well. It may be that they won't have a purpose in life if they don't have somebody on whom to focus. I've seen parents totally unaware, or seemingly unaware, of how to make their children feel better. Some parents just know what buttons to push to cause a temper outburst or a fight.

This was the case with the family in which Maryanne, now thirty, grew up. Her mother, who was born in South America, was by any measure the long-suffering fulcrum of the family. Her father, who had been brutally beaten in childhood by his own father, never raised a hand, or his voice, to his kids. Instead, he left the parenting to his wife, oblivious to the madness that spun around him.

One of their two sons, Vince, was diagnosed at eighteen as schizophrenic, and was about as threatening as a kitten. The other son, Tommy, then twenty, was a bully, enraged by his ill brother's mumbling and bizarre behavior. Then there was sixteen-year-old Maryanne, who, as the only girl, in true Bystander form, was both brothers' prey.

Maryanne gives the following slice-of-life example of daily life in her house when she was a child.

> Nobody in my family ate together. My mother would cook everyone separate meals. One night, my parents and I were in the den watching TV. Both my brothers were in the kitchen, yelling for Mom to fix them a snack. My whole body tensed up because I knew they'd get into a fight. The next thing I knew, pots and dishes were crashing against walls. My mother jumped up to stop the fight and clean up the mess. My dad just lay on the couch. He never got involved in anything.

Maryanne never had any privacy. Both her brothers were constantly intruding on her. If she took a shower, Tommy would walk into the bathroom, pull away the shower curtain, and grab her breasts. Vince would stand outdoors, peering at her through the window. Sometimes Tommy would sneak into her bed at night and rub against her until he had an orgasm. Maryanne was so terrified of him that she'd pretend to be asleep. Other times Vince would wander into her room and sit naked on her bed.

There were virtually no consequences for either brother's behavior. It was as though her dad tacitly encouraged it. Her mother was hardly more helpful. For example, when Maryanne told her about Tommy's sexual abusiveness, she said, "Well, he's just an unhappy kid." Says Maryanne:

I've decided that my mother is as sick as her husband and her sons. This wanting to be "needed" by them, and not having an identity apart from that, is just crazy. There were a thousand things my parents could have done to make things better, and they never did anything. Was it because my father was abused as a child? Was it because my mother was trying to have an important role? Who knows? And at this point, *who cares*? All I know is that I can't have a relationship with anyone in that family.

In other cases, undermining of health can occur because a child's illness is the mortar of an unhappy marriage. If the attention is focused on the disturbed child, then parents can avoid a sense of complicity in their own misery by unconsciously impeding that child's recovery. Says Dr. Elkind:

Certainly there are cases where mental illness is genetic. But children's problems usually reflect problems between parents. In some cases, if the ill child gets better, often the family gets worse, because the child is the vehicle for resolving family problems. Let's say a mother is unhappy with her husband, but has difficulty expressing that, so it gets translated into anger at the child. Then the father defends the child. The child becomes the medium for this battle that can't be fought directly. In other words, as long as that child is ill, the family can function.

LIFE-THREATENING SECRECY

"Silence breaks the heart," wrote poet Phyllis McGinley. Nowhere is this more evident than in chaotic families of the mentally ill. The single greatest source of distress for the offspring and siblings I interviewed was not so much the presence of mental illness but that no one talked about it and no one explained it.

In chaotic families, however, mental illness was simply one of many family secrets that were covered up. Alcoholism, obviously, was one such secret. Incest abuse, primarily between siblings, was another. In these families, it wasn't only that such secrets were hidden from the outside world. Some were secrets children kept from their parents because if they were revealed, all hell would break loose. For example, for a child to "rat" on an abusive sibling often invited a torrent of parental fury toward the abused child. Said one woman:

> It wasn't just that we didn't talk about my brother's illness. We didn't talk about anything. There was too much other garbage going on. My dad was a control freak. He couldn't stand failure. So if you told him something like my brother was molesting me, he'd beat the shit out of you. My mother covered for my brother because she was afraid my dad would beat him up. Guess who got left out in the cold. I had no one to confide in. So I just zoned out. I learned to feel nothing. The reason I fooled around with drugs as a teenager was to try to feel *something*.

Dr. Julius Segal, an authority on prisoners of war and concentration camp survivors, observes that it isn't stress or captivity per se that is so devastating to the human spirit. Rather, it is *the lack of communication*. Indeed, the urgent need for human contact, and the ability to be heard, can be lifesaving. For instance, American prisoners of war in Vietnam would "talk" to one another by tapping on walls, even by belching or scuffing the floor with their sandals in code. By one estimate, when stress levels are high, people who have no emotional support suffer *ten times* more physical and emotional illness than those who have someone to confide in.

Being heard is essential to survival. When Linda Gray Sexton, daughter of the Pulitzer Prize–winning poet Anne Sexton, permitted her late mother's therapist to reveal to a biographer the dark side of her mother's mental illness, Linda was excoriated by her mother's relatives and devoted fans. As a consequence, Linda herself became extremely depressed. Only by speaking the truth of her experience in her memoir, *Searching for Mercy Street*, was she able to get beyond her depression. She writes:

> I have only just discovered how much I need to regain the power taken from me so many years ago, when I was a frightened and guilty child. . . . Power accompanies words: the ability to speak your mind, to tell your own story, to say what you want. . . .

Not speaking your mind, suffering in silence, can crush one's core sense of self. Several siblings and offspring told me that keeping terrible family secrets stifled their ability to perceive their experiences accurately. The only way to maintain their silence was *to pretend the "secret" events weren't happening.*

When parents do not talk about a family member's mental illness, or about any other serious problems, they endanger their children's emotional and physical health, and sometimes their very lives. As one woman, the daughter of a manic-depressive mother, told me:

> My mom was violent toward us kids and all my dad ever said was, "Keep an eye on her, make sure she takes her pills." He wouldn't talk to any doctors, he wouldn't get her hospitalized, and he'd *never* discuss her illness with us. So I had to deal with her. When she got violent, I'd try to call the police, and the next thing I'd know, her hands would be around my throat. By the time I was fifteen, I was suicidal. I used to pray every night for God to take my life so I wouldn't have to live through this for one more day.

Breaking The Silence: The "Messenger Theory." As these case histories demonstrate, life-threatening secrecy can create such an accumulation of stress and anxiety that something has to give. It's like metal fatigue—eventually the structure falls apart. So it is with chaotic families. It's only a matter of time before someone snaps and their secrets break out.

What usually happens is that one child gets into so much trouble that outside attention is brought to bear upon the family. The child could be mentally or physically ill, or could commit a crime, or could be chronically truant from school. These "problem children" are frequently their families' salvation, for were it not for them, the family might never get help.

Dr. Jane S. Ferber calls this phenomenon the "messenger theory." As she explains it:

> Very often the person who appears in the emergency room or clinic or police station is not the person in the family in the worst trouble. They're usually the person most sensitive to the stress in the family. Somehow, it seems to be their function to bring a message to the outside world that something is wrong in the family, and to get the attention of outside helpers. They may do it rationally by saying, "Everyone's crazy in my family," or they may be hallucinating themselves. It doesn't really seem to matter. What matters is that their behavior mobilizes the family to get outside help.

In some cases, the messenger in the family is the only one helped— the rest of the family simply will not follow through. Vera, mentioned earlier, had a nervous breakdown and went into therapy, but her family did not. Daphne got help after her brother attacked her, while her siblings and parents retreated deeper into their own symptoms. Neither of these two women was the most psychologically disturbed family member. The point is that they broke the silence and saved themselves.

Maggie, on the other hand, is becoming an effective family messenger. The more desperate she feels, the louder she yells at her parents to get help for themselves and their son, and the more she gets involved in the mental health system. For example, she recently joined a support group for siblings and offspring of the mentally ill and is beginning to bone up on community mental health facilities. Her motivation in breaking the gridlock of family silence and secrecy is not, however, mere altruism. As she puts it, "I want my chance to have a life."

THE WALKING WOUNDED: THE LEGACIES OF CAPTIVITY

In her book, *Trauma and Recovery*, Dr. Judith Lewis Herman describes the lingering devastation of literal and psychological captivity:

> When neither resistance nor escape is possible, the human system of self-defense becomes overwhelmed and disorganized. . . . [T]he victim of chronic trauma may feel herself to be changed irrevocably, or she may lose the sense that she has any self at all. . . . Chronically traumatized people no longer have any baseline state of physical calm or comfort.

When survivors of childhood captivity reach adulthood, even if they physically escape their family torment, "invisible barriers" to emotional escape may remain in the form of complex post-traumatic stress disorder. The symptoms of this disorder, writes Dr. Herman, fall into three categories:

Hyperarousal. The person is on constant red alert, prepared for danger—easily startled, or easily provoked, or unable to sleep soundly.

Intrusion. The person relives the trauma either consciously or subconsciously. Consciously, survivors sometimes have flashbacks, or fantasize about changing the outcome of traumatization. Subconsciously, memories linger in bodily sensations, or in nightmares. The person is paralyzed emotionally, as though caught in a traffic jam, unable to move forward or backward.

Constriction. The person surrenders to feelings of powerlessness and defenselessness. Some survivors "escape" by going into an altered state of consciousness. Another term for this symptom is "numbing." Emotional deadening causes a kind of trancelike immunity to stimulation of any kind. The traumatized person loses a sense of time, as well as awareness of what is happening around him or her. Such feelings are beyond simple indifference; they are a disconnection of the mind, soul, and body, which makes the person vulnerable to further harm.

Those who cannot summon this kind of dissociative fugue state sometimes resort to alcohol or drugs in an attempt to induce it, Dr. Herman reports. In the worst cases, they develop multiple personality disorder. They divide themselves up into tiny bits of coping, each "alter" taking care of one piece of the emotional or physical pain.

In these three ways, victims of traumatic captivity die a little—or a lot—inside, to the detriment of their future relationships, as we shall see. Some victims recoil from any attachments. Intimacy feels life-threatening, even if the victim can no longer remember exactly why. Others repeat the past by getting involved with abusive partners.

Dr. Herman's "captivity" model explains, among other things, the almost clinical detachment with which many of the people I interviewed raised in chaotic families told their chronicles of torment and deprivation. Their words painted pictures of agony, but their tones of voice and vocal inflections were unmodulated, revealing nothing.

One woman, now forty-one, the daughter of a bipolar mother, has yet to shed a tear about the extreme isolation and silence in which she grew up. This woman, alarmed by her own emotional flatness, is in therapy with the sole purpose of being able to weep for the first time. She is an example of "constriction."

Other survivors, however, appeared to be in a state of "hyperarousal." It didn't take much for them to all but literally jump out of their skins when they were being interviewed, perhaps because in telling their stories they were reliving them physiologically.

Their nervousness might also be a function of "kindling," a concept introduced by Dr. Robert M. Post and his colleagues at NIMH. When the brain is subjected to repeated, traumatic stimulation, in time that stimulation takes on a life of its own, long after the original stimulation has stopped. Another name for this process is "sensitization."

Children who are timid to begin with, and who are raised in stressful environments, are especially likely to experience "spontaneous attacks of anxiety" and to suffer panic attacks in adulthood, according to Dr. Jerome Kagan. He writes, "[F]rightening environmental event[s] might function as a kindling stimulus. The anxiety-arousing events might include . . . marital quarrels [or] attacks from a sibling or older child. . . ."

Thus, even an event as relatively innocuous as an interview with a sympathetic journalist might be a "kindling stimulus." Talking about one's painful history can add fuel to the emotional fire.

WHEN DEFENDING STOPS
AND COPING BEGINS

As we have seen, the outcomes of offspring and siblings of the mentally ill are directly related to how well their parents coped both with a relative's illness and with the parents' own unfinished emotional business. Numerous studies have shown that the children of the mentally ill who fare best are those who have family supports and access to counseling and other mental health services. Neither of these attributes characterizes chaotic families.

Of all the seventy-five siblings and offspring I interviewed, the ones who bore the deepest scars were those who were captives of family chaos. In childhood, these young family members, traumatized by neglect or abuse and muzzled into secrecy, had but three alternatives: to act out their anger and pain, to tune out their anguished perceptions, or to break down themselves and even attempt suicide.

When parents cannot cope, neither can children.

CHAPTER 8

When Families Can Cope

The older I get, the more I admire my parents. My father deserves so much credit for his strength and commitment to his family. And my mother has been heroic in maintaining her love for us, even though the voices in her head keep whispering about dreadful possibilities, threatening and conspiring against her. My parents have not had an easy life, my mom because of her illness, my dad because of his wife. Yet in spite of everything, they successfully raised their children. We've always loved and supported each other. And that's been very sustaining.

—Cathy, 37

It's hard to come up with a better example of good coping than Cathy's family. In ways they are an *ideal* family. The only wrinkle in it is her mother's severe mental illness. But the illness has not destroyed them. On the contrary—it has brought them closer than ever, closer, it could be argued, than most "normal" families.

You may recall Cathy, mentioned in chapter 1, who at the age of eleven was the first member of her family to notice that something was wrong with her mother. What was "wrong," according to the psychiatrist who diagnosed the mother the next day, was that she had late-onset schizophrenia.

Since that day twenty-six years ago, her mother's illness has gotten progressively worse. The medications she takes must be kept in relatively low doses because of their horrible side effects. Consequently, while she is rarely totally out of touch with reality, she is delusional

172

most of the time. She thinks her husband, an attorney, is actually the CEO of IBM, that she's the president of the company, and that each of their three grown children are captains of assorted industries.

But she does not consider herself to be mentally ill. Rather, she is convinced that she simply has amazing mental capacities, which she calls being "on line." She has regular conversations in her mind with various kings and queens around the world. She also has talks with her many "employees," one of whom keeps sabotaging the "business" by telling lies and spreading vicious rumors. When she catches this phantom employee saying terrible things about her, she sharply reprimands the person, although not in public. Her family encourages her to keep her on-line activities confidential.

Every so often, however, they slip out. When she and her husband visit Cathy, occasionally she'll say something preposterous to her grandchildren, such as that Cathy is producing a major motion picture and everyone's invited to the gala opening. Cathy then quietly explains to her kids, "That's only in grandma's mind," to their disappointment. Or the mother will get agitated about something that's happening in her mind and call the police. Cathy's father will tell her to put down the phone, and her grandchildren will chorus, "Don't be mean to Grandma!"

Through it all, Cathy and her family have rallied protective forces around her mother, drawing on the mutual caring and warmth that were firmly rooted long before the illness erupted. Says Cathy:

> I have really good memories of my mom, from always. I don't remember her ever yelling at us when we were little kids. She was very sweet-natured, sometimes too much so. My dad was a pretty dominant character—he was a litigator! And he was gone a lot, so she had to handle everything. But she was real gentle. A real, *real* nice mom.

During those early years, Cathy's father was making quite a name for himself, attracting a roster of well-heeled clients. After his wife became ill, however, he felt an urgent need to accumulate a portfolio of investments so that his children would never have to support their mother, and so that she herself would always have the best medical treatment.

He had to make a choice. Either he could be around more to take care of his wife or he could plan for the future by piling on more legal work. Since he knew that Cathy, the firstborn child, was unusually level-headed and mature, and because his wife, under constant psychiatric supervision, was never violent, he chose the latter course. It was a judgment call, and it worked. Somehow, Cathy's mother managed to hold herself together most of the time, even as the voices in her head grew louder and more demanding.

This is not to suggest, however, that life on the home front was altogether tranquil. Sometimes, when Cathy walked home from school with the other kids in the neighborhood, her mom would be sitting on the front lawn wearing her nightgown, and Cathy would be mortified. Other times, Cathy would have to ask her mother the same question six or seven times before she'd get her attention.

And there was something else, something really "odd," says Cathy, because she's never read or heard about anything quite like it: She could tell the instant she woke up in the morning if her mom was going to have a really bad day. *She could smell it.* Says Cathy:

> There'd be a heavy, sweet odor in the house. I could literally smell her fear. Invariably, it would be when my dad was out of town. And then I'd be filled with dread. I'd think, Oh no—what am I going to have to handle now? Sure enough, when I came down for breakfast, her body movements would be real jerky and she'd be withdrawn or very distracted. I don't remember too much more about those early episodes, though, because I was so busy. I had to cope because there were a lot of people counting on me to cope.

One reason Cathy was so busy was that she had to take care of her younger sisters, then nine and five. She'd say to her mother, "Why don't you go lie down? I'll keep the kids occupied." The middle sister was a bit fearful, and the youngest one seemed somewhat bewildered. Yet all three children were remarkably free of serious signs of stress.

Even more remarkably, the mother was still able to function in many ways. She continued to do the marketing, make the kids' lunches, cook dinner, and keep the house reasonably tidy.

Cathy credits her dad for the family's ability to function so well. As a parent, she says, he was everything a child could wish. He was endlessly patient. He was always available to talk to his kids about their mother's illness. True, in the beginning he had a hard time accepting it. But he had quickly faced the reality that his wife was incurably ill, and that he would have to pay as much attention as possible to his children in the limited time available to him. Regardless of his exhaustion, each night when he was home he'd read to them or help them with their homework; if he was out of town, he always telephoned.

And although he could have hired a housekeeper to cook and clean, he wisely chose not to. He did not want his wife to feel that her domestic role had been usurped, nor that he perceived her to be a hopeless case. Says Cathy:

My dad had this instinctive store of wisdom. He always expected my mom to be as good a mother and homemaker as she was capable of, and she pretty much lived up to his expectations. It's not like he walked around with a white glove, checking the tops of cabinets. And he certainly didn't expect gourmet meals. He'd tell me, "Boy, sometimes the food's pretty bad around here. But I'll be damned if she's going to sit around all day." So even though food got burned, because she'd forget what time she put the oven on, he never complained to her. And he was always solicitous toward her. He'd say to me, "The most important thing I can do is to keep your mother happy, because if she gets angry with me, she might leave or decide some day to move in with you kids." So he's been willing to put up with all kinds of things. My dad is a saint.

Because he and his children have been so accepting and encouraging of her, the mother has bent every effort to control her symptoms, even if she doesn't identify them as such. Cathy once asked her about her delusions. Her mother explained that sometimes she has to concentrate hard on what people are saying because the voices keep interrupting. If she's really interested in the topic of conversation, she can turn down the volume of her voices. But if she's tired, or if the conversational subject is of little interest to her, the voices crescendo.

As the years have gone by, the family has maintained its openness and intimacy. The parents spend several weeks each year at their children's houses. They always gather for Christmas and other celebrations. And they have made plans as a group for "in case." If their father should die before his wife does, they've agreed that the mother will live with Cathy. To help pay for her mother's upkeep, they've agreed, too, that Cathy will inherit a larger portion of her father's estate. To give Cathy some respite, the other children will continue having their mother visit them. And should the voices in their mother's head ever command her to harm anyone, they are prepared to have her hospitalized. In the twenty-six years of her illness, however, she's only had to be committed four times.

Why does it all work? Cathy can think of a number of reasons: her father's financial planning and emotional availability; their mother's ongoing domestic role; the joint decision making; the fact that each of the daughters married decent men who encourage their emotional support of their parents.

If Cathy had to single out any one thing, though, it would be the woman behind the illness herself who has valiantly struggled to reciprocate her family's devotion. Says Cathy:

I remember after my first child was born, I was nursing the baby, and my mother, who had come to help me, was standing there smiling. And I thought, Now I understand my mother. She feels about her children what I feel about this baby. I realized that for all the problems we've had over the years and all our strange role reversals, my mother has always been there for us. If the day ever comes that she has terrible delusions about me, that I'm poisoning her or something, I'll always know that that's the illness, and that the real person loves me completely. There have been times when she's been wigged out and I couldn't wait for her to go home. But for all her limitations as a person, we have never doubted her love. I know people with normal parents who can't make the same claim.

A UNITED STAND

If ever a case could be made that mental illness is biological in origin, families like Cathy's provide ample evidence. Prior to the eruption of her mother's schizophrenia, nothing in this family's behavior suggested anything but mutual caring and respect. There were no environmental triggers for the illness, which may explain its late onset—the mother was thirty-seven.

Nothing about the family dynamics *after* her diagnosis necessitated anyone's defensive emotional distancing. Since the illness was so clearly a matter of terrible biochemical fate, and since the family was close to begin with, they were able to combine their efforts harmoniously. They saw the illness as an opportunity to learn more about how the brain works, and to understand themselves and each other better.

Thus, in keeping with Alice and Peter Rossi's theory that parents' nonemotional problems tend to unite families, as described in the previous chapter, this family has come through with flying colors. Mental illness simply brought out everyone's best.

When Coping Comes Naturally. Agnes Hatfield, Ph.D., has defined "coping" as "those efforts persons make to master conditions of threat, harm, or challenge when the usual strategies are insufficient." Good copers are not destroyed by tragedy—they see it as a challenge to find solutions.

Some families seem to be inherently good copers in the face of adversity, and researchers have come up with various theories about their resilience. As has been mentioned, black families tend to extend help to one another more readily than white families because such help is a cherished value. This mutual caregiving may be one reason why mental illness is less common among blacks than among whites. According to a recent national survey conducted by Dr. Ronald C. Kessler and his colleagues at the University of Michigan Institute for Social Research, blacks, including young blacks, have lower rates of affective disorders and substance abuse disorders than whites.

Education is another predictor of good coping. According to Dr. Kessler, although people with mental illness tend to cluster in lower income groups, wealth per se is less protective than education. Paradoxically, research shows that wealth can sometimes *impede* good coping. Whereas rich people can afford to hire outside help, in economically strapped families, everyone, including a mentally ill relative, must share the load of chores. The result is that the ill person simply functions better.

Good family coping has much to do with how children raised in difficult circumstances ultimately turn out. Studies demonstrate that resilient children often have families that are warm, close-knit, and relatively free of conflict.

But resilience is not a static, preexisting characteristic; rather it is a *process*, according to London psychiatrist Michael Rutter, who has conducted studies of hardy children. In his view, resilience is the result of having made adaptive changes and *done something* about one's problems. The best predictor for future coping, then, is having coped well in the past. It helps, Dr. Rutter adds, to have a family in which there is the opportunity to cope successfully—that is, where children are loved, valued, and consulted. Cathy, mentioned at the beginning of this chapter, grew up in such a family.

Among the siblings and offspring I interviewed, those who fared best were raised in families with at least one of the following three characteristics: a lack of secrecy, encouragement of the well children's outside roles, and parental responsibility for the ill member's care and behavior.

Lack of Secrecy. When children are kept in the dark about mental illness, they fumble for explanations that may be harmful to them— for example, that they caused it. While many parents feel that they need to protect their children from unpleasantness or sorrow, in the case of mental illness it is imperative that children be informed about the illness. It is impossible to overstate the importance of this openness for younger family members.

Naomi, thirty, says that of her parents' many virtues, it was their candor about her older sister's paranoid schizophrenia that helped her most. She recalls:

I vividly remember the day my sister had her first psychotic break. It was a bolt from the blue, and my parents had to hospitalize her. I was fifteen. I didn't find out about it until I got home from school. My parents were sitting there crying—they were just devastated. But they were wonderful about telling me what was going on. Their belief was that I needed to know, and that I could handle it. It was horrible to find out that she could be violent. But knowing about her illness helped me be prepared for when she started getting paranoid. I knew exactly what to do. The way my parents protected me was to keep me informed.

Encouragement of Outside Roles. We have seen the value to siblings and offspring of the mentally ill of having parallel lives outside the family. In families that cope well, these outside roles are more than just escape—they are actively endorsed by parents. Thus these younger family members do not feel ambivalent about their victories beyond home. As one man, whose brother has severe manic-depression, put it:

My parents were very big on seeing that I didn't have to get too involved in my brother's illness. By that I mean that I wasn't expected to be his caretaker. They realized that my brother kind of captured the family agenda. So they encouraged me to be independent. My mom said, "You can't live your brother's life. You have to live your own life." She was really supportive when I went out for sports, or got involved in student government. I think that helped her to feel less guilty about not spending enough time with me. And I'm grateful for it. It helped me to be really autonomous, to feel I could do anything I set my mind to.

Parental Responsibility. The third key component of good family coping is parents' making clear to their well children that responsibility for the ill person belongs to the adults. This point may seem obvious, but in many families of the mentally ill, parental responsibility is fuzzy.

This is not to say that many of the young family members I interviewed did not help shoulder that responsibility. But in stable families there was no question about who was in charge of protecting the children against harm, of making sure the ill person got treatment, and, when necessary, arranging for the ill person, if he or she was persistently out of control, to be moved to a residential facility or asked to leave. These parents did not give guilt-inducing messages to the well children to pay more attention to the ill relative. They took particular pains to explain to their children that they, the parents, were the primary caregivers.

Laurie Flynn, executive director of NAMI, whose daughter has mental illness, is an example of such foresight. She says:

> I never wanted my other children to feel they had a special obligation to their ill sister. You can't do that to people growing up. You can't hand off that job. I have an obligation as a mother to my ill child. My children don't. It's important for them to have their own lives. Family ties cannot be chains—they have to be elastic. Children have to be who they are.

While any one of these three characteristics helped to improve the outcome of the siblings and offspring I interviewed, those whose parents had all three qualities fared best of all.

For four years, Jarred, twenty-five, mentioned earlier, served as his mother's protector against his ill brother when his dad was out of town on business. Yet never has Jarred felt resentment toward his parents for his having had to assume that role. Says Jarred:

> My parents are my best friends. It sounds sick, but sometimes we joke about how lucky we were to have mental illness in the family, because it taught us how much we mean to each other. My dad's a really gentle, strong guy who always let me make my own decisions. My mom was the rock of Gibraltar. She was really aware of my needs. She'd push me out the door and say, "You don't need to protect me all the time. Go out with your friends. Go have a normal life." They both always kept me informed about my brother's illness. I even went with them to talk about it a couple of times with his psychiatrist. We were always just really up front and supportive of each other.

Alas, not all families have these inherent emotional gifts.

Learning the Hard Way. Many families do not initially cope easily or well with tragedy. They must learn to do so in painful, incremental steps. Often, their eventual good coping is preceded by an extremely rocky, even dysfunctional, transition period. In this case, family resilience is an acquired talent—the end result of having fallen apart when tragedy occurred, and reinventing itself in the aftermath.

Psychiatry professor Frederic Flach calls this phenomenon of falling apart and regrouping the "law of disruption and reintegration," referred to earlier. To survive long-term tragedies such as a family member's mental illness, it is not enough simply to deal with periodic emergencies in bursts of activity and afterward resume one's previous behavior as though nothing had happened. Rather, to cope well over the long haul, one must change *down to one's bones* so that subsequent crises can be prevented or handled with greater equanimity. Since life as family members knew it is over, it is necessary to find a new "homeostasis."

For some people, pain is the *only* mechanism by which such profound and lasting change can take place, Dr. Flach argues. Suffering is simply the first step—it gets one's attention. One must then integrate the pain by talking about it with others. Survivors of adversity who do best are those who reveal their feelings to sympathetic relatives, friends, or mental health professionals.

In the process of such revelations, survivors often discover hidden sources of unhappiness or self-destructiveness. Survivors who do less well are those who deny or cover over the pain; they remain perpetually vulnerable. In ignoring pain, they have scant incentive to put the pieces together again in such a way that they are even stronger than before.

Resilience, as Dr. Flach summarizes it, "depends on our ability to recognize pain, acknowledge its purpose, tolerate it for a reasonable time until things begin to take shape, and resolve our conflicts constructively." Thus, for example, the person who, owing to an automobile accident, must give up tennis may regroup by joining a gym and learning how to lift weights. The person whose occupation has become obsolete may regroup by going back to school to acquire a new skill. The person who has been scared to death by a relative's mental illness may regroup by reading about brain disorders and joining a support group.

While one would hardly recommend it, mental illness can be a catalyst for change in families that are not cohesive or do not have good coping skills to begin with. For these families, there are two primary paths to reintegration and resilience. One path is introspection and insight. A family member, in reaction to a relative's mental illness, has an epiphany and undergoes a metamorphosis. In such situations, people often turn to psychotherapy to help implement their new awareness. They change from the inside out, which has a positive effect on their families.

Other families change from the outside in through what is called "psychoeducation." These families alter their behavior through practical knowledge, whether by reading about brain disorders on their own or by taking a formal course tailored to families of the mentally ill.

In these two ways, many families discover or learn new coping strengths, born of dreadful necessity.

EPIPHANIES: CHANGING FROM THE INSIDE OUT

In recent years, increasing numbers of clinicians and theorists have decried the application of the term "dysfunctional" to families of the mentally ill because the word connotes fault-finding, which does nothing to ease the burden of caregiving. Moreover, these theorists argue, to the extent that family dysfunction exists, it is not the cause of brain disorders. Rather, it is primarily the *result* of living with people who have them.

While there is much merit in these theories, they cannot be universally applied, as we saw in the last chapter. When families of the mentally ill completely ignore the *possibility* of preexisting family or individual problems, they often compound their difficulties. Dysfunction, as has been mentioned, is a signal that something is wrong. Picking up on that signal—whether or not it is in reaction to a mental disorder—is critical to family survival.

Many of the siblings and offspring I interviewed whose families ultimately coped well said that a key ingredient in their adaptation was the ability to *zero in on what they were doing wrong in order to understand what they could be doing right.* Such painful self-assessment made it possible for their families to settle their differences and then focus on a higher purpose: pulling together for everyone's sake. The following case history illustrates the point.

Josh, forty, a high-functioning victim of schizophrenia, believes that his illness, while biological in origin, was, in large part, triggered by his chaotic family. He goes further. He strenuously makes the point that *but* for his illness, his family, and in particular, his mother, might never have relinquished the corrosive patterns of their complicated love for one another.

Until Josh had his first psychotic break at the age of twenty-four, *he* was the most resilient member of the family. His mother, whose own father had schizophrenia, was a woman of enormous personal and professional frustration who was given to violent outbursts of temper. Josh's father was by nature extremely anxious. Of his parents, Josh says:

> My father was someone who would literally cry over spilt milk. Both my parents were out of control most of the time when I was very young. There are few things as frightening to a child as that.

The last born of four children, Josh was the family peacemaker. He was able to jolly his mother out of her black moods, listen sympathetically to his father, and be the charismatic buffer between his embattled older sisters who adored him but did not get along with each other. To get some nurturing for himself, Josh sought surrogate parents outside the family. Often he'd stay for days at a friend's house on some pretext, such as a school project, in order to have a measure of affectionate adult attention. Through the years he has acquired countless friends who have been his constant support. It's easy to see why. He's hilarious. He's also a genius. "Certified," he deadpans.

Josh was the family *wunderkind*—a straight-A student who scored a perfect 1,600 on his SATs and whose IQ hovers around the 200 mark. At eighteen he was offered full scholarships by eight top-ranked colleges and universities. It was while he was breezing his way through college, easily maintaining a 4.0 average, that he began having terrifying symptoms. He thought his phone was being tapped and that he was in mortal danger.

During a visit home at Thanksgiving, an old family friend, who happened to be a psychiatrist, came to the house one evening for dinner. Josh described the elaborate plot he believed had been hatched by secret agents to destroy him. The psychiatrist looked at him and said, "You have to get into treatment immediately. You're crazy." Because both Josh and his parents utterly trusted this man, Josh agreed to be hospitalized. It was a total leap of faith because Josh didn't think anything was wrong with him. He recalls:

> I was completely out of touch with reality. My reality was what was going on in my head. That's something many doctors never grasp, that the interior life of a schizophrenic is just as real as the lived experience. I still have post-traumatic stress disorder from being in the hospital, because I believed I was in a concentration camp. I truly thought I was going to die.

While he was in the hospital, among his delusions was his certainty that his parents had been exterminated and replaced by assassins who had undergone plastic surgery to *look* like them. Whenever his mother came to visit him, Josh accused her of being a murderer.

The effect on his mother was instantaneous—one might say, miraculous. Her rages simply ceased. From then on she threw all her energies into helping her son, which in turn had a calming effect on her husband and daughters; somehow, their individual grievances no longer seemed important. Says Josh:

What's been interesting to me is how drastically my parents changed. My father became extremely supportive. And my mother became this rock of strength. She visited me every day for the seven months I was in the hospital. She'd stay with me even when I was lunging at her, screaming, "Get out! I'm not going to let you kill me!" She'd weep and say, "Don't you know me? I'm your mother. Who else could I possibly be? Who else could *fake this*?" We laughed about it. My mother grew as a person. I think she found herself to be an incredibly nurturing presence, and she performed that role for me with enormous skill and power. She had been capable of it all along, but it wasn't evoked until I got sick. My mom couldn't stop the illness, because it's in my genes. But she did a great deal to ameliorate its effects.

After Josh was discharged from the hospital, he entered graduate school, from which he received a Ph.D. and every academic prize the school could confer. He is now a contributing editor at a prestigious magazine. No one there knows of his schizophrenia. Nor has he ever had to be rehospitalized. By taking his medications faithfully, and by remaining in psychotherapy, most of the time he's able to stay in touch with reality and deflect his constant delusions and hallucinations.

His mother has encouraged his efforts at every turn. Whenever Josh's symptoms overwhelm him—for example, suddenly he will see a circle of swords around him—he calls his mother, who talks him through his terror, through the swords, assuring Josh that he won't be slashed. The new bond between mother and son has been Josh's lifeline. But for his mother, Josh is convinced that he'd either be locked away in the back ward of a mental institution, living on the streets, or dead.

Of course, his mother's willingness to shift gears abruptly was helped enormously by her belief in the value of psychiatry and other pursuits of the mind. Josh himself intends to stay in psychotherapy forever because it helps to give him insights about himself and his illness. It's the one sure way, he says, that he'll never have to go back to the hospital.

Insight and psychotherapy worked for this family, transforming it from chaotic to having a passionate unanimity of purpose. But such approaches are not for everyone.

PSYCHOEDUCATION: CHANGING FROM THE OUTSIDE IN

Many families take a dim view of psychotherapy and psychiatry, according to my interviews. Some regard the need for a "shrink" as a sign of weakness. Others understandably recoil from guilt-inducing, parent-blaming traditional psychoanalytic theories. Still others are put off by the power imbalance implicit in the doctor-patient relationship, and by the condescension with which some professionals address the less academically credentialed. And always there is the fear of stigmatization in volunteering to have one's head examined.

Consequently, these families—members of which may be more insightful than some of the "experts"—may respond to mental health professionals by saying, in effect, "Spare us your theories. We've got enough problems," and beat a hasty retreat.

How, then, to reach such families? Here we return to the same theorists who abhor the term "dysfunctional." They make another compelling argument—that without the *collaboration* of families, few people with mental illness improve. According to this line of thinking, the best way to help families is to give them information. There are biomedical reasons for the behaviors of the mentally ill and practical ways for families to manage and adjust to them. At the same time, families can be of immeasurable help to mental health professionals who, after all, do not know the ill person as well as relatives do.

Many of these theorists believe that families of the mentally ill face two challenges. The first, of course, is the illness itself and their reactions to it. The second—and *as important*—is the families' reactions to one another, and not just to the ill person. "Coping" entails more than simply managing symptoms. It also means recognizing the difference between behaviors that are volitional and those that are driven by illness.

Psychoeducation is an ingenious, no-fault format in which to meet those challenges. The psychoeducation model was developed by Dr. Carol Anderson and her colleagues at the University of Pittsburgh in the late 1970s. The researchers found that when families were educated about schizophrenia, and when the ill person received proper medication and social-skills training, the relapse rate fell to zero for the first year after the combined approaches were implemented. Patients functioned better, families were less anxious, and their confidence and ability to manage the illness rose.

At its best, then, psychoeducation addresses both issues—the medical and the psychodynamic—in a blame-free way. By teaching rather than *treating* these families, the families are more responsive to the learning process. And their relationships to one another improve.

When Doctors Teach Families. When Demitri Papolos, M.D., a leading authority on affective disorders, was an attending physician at a New York hospital early in his psychiatric career, he and his colleagues were alarmed by the "revolving door" of psychiatric rehospitalization. Within months of being discharged from the hospital, patients would be back in. The doctors realized that mental illness could not be treated in a vacuum. To prevent relapse, families needed the tools to deal with the ill person and with each other.

Drawing on Dr. Anderson's model, Dr. Papolos and his team put together a psychoeducation course for families. Parents, siblings, and offspring of psychiatric patients would come to the hospital for a series of classes to learn, among other things, how the patterns in their interactions might have calcified around the ill member's behavior. The families knew something was wrong with their relatives, but the families had not yet been informed of the relatives' specific diagnosis. Says Dr. Papolos:

> We wanted to find out what the family thought had happened to the ill member—why the person got sick. So at first we didn't tell the family what the diagnosis was. Instead, we said, "We really need your help in understanding what you think has gone on. We think we have an idea of what the problem is, but we don't really know." And we'd go around the room and say, for example, "Well, Joe, what do you think was wrong with your sister?" The brother might say, "Well, she was hanging around with a bad crowd in the last two years. She was smok-

ing marijuana, that's what caused this.'' We'd say, ''Okay, that's good,'' and we'd go on to the next person. Everyone would have a different idea of what happened.

Then the doctors would tell the family that they'd noticed certain patterns in the ill person's behavior, and ask the family if they could confirm those patterns. The doctors posed such questions as, ''Did you ever notice that she talked so fast that you had to tell her to stop talking?'' Or, ''In the winter, does she get real depressed?'' Or, ''Does she sometimes go out and spend huge amounts of money?'' Or, ''Is she usually sluggish or sad in the morning, but by nighttime she kind of perks up?'' The family would nod and say, ''Oh yes, all the time.''

Having gathered all this family confirmation, the doctors would then give the punch line: ''Did you know that these behaviors describe a particular condition?'' and tell the family that the condition was manic-depression. By approaching the family from the point of view of collaboration, rather than accusation or power imbalance, family members were able to absorb the diagnosis. They were also able to rethink the ill person's behavior as a medical disorder rather than as a character flaw.

Dr. Papolos's psychoeducational approach had other positive effects on families. Occasionally, family members would notice similar behaviors in themselves and realize that they, too, had a treatable disorder. Or they'd recall that a grandparent or an aunt had acted the same way as the ill relative and probably had an undiagnosed mental illness, when all along the family had thought the person was simply lazy, or deliberately mean-spirited.

Of paramount importance was that families began to view the ill person with much more compassion. For example, Dr. Papolos worked with a close-knit, European family of a young woman with manic-depression. When the daughter was in a manic state, she'd become hypersexual—a symptom of the disorder—and proposition her father's friends. When her authoritarian father got wind of this seductiveness, he beat his daughter unmercifully. But once he understood that her behavior was a hallmark of illness, he was able to stop judging her harshly. He apologized to her for his abusiveness and started serving as part of her early warning system and network of loving support.

When Families Teach Families. Most psychoeducation courses are taught by mental health professionals, usually in hospitals or clinics. However, the National Alliance for the Mentally Ill endorses a course taught by relatives of the mentally ill called "The Journey of Hope: Family Education and Family Support" developed by psychologist Joyce Burland, Ph.D., in 1991. As its name implies, the course offers both knowledge and emotional sustenance. Its curriculum, which includes the latest information on drug treatments and research, focuses primarily on three disorders: schizophrenia, manic-depression, and major depression.

Among the skills that are taught are how to communicate effectively within the family, how to set limits with the mentally ill, how to motivate the ill person to function better, and how to retain a sense of self. And among the decisions it helps families to reach is determining when an ill relative may be too disturbed to continue living at home.

The twelve-week course is taught in neutral settings, such as churches or libraries, to avoid the stigma families may associate with mental health facilities. The support group is ongoing, giving family members the opportunity to comfort one another and swap practical coping tips. The course is free, funded primarily by state mental health departments.

Since its inception, the Journey of Hope program has been implemented in thirty-two states across the country, four metropolitan areas, and two Canadian provinces. Currently, 850 family member teachers have been trained in 400 different locations. At least 12,000 people have taken the course.

The power of the course, says Dr. Burland, is the empathy and hands-on experiences of the family members who teach it. "Family members are wonderful teachers," she says. "They taught me nearly everything I know. A lot of people who take the course say, 'This just changes my whole attitude. I'm so much more accepting.' And, of course, that helps the family to function better.''

Rochelle, fifty-two, who took the course, says that it changed her life. When she was in her thirties, her mother died and her father, a taciturn and self-absorbed man, had a nervous breakdown. From then until his own death two years ago, he was in and out of various psychiatric hospitals being treated for schizoaffective disorder. In all those years, says Rochelle, no one in the hospital told her what was wrong with him. And no one told her how to reach him emotionally. Says Rochelle:

> One thing the course taught me was how to establish boundaries. My father was an angry man who I didn't know how to say no to. I learned that to deal with him, I had to leave my own anger at home and say to myself, "How do I get through to him?" When my father criticized me or called me terrible names, I could look him in the eye and say, "Excuse me, Dad, I will not sit here while you tell me I'm stupid. If you do that again, I will pick up and walk out." That was hard for me because the way I survived when I was a kid was by tuning him out. This is not easy stuff. You're doing constant figure eights—weaving in and out of your own emotions, from anger to forgiveness. It takes tremendous strength and perserverance to communicate with someone who's mentally ill and to remember that they're sick. The course helped me to do that. But I still have to work on my own problems. I still have to deal with the losses, which when your father is mentally ill happen every day of your life.

The Journey of Hope course addresses such losses in an extremely effective way. One of the class sessions is devoted to making lists of the most difficult aspects of living with mental illness. In this session, the class is divided into small subgroups according to family position—parent, sibling, or offspring. Each group makes its own separate list, and then the entire class comes back together to compare lists.

Dr. Burland recalls one such session that was particularly revealing of the unique problems of siblings and offspring. When the subgroups reunited at the end of the session to read their lists, *none* of the parents mentioned anything about their well children. Says Dr. Burland:

The sibs group, of course, got really mad. They said, "See? This is what we've been telling you! Even here, even with all this work we're doing in this course, you don't even *see* us. So the first thing we're going to add to our list is *that you did not put on your list that you're worried about us!*" And the parents just said, "Oh my God. You're right. You're right." They got it.

Psychoeducation helps families discover ways to settle their conflicts so that they can collectively weather the storms of mental illness. However, it must be remembered that these courses are oriented primarily toward helping the *sick*, not the well. As Dr. Hatfield has written, "The well-being of other family members is secondary in psychoeducation approaches."

BEYOND FAMILY COPING:
UNFINISHED INDIVIDUAL BUSINESS

No matter how loving, enlightened, or educated the family is as a group, no matter how well they may have adapted over the years, offspring and siblings of the mentally ill will nevertheless emerge from the experience with certain wounds. Family survival required that these young family members take a backseat to illness. And while many of them willingly did so with poignant awareness of their parents' staggering burdens, most of these young people bear scars inflicted by that very invisibility.

Once they reach adulthood, the experience of mental illness leaves long shadows over their lives. For these offspring and siblings, it is not enough simply to have coped within the family. Adapting to illness is not the same thing as adapting to life beyond home. And it is beyond home that the legacies of their experience will emerge.

Some of these legacies have been mentioned in earlier chapters. It's worth reviewing them here:
- the fear that they are next in pathological line;
- the fear that they will be "put away" if they do anything wrong;
- the fear of the mentally ill relative him- or herself;

- the fear that they will one day have to take care of the sick relative;
- the fear of having children;
- the fear of telling lovers or friends about mental illness in the family;
- guilt for feeling angry at their parents for not paying more attention to them;
- inhibition and lack of spontaneity;
- an inability to set limits—not knowing how much is enough;
- a lack of pride in their own talents and skills;
- the pressure to be perfect;
- embarrassment and shame about a relative's peculiar behavior;
- sorrow over the loss of the ill relative's mentorship, or companionship, or competitive spark;
- grief over never having had a childhood;
- the uncertainty of how involved to be with their families of origin and in particular with the ill relative;
- anger at being denied, by virtue of "wellness," the same importance to mental health practioners and policy makers that the ill relative received.

These legacies can become land mines in one's adult life and attachments.

PART THREE

FLASH POINTS:
The Long Shadow of
Mental Illness

CHAPTER 9

Risks:
Am I Next?

I've always gotten a lot of mileage out of being nice, never saying what I really think. It's a facade. I have this funny thing I've always done when I feel anxious or intimidated. I put my hand over my mouth. I was a really angry kid growing up, but no one knew because I kept it all inside. I was afraid to let anything show. I think that covering my mouth was a kind of numbing, a way of silencing myself. It was all related to the fear that I would become mentally ill, like my mother. I was afraid that all the anger would come out, which would mean, of course, that I was sick, too.

—Nadia, 50

I am sitting in the coffee shop of a sprawling Washington, D.C., hotel crammed with people attending the 1995 convention of the National Alliance for the Mentally Ill, now in its third day. Across the table from me is Nadia, smiling brightly and waving to a group of people on the other side of the room.

"Sorry," she says. "Those are some of my buddies from my NAMI group back home. I don't know what I'd do without them."

Undoubtedly the feeling is mutual, since it is impossible not to be drawn to this gracious, soft-spoken woman. She exudes warmth and concern. You feel as though you could tell her anything, perhaps because she is a hospice worker, practiced in the gentle art of comforting others and putting them at ease. More likely the attraction is that she herself is so open about her experiences growing up with a manic-depressive mother. Nadia is a journalist's dream, and I tell her so.

"Believe me, that's new," she says, laughing. Her candor has been a long time coming, she explains, the result of slowly, deliberately forcing herself to emerge from the cocoon of silence in which she wrapped herself after her mother had her first breakdown over forty years ago. Of that day Nadia says:

> It's the usual story—I'm sure you've heard it before. My brother and I were walking home from school, and outside our house we saw a crowd of neighbors, a police car, an ambulance, and a doctor. My mother was standing in the driveway, screaming and shoving people. The police had to wrestle her to the ground and put her in a straitjacket. They took her to a hospital. She didn't come home for two years. My family just blew apart.

During their mother's long absence, Nadia's older brother, then sixteen, quickly fell into the Custodian role, serving as surrogate parent. Nadia adopted the Bystander role, retreating deep within herself and keeping a low profile in the family. To the world at large, she was the stoic family ambassador. "I was an excellent student," she says. "I was going to show everyone that everything at home was just fine, thank you, and that no one should feel sorry for me."

Like many offspring of the mentally ill, Nadia felt empty on the inside, brittle on the outside. Throughout her growing up years, she had to weather her mother's highs and lows—the being "there" and "not there," the repeated hospitalizations, the constant good-byes.

But Nadia isn't convinced that her own fragility was entirely, or even largely, a consequence of her mother's illness, shattering as that was. Nadia had another, even more distressing problem. As she describes it:

> I have wonderful memories of my mother in between her episodes. She was exceptionally bright, and could be great fun. So my hopes were constantly raised and then dashed. Each time she came out of the hospital I'd think, "Oh, maybe this time I'll get my mother back." And, of course, she'd get sick again. So I had to distance myself from her, and from my own feelings. But that wasn't the worst of it. The more

difficult relationship was really with my father. He was a bitter, angry man who used to humiliate me and beat me for reasons I could never understand. I was always just trying to stay out of his way.

One day when Nadia was fourteen, her father slapped her hard across the face. This time, something in her snapped. Suddenly she raced into the kitchen, her father at her heels, and grabbed a knife. "I stood there holding this knife, thinking, If this guy doesn't back off, I'm gonna kill him," she recalls. "He must have seen the look in my eyes that said I'd had enough. He never hit me again."

Somehow, Nadia managed to hold herself together for the next four years, maintaining her vigilance at home and feigning composure at school. At eighteen, she ran as far as she could from her family. But the defenses that had served her in childhood betrayed her in adulthood. Having protected herself for so long by emotionally withdrawing, she found it hard to reverse the pattern. Little by little, she herself began to fall apart, colliding into dead ends of her own making.

Although she had the grades and family connections, she chose not to apply to college because she was afraid of having everyone know her. Instead she became a secretary at a large corporation where she could be anonymous. At twenty-two, she married a man who, she hoped, would make up for all that she had missed, someone to nurture and take care of her. But she couldn't let down her guard with him. She was unable to trust that he wouldn't harm her.

When her son was born, she was terrified that she'd either kill him, or that he, too, would become mentally ill. Her marriage was in tatters. And she thought about suicide constantly.

In short, the life she had created for herself was beginning to bear a striking resemblance to the life she had fled, and this recognition catapulted her into intensive psychotherapy. For eight years she painstakingly pored over her own feelings of despair and loneliness and disconnection.

Therapy helped to repair her broken spirit, but it couldn't change the reality of Nadia's possible biological vulnerability to madness. Only time would settle that score. As the years went by, she nervously checked off the anniversaries of events in her mother's psychiatric history. At thirty-five, Nadia was the same age her mother was when she had her first psychotic break. At thirty-seven, her son turned nine, the same age Nadia was when her mother crashed. At forty-eight, she was the same age her mother was when she died in a mental institution.

Now those anniversaries have all passed and she still hasn't become mentally ill. She is on uncharted territory. It is as though she has held her breath for half a century and is able to exhale at last. Having beaten the odds of cracking up, she is putting the finishing touches on her re-created self.

Recently, she started to "come out," as she puts it. She began telling friends and colleagues that her mother was mentally ill. For Nadia, it is a daring move—speaking up without worrying that people will judge her harshly or think that she is "sick."

Nadia drains the last of her coffee and prepares to depart for the afternoon session of the NAMI convention. As we leave the restaurant, I remark to her that not once during our interview did she revert to her old habit of clasping her hand over her mouth.

"It never happens when I'm with my NAMI friends," she says. "Here, I don't feel any tension. I can be myself. I *love* these conventions. I almost hate to go home."

FEAR OF BREAKING DOWN

The most fundamental difference between parents and children of the mentally ill is the constant terror of going mad oneself. This difference is crucial.

Parents of psychiatrically disturbed children may be enormously relieved to learn that their children's disabilities are based primarily upon biology rather than bad parenting. But for offspring and siblings of the mentally ill, the biological model is very cold comfort. Because if mental illness is genetic or biochemical in origin, that means that you could get it, too. You might not have it *yet*. But the biological clock is ticking.

There is, indeed, a statistical chance that this fear will become fact. Before we delve into the numerical odds, however, it's important to set the stage with two caveats—one cultural, the other psychological—which inform those odds.

A Generation at Risk. According to sociologist Ronald C. Kessler, Ph.D., formerly of the Michigan University Institute for Social Research and now professor in the department of health care policy at Harvard, mental illness in the United States is on the rise. He explains:

> There are more people with mental illness now than there used to be. This is not an age effect. This is what we call a "cohort effect." Among people born after World War II, there's been a lot more access to drugs. Adult sex roles have shifted. Changes in women's status in society have led to more pressures on them, which means that more women are drinking and using drugs and becoming depressed. But men have gotten more anxious and depressed, too. And the suicide rate has gone up and up. So it seems pretty clear that rates of mental disorders of a wide variety have been increasing since the early 1950s. People in their thirties today are in worse shape than thirty-year-olds were ten years ago.

Add to Dr. Kessler's dire cultural diagnosis the increasing reluctance of policy makers to address this epidemic in the making and you begin to appreciate what siblings and offspring are up against. Fear of going crazy is not all in their heads. People around them, people they know and work with, are becoming mentally ill, and less and less is being done about it.

Which leads us to the second caveat: A lot of the fear *is* in their heads and can be as devastating as any biogenetic booby trap that may lurk within their pedigrees.

Most siblings and offspring burn up tremendous stores of energy trying to beat the odds that they will become mentally ill, which only adds to their vulnerability. Such fear can be a vicious cycle, if not a self-fulfilling prophecy. Each discomfiting thought or angry feeling produces a rush to psychological judgment: I must be going mad. As one forty-year-old woman whose brother has schizophrenia told me:

> Do I worry about becoming mentally ill? Only all the time! Sometimes when I'm reading a complicated book, or a really technical article about cars or something where nothing is sinking in, I think, Oh my God, why am I not grasping this? Does this mean I have neurological problems? It doesn't occur to me that maybe the writing stinks. I immediately figure that there's something really wrong with my brain.

Defending Against Madness. As we saw in part one, children who lose a close relative to mental illness construct all kinds of elaborate defenses against the anguish of future abandonments. But when "loss" includes the possibility of *losing one's own mind*, the double dose of pain is almost unbearable. Children must defend against *themselves*—the enemy is within. They will push aside their own natural emotional inclinations—their unruly feelings, their wild imaginings—and pretend to be normal, hoping that the charade will forever make it so.

For children of severely mentally ill parents, the problem begins with attempting to be acceptable to those parents. To be acceptable to a psychiatrically impaired mother or father—that is, to adhere to the dictates of madness—is virtually impossible for a child. For one thing, you can't fathom the "rules" of delusional thinking or anticipate dizzying mood swings. You can't grasp exactly what the parent wants, because it keeps changing. Plus, the attempt to fit in with a symptomatic parent can be a kind of psychic suicide. To make the unreal real, to suspend disbelief, is to imperil one's own sanity.

Pamela, sixty, says that throughout her childhood her sanity hung by a thread. Since her father worked long hours, when Pamela wasn't in school she was in her bipolar mother's nearly constant company. Slowly, almost imperceptibly, Pamela began to take on some of her mother's characteristics. Says Pamela:

> I desperately wanted my mother's approval, but nothing I did was good enough. Sometimes I'd turn on the radio to get an idea of what other

kids' families were like. When my mother was delusional, I'd listen to
shows like *Ozzie and Harriet*. My mother and I had something in common—we were both in a fantasy world. She was having hallucinations
about people who weren't there while I was dissociating into these
radio shows. After a while, I became convinced that if I didn't get out
of there, I'd crack up myself. When I was eighteen, I was offered a
full scholarship at a college on the other side of the country and I
grabbed it. I was determined never to go back home.

Trying to be acceptable to a mentally ill sibling can exact a similar
price. Sheila, thirty-nine, says that her relationship with her older
brother, who has schizophrenia, was the defining attachment of her
life. Of her childhood with him she says:

> I had no concept of what was normal. I was not aware that my brother
> was sick. He was a real bully, and I was kind of his little disciple
> because we were very close. He could control me, and he was incred-
> ibly manipulative. Whenever he'd hit me and I'd scream for help, he'd
> say to my parents, "I didn't do anything." I kept thinking, How con-
> vincing can I be? Who's going to believe me over him? So I got to be
> pretty bizarre myself. I changed from an introverted little kid to a wild
> kid. No one who knew me back then would ever tell you, "Sheila was
> a normal child." For years, I just raged and raged, because to me, that
> was normal. I didn't find out until I was sixteen that he was mentally
> ill. After that, I turned into superkid. I was going to be an astronaut
> and win prizes. I mean, nothing was going to stop me. I was *not* going
> to be like my brother.

Thus offspring—and to a large degree, siblings—of the mentally
ill fashion a "false self" of being weller than well, tougher than
tough. To seal the bargain, they will turn off their own awareness and
become numb. Still, the fear that they are a breath away from falling
apart themselves haunts them.

The irony is that, in a sense, they have *already* broken down. They
just don't know it yet. In a classic paper called "Fear of Breakdown,"
noted British psychoanalyst D. W. Winnicott advanced the theory that
when children are forced to construct false selves to defend against

madness, the worst has already happened: They've buried alive their authentic selves by shutting off conscious recognition of their genuine feelings and reactions. The trick is to keep them buried.

"Anxious" does not begin to describe their chaotic emotions, says Dr. Winnicott. However, "primitive agonies" does. It is the terror of *reexperiencing* the loss of self—a kind of death—that children of the mentally ill defend against so strenuously.

Thus the fear of breaking down is actually the subconscious fear of psychologically "dying" again. Winnicott calls this "the death that happened but was not experienced. . . ." And when it is not experienced, the child cannot mourn. Rather, the child remains emotionally at loose ends, unable to pinpoint the source of distress and unwilling to get close to anybody.

It is this phenomenon of emotional numbing and distancing that parents find hardest to grasp, especially those who are dismayed by their well children's "neglect" of and "insensitivity" toward an ill relative or toward the family as a whole. For many siblings and off-spring such distancing was essential to their emotional survival in childhood, and, often, is essential in their adulthood as well. Only in mid-adulthood—if then—is it safe for these young family members to exhume their buried selves, to complete the mourning process, and to build bridges back to their families.

In the meantime, many believe that they are living on borrowed psychological time. Because if mental illness could strike once, it could strike twice. And they are next in line.

THE RISKS OF BREAKING DOWN

Mental illness runs in families. On this point, most investigators agree, which gives them more than a passing interest in how the siblings and offspring of the mentally ill turn out. The results of the first family study of schizophrenia, for example, were published in 1916. Young family members have been a source of endless scientific fascination in terms of their risks of developing a brain disorder.

There are two primary ways of investigating this risk. One is from the standpoint of pure genetics—that is, estimating what percentage of children will break down if one parent is ill, if two parents are ill, if a sibling is ill, and so on.

The other way to evaluate risk is in terms of environmental factors. In this case the unit of measurement is not of genes or biochemistry but of other variables, such as socioeconomic status. This latter approach takes genes into account, chiefly by ruling them out as *definitive* risk factors. Even if you carry a gene for mental illness, the gene may not be expressed. Thus it is not enough simply to know the genetic odds. More important, according to this view, is to know the *means of transmission* of illness—genetic, biochemical, environmental, or some combination. For example, certain traits, such as height, are flat-out genetically determined. But even that trait is subject to such environmental influences as malnutrition.

To reiterate, the statement ''mental illness runs in families'' is true. *Why* it's true is the controversial heart of the matter.

GENETIC RISK

Mental illness doesn't just run in Carolyn's family—it races in packs. Carolyn, fifty-two, is one of sixteen first cousins in her family. Of the sixteen, four have been diagnosed with paranoid schizophrenia.

Carolyn's brother, now forty-eight, was the first of the cousins to break down. He had always been hot-tempered, but his anger broke all bounds when he was a senior in college. Obsessed with the delusion that someone was going to kill him, he stole a gun from a store. The police were called, and as they tried to arrest him, he shot and killed one of the officers and was himself wounded by a bullet.

He was declared criminally insane and spent the next fifteen years in a hospital jail. Today he lives in a halfway house, compliantly taking his medicines, aghast that he could have done something so terrible and that his whole life has been smashed by madness.

Carolyn is convinced that her brother's illness is entirely genetic in origin. For one thing, there's the historical evidence of a 25 percent illness rate among her cousins. For another, her family has always been exceedingly close and mutually supportive. Says Carolyn:

> I feel like the luckiest person in the world. I've never needed therapy because we were always there for each other. There was always somebody to take your problems to. And my parents were great people. They did everything they could to protect me. None of what happened to my brother is their fault.

The Search for Genetic Markers. Families like Carolyn's fuel scientific hopes of finding a specific gene, or cluster of genes, which would predict mental illness and prevent it from erupting, or at the very least ease its potential damage by early treatment. But since there is no diagnostic test or technical device to determine conclusively whether or not one has a biological propensity for madness, many investigators rely on retrospective or cross-sectional studies and surveys. From the data gathered, scientists simply count the heads of those who have been diagnosed with mental illness, their well and/or ill children and other relatives, and hazard an educated, predictive guess.

These percentages depend on who's investigating, and which methodologies they use. The following statistics, then, are ballpark figures, or "robust" suggestive evidence, as scientists put it, of a genetic link. The scientists who publish them almost always cautiously note that they can't say *for sure* that these illnesses are genetic in orgin. Again, we're talking about odds. (You may wish to refer back to chapter 1 to review the symptoms of these disorders.)

With regard to *schizophrenia,* the odds in the general population of developing the disorder are an estimated 0.7 percent. What this means is that if your parents and grandparents and as far back as you can go appear to have been normal, the chance of your getting schizophrenia is under 1 percent. But there's still a chance, perhaps due to birth complications or a maternal virus during gestation, for instance.

Those odds rise considerably if you have a relative with schizophrenia. According to Irving I. Gottesman, Ph.D., if one parent has the illness, a child has a 12.8 percent chance of getting it. The figure jumps to 46.3 percent if two parents have the disorder. If a sibling has the illness, the risk to his or her siblings is 9.6 percent. The risk for grandchildren of schizophrenics is 3.7 percent. (Some scientists believe these statistics, published in 1984, are open to revision because of improved study and diagnostic methodologies since then.)

Affective disorders, such as major depression and manic-depression, also are said to "breed true." Recent studies show that in the general population, the lifetime risk of developing these illnesses is approximately 19.3 percent. Here again, these rates are higher if one has a relative with these disorders. Dr. Nancy C. Andreasen reports that the rate of affective disorder among siblings of people with this diagnosis is around 30 percent. Adoption studies have found that if one identical twin has a mood disorder, the odds that the other twin will develop it is approximately 66 percent.

As for offspring of parents with mood disorders, Dr. Constance Hammen and her colleagues at the UCLA Family Stress Project found that children of afflicted mothers have a 72 to 82 percent chance of themselves developing a diagnosable mental illness, compared to 22 percent of the children of normal mothers.

Affective disorders come in several forms, and risk estimates depend in part on which form you're talking about. For instance, Kay Redfield Jamison, Ph.D., of Johns Hopkins University believes that the genetic basis for bipolar disorder is "almost incontrovertible." If one identical twin has manic-depressive illness, she reports, the other stands a 70 to 100 percent chance of getting it. If the twins are fraternal and one is ill, the other twin runs a 20 percent risk of becoming ill.

You may be at genetic risk even if neither your parents nor your siblings have mental illness. According to behavioral geneticist Dr. David C. Rowe, an unexpressed gene in the current generation and immediate past generation may find its "voice" in the third generation. So you have to look to your grandparents, and not just to your parents, to determine the possibility of inheriting a gene or of passing it along to your offspring.

"High-Risk" Studies. Another way scientists look at genetic risk is prospectively, that is, by identifying the children of psychiatric patients early in life and then examining these children at periodic intervals *while they are growing up*. These studies are called "high-risk" studies.

One of the most exhaustive of such studies in terms of sheer time is the New York High-Risk Project, begun in 1971 and spear-headed by L. Erlenmeyer-Kimling, Ph.D., acting chief of the department of medical genetics at the New York State Psychiatric Institute and a professor at Columbia University's College of Physicians and Surgeons.

The New York High-Risk Project has followed 188 (originally 206) children of three white, English-speaking diagnostic groups: parents with schizophrenia; parents with affective disorders; and a control group of parents with no psychiatric impairments, or "normals." As of 1995, the "lifetime prevalence" rates of psychotic disorders among the children—at the time of assessment, between twenty-eight and thirty-five years of age—of these parents are as follows:

• Children of parents suffering from *schizophrenia*: About 22 percent have developed a psychotic disorder, primarily schizophrenia-related psychoses, but *none* have developed bipolar disorder;

• Children of parents with *affective disorders*: Close to 15 percent have developed a psychotic disorder, primarily schizoaffective disorder, followed by affective disorders, but *none* with schizophrenia;

• Children of *normal* parents: *None* have developed schizophrenia, whereas about 2 percent have developed schizoaffective disorder or another psychotic disorder not related to schizophrenia.

As these figures demonstrate, there appears to be a large genetic component, or "genetic loading," to schizophrenia and affective disorders. "Our data merely help to confirm what has been found previously in a large number of other studies," says Dr. Erlenmeyer-Kimling, "including twin, family, and adoption research designs."

What makes Dr. Erlenmeyer-Kimling's study of particular importance is that most of these offspring have passed through the highest risk period for schizophrenia (late teens through mid-thirties), although not for major depression nor for bipolar disorder. Thus, from a purely statistical standpoint, the offspring of people with schizophrenia who have not become psychiatrically disabled appear to have made it through the high-risk woods. Says Dr. Erlenmeyer-Kimling:

> If by the time you've reached your mid-thirties and gone the usual course of establishing a career, getting through college perhaps, had a reasonably normal social life and gotten along in a fairly normal fashion without serious symptoms, your risk of developing schizophrenia is much lower. I can't say that about depression. But with schizophrenia, notwithstanding cases of late onset, the individual is largely in the clear by the mid-thirties.

Dr. Erlenmeyer-Kimling hastens to add that this study does not prove *causality*, teasing out nurture from nature, since the children in the two high-risk samples were, after all, raised by mentally ill parents.

The Importance of Genetic Risk. Nevertheless, knowing that one is at genetic risk is extremely important to offspring and siblings. For one thing, it can explain dysfunctional behavior that appears to have no psychodynamic or other environmental cause. Moreover, should family members suspect they have one or another form of illness, by treating it early they can reduce further biological and emotional damage. In addition, they may wish to give serious thought to whether or not they should have children, especially if their mates also have a family history of mental illness. Family members in this case might want to consult with a geneticist.

These vital points were brought home to me by Doris, a thirty-year-old woman I interviewed who was adopted at birth by loving, supportive, well-to-do parents, and who knew from early childhood that she was adopted. Despite her all but perfect childhood, Doris was always subject to terrifying mood swings. In her teens, she figured that she was merely a temporary hostage of raging pubertal hormones. But as she entered and went through her twenties, the mood swings did not settle down. Rather, they began to pick up steam. By the age of twenty-seven, she was, she says, "a mess."

> I was about to marry this wonderful man. I had this fantastic job in the research department of a foundation. I had a million friends. Yet every

morning I would just curl up in my bed and cry and not want to get up. I said to myself, This is ridiculous. This has nothing to do with your life. So I went to see a psychiatrist, who put me on antidepressants, which helped enormously.

Still, Doris couldn't understand the *need* for medication, given all her advantages, and she kept searching for explanations. "I'm a researcher, for God's sake," she jokes. "The unexamined life is not one of my problems."

Then one day she got a phone call from a woman claiming to be her biological mother, who somehow had tracked her down and wanted to meet her. With some trepidation, Doris drove to the woman's apartment in a city seventy-five miles away. The woman she met told her about her long history of severe bipolar disorder. She had attempted suicide in early childhood and had been in and out of mental institutions ever since (this information was later confirmed by Doris's adoptive parents).

Although the woman was so disturbed that Doris chose not to see her again, just meeting her and learning about her history solved a lot of mysteries. Says Doris:

> It just cleared up the whole nurture/nature aspect of my moodiness. I got my "nature" from my birth mother. But I got incredible nurturing from my adoptive parents. In finding out I might have a genetic predisposition for manic-depression, I realized how important it was to have caught it early. Still, of the two, nurture or nature, I'm convinced that nurture had the greater impact. I will never be as sick as my biological mother is. But because of my "nature," and because there's mental illness in my husband's family, we've decided to adopt children.

ENVIRONMENTAL RISK

One could argue that good nurturing makes imperfect nature bearable. Genetic "risk" is not certainty. Doris's case makes the genetic point. But it also makes the *environmental* point: You may be genetically vulnerable but be environmentally protected. Thus, you may have a relatively low actual risk of becoming severely mentally ill.

Many scientists argue that a diagnosis of mental illness in a parent or sibling predicts very little for their offspring. Of greater importance are the *other* characteristics of these children's lives. As Drs. John Richters and Sheldon Weintraub of the Stony Brook High-Risk Project have written, "... an individual's chances of succumbing to psychopathology or maladjustment are influenced by the patterns of the individual's life. . . . *The fact that someone has a schizophrenic parent implies nothing necessarily about that individual* beyond the fact that he or she has a schizophrenic parent [italics in the original]."

The Search for Environmental Markers. The importance of environment is the focus of the Rochester Longitudinal Study, an examination of the development of children of mentally ill mothers of assorted ethnicities and socioeconomic statuses. Dr. Arnold J. Sameroff, the lead investigator of this study, believes that gross percentages of the nose-counting variety can be misleading. Says Dr. Sameroff:

> Every family has a different story. When scientists look at 1,000 people, they say, "on average" this or that is a risk factor. But when you look at an individual family, it may be that it has two risk factors, and another family might have different risk factors, or no risk factors.

Some family characteristics, says Dr. Sameroff, put children "at risk," while others may be "protective." What matters may not be any particular risk factor, but *how many* risk factors there are. Among the characteristics of mentally ill mothers that put their children at risk are:

• history of maternal mental illness (that is, the frequency and duration of episodes);

• high maternal anxiety;

• parental perspectives (such as inflexibility, or valuing conformity);

• few positive spontaneous interactions between mother and child during the child's infancy;

• minimal maternal education;

- unskilled occupation of the head of household;
- disadvantaged minority ethnic status;
- little family support (father absent);
- stressful life events;
- family size (four or more children).

The more risk variables the children in this study were exposed to, the worse they performed cognitively and in terms of social and emotional competence. Children who were living in high-risk environments at age four and were still living under those circumstances at age thirteen had consistently low performance scores. The children who were living in families with few or no risk factors had much higher scores; in the case of IQ, thirty points higher than children in multi-risk families.

The bottom line of this study was that the greatest danger to these children was *poverty*, not their mothers' diagnoses.

THRESHOLDS OF HOPE

What all these high-risk studies demonstrate is that while mental illness, especially schizophrenia, cannot *always* be prevented, the odds of breaking down, or of having repeated breakdowns, can be greatly reduced provided the circumstances in which one lives are benevolent. "If environments change," writes Dr. Michael Rutter, "so will the potential alter." Herein resides a vast reservoir of hope.

When the environments in which junior family members choose to live in adulthood offer opportunities to succeed, emotionally or otherwise, their chances of breaking down begin to dwindle accordingly. That's because the human mind wants nothing so much as to be healthy. To that end, nature has endowed the brain with an extraordinary range of ways in which to repair itself.

Plasticity. In a fascinating 1995 *National Geographic* article, Joel L. Swerdlow writes of a typical American kid—a boy in the second grade whose school marks and general deportment indicated rampant normalcy.

Yet two years prior to the boy's interview with Swerdlow, nearly half the boy's brain was removed by surgeons because of a devastating, rare, and incurable illness called Rasmussen's encephalitis. The surgeons did not excise those parts of the brain that govern such functions as bodily movement and emotions. Although the boy was left with a slight limp and some peripheral vision problems, he was otherwise in remarkably good shape.

The reason: the brain's self-healing processes. As the boy received speech and other therapies, his brain grew new cellular properties, in a sense filling in for the portion of the brain that was gone. This boy's postoperative recovery is an example of the amazing flexibility of the human brain.

To get an understanding of this flexibility, I interviewed neuroanatomist Jill Bolte Taylor, Ph.D., codirector, Harvard Psychiatry Brain Collection, at the Harvard Medical School. The organizing principle of her explanation is to be found in the brain's built-in redundancies. Says Dr. Taylor:

The beauty of the human system is something we call "plasticity." When you look at actual brain cells and how they're communicating, the cells are constantly reaching out to one another, giving and receiving information in a huge network of brain circuitry. As long as a cell is providing stimulation to another cell, then the connection between them will be maintained. However, if something happens to a cell within a circuit and it no longer works, then the other cell will withdraw and form new circuits. Another feature of the brain is called "lateralization." Both hemispheres of the brain have specific cells which are capable of the same responsibilities, such as language, and in general the cells in one hemisphere will be developed. But if for some reason—a stroke, for example—the cells on one side die, the comparable cells in the opposite hemisphere can be stimulated to take over. Because of plasticity and lateralization, the human brain is quite capable of adaptation to the environment.

Extreme stress, Dr. Taylor says, can have a devastating effect on the brain and its functioning. Environment plays an enormous role in neural connections. For example, scientists have discovered that psychological trauma can cause memories to be "encoded" powerfully—relative, say, to an unexceptional or benign experience—although memories may remain unconscious or be recalled only in snatches. In addition, prolonged "fight or flight" hyperarousal can cause certain brain cells to remain excessively excitable or to die.

Yet once the person has removed—or been removed from—the source of stress and perhaps gotten loving care or therapy, the brain can repair itself with these miraculous backup systems. Thus, some people with schizophrenia can compensate for certain cognitive deficits by using other parts of their brains. So, too, can people with affective disorders.

And so, especially, can siblings and offspring of the mentally ill who have been exposed *genetically* and *environmentally* to mental illness. For it must be remembered that while they may be "at risk," between *85 and 90 percent of these junior family members will never become severely mentally ill.*

CHAPTER 10

Effect on Relationships

*It took me a long time to realize that my ex-husband was mentally ill—
I was very good at papering things over. He overflowed with self-pity,
but he wouldn't do anything to help himself. He behaved abominably
toward our children, and I was forever trying to make him feel better.
It was only after his second suicide attempt that I woke up and said,
"I cannot put my children and myself through any more of this." So
why did I stay with him so long? I think it came out of my relationship
with my brother, who was manic-depressive. I stayed because I believed
that, somehow, I could fix it the second time around.*

—Simone, 57

The word "survivor" aptly describes people like Simone. Both her
mother and her brother had severe bipolar disorder and died, in 1972
and 1994 respectively, in the same mental hospital.

The term "survivor guilt" even more aptly describes people like
Simone. From the time she was twenty-five, when her father died,
Simone's brother, George, then twenty-three, was her responsibility.
Although he had been diagnosed in his teens, he managed to graduate
from college, live independently, and hold down an undemanding job.
But he refused to take his medications and became increasingly hostile
and delusional. By the time he was in his thirties, he was no longer
able to work, and he began squandering on travel the small bequest
left to him by his parents.

His life in ruins, George was consumed by the unfairness of his
having apparently inherited his mother's illness, while his sister, a

213

successful business executive with a family of her own, had gotten off scot-free. Thus George felt he had every right—indeed, the moral entitlement—to invade Simone's life as though he owned it. He'd call her at all hours of the day and night, enraged by the terrible circumstances of his existence, and demand that she do something. She found it nearly impossible to say no.

Every so often Simone would get a call from a police officer in some exotic locale—it could be the Bahamas or Hawaii—informing her that George had been found wandering on a beach, hallucinating and frightening people. She'd have to stop everything and make arrangements for him to be sent home and committed to a psychiatric hospital. Soon he'd be discharged and back in her life. On one occasion he barged into her house while she was giving a dinner party, trashed her living room, and stormed out. She never pressed charges.

Things went from bad to worse. After George's money ran out, Simone paid the rent on his shabby apartment. At his insistence, once a week she'd bring him groceries and—this was the revolting part—clean up after him. She recalls with a shudder:

My brother was militant about wanting to be taken care of, and God knows I tried. When I'd visit him, there'd be food and filth on the floor. He wouldn't bathe or even use the toilet, so I had all this muck to get rid of. He'd be horribly verbally abusive to me. I was terrified of him because he was so jealous, and because he was *big*. One day I was telling my therapist about all this, that my brother was constantly preying on me. The therapist said, "You are pathologically guilty about your brother's illness." A big light went on in my head. Because it explained my marriage, too.

With her therapists's help, Simone gave up feeling remorse over the fact that she was sane. Less easy was learning to "quit being so damned capable," as she puts it, particularly with regard to her needy husband, who was far less incapacitated than her brother. It was her very competence and survivor guilt that landed her in her disastrous marriage when she was thirty and kept her in it for nearly a decade. Says Simone:

The old Freudian saw of "marrying" your father did not apply to me—would that I *had*. I "married" someone like my brother, and waited on him hand and foot. Even after I divorced my husband, I kept making excuses for him to our children. I think I behaved quite unforgivably by not telling them at the time that he was really a son of a bitch who wouldn't take responsibility either for himself or them. He virtually ignored them. But I didn't want them to feel disloyal. If I had it to do over, that's the thing I would change. I wouldn't have covered for him.

Simone has never remarried. When her brother died two years ago, she felt nothing but relief. She appears to have had her fill of togetherness. For the first time in her life, she is free of the burden of caretaking and at last has the time, literally, to tend to the garden outside her lovely New England cottage.

Interestingly, Simone has never worried that either she or her children would become mentally ill. On the other hand, she *is* uneasy about one pattern in her life that seems to have carried over to the next generation. Her son also married someone with mental illness. For all Simone's candor about other aspects of her history, on this particular subject she prefers not to elaborate.

"I guess I'd just as soon paper that over, too," she says, laughing edgily. "I'd hate to think it was because I didn't divorce sooner. But, of course, it's entirely possible. Maybe my son is trying to 'fix' his father's illness the way I tried to 'fix' my brother's. Heaven help him."

TOO CLOSE FOR COMFORT: THE SLEEPER EFFECTS OF MADNESS

Nowhere is the effect of mental illness on young family members more apparent than in their attachments, or lack of attachments, to romantic partners and to children.

As we have seen, surviving mental illness in the family takes enormous ingenuity and perseverance. One way or another, most of the siblings and offspring I interviewed were able to protect themselves when they were children through various forms of escape. Emotional detachment became second nature to them.

By the time they were adults, however, this detachment became a handicap. Distancing of others was so ingrained that for the majority, their judgment in their personal attachments had become blurred. Intimacy felt unnatural, like speaking a foreign language. Their early losses had caught up with them.

One of the surprises in my study is the similarity of the romantic track records of offspring and siblings. I expected greater variation. For one thing, the parent-child relationship is qualitatively and quantitatively different from the sibling bond. And, as has been mentioned, nearly half of the offspring of the mentally ill in my sample witnessed their parents' divorces, compared to 30 percent of the siblings of the mentally ill.

Nevertheless, the marriage rates of the two groups are nearly identical: 45 percent of the offspring, and 44 percent of the siblings are married. By contrast, in the general population, 61.2 percent of people eighteen and over are married.

The divorce rates of junior family members are also remarkably alike: 31 percent of the offspring and 28 percent of the siblings have been divorced one or more times. (According to the Census Bureau, there are no available statistics on how many Americans have ever been divorced.)

Moreover, 24 percent of the offspring in my sample have never married, nor have 28 percent of the siblings. This is slightly higher than the national average—22.6 of all Americans have never married.

The biggest surprise, however, has to do with having children. In the United States general population, 42 percent of women have never given birth. By contrast, over *half* of the women and men in my sample do not have children, and, with few exceptions, do not plan to have them. Again, there are similarities between the two groups. Of the adult offspring, 55 percent are childless; of the siblings, 53 percent. Socioeconomic and educational status have something to do with this trend. The more educated and financially secure their families were when they were growing up, and the more they themselves were educated, the less likely these young family members were to reproduce.

One way to interpret these trends is that in romantic attachments there are always options. Either a relationship can be improved, or one can move on to another partner, or one can opt for solitude. The same latitude does not apply to childrearing. Biology is too wild a card—you can't "fix" a child's genetic makeup, nor guarantee that the child won't develop a brain disorder. Moreover, you can't (or shouldn't) walk away from your own progeny. Consequently, having children is a gamble the majority of these young family members are reluctant to take.

Let us examine these sleeper effects of a relative's madness one at a time.

EFFECT ON ROMANTIC CHOICES

Intimate relationships are the one arena in which siblings and adult children cannot easily disguise either their family histories or their own vulnerabilities.

Allan, twenty-seven, says that the most painful legacy of his brother's mental illness has been Allan's fear of telling people about it. But he couldn't duck sharing this fact of his close-knit family's life with Laura, the woman he ultimately married. He recalls:

> I had been dating Laura for several months, but I kept postponing telling her about my brother. You never know how people will react. I was afraid she'd think my family was all messed up and not want to see me anymore. Finally I just bit the bullet. I sat her down and started fumbling around, trying to find the words. She said, "What are you getting at? That there's mental illness in your family?" I said, "Yes. My brother's schizophrenic." Her reaction was great. She said, "So what? I think you're wonderful. I can't wait to meet your family. This doesn't change how I feel about you." We laugh about it now. But that day, I was sweating blood.

Christina, thirty, has had an even harder time coming clean about her mother's bipolar illness. Christina's parents fought bitterly throughout her childhood, and they either ignored her or treated her harshly. Christina spent her early dating history "sleeping around," she says, trying to get a measure of affection to make up for the years when she received none at home.

Once she felt ready to settle down, however, she went in the opposite direction. She decided not to go to bed with anyone unless the person was truly in love with and wanted to marry her. "Antediluvian," she jokes of her neo-chastity years. But she was determined to test the men in her life to see if their feelings for her were genuine. The quickest way to find out was to refuse to have sex with them. She recalls:

Most of the men I dated said something like, "You've got to be kidding," and took off. But there was one man who didn't, and that's the man I married. He passed the test, and believe me, I tested him plenty. When he asked me to marry him, I said, "Hold it. Before we decide on anything, you have to meet my mother. I don't want you holding her craziness over my head." He said, "Don't worry. We'll deal with this together." He's the first man who ever said that. My husband is a gem. I never experienced anything like this in my life, this complete love.

These two stories represent romantic gambles that paid off handsomely. Both of the chosen partners are loving and steady, and neither has a family history of mental illness or dysfunction. Such wise, well-planned romantic choices, studies show, have extraordinarily beneficial effects on young family members, providing a loving, steadying atmosphere in which to recover from their early losses.

However, choosing a partner wisely and well, at least the first time around, was relatively rare among the offspring and siblings I interviewed. Most have had complicated love lives, which more closely mirror their own fragmented histories and identities. The patterns in their romantic choices tend to cluster into four categories:

- avoidance of attachments;
- incomplete attachments;
- abusive attachments;
- attachments to mentally ill partners.

Avoidance of Attachments. Of course, being single and postponing marriage are common cultural occurrences in this country. For some siblings and offspring, however, being unattached is a way of life. They often claim that they yearn for a monogamous relationship. It's just that they've never found the "right" partner, or it's been a very long time between engagements. The difficulty, they say, is that intimacy has always been a frightening enterprise, since it came at such a high price in childhood. Being "mad" about someone has a painfully familiar ring.

Michael, forty-seven, is the only member of his immediate family (other than his father) who does not have mental illness. When he was growing up, he was surrogate parent both to his mother, who had a delusional disorder, and to his younger siblings, one of whom, a suicide, was bipolar, the other, a victim of chronic depression. Michael has never married. He's never even had a long-term relationship. As he explains it:

It's a trust issue. It's hard to trust anybody when the people you were closest to as a kid could just go away. What that teaches you is that the world is not a safe place. So you become emotionally removed. Yet I never thought I'd reach the age of forty-seven and still be unmarried. I'd really like to have a woman in my life. But somehow, I don't do anything about it. I can't figure it out.

When I suggest that he might want to consult with a psychotherapist to sort out his ambivalence, he responds as though he'd been struck. "I think there's something fundamentally wrong with saying, 'I need therapy' or 'There's something flawed in me,' " he says heatedly. "I don't think I'm broken. I'll admit, I feel plenty disjointed. Perhaps I'm splitting hairs."

Perhaps he is. Yet he is far from unique in his wariness. Virtually all of the young family members I interviewed said that the most costly legacy of their early experiences has been the "trust issue." Some can't let their guard down with friends, let alone lovers. This wariness *especially* applies to therapists, whose job, after all, is to get you to spill your guts as if on cue, and to a relative stranger at that.

Many of these survivors are reluctant to examine their tendency to keep others at an emotional distance. After all, it's a defense that got them through in the first place, and it is not to be parted with lightly or easily, as we shall see in chapter 13.

A forty-two-year-old divorcée, whose mother had schizophrenia, told me that the reason for the failure of her short-lived marriage when she was in her twenties was not necessarily because of the man she picked. He was "okay"—maybe a bit dull, but by no means the worst person she ever met. Rather, the marriage foundered because it never really got started. She blames herself.

> It's amazing I got married at all, because I have such a fear of intimacy. As soon as I become vulnerable enough to want to be close to someone, I always think that the person will be gone, maybe not physically, but certainly emotionally. That fear created a lot of distancing on my part in my marriage. I think my husband just got tired of being shut out. I don't do that with friends. It only happens with men. I'll probably never get married again.

Of such intimacy avoiders, Clarice J. Kestenbaum, M.D., director of training in the division of child and adolescent psychiatry at Columbia University's College of Physicians and Surgeons, has this to say:

> There are some children who run away as fast as they can and never look back. It was so hard growing up with their relatives' mental illness that they can't deal with it anymore. And why should they? Running away saved them. But in adulthood, it's not a very good defense, because you run right into other situations where once again you don't know how to cope. You'll think the solution is to escape or just get rid of a relationship, instead of working problems through.

As these unattached family members get older, however, they often find that they are increasingly lonely. Some are simply tired of keeping their dukes up. Others are discouraged that all their romantic encounters are of the identical brief, unsatisfying sort, and they can't seem to break the pattern. Yet many of these people reject partners who, in fact, are *right* for them and whose primary flaw is that they got too close.

It's more than just a trust issue. It's a *boundary* issue. They are often afraid that if they allow themselves to be at all vulnerable, they won't be able to maintain a separate identity.

Several people in this category recognized their off-putting qualities and, in midlife, did something about them. For example, one woman whose sociopathic brother was both terrifying and exhilarating, spent most of her twenties and thirties bouncing between "exciting bad guys" and "boring good guys." There seemed to be no happy medium, and she went into therapy to sort out why. Then, when she was forty-two, she met Ben, whom she ultimately married, and the pieces of her romantic history fell into place. She says:

It took a lot of therapy for me to be able to see my brother's good side. He was a bully, but he was also a genius who had this fascinating "take" on things. He abhorred fuzzy thinking. Any comfortable assumption you had, he'd say, "Well, wait a minute. Let's examine this." Ben has the same quality. After we'd been dating for a while, I thought, God, I've hit the jackpot with this guy. He has all my brother's energy, with none of the craziness! I always wanted to be with someone who makes me feel excited and alive, who's a bit of a maverick, but who is essentially sane and trustworthy. I was finally able to have both with Ben.

Incomplete Attachments. The second romantic pattern among young family members is the tendency to form and stay in relationships in which they themselves are less than giving, less than trusting, and, sometimes, unfaithful. These survivors frequently select their partners well—that is, they choose mates who are stable and loving and committed to them. But the survivors are unable to reciprocate that ardor and commitment.

Claudia, forty, whose bipolar father was violent to her during her childhood, is on the brink of collapse because she's involved in an extramarital affair that she knows can lead nowhere. Yet she is unable to part with her lover. At the same time, she does not want to leave her husband either.

She realizes that her ability to love is marginal, that her infidelity is sabotaging her marriage, and that her own behavior bears a terrifying resemblance to her father's—in some ways, she's as controlling as he was. Says Claudia,

> I picked a "safe" man to marry. My husband is incredibly attentive and will do anything for me. But I have a hard time showing him my emotions. I can be open with my lover, because I'm not married to him, which is kind of sick. Partly it's because I never really put down emotional roots anywhere. I'm not really close to anyone. I have a horror of going into therapy. With all these pressures I've put on myself, something's bound to give. Already I'm getting panic attacks and having other health problems.

Abusive Attachments. The third romantic pattern among young family members is a tendency to connect quickly and intemperately. In seeking respite from their painful family experience, in their teens and early twenties they plunged recklessly into dangerous liaisons, recreating the very relationships they left behind. These hasty connections were fueled by lingering fears of abandonment. The paradox is that such fears often became self-fulfilling prophecies.

People in this category were unable to spot serious trouble early in their relationships. Having bonded traumatically or incompletely with a mentally ill parent or sibling in childhood, these survivors knew no other way to bond when they became adults. As a result, many of them became victims of emotional or even physical abuse.

This tendency to form destructive relationships, says Dr. Kestenbaum, is common among siblings and offspring of the mentally ill. These family members grew up with and learned to "normalize" pathological behavior, and were inured to "deviance." Since the objects of their adult romantic affections weren't perceived as *blatantly* unstable, the subtler signs of that very instability simply escaped them. Says Dr. Kestenbaum:

> These people will be much more accepting of craziness and often don't take it personally. They'll say, "Oh, that's just that person's way." Often they'll marry spouses who are just like the ill relative who screams or is abusive. To these people, that's the norm.

Paula, twenty-five, whom we met in an earlier chapter, recognizes that the legacy of growing up with and eternally forgiving her abusive schizophrenic brother lingers in her dreadful romantic choices. Says Paula:

> I can see the patterns in the men I've dated that directly result from my relationship with my brother. Every one of them has abused me emotionally. But I've just taken it, like nothing could get to me. I've spent the majority of my life acting like nothing's wrong. If you hurt me, I'd probably make a joke of it, and I'll *never* let on that it bothers me. I don't know what it is. These guys just seem to find me. And I keep letting it happen.

Loretta, forty-eight, saw a similar self-destructive pattern in herself, but in her case, awareness of it came only after her ten-year marriage broke up. To avoid making the same mistake twice, she went into therapy to figure out what attracted her to her husband in the first place. Says Loretta:

> The man I married was just like my unpleasable, manic-depressive mother. I was very clear about not wanting to marry a sweet guy like my dad because he was always kowtowing to my mother and I couldn't bear to see him so demeaned. So when Irving the nice CPA asked me to marry him, I said, "I'm sorry, no." When Bernie the adorable dentist proposed, I said, "I don't think so." Then into my life came Barry, the debt-ridden sadist. I said, "*This* is the man for me." When your mother says you're stupid and you're fat every day for eighteen years,

you believe it. I figured, So what if my husband is difficult? My mother was, too. I can handle it. But of course, I couldn't handle *him*. He was a liar, a cheat, and a thief. I was programmed for him. I was always taking on difficult people and striving to make things better. At the age of forty I had to be taught not to let people walk all over me.

In some cases, this tendency to minimize or ignore troubling behavior in a partner seems to run in the family. In chapter 2, we met Rachel, twenty-five, and her brother Mark, thirty, whose schizophrenic father repeatedly threatened to kill their mother, finally causing the mother to take her children and run for her life.

Today, both siblings are also in miserable marriages. Rachel is an emotionally battered wife who is trying to persuade her husband to go into therapy. Mark's wife is similarly hostile, and he's hoping that if he's sufficiently loving, she'll come to her senses and treat him more kindly. In each case, the siblings keep excusing their partners' behavior. Says Mark:

My wife had a really terrible childhood, which I think is why she has such a temper. She's happy when things are going her way. But if you criticize her, you gotta duck, because objects start flying at you. It's like you don't want to step over the line because she'll really blow up. The only way to prevent it is to apologize ten times for something you didn't do or that wasn't so terrible. But I think deep down she really cares for me. Women have always dumped me. She's the only one who didn't walk away. So it's kind of hard for me to think of leaving her.

Rachel also hopes to be the agent of her hotheaded spouse's reform. She says:

My husband's childhood was much worse than mine—it was really tragic. His mother was killed by a drunk driver when he was a little kid. It's amazing that he's coped as well as he has. He's extremely reliable and hard-working, and I know I'll always be taken care of financially. It's just that he has this uncontrollable rage. Lately he's started to open up a little about his childhood. Every time I suggest he get some help, though, he just loses it. Still, he keeps telling me how much he needs me. I'm keeping my fingers crossed.

Family members are not all helpless victims, however. Sometimes, they are the abusers, either physically or verbally. One woman I interviewed admits to both tendencies during her first marriage. She thought she had constructed a perfect life—a dependable spouse, two healthy kids, a house in the suburbs—only to discover that she was becoming just like her schizoaffective mother.

I was creating the same nightmare, only I wasn't crazy. When my husband and I would fight, I'd rant and yell and scream, break dishes, throw things at him. I didn't know how to behave. My temper caused me problems in my jobs, too. It never occurred to me then that I drove people away by being so aggressive. I was my own worst enemy. It cost me a lot, my marriage especially.

Attachment to Mentally Ill Partners. The fourth pattern of romantic attachments among siblings and offspring of the mentally ill is the tendency to be drawn to partners who have psychiatric disorders.

Several of the people I interviewed in this category knew about their partners' impairments before they married, while others didn't find out about them until afterward. As we saw with Simone at the beginning of this chapter, choosing a partner who has mental illness can be a way of assuaging one's survivor guilt. But it can satisfy another goal as well. In caring for and possibly "curing" an ill partner, siblings and offspring feel a measure of control over the outcome of mental illness, where in childhood, they had no such control. Says psychiatrist Jane S. Ferber, M.D., director of the Family Training Center at Creedmoor Psychiatric Center in New York, "Being a caretaker helps to heal the tremendous feelings of helplessness they had growing up."

Much depends, of course, on whether or not the partner *wants* to be helped, or thinks there's a problem in the first place. Most of the people in this category eventually were divorced, largely because their partners either refused to admit they were mentally ill or because they would do nothing to help themselves.

Of those who remained married, the ill partners have, in fact, made huge efforts to manage their disorders and monitor their symptoms. Many of these afflicted partners have been chastened by their afflictions and are more compassionate toward others as a result. Thus they have much to give.

Theresa, now forty-five, is married to such a person. Theresa grew up with a schizophrenic mother who committed suicide soon after Theresa left home at eighteen. For years afterward, she kept people at an emotional distance and focused all her energies on her career. She had no close friends, and almost never went out on dates. By the time she hit thirty-five, however, she felt that she was coming apart at the seams. Says Theresa:

> I had this hard veneer that I showed to the world, and I kept my emotions held tight inside. But it was getting harder and harder to maintain this "split," as my therapist called it, and it was exhausting me. I had no people skills because I wouldn't let anyone in close. Therapy gave me a safe zone to have some feelings, and I began to reach out to people.

During this period, she met Frank, the man who became her husband. She knew when they were dating that he had "a psychological condition" for which he was taking some kind of medication. Frank did not know what the "condition" was because his psychiatrist, not wishing to "label" him, never gave it a name (this is a shockingly common phenomenon—see Notes). Since he was working full-time, and was so attentive and tender toward her, Theresa didn't give it much thought, and the couple married.

Within a year, Frank began complaining that the TV was talking to him. Since she had grown up with her mother's similar delusions, Theresa immediately took Frank to see another doctor, who gave her husband's condition a name: paranoid schizophrenia. The couple left the doctor's office, went to a bookstore and bought everything they could find on the subject, determined, she says, to "fight this thing together."

Since then, Frank's illness has progressed to the point where he is unable to concentrate enough to hold down a nine to five job. And while he is intellectually aware that he has an illness, he still operates under the assumption that the world has formed a conspiracy against him. Theresa realizes that she can't talk him out of his delusions. But she can't lie to him either, and just humor him. So the couple have reached a mutually acceptable accommodation. Says Theresa:

> He gets to believe the house is bugged, and I get to say, "I don't think it is." I'm Frank's reality check. Once in a while he'll ask me things like, "Is that newspaper headline written just for me?" I'll say, "No, that headline is written for everyone."

How, I ask her, could any sign of such a devastating illness have eluded her when they were dating? And once she knew the diagnosis, what kept her in the marriage? She replies:

> You have to remember that I grew up in a family where there was no affection. My mother was usually catatonic, and my father wouldn't talk to me about anything. When I met my husband, I was in my own recovery phase. I was beginning to allow myself to have feelings, and with him they were warm and fuzzy and wonderful. Frank meets my emotional needs. He takes total responsibility for his illness and treatment. And he gives me a lot of space, which we both really need. Schizophrenics don't like to be crowded, and neither do I. What can I tell you? It works really well.

Compromising Positions. When it comes to the reasons for these four romantic patterns, once again researchers are divided between the nurture and nature camps, the psychological and the biological.

The "Repetition Compulsion." The tendency to repeat the painful past in one's adulthood is known in the psychological community as the "repetition compulsion." It's not so much the desire to be hurt again that drives this behavior. Rather, it's a response to the familiar and perhaps a chance, this time, to fix it, or to respond to it differently.

As we have seen, many siblings and offspring of the mentally ill were exposed to repeated disruptions and confusion early in their lives. They witnessed and had to adapt to their relatives' sometimes terrifying behavior and frequent absences. These traumatizing experiences, and their reactions to them, often echo in their romantic choices. In choosing to remain alone, they could sidestep the whole loaded issue of intimacy altogether. In forming emotionally or psychologically unbalanced partnerships, *they knew what was expected of them* and could deliver it.

According to Dr. Judith Lewis Herman, children who were raised in abusive emotional "captivity" learned to tune out their own feelings. In their adult relationships, they frequently do so again in a kind of emotional short circuit. At the first whiff of trouble, they switch off their *conscious* awareness of it, which makes them vulnerable to further traumatization.

Many of the siblings and offspring I interviewed described similar short circuits in their romantic partnerships. In their families, they often were uncomplaining, good copers. In adulthood, many of them automatically responded to cues of a partner's neediness or abusiveness and tried to "fix" it rather than recognize that they had waded into troubled romantic waters. Others tried to change the outcomes of their childhoods by dominating their partners.

When, almost inevitably, these relationships failed, many of these junior family members were left with an anguishing sense of complicity in their romantic disappointments. In hindsight, they realized that the partnerships of their choosing were as lacking in reciprocity as their relationships with their afflicted kin.

"Assortative Mating." History may indeed tend to repeat itself in the romantic lives of siblings and adult children, but the reason may have nothing to do with psychology. Rather, it may have to do with biology. Researchers call the tendency to pair off with people like ourselves, or with people who resemble the relatives we grew up with, "assortative mating." In this case, the lure is *genetic sameness*. Says Demitri Papolos, M.D., codirector of the program in behavioral ge-

netics at the Albert Einstein College of Medicine/Montefiore Medical Center in New York, "You respond to that which you know most intimately, and part of that response may be genetic."

According to Dr. Hans J. Eysenck of the London Institute of Psychiatry and his colleagues, when it comes to romance, "[T]here is not the slightest suggestion that 'opposites attract.' " Rather, say the researchers, we pick our partners based upon our genetic endowment. Marriage and other "random" choices are not so random after all. Instead, they are forums, or "niches," within which our innate temperaments are reinforced.

The genetic viewpoint has its critics because it doesn't take into account the fact that not everyone has the same *opportunities*. As Dr. Arnold J. Sameroff has noted, ethnicity, gender, and social status play an enormous role in one's *access* to certain environments.

Obviously, the stigma attached to mental illness in one's family also does nothing to improve one's romantic chances. For example, several offspring and siblings told me that when they told their lovers they had a relative with a psychiatric disorder, these lovers disappeared. In other cases, the lovers' families put enormous pressure on the couples to break up. Thus, the romantic "environments" that are *available* may be restricted.

A Hybrid Hypothesis. Somewhere between these two approaches— the psychological and the genetic—is a combined view: Genes may play a part in our romantic choices, *but so, too*, does painful or happy experience. In the long run, research demonstrates, it is the latter that has the greater influence, perhaps because it is the one thing we can change.

A groundbreaking study of older identical and fraternal Swedish twins—the average age was fifty-eight—who were raised either separately or together produced interesting and heartening results. The researchers found that the effects on personality both of genes and of early family environment tend to wane over the life span. More lasting are the influences of non-family, or "non-shared" environments, as researchers call them. Once we are grown, we continue to develop and be shaped by the partners we select and the environments in which we choose to live.

In my own study, age was an important factor in the romantic patterns of the siblings and offspring. There was a limit to how much "sameness" to their painful childhoods these people could tolerate over the long haul. Given enough seasoning, and, often, with professional or other forms of help, many of these family members eventually were able to improve their romantic choices. They learned to relinquish the self-protective, distancing survival strategies that once served them well, but which now, in their intimate attachments, were becoming a liability.

Unfortunately, others, unable to recognize the ways in which they contribute to their own unhappiness, seem condemned to keep repeating history. It's easier to stay with self-destructive patterns than to examine their origins. This reluctance to probe the painful past can have terrible consequences for the next generation.

EFFECT ON CHILDBEARING
AND CHILD-REARING

As has been said, over half of the siblings and offspring in my study do not have children of their own, primarily because they are afraid of producing a mentally ill child or of doing something that might *cause* a child to break down. One woman whose father has schizophrenia married a man whose parents are both alcoholics and have diabetes. She says, "The sick joke in our house is that if we had kids, they'd all become alcoholic, insulin-dependent schizophrenics. So we raise horses instead."

Those junior family members who decide to take the procreative risk do so with enormous trepidation. Many of them had little or no idea how to be good parents when they began raising their children, since they frequently had abnormal or intermittent parenting when they were children. To illustrate the point, Dr. Jane S. Ferber tells of a woman she treated who was the daughter of a schizophrenic mother. The woman had recently given birth, and didn't have the vaguest idea of how to take care of her baby. Says Dr. Ferber:

She survived her mother's schizophrenia, but she was terrified that her child would get it. So for the first eighteen months of the baby's life, she brought her baby in to see me once a week. I would teach her such things as how to hold the baby, how to soothe it, how to feed and play with it, just basic parenting lessons.

Several people told me they had difficulty nurturing their children because they themselves had not been nurtured in childhood. As one woman said of her relationship with her twenty-two-year-old daughter:

I was not a very good mother to her—she turned out well *in spite of* me. We are great friends today, but we had to work very hard to develop that friendship. As a mother I did what was expected of me, like giving her music lessons and all that. But I didn't really hug her until she was six years old. I wasn't hugged myself by my schizophrenic mother. I didn't have a good role model.

In becoming parents, many of these family members reexperienced the very fears and anxieties that haunted them as children. Some were hyper-vigilant, monitoring their children's day-to-day progress, looking for the slightest clue of instability, just as they had once monitored their ill relatives. Occasionally, they found trouble where none existed. A woman whose brother has schizophrenia told me:

About ten years ago, something happened with my son that made me realize how emotionally bound up I still was by my brother's illness. My son, who was then seventeen, was in an automobile accident in which his best friend was terribly injured. It devastated my son, and I took him to see a therapist. One day soon afterward, I heard my son laughing. It sent a chill through my whole body because my brother used to laugh exactly the same way. I called my son's therapist and just sobbed. I said, "I thought I did everything right. The monster has hit, and I couldn't prevent it." I really overreacted because my son turned out splendidly.

Such fears also haunt a thirty-year-old man I interviewed whose mother had chronic depression. He has always been terrified that he'll break down. Four years ago, after his wife gave birth to their child, his fears increased exponentially—he's panic-stricken that the illness will show up in his daughter. In fact, he says, it's all he can do not to put her into a protective bubble. Says this father:

> There are times when my daughter and I are in the park, and I'll see her watching other children. I'll notice that she's longing to play with them but can't work up the nerve to go over to them. She'll turn away and get this sad look on her face. I'll choke up and think, Oh God, there it is. Someday she's going need treatment for serious depression.

This kind of parental vigilance opens up a new calendar of anniversary reactions for siblings and offspring of the mentally ill. Now they wonder if, and when, their *children* will crack up.

Other parents go in the opposite direction and behave as many of their own parents once behaved. Rather than overreact, these young parents underreact. They ignore, minimize, or deny that their kids have any problems because the anguish of having a flawed child is too much for them to bear.

With regard to the actual risk that these children will develop a psychiatric disorder, there is much good news. Says Dr. L. Erlenmeyer-Kimling, director of the New York High-Risk Project:

> If you just look at the statistics, the grandchildren, nieces and nephews of schizophrenic patients have about a 5 percent risk. But even that can be lower in many cases. First, remember that this figure—5 percent—is an averaged statistical risk for these groups. If the grandchildren, nieces, or nephews have parents who themselves are free of schizophrenia, the risk is expected to be lower—more like 2 percent. Second, there are certain childhood cognitive dysfunctions that are often seen long before kids develop symptoms of actual illness, and if these are not present, the risk is, again, probaby lower than 5 percent. Also, with interventions such as cognitive therapy that may improve the child's ability to process information, it's possible that more severe manifestations of illness later on may be prevented. So there's a lot of hope.

Triumphs of Hope. Simply being aware of this relatively remote risk has made many of the young family members I interviewed more tolerant of and sensitive toward their children, and much better parents. These siblings and offspring have a heightened appreciation of what's truly important in life.

Corinne, fifty, whose mother was bipolar, has aged out of the risk period for developing the disorder. However, her son, twenty-eight, has *not* aged out of it. Recently he solemnly announced to her, "Sit down. I've got something to tell you." Corinne's heart rose into her throat. "What's wrong?" she asked. He took her hand and gravely announced, "I'm gay."

"Is *that* all?" she replied, heaving a relieved sigh. "Thank God! I thought you were going to tell me you're mentally ill."

More than anything, I have been impressed by how seriously, albeit sometimes urgently, most of these young family members take their parenting responsibilities. They have survived what can happen when mental illness is "normalized," or untreated, in their own families. And they are determined *not* to let the past repeat itself in the next generation. For them, having children is, indeed, a triumph of hope over experience. As one mother of three put it:

My husband and I both come from families with mental illness in them. When we decided to have kids, it was really important to us that they get a lot of attention. We feel that if we give them a solid childhood where they really feel loved and nurtured, that's by far the best thing we can do for them if these illnesses ever rear their ugly heads. Just the feeling of having people you can depend on and who you know love you makes all the difference in the world.

CHAPTER 11

Effect on Achievement

I don't know what drives me, but I'm constantly pushing myself. It's almost a form of illness in response to my mother's illness. I work eighty hours a week, to the point of getting physically sick, just to see how much I can put up with. My work consumes me, which has had major consequences in my life. I don't take failure well. I have no social life. Everything I do revolves around my career. It's all a matter of proving that I won't break down mentally. I try not to think about it too much—that's why I stay so busy.

—Robert, 53

The people who work with Robert consider him to be a kind of legend. A neuroanatomist who teaches at a large university, he seems to thrive on no sleep. He's a member of a team of investigators involved in psychiatric research. He's the author of five books. And he serves on the boards of a variety of health care agencies and government commissions.

Yet Robert can hardly find a kind word to say about himself. Words like ''should'' and ''ought'' punctuate his punishing self-appraisal. He ''should'' be more attentive to his ailing father. He ''ought'' to be more patient with his students. He ''should'' get more exercise. He ''ought'' to have published more books.

But then, Robert was trained in reproach—verbal assaults from his manic-depressive mother were the leitmotif of his childhood. She couldn't find a nice word to say about anyone. "Her opinions terrorized the roost," he recalls.

Robert's fondest childhood memories are of the times when his mother was locked away in a psychiatric hospital. Only then did he get the undivided attention of his gentle father, whom he adored. The rest of the time was pure hell. "I was the house slave," he says. By the time he was in the fourth grade, it was Robert's job to baby-sit for his younger sister and keep the house tidied up. If ever his chores fell short of his mother's exacting standards, she'd reach for a leather strap that she kept hidden from her husband in a closet. She never actually used the strap on her children—she didn't have to. Says Robert:

> My mother had a way of enunciating words that scared the hell out of me. I can remember her saying to my father, "I can't stand the sight of those kids!" Everyone in the neighborhood knew about her, because she was always calling the police to complain about something. My sister and I were known as "the kids with the crazy mother." You had to walk on eggshells, because any little thing you did could bring about a rage in her. She was always making us apologize, and if you didn't cry, she'd punish you. I never felt any bond with her whatsoever. Nor do I now, sad to say.

Robert's escape, he says, was school. There, at least, he could play ball during recess or hole up in the library. Although he loved to read, his grades were always only so-so. But when in his sophomore year in college he decided to become a scientist, he began to apply himself more diligently to his studies. He went from Cs to straight As. "All of a sudden, I had to be the best at everything," he says.

In medical school, he became interested in the biochemistry of brain disorders, partly because he was trying to get a handle on his mother's illness, and partly because of his fear that he might inherit it. The world of the laboratory, and the mysteries of the mind, enchanted him. He became obsessed with the idea that maybe he could be of help to others, and he determined to devote his life to research.

While his devotion to his work has an undeniable nobility to it, his zealous quest to cure people has exacted a harsh price. He has little ability to put limits on himself. When asked to advise a colleague, or give a paper, or consult on a particularly difficult case, he finds it nearly impossible to say no. Nothing he does ever quite measures up to his own exalted standards, which forces him to work even harder. He hasn't taken a vacation in years. Last but by no means least, he was married once, briefly, never remarried, and has no children.

Yet despite his lopsided life, there is one aspect of it that fills him with pride: his talent for divining the secrets of the brain's inner workings. When it comes to research, he seems to have a magic touch. Says Robert:

> My work sort of validates that I have something worthwhile to give. I may be better at helping others than helping myself, but the fact remains that what I do, in all immodesty, changes people's lives. The satisfaction I get out of that is immeasurable. I can make a difference. That's what keeps me going.

PROVING GROUNDS: THE ROLE OF WORK

As we saw in the last chapter, the intimate attachments of offspring and siblings of the mentally ill reveal a great deal about the impact of their family histories on their private lives.

Perhaps more telling, at least to the world at large, are the public faces of these family members—specifically, their occupational choices. Just as they carved out separate identities for themselves apart from their families in childhood, in adulthood most of them continue to do so, refining these outside roles. Indeed, they frequently feel more alive in their work than anywhere else.

Losing oneself in work is a hallmark of siblings and offspring of the mentally ill. At work, they have an identity they can rely on, a chance to feel valued on their own terms. On the job, they often experience a sense of control, of opportunity, even of purpose, that they lacked with their kin and may lack in their personal attachments.

Achievements at work can compensate for many of their losses in childhood. Perhaps this time, they'll have an influence on others. Possibly they'll find a structured occupational cover for their disorderly feelings. They may even discover their own strengths.

But there is a rub. Work can become the *only* thing that matters, the very core of their identities, eclipsing their private lives and undermining their emotional and physical well-being. Should they lose their jobs, they may undergo a frighteningly familiar sense of helplessness and failure.

Patterns of Achievement. In my study, there are intriguing patterns in the occupational choices of siblings and offspring of the mentally ill. Three trends in particular stand out. Of the total sample, 26 percent work in the arts in such capacities as writer, editor, musician, agent, or painter. Of the people in these occupations, roughly half are siblings and half are offspring.

Another 31 percent of the total sample are in the helping professions, such as medicine, social work, research, psychotherapy, and teaching. Here there are wider differences, depending on their position in the family. Twenty-four percent of the offspring and 35 percent of the siblings are in these fields.

One other occupational pattern is noteworthy. While only 8 percent of the total sample toil in well-paid, non-health care, white-collar professions such as the law, finance, or upper corporate management, there are *three times* as many offspring (14 percent) as siblings (5 percent) in this category.

Some inferences can be drawn from these three patterns, which collectively represent two thirds of the total sample. For instance, it is striking that a larger percentage of siblings than offspring work in the helping professions. One possible explanation is that siblings— who identify so strongly with one another—are more likely to suffer survivor guilt than offspring. Consequently, siblings may feel a greater compulsion to help others as recompense for their fallen siblings' unrealized promise.

It is also striking that many more offspring than siblings are in highly remunerative non-health care professions. These offspring may feel a greater need to ensure their own autonomy, and, through financial success, to reflect well on their parents.

As for the remaining 34 percent of the total sample, their jobs cover a wide range, including blue-collar workers, secretaries, and housewives. Although many are perfectly content with their occupations, the majority appear to be in a state of drift, for reasons which will be explored in a moment.

Whatever their career choices and motivations, however, siblings and offspring share one characteristic: Work is a relatively neutral zone within which to escape, and possibly repair, their emotional fragmentation.

THE ARTISTS: REFLECTIONS OF MADNESS

Throughout history, people have been fascinated by a possible link between creativity and insanity. As Kay Redfield Jamison, Ph.D., notes in her book *Touched with Fire: Manic-Depressive Illness and the Artistic Temperament*, the poet Lord Byron once said, "We of the craft are all crazy." Such legendary figures as Vincent van Gogh, Ernest Hemingway, and Sylvia Plath all had severe mental illness, which ultimately led to their suicides. It is tempting to hypothesize that artistic immortality is nature's way of apologizing for psychological torment.

So, too, may creativity be the providential reward to family members for having to endure their siblings' or parents' mental illnesses. While the theoretical connection between creativity and madness has long been the focus of scientific studies, in recent years investigators have widened their scrutiny to include artistically gifted relatives of the mentally ill.

In her book, *No Voice Is Ever Wholly Lost*, Louise J. Kaplan, Ph.D., states that art is a place where offspring of the mentally ill can "find a home for [their] tears—and rage." Among Dr. Kaplan's examples is René Magritte, whose paintings of featureless faces and floating body parts bear silent witness to his "derailed dialogue" with his chronically depressed and suicidal mother, who drowned herself when he was thirteen.

Magritte's work vividly depicts the disturbing frontier between physical life and psychological death, as well as the artist's own repressed emotions. Having "lost" and been "lost by" his mother, his paintings bear chilling testimony to the ravages of those losses. Writes Dr. Kaplan:

> Art would become the solution to working through the emotional perplexities surrounding his "dead mother." . . . An artist could be a detached observer of death. An artist might even resurrect a dead mother in his paintings—over and over again. And an artist had permission to express his rage by distorting and mutilating as many bodies as he wished.

Searching for an Audience. For creatively gifted siblings and offspring of the mentally ill, art can serve another purpose. It satisfies their *need to be heard*. This need is particularly urgent among siblings of psychologically disturbed artists, according to psychiatrist Nancy C. Andreasen, M.D., of the University of Iowa College of Medicine, who also has a Ph.D. in English literature.

In a seminal fifteen-year investigation, Dr. Andreasen studied thirty well-known writers (twenty-seven men, three women) who had taught at the prestigious Iowa Writers' Workshop. Such writers as Philip Roth, John Irving, Kurt Vonnegut, and John Cheever have participated in the workshop.

Dr. Andreasen evaluated the creative patterns and psychiatric histories of workshop participants, and of their parents, siblings, and offspring. She also studied these traits in a group of thirty highly intelligent "controls"—who work in noncreative fields—and their first-degree relatives. Her findings, published in 1987, were stunning. While none of the workshop participants had schizophrenia, *80 percent*, compared to 30 percent of the controls, had had an episode of affective illness, such as major depression and especially manic-depression.

Of even greater significance were Dr. Andreasen's findings regarding the patterns of mental illness and creativity among the closest relatives of these writers. Forty-two percent of the parents, and 43 percent of the siblings, had had some form of mental illness, compared to 8 percent of the first-degree relatives of the controls. As to creative output, *twice as many siblings* (41 percent) as parents (20 percent) of workshop participants labored in such fields as dance, painting, music, and writing, or made "creative" contributions to the sciences. Nearly half of the creative family members were widely recognized and respected in their chosen fields. By contrast, only 18 percent of the "control" siblings, and 8 percent of the "control" parents, were in the arts. (Results for offspring were not listed in the published study.)

From this study, Dr. Andreasen concluded that both mental illness and creativity seem to run in families. She believes that this pattern strongly suggests a genetic transmission of these traits, rather than mere role-modeling. For example, creativity in siblings covers a variety of talents, and not just the literary arts.

In a follow-up paper, Dr. Andreasen and psychiatrist Ira D. Glick, M.D., discussed the link between affective disorders and creativity, focusing on the illnesses' arguable benefits. During episodes of crushing depression or feverish mania, creative people have trouble concentrating on their work. It is then, the researchers believe, that artists' ideas incubate, and their sensitivity about the human condition is heightened. In between episodes, however, these people are energetic and disciplined, able to concentrate for long stretches on a project. Their work is a monument to powerful sensibilities born of mental anguish.

The same might be said of creative siblings and offspring of the mentally ill.

Saving Graces. All of the people in my study who have careers in the arts said that their work was inspired by their experiences with their afflicted kin. Some felt that by creating something of lasting, if troubling, beauty, they were able, in a way, to memorialize their families' tragedies.

This was not, however, the primary motivation for their creative endeavors. Rather, it was to *harness and make sense of their own sorrow and confusion*, containing them inside the borders of a picture frame, or between two book covers, or within a finite space (dance) or set amount of time (music). Artistic expression served as interpretation and controlled emotional release.

A poetry professor told me that his highly structured writing is his way of organizing his complicated feelings about his chronically depressed mother. As he describes it:

> My mother's illness certainly has made me interesting in a peculiar sort of way. I have all these fascinating images that come directly out of my childhood. Yesterday I wrote a particularly good piece and I thought, Damn, this is great. I get to vent all these feelings, and it's really good material. I'm not a poet solely because of all the craziness in my family. But clearly, poetry is a useful way to survive. You get to be heard. And you get to explore. I mean, most people don't know what goes on in life. I was lucky. Somewhere there was a longing to understand things. I don't want to romanticize this, but my work has taught me that I wasn't meant to break.

Other creative family members spoke of the "authenticity" of their work, contrasting it to their "artificial" behavior with their mentally disturbed relatives, with whom they dared not be themselves. In their families, they had to be careful, vigilant, good copers, muzzled by the dictates of madness. In their work, their pent-up anger, sadness, terror, and bewilderment found expression. In the case of agents and editors, these emotions were "voiced" by the artists they represented, who "speak" for them.

Sometimes acquaintance with a relative's madness can result in a performance of scalding wit. A stand-up comic I interviewed draws upon his chaotic family's dysfunction, and his father's terrifying manic-depression, for material. He says:

> I've always had a kind of sick sense of humor, and I can appreciate the ironic paradoxes of human behavior. For instance, I have a fear of commitment, but I also have a fear of abandonment. I have a fear of failure, but also a fear of success. Recently I tried out a routine where I gave all my fears distinct personalities and had them fight with each other. My siblings always thought I'd be the first of us kids to go

insane. They're not far from wrong. I'm twisted, that's for sure. My comedy is a way of getting even.

One last benefit accrues to the artistic life of the people in my study. However wide their audience or exhibitionistic their work, it is in actuality their private sanctuary—a way of connecting to others *indirectly*. They expose their deepest selves, but artfully dodge intimate involvement with their audience. They can be heard, but from a well-defined distance.

It must be added, however, that while these people may have been inspired by their painful family experiences, most of them probably would have become artists anyhow. Temperamentally, they are intense, passionate, exquisitely sensitive people, capable of spending endless, solitary hours agonizing over their work.

Still, for the creative people I interviewed, a life in the arts is emotionally punishing and, for the vast majority, financially and often socially impoverishing. For this reason, it requires a certain masochism, a sort of "bent" world view, a touch of madness. As the comedian caustically put it, "You don't *have* to have mental illness in your family to become an artist. But, you should pardon the expression, it couldn't hurt."

THE HELPING PROFESSIONS: THE SOUL'S WELFARE

Of course, creativity is not only the provenance of artists; it is also the wellspring of innovative scientific research, effective therapy, and inspirational teaching. The soul's welfare requires a kind of vision on the part of the healer or educator, a way of connecting so that the people in need of such services can be reached, understood, and, perhaps, transformed.

The people I interviewed in this occupational category bring a particular sensitivity to their work, having tried, with varying degrees of success, to connect with their disturbed relatives. Such acquaintance with madness is common among members of the helping professions. Says Clarice J. Kestenbaum, M.D., of Columbia University:

> Many children of psychotic parents are quite brilliant and marvelous at reading cues. They know how to "read" their parents and how to take care of them. They frequently become doctors and nurses or mental health workers because they were trained from early age to cope with family members who are sick. These people have a tolerance for the mentally ill and have incredible knowledge and insight in dealing with them. I have many colleagues who have very ill parents and siblings. One reason they went into the field was to try to find a cure for their relatives. They're able to think something through, to size up a situation, not be impulsive, and to find more adaptive solutions to problems.

The family members I interviewed who are physicians, psychiatrists, psychologists, social workers, nurses, and teachers are fueled by tandem imperatives: the need to *give* and the need to *effect change*. How these needs are expressed occupationally depends to a large degree on the individuals' inherent dispositions.

In *Converging Themes in Psychotherapy*, Marvin R. Goldfried, Ph.D., and Wendy Padower offer the theory that temperament governs health care specialization. "It may be," they write, "that two basically different types of individuals are involved in these two enterprises, with the clinician being a 'warmer' and more interpersonally oriented person and the researcher tending to be more aloof and task oriented."

Borrowing from the authors, the people I interviewed who work in these professions could be divided into two groups: those who are "people-oriented helpers" and those who are "task-oriented helpers."

People-Oriented Helpers. Siblings and offspring in this category tend to be extremely demonstrative and empathetic, and like the structured intimacy of helping people one-on-one.

Anne, thirty-seven, says that the reason she became a psychotherapist is because "I've been a 'shrink' all my life, ever since I was nine years old and I figured out that my youngest brother was headed for mental illness." She continues:

I was the firstborn and only girl. After my brother was born, I noticed that my mother behaved differently toward him than toward me. There was just this bad chemistry between them. I knew I was her favorite and that she alienated him. He was a difficult kid, but he was just a *kid*. The more she criticized him, the more he acted out his anger. It was just this vicious cycle, and he got more and more disruptive. So when he was diagnosed as schizophrenic in his teens, I was the only one in the family who wasn't surprised.

Anne's attachment to her brother also informs her professional specialty—she works almost exclusively with manic-depressive clients. She explains:

I love working with bipolars because their psychoses are different from my brother's. They can be just as frightening, but they have a way of relating that kind of ameliorates some of the craziness. It's a two-edged sword because you get seduced by their people skills. Schizophrenics, on the other hand, are hard to treat because their thinking processes aren't quite human. It's hard to make them laugh, it's hard to know what's going on in their minds. There's that flat affect. I hate that. *I hate that!* That's what was so hard about living with my brother. When he was psychotic, you couldn't get through to him. I'm certain that part of why I went into this profession was because I felt somehow responsible for making his illness worse by being normal. He always tried to compete with me and, of course, he just couldn't. It was a great wound to my ego to be unable to prevent his illness. Being a therapist has helped me to understand him better, and to forgive myself.

As this case history illustrates, health care workers who have mentally ill relatives often have their own "boundary issues." Their family histories and residual anxieties can seep into their work, flooding them with emotions, and they must struggle to keep the appropriate professional distance. Sometimes they simply can't, and must recognize when a case compromises their therapeutic effectiveness. As a psychiatrist, whose schizophrenic brother killed himself, told me:

Suicide is a hot button for me. If someone comes to see me who's depressed, I'll say, "Look, I need to know up front how much I should worry about you. Are you sitting there thinking, To be or not to be?" For some therapists, if they've never had suicide in their families, self-annihilation is theoretical. For me, it's the reality. If a patient is suicidal, it taps too much into my personal pain and I cannot be objective. I can't be a good therapist to these people. I refer them to someone else. And I tell them that it's because of my own family history.

Task-Oriented Helpers. The people in my sample who work in research or policy making tend to be introverted and restrained. For many of them, intimacy, even professional intimacy, may simply be too threatening.

Victor, a pathologist who performs autopsies in a large urban hospital, sidesteps these painful issues altogether in his work. The son of a schizophrenic father, he spends his days trying to figure out why people got sick in the first place. There is something about a morgue, he says, that he finds peaceful—and which, he confesses, is fodder for his mordant wit.

> I like 'em dead. Corpses don't complain, they don't sue, and they have so much to tell us. These are beautiful anatomical specimens who help us to learn and grow and try to understand. Another reason I love my work is because I'm an introvert who doesn't like supervision. I am very intuitive, very intellectual, and I need a lot of freedom, which is why I'm good at what I do. Don't say the word "should" to me. Don't give me rules. I had so many weird rules growing up—such as don't do anything to set your father off, keep your mouth shut—that I don't take to being closely watched. I work best when I'm charting new ground, being scientifically rebellious, and doing it alone.

Dr. Jerome Kagan must have had people like Victor in mind when he wrote about scientific creativity in his book, *Unstable Ideas: Temperament, Cognition, and Self.* To be innovative, Dr. Kagan argues, requires a certain "hostility to peers," a trace of insecurity, and a wish to have "psychological power" over people. Scientific pioneers have no trouble upsetting the theoretical or intellectual order of things and challenging the status quo. They long to "replace established beliefs with fresh ones," Dr. Kagan writes. A degree of "uncertainty," a need to prove one's intelligence and virtue, the ability to take risks, all combine to produce new scientific discoveries.

For the professional caretakers in my sample, "uncertainty" was the given of their relationships with their mentally ill relatives. Resolving uncertainty is the cornerstone of their work.

THE FINANCIAL SUCCESSES: HOSTAGES OF FORTUNE

Like many people on the fast occupational track, siblings and offspring in this category are a restless group. They yearn for financial security and the prestige that is attached to such titles as "senior vice president," or "attorney-at-law," or "regional manager." To that end, they often jump from job to job as they hop up the occupational ladder.

Many of these family members complained that even though they were financially successful, they were nevertheless occupational misfits. Their career choices initially satisfied their need for structure—a haven in which to repair their fragmented identities—yet in the long run were neither emotionally nor intellectually rewarding.

Norman, forty-two, went to law school because he wanted the safety of other people's rules—statutes, torts, legal precedents gave him the rigid framework within which to recover from his chaotic, unpredictable childhood. Both his parents were alcoholics, and his mother was a chronic depressive who refused to take her medications. But now, he wishes he'd gone into another line of work. Says Norman:

> I knew from day one growing up that I was basically on my own. I was *determined* not to be dependent on anyone. Since I was always a good student, I sailed through college and law school, and joined a top firm. Law gave me an incredible sense of control. My addiction was work, staying in my head. I felt as long as I was doing well in my career, I wouldn't crack up. But now I wonder if I made the right

choice. Often I think I should have followed my real dream, which was anthropology. I mean, that's where I belong.

For some people in this category, their business judgment has often been jeopardized by their unresolved feelings about their mentally ill relatives. A forty-three-year-old man I interviewed, whose mother has schizophrenia, became extremely successful in his own housewares company, building it up from one store to a state-wide chain. In order to bankroll this expansion, he took on a partner. That's where the trouble began. The person he chose to do business with was a clone of his mother, and the partnership proved to be a disaster. He recalls:

> You have to understand that I was raised with a mother whose every behavior was inappropriate. I mean, anything you said or did got a response that made no sense. I learned to tune out. I didn't "hear" other people's abusive behavior. Even now, after years of therapy, I still have to work very hard to pay close attention to what people say because otherwise I won't recognize when I'm being exploited. My business partner treated me horribly, both in word and deed, and for a long time *I never saw it*. By the time I realized what was happening, the guy had just taken over the company. I was shut out of day-to-day operations. All our clients wanted to deal only with him, not with me. Finally I sold him my interest in the company. Now I'm thinking of going back to school and becoming a social worker. I really think I could be of help to people.

In talking to these people about their work, there seemed to be a missing piece. Why was it that none of them felt satisfied in their careers? Are *all* family members who are financially successful similarly unhappy in their occupations? Isn't financial success the American dream? To solve this puzzle, I went back to the seventy-five transcripts of the people I interviewed, and there I found the answer.

Walls of Wealth. Many of these family members had *siblings* who have scored big in business. However, unlike the people who participated in my study, their siblings were *not* inclined to talk to me, or anyone, including kin, about their mentally ill relatives. I had asked all my interview subjects to poll their siblings to find out if they, too, would be willing to discuss their histories with me. None of these well-heeled brothers and sisters of my interview subjects wanted to be reminded of the painful past; they declined the invitation.

A poignant explanation for this reticence was given to me by a woman who suffers from schizophrenia and whose sisters are both extremely successful in business. Said this woman:

> My siblings love me deeply, but they have tremendous difficulty with illness. Prior to my getting sick, I was always their big, protective sister. I helped them get into college. I was this parental figure. Then, when I was twenty-six, I collapsed completely, and I let them down. I think it was terrifying for them. I think they were very afraid it would be catching. My illness enabled them to stop respecting my opinions. Some people are good with illness. My sisters, unfortunately, aren't. They just backed away. I seldom hear from them. I rocked their world view, their coherent frame of reference. I think that's why they became workaholics. They've just buried themselves in their careers.

Siblings who go on to fame and fortune tend to be unavailable to the relatives they left behind. To help their families, they may occasionally write a check, or use their influential contacts in the legal, political, or medical professions to twist an arm or bend a rule. But for the most part, they avoid contact with their kin.

While obsessive devotion to one's career may result in the fraying of family ties, it should not automatically be construed that such devotion connotes emotional or moral bankruptcy (although it may). Another way to look at this ambitiousness is that it may be psychologically lifesaving.

It's not so much financial success or prestige that matters to most of these people; rather, it's *the ability to surmount difficult challenges*. In pursuing, and persisting in, their career goals, and in overcoming obstacles, their self-esteem is enormously enhanced. Their success goes a long way toward repairing the sense of failure they felt, or may still feel, within their families. At least in their work they've been tested and have prevailed.

In his studies of resilient people who endured numerous tragedies in their childhoods, psychiatrist Michael Rutter, M.D., has found that two kinds of experience can ameliorate the damage of those tragedies. One is having a loving and secure relationship. The *other* is "success in accomplishing tasks that are identified by individuals as central to their interests." Such accomplishment, Dr. Rutter believes, can compensate for and "neutralize" setbacks in other areas of life.

Thus, what is good for the successful family member who "escapes" through achievement, and who continues to be drawn to occupational challenges that bolster self-regard, are not necessarily strategies that will foster intimacy with the person's family of origin. Yet such escape may be essential for these family members. As we shall see in the next chapter, career "success" can make it possible for them to feel secure enough in later life to build bridges back to their families.

THE DRIFTERS: QUIET DESPERATION

Finally we come to the people who are either just getting by in their jobs, living from paycheck to paycheck, or are still experimenting and haven't settled on a career trajectory. These, of course, are vastly different situations, which depend, in part, on the accumulation of stress in their lives over time, and, in part, on their own personalities.

Dreams Deferred. Several of the "drifters" in my sample had to quit school because their parents did not have the finances to pay for both psychiatric treatment for ill children and college tuitions for the well ones. This lack of financial family support was not, however, enough to deflate the dreams of other people in my study.

Many of the drifters I interviewed seemed to be suffused with feelings of worthlessness, and didn't even dare to have dreams for themselves. This was particularly true of family members who had not escaped but, instead, continued to be closely involved in the lives of their mentally ill siblings and parents.

A thirty-five-year-old woman I interviewed who is a housewife and part-time secretary, and whose brother has schizophrenia, has in many ways been defeated by her brother's illness. She says:

> When I see how my brother's mind has deteriorated, it makes me wish I had become a scientist. But I have always tended to take the easy path. There is for me the sense of never starting with anything long term, because one never knows if it can be finished. A crisis may strike and the job will never get done. I find it very difficult to step back from all this and live my life. There's this voice in my head that says, "What could I do?" and I never seem to get anywhere. The mountain starts to look too big to climb.

Roadblocks to Achievement. Other "drifters," who had been given every financial and educational opportunity by their parents, were in a state of occupational flux because they felt defeated by their parents' unrealistically high expectations of them. Indeed, many had been pressured by their parents—especially by fathers—to succeed in school and in their careers in order to reduce the parents' own sense of failure in having an ill child or spouse. It was up to these well offspring and siblings to offset those losses by measurable financial success. They felt unequal to the task.

One twenty-eight-year-old man, whose mother has severe bipolar disorder and whose parents divorced when he was twelve, said that he had wanted to be an artist, but his father insisted he go into the family banking business. Says the young man, who currently works as a waiter in a restaurant:

> Any idea I ever came up with for a career—other than banking—my father always said, "What the hell do you want to do that for? You can't make any money." So I went into my dad's business. I did extremely well. The trouble was, I was fulfilling his expectations of me, but not my own. So I finally quit. The only thing he cares about is money. He doesn't approve of me. I think part of his disappointment is that I look just like my mother. I think I remind him of her. I wish I didn't give a damn about his opinion, but I do. What he doesn't realize is that once I set my mind to do something, I do it well. I just haven't

figured out what I want to do next. But I will. I'm considering going to art school after all. I just wish my father had more faith in me.

Self-Sabotage. For many junior family members who grew up with family chaos or parental harshness, there is often a delayed response to their unhappy childhoods. Offspring and siblings whose needs were not met in the family, and who had no outside mentors, sometimes express their feelings of sadness or rage through self-destructive behavior beyond home. This behavior, and lack of opportunity, can result in their checkered or lackluster careers.

In their examination of explosive children and of extremely shy children over the life course, Drs. Avshalom Caspi, Glen H. Elder Jr., and Daryl J. Bem have found that such children often have difficulty in their work lives when they are adults. Family dysfunction, the researchers report, can create and *sustain* children's aversive behaviors. Volatile kids become aggressive. Shy kids become withdrawn.

Once these behaviors are established, they are reinforced by the choices offspring make in the course of their lives. That is, they select situations—such as partners or jobs—which re-evoke their childhood emotional responses, setting into motion a vicious cycle. The researchers call this lifelong aversive behavior "cumulative continuity."

For example, explosive boys were still "ill-tempered" at thirty and forty years of age, and had more erratic work lives than their even-tempered peers. Explosive kids raised in middle-class homes became working-class adults. These angry men tended to drop out of school and to experience more unemployment than their peers. The hot-headed women in this study, who came of age in the 1940s, did not have the same occupational fate but were more likely to have married men in lower socioeconomic classes, and to be divorced, than their less excitable peers. These angry women often were angry parents to their children.

As for the shy children studied over time, they, too, continued to select environments in which their temperaments were reinforced. The most striking finding regarding shy men was that they often delayed getting married, becoming parents, and establishing stable careers. As a result, there was a pileup of these roles relatively late in life, putting the men under extreme stress. They tended to have low expectations of themselves, which was underscored by their inability to assert themselves. Thus, their careers were unremarkable. (The timid women in the study were less likely than their even-tempered counterparts to be in the workforce and, interestingly, frequently married into a higher socioeconomic status.)

Chain Reactions. As these and other studies demonstrate, an adverse chain reaction can be set into motion if, beginning in childhood, people are unable to cope with their environments. To restate an important point, children who endured their parents' mental illness, marital disruptions, low socioeconomic status—*and who had no outside supports*—are less likely to overcome adversity in adulthood than those who had fewer such experiences. These unhappy survivors frequently will bring trouble upon themselves in their work lives.

Hence, while mental illness in the family per se does not foretell a life of economic failure for offspring and siblings, when combined with other disquieting aspects of their lives, and their own aversive personalities, they may well squelch, or squander, their job opportunities.

UNBALANCED LIVES

As all these interviews and studies demonstrate, acquaintance with madness permeates the occupational choices of siblings and offspring of the mentally ill.

Trudy L. Mason, who agreed to be interviewed by me on the condition that I use her real name, and whose sister, Maxine, recently died in a psychiatric hospital, has spent the bulk of her life working in the spotlight. A public relations consultant and ardent advocate for the mentally ill, Trudy has been an official in New York City and state government, run for public office, and is presently a New York State Democratic committeewoman. She herself figured prominently in Susan Sheehan's book, *Is There No Place on Earth for Me?*, which, using pseudonyms, chronicled the torments of Maxine's schizophrenia, and of the siblings' anguished relationship.

Trudy could well have been speaking for most siblings and off-spring I interviewed when she told me:

You want to know the effect of Maxine's illness on my life? Start with functioning as a parent to my sister, constantly being on call for her, whether she was in hospitals, living on her own, or living with my parents when they were alive. Add my fighting to get her good care—even with all my connections I couldn't get her the right treatment or prevent her death. Other effects? I never had any children. My relationships with men suffered greatly. I felt I had to fulfill the role of being the family achiever and "shining star." My parents needed it, and Maxine resented it, because I was everything she could never be. After ten years of therapy, I now understand that I suffered from survivor guilt and viewed myself as a failure. Even though the outside world and my family viewed me as a "great success," I thought it was all a sham and that at any moment I could turn into Maxine. It took me a long time to get a sense of balance in my life. My being in the public eye is very positive in that it enables me to advocate for many causes, especially the mentally ill. I used to think it was a negative because I could not affirm myself and needed the public's applause and approval. That's what having a mentally ill sibling does to you.

CHAPTER 12

Family Ties: Responsibility, Obligation, and Accountability

It's been six years since my mother killed herself, and I still have nightmares about it. In my dreams she comes back and is angry with me because my husband and I moved away and didn't take her with us. I was always afraid of her, even as an adult, and I just couldn't put myself through it anymore. If she had been stabilized and capable of rational thinking, it would have been different. The objective side of me knows I have nothing to feel guilty about. But the daughter in me feels that I'm a bad person for wanting to have a life.

—Samantha, 36

By any yardstick, Samantha was always a "good" daughter. The eldest of three children, she was the bulwark of her family. Even in grade school, she kept track of her schizophrenic mother's symptoms, cooked the meals, and baby-sat for her younger brothers while her dad worked twelve hours a day in a television repair shop near their Kansas City home. Whenever her mother got paranoid, threatening her children with a knife, Samantha had a knack for calming her down.

After Samantha graduated from college, she got an apartment near her parent's house so she could continue to be available to them. And when she fell in love with the man who was to become her husband, she accepted his marriage proposal under one condition: She would always have an obligation to help her family, and he must never ask her to choose between him and them. In exchange, she would never allow her mother to live with them. He agreed to her terms.

254

Shortly after their wedding, while having dinner with her parents, Samantha's father said to her, "You know, I'm not going to live forever. You must promise me that after I'm gone, you'll take your mother in. Promise." Says Samantha:

My father really put me on the spot. Somehow I worked up the nerve to say, "I can't promise you that, Dad. I'll always do everything else possible, but that I can't do. I'm married now, and we're planning to have kids right away." My father was furious. From that moment on, he didn't want to have much to do with me.

Samantha's husband was offered a plum job in New York, and the couple relocated. She felt uneasy about the move but comforted herself with the knowledge that her youngest brother, then twenty-two, still lived at home and could be a support to their parents.

A year later, however, her father had a fatal heart attack. Samantha flew in for the funeral and began looking for a residential care facility for her mother. Unfortunately, her mother had a psychotic break during this period and had to be hospitalized, which made her ineligible for supervised housing. Samantha returned to New York and continued, by telephone, to try to find a suitable place for her mother to live.

When her mother was discharged from the hospital, Samantha's brother quickly realized that he was out of his depth. The mother wasn't sick enough to be rehospitalized, but she was too delusional to be left alone, and he couldn't afford to lose his job. He kept calling his sister for advice on handling such crises as the mother's refusal to take her medications, or her bizarre behavior. And then Samantha got the call she had most feared. She recalls:

It was my brother, crying hysterically, and I instantly knew my mother was dead. He had just come home from work and found her lying in bed with an empty bottle of sleeping pills next to her. I tried to console him, saying, "It's not your fault. You couldn't watch her twenty-four hours a day. If anything, I'm to blame. I shouldn't have left until we had her set up somewhere." The guilt still eats at me. I feel guilty because my brother stayed and I ran. I feel guilty because her death was a relief. More than anything, I feel guilty for having been afraid of her. It's hard to keep loving someone who's traumatized you and endangered your life. I keep thinking that if I had been a better person, a stronger person—if I had loved her more—maybe she'd still be alive.

PASSING THE TORCH:
WHO WILL TAKE RESPONSIBILITY?

Of all the dilemmas confronting adult children and siblings of the mentally ill, few are thornier than these: What will become of the sick one when the parents or partners are no longer able to provide care? Who will decide about treatment, or battle the mental health system for housing, rehabilitation, insurance benefits? Who will fight the legal system to get the person involuntarily committed, if necessary, or, in the case of criminal acts, to try to ensure that the person gets a fair trial and medical attention in prison?

Such questions haunt families and, with tragic frequency, divide them, for they raise a host of other questions. For example, do parents have a right to expect their well progeny to share—and one day shoulder—the burden of caring for their disturbed kin? Are siblings and offspring morally obliged to do so? Who's to say what kind of "help" they should give, or how much, or when?

And what of the mentally ill themselves? Should they be held accountable for their behavior, regardless of the severity of their disorders? Should they be required to make an effort to control their impulses, to get treatment, and to suffer the consequences if they do not? Or are they blameless, helpless victims of their illnesses? Are they absolved of all responsibility and entitled to their siblings' and childrens' unconditional love, tolerance, and care?

These are the questions I asked parents, siblings and offspring, and consumers (people with mental illness). Depending on their position in the family, their answers varied widely.

Parents. When it comes to filial and sibling responsibility, parents fall into three camps: those who feel strongly that their well children

have a duty to help their ill relatives; those who are torn by the recognition of everyone's needs; and those who are estranged from their
ill children and who may or may not expect their well children to step
into the void.

Duty-Oriented Parents. Harriet, fifty-four, a widow, is deeply dismayed that her sons do not include her schizophrenic daughter in their
lives, and is terrified that once she dies, they will utterly abandon their
sister. Says Harriet:

> They don't even call her up to ask how she's doing. It infuriates me
> that they're so self-centered. I must have made some big mistakes to
> have raised such insensitive kids. My daughter can't help being sick,
> and she truly needs all the support she can get. It breaks my heart to
> see how hurt she is by them. They just don't seem to care.

Ken, fifty-seven, whose younger daughter has severe bipolar disorder, is similarly critical of his firstborn daughter. To illustrate the
point, he tells me about a recent argument they had about money—
specifically, about his and his wife's wills. The bulk of their estates
will be held in trust for their mentally ill daughter. Says Ken:

> When I told my older daughter about this, she became enraged. She
> said, "I don't think that's fair. It should be divided equally." I tried
> to conceal my anger, but I thought, She doesn't understand. She's
> greedy. I said, "You know, you've got a great job, someday you'll get
> married, and I have no doubts that you're going to be okay. But I can't
> say that about your sister. I don't know that she'll be okay. And when
> we're gone, we want to make sure she's taken care of." We haven't
> had another conversation about it. It's a sore point.

Ambivalent Parents. Parents in this category are achingly aware of
the ways in which, of terrible necessity, they have been unavailable
to their well children through the years. At the same time, these parents agonize over their most vulnerable offspring. If only their well

kids could be a little more compassionate—but then, they have a right to their own lives, too.

Delia, fifty-seven, whose daughter has schizophrenia, is bedeviled by such ambivalence. She wishes her twenty-eight-year-old son had more time for his sister; on the other hand, she understands it. She says:

> It's been rough for him to have a mentally ill sister. He's embarrassed to be seen with her. He's had a hard time because she's so irritable. Still, I wish he'd take her to the movies or out for pizza once in a while. I think one reason he doesn't is that he resents my relationship with her. I cater to her. I make excuses for her. I say, "She can't help the way she acts—she's sick." He wants me to be more strict with her. He thinks he has all the answers, and so does my husband. I've tried to get them to go with me into family therapy to talk about this stuff. But they refuse.

Other parents have dealt with their ambivalence by striking bargains with their well children. Says the father of a schizophrenic son:

> My wife and I have told our other kids that they should get on with their lives. But once in a while, if we have a real emergency, we'll send up a red flag and ask them to lend a hand—for instance, if our son ever ran away and we needed help finding him. They were very relieved to hear that we don't expect them to do more. It's only fair, because they really got the short end of the stick. I bet if you talked to them, they'd tell you that we've been totally absorbed by our son's illness. They'd be right.

Estranged Parents. A minority of parents have minimal or no contact with their ill children, some because these children want nothing to do with them, others because the parents prefer to keep their distance. Either way, their well children often feel compelled to pick up the caretaking slack.

Parents in the former category have been rejected for a variety of reasons, and often are perceived by their ill children as the enemy. In some cases, afflicted children cannot forgive their parents for having once, or more than once, involuntarily hospitalized them. In other cases, the disturbed children often lack insight into their illnesses, or refuse treatment. In still other cases, these offspring had extremely unhappy childhoods.

Most rejected parents are tormented by worry and self-blame, which affects their relationships with their other children. For example, Selma, sixty-eight, a widow and mother of two—a son and daughter—has not laid eyes on her mentally ill son in over a decade. While she takes great pleasure in her daughter and grandchildren, her son is never far from her thoughts. Every so often she hires detectives to track him down, just to make sure he's still alive and not in need of money or medical attention. The son bitterly resents these intrusions, and always sends back the message that he wants his family to leave him alone. Says Selma:

> What kills me is we had an extraordinarily warm relationship when he was a little boy. As time went on, there was increasing friction between us, partly because I worked full-time and the nanny I hired—whom I fired—was a horror, and partly because my son was completely undisciplined. I tried many times to get him into therapy, but he wouldn't cooperate. And then one day when he was around thirty, just like that, he disappeared. The word I get is that he's convinced he had a miserable childhood. I have done all the mea culpas, apologizing, soul-searching. I lie awake at night worrying about him. The grieving never ends. And, of course, it upsets my daughter to see me so upset. She feels as helpless as I do.

Parents who choose to retreat from their disturbed children, however, are another matter. Such parents put their well children into untenable positions. If these younger family members take on the total burden of their afflicted kin, they jeopardize their own careers and marriages. If they don't, the ill relative could end up on the street, or dead.

Millie, thirty-five, who herself has young children, has come to the fore on behalf of her manic-depressive sister because her parents have essentially given up on the sister. Says Millie:

> I know it pains my parents to have lost a child to mental illness. Maybe they're burned out. But they've totally turned their backs on her. Dealing with my parents has been a lot harder for me than dealing with my sister. I'm really her only support. It's hard to keep explaining to my husband and kids why I'm always running over to my sister's place, and why I'm always so sad. Everything I give to her, I take from them.

Siblings and Offspring. As these case histories illustrate, the pressure on junior family members to provide loyalty and support to their parents and ill relatives can be staggering. Most siblings and offspring look to the future with dread, because it's only a matter of time before they'll have to decide whether or not to assume responsibility for their ill relatives' welfare.

For instance, when I asked an African-American woman, whose brother has schizophrenia, "What happens when your parents die?" she replied:

> Oh God. Just the thought of it sends a chill through my body, that's how frightened I am. I'm desperately trying to raise my own children and keep my marriage going. I feel great resentment that my parents, who always gave all their attention to him, expect me to jump in when they die and take over, no questions asked. Sometimes, when he's really berserk, I think, Why can't he just be taken off this earth? I know he's miserable. What makes it harder is that in the black community, mental illness is kept in the closet. You surround yourself with relatives and friends and don't get professional help. My parents are very active in their church, and the advice they get is, "Just pray on it and it'll get better." I keep trying to get them to reach out to the mental health community for help, and that comes across as disloyalty. I shudder to think what will happen, because he's getting worse and worse.

Such resentment can be even greater among adult offspring of the mentally ill. Filial "responsibility" seems particularly unjust because it violates the natural order of things. Able-bodied parents are supposed to help their kids, not the other way around. And should one child assume all or most of the responsibility, while his or her siblings do less, the tension between them can reach the breaking point.

Resentment can turn to rancor if the ill parent was abusive to the caretaking child when he or she was growing up. This was the case for Lonnie, forty, the eldest of two children of an extremely hostile, bipolar mother. Lonnie's parents divorced when she was twenty, and everyone in the family parted company. Her mother went back to her parents to live, her brother moved abroad, and Lonnie fled into early marriage and parenthood.

Then one day about ten years later, Lonnie got a phone call, out of the blue, from her maternal grandmother. Says Lonnie:

I was told, "We're putting your mother on a plane tomorrow. She's your responsibility now." My grandparents were getting too old to take care of her anymore, so I had no choice but to let her come. I knew nothing about the mental health system, so I asked a social worker for advice. She said, "Do not take your mother to your home—you'll never get her out." She found a decent full-care boarding house, and the next day I picked my mother up at the airport and took her directly there. Until her death last year, I visited her constantly, washed her clothes, fought with her doctors. My husband finally said to me, "Who's more important? Your mother or us?" I said, "I can't abandon her, even if she never loved me." The only time my brother ever showed up was at my mother's funeral. We had, shall we say, "words." I tore his head off.

Consumers. At the center of these family disputes, of course, are the mentally ill relatives themselves. Frequently they are mortified to be dependent upon others because it goes against the grain of normal adult development. It is doubly humiliating for them to have to lean on their siblings or children. Many consumers, despite their illnesses, are able to forge independent lives. But even they don't know what the future—or their brain chemistry—holds in store.

Jeff, a forty-seven-year-old divorced father of three grown children, has been struggling with chronic depression since his twenties. In recent years he has been unable to hold down a full-time job because his fluctuating moods have gathered momentum, wreaking havoc on his concentration. To supplement his meager Social Security disability benefits, he works part-time, off the books, at a diner.

Of all his difficulties, it is the thought of being dependent on his kids that brings Jeff to his knees. He'd rather die than be perceived by them as a hopeless case. Consequently, he is passionate about adhering to his treatment regimen and maintaining his independence. It's the only way, he says, that he'll have a shred of dignity.

> The worst thing in the world is to be pitied. As long as you're treatable, you're responsible. I can't help being sick. But I owe it to myself to do what I can to deal with my illness, because if I don't, I diminish myself. I have no guarantees that I won't break down again. Still, there are ways of coping with depression. I take my meds. I see a therapist. I'm in a support group. That's what keeps me out of the hospital. And that's what will keep me from becoming a burden to my kids.

Abe, thirty, who has schizoaffective disorder, is equally vigilant about his symptoms. He, too, does not relish the idea of being dependent upon anyone. However, his illness has already created cracks in his relationship with his sister—she has begun distancing herself from him—because someday, it will fall to her to make decisions about his treatment should he be unable to make them himself.

Compounding matters, the stigma of his illness makes it virtually impossible for him to land a decent job, even though his pre-illness résumé is studded with illustrious job titles. At the moment, his future, both personally and professionally, looks murky. Says Abe:

> My sister and I may have drifted apart, but she'd never abandon me. It's a great comfort to know that she will do her utmost to see that I'm never on the street. For me, though, that's such a limited aspiration. That's why I'm trying to build a life for myself so I can provide my own clothing and shelter. The problem is, I can't string together a lot of good days. I'll get more done in a week than most people, and then I'll have two days where I can't move. That makes it hard to find a

good job with flexible hours. Once you say the words "mental illness" to prospective employers—which would explain your need to set your own hours—they don't hear anything else. You're Norman Bates in *Psycho* even if you have solid credentials, are in treatment, and haven't been hospitalized in years.

Other consumers are less fortunate than Jeff and Abe. The unlucky ones are those who are most acutely disabled, and who feel they have no alternative but to turn to their siblings, or children, for emotional support, if not full-time caretaking.

Ellie, a fifty-year-old woman with paranoid schizophrenia, is such a consumer. She allowed me to interview her with her sister, Rose, so that I could get a better idea of their relationship and how her illness has affected it.

Until recently, Ellie was unable to live on her own. She tried working so she could live independently, but either her voices kept intruding, or she'd say things that were "nutty." She was briefly married in her twenties and had a child. But due to her constant hospitalizations, the marriage foundered, she lost custody of her child, and she had to go back to live with her parents.

As she has gotten older, her illness seems to have settled down. Currently she lives in a rooming house, doing domestic chores in exchange for a break on her rent. Her closest friend is her sister, Rose, whom she visits nearly every weekend.

Their relationship is uncommonly close, the primary reason being that they have always been honest with one another. During the interview, I asked them how they've handled the issue of sibling "responsibility." Here are their responses.

ELLIE: It took me a long time to get my symptoms and my medications under control. Sometimes my sister and I talk about my living with her, but it would be hard on her. She'd have to hide her emotions if she didn't feel like being with me.

ROSE: I couldn't do it. I'd break.

ELLIE: You'd never break.

ROSE: I would. It makes it tougher to live with an ill person you love. I'm more emotionally invested. I could only take it in little blocks of time. Remember how scared I was of you when you first got sick?

ELLIE: You were?

ROSE: Yes. I was scared I'd get sick, too. I was scared of saying the wrong thing. I stayed in my own corner. And the guilt of not being sick myself was terrible. Every time I had a success, I felt guilty.

ELLIE: That's crazy!

ROSE: Of course! You have crazy reactions to something you can't do anything about.

Most of the siblings and offspring I interviewed have not reached this level of openness with their ill relatives. Rather, they grope for a sense of balance between intimacy and escape, between insight and denial, between loyalty and self-preservation.

Laurie Flynn, executive director of the National Alliance for the Mentally Ill, one of whose children has a brain disorder, understands the dilemma that siblings and offspring are in. She says:

> I have told my other children, "Go live your life. The only thing I ask is that you be kind to your sister. You have to make your own choices, and do what will make you happy and comfortable. You have a right to that." I would not want my kids to think they have some special responsibility—it's not their job. Children have to be allowed to give when they can, where they can, if they can, and how they can. To make judgments about their level of involvement is limiting to what their futures can be. They need to be who they are first.

Siblings and offspring may not be responsible for their ill kin, but that doesn't mean they are devoid of *feelings of obligation* toward them. That's where the trouble is—they're not sure what that obligation should be.

RECKONINGS: THE ROOTS OF OBLIGATION

According to sociologists Alice S. Rossi, Ph.D., and Peter H. Rossi, who have studied the parent-child relationship across the life span, obligation toward kin is determined by two primary variables: how closely family members are related to one another biologically, and the tenor of their family ties when the offspring were growing up.

In general, "kinship obligation" follows vertical lines. The highest sense of obligation is toward "primary kin," one's parents and one's children. Siblings consider each other "secondary kin," and their sense of obligation toward each other is correspondingly less than toward their parents and progeny.

Moreover, kinship obligation tends to favor younger relatives—parents help their children, aunts and uncles help nieces and nephews, and so on. More women than men feel high obligation toward their families, and do most of the helping. As to intensity of obligation over the life span, it peaks between the ages of nineteen and thirty, drops off in the thirties, plateaus in the forties, and declines precipitously after age fifty, presumably when parents die off and when it is necessary to conserve one's resources.

The other important variable of obligation, say the Rossis, is the degree to which offspring felt loved and valued by their parents when they were growing up. The more affectionate and accepting the parents were, the more their children express strong obligations toward them and toward other family members in adulthood. Conversely, the more difficult or hostile the parent-child bond, the less these offspring feel obliged to their parents and their siblings. Put another way, the greater the family dysfunction early on, the looser the family ties, at least on the parts of junior family members. Some parents may "forgive and forget" and find diplomatic ways to relate to their adult children. Offspring, on the other hand, have very long memories. "For them," write the Rossis, "the past colors the present."

Other investigators corroborate many of the Rossis' findings—in particular, the ways in which the sibling bond is influenced by parents.

In his studies of siblings, Victor G. Cicirelli of Purdue University has found that when children feel warmly toward their parents, that warmth radiates to their siblings. But if siblings were constantly at odds in childhood, perhaps due to parental favoritism or neglect, their rivalry can lie dormant in adulthood, only to be reactivated by later family emergencies. Such crises include caring for elderly parents or carrying out the terms of their wills. Presumably, being asked to assume responsibility for a mentally ill relative could qualify as an "activating" source of hard sibling feelings.

Age has a profound influence on sibling attachments, Dr. Cicirelli reports. In early adulthood, siblings are in the "exploration" stage of life—focusing on their jobs and romantic relationships—which weakens family ties. Later in life siblings pay more attention to their family attachments and are more "protective" of them.

Nevertheless, says Dr. Cicirelli, *siblings tend to maintain in adulthood the relationships they had to one another in childhood.* These relationship patterns have an enormous bearing on how involved siblings are in the lives of their mentally ill relatives.

Variations of Involvement. In a study of siblings of people with schizophrenia, Laina M. Gerace, Ph.D., R.N., professor of psychiatric nursing, and her colleagues at the University of Illinois College of Nursing identified three patterns of involvement: "collaborative," "crisis-oriented," and "detached" (helping only from a distance, such as by giving advice). These patterns, say the researchers, are reflections of family cohesiveness early in the siblings' lives. The closer the family, the more members will collaborate on behalf of an ill sibling. The more troubled the family, the greater the siblings' need to "help" only when absolutely necessary, or from afar.

In my study—which differs from the Gerace study in that it included offspring as well as family members who have severed their family ties—I found similar, although not identical, patterns. Current family "involvement" often, although by no means always, is an extension of the roles these people adopted in childhood. I have termed these roles, outlined in chapter 6, *Custodian*, *Bystander*, and *Adversary*.

Custodian. Forty-eight percent of the offspring in my sample and

37 percent of the siblings are closely involved with their ill relatives, providing emotional and caretaking support. In no case, however, are their psychiatrically disturbed relatives currently living with them. (One man took in his mentally ill brother for a time, but the "experiment" failed when the brother attempted suicide; he was asked to leave.) While some Custodians assume this role grudgingly, most feel a strong sense of obligation toward their parents and/or the ill person.

Bystander. Seventeen percent of the offspring in my sample and 30 percent of the siblings play a less active role in their ill relatives' lives. They are available for emergencies, consultation, and all-round morale boosting. Even those who harbor grudges toward one or more of their kin feel morally bound to help to some degree. But they are not directly involved in the day-to-day care of their afflicted kin.

Adversary. Thirty-three percent of the siblings and 34 percent of the offspring fall into this category. These family members want little or no part of their ill relatives' lives, and are not particularly close to the rest of the family either. Most Adversaries grew up in chaotic or dysfunctional families and fled from them in early adulthood. Others are simply burned-out former Custodians. Some Adversaries occasionally send money to the ill relative, or pull legal or medical strings on their behalf. In general, however, they are not on good terms with their parents and keep a great emotional and, usually, geographic distance from their families.

Role Transitions. These family roles are not set in stone—often they are tempered by the passage of time. For example, some of the people I interviewed pulled away from their families in early adulthood in order to build their careers, find themselves, and repair their own sense of fragility. But now, as they approach middle age, they are softening.

In a serendipitous stroke of journalistic luck, I interviewed a thirty-seven-year-old woman who had only the month before reunited with her schizophrenic mother, having seldom seen or talked to her in over twenty years. Said the daughter:

> My mother called me to tell me that she was considering committing suicide. She wasn't being manipulative. She was just worn out by her

illness. I found myself blurting, "Well, before you do that, why don't you come visit me? Let's get to know each other." I suppose I was just ready to let her back in. As a kid I was her caretaker because my dad always dumped everything on me, and at eighteen I ran away. I started my own business, got a lot of therapy, and began reading books about mental illness. By the time she came to visit me, I was able to relate to her as a human being rather than see her as just a crazy person. It was wonderful. She asked me about my life. She told me about her childhood. She hadn't really changed—I had. Now I'm toying with the idea of having her move nearby so that maybe she'll decide to hang around and live a somewhat okay life. I'm still terrified. I still want to be on the outside and not get involved. But each baby step I take makes it safer to take the next step. I guess what's different this time is that I have a choice in the matter—it's not being forced down my throat.

Other people in my sample are also changing their family roles, in this instance, from total involvement to a more circumspect distance. These family members are focusing on their own needs, often for the first time, and learning to say no both to their parents and to their mentally ill kin. Again, the approach of middle age has a great deal to do with this change.

Terry, fifty, became her schizophrenic brother's caretaker eight years ago, when her parents became too frail to cope with him anymore. Her brother lived in a trailer—when he wasn't in the hospital. Looking after him consumed Terry's life. She kept bailing him out of jail after his myriad public disturbances. She wrangled with the mental health system about getting him disability benefits, treatment, and rehabilitation. She took his dozens of daily phone calls. She nagged him about his refusal to bathe or to take his medications.

And then Terry decided to stop being so long-suffering. She told her brother that if he didn't shape up, she wouldn't have anything to do with him. The announcement transformed her brother, and their relationship. Says Terry:

I guess I just snapped, because nothing I did made any difference. I said to him, "That's it. You're on your own. You can figure out how to get your Social Security payments, where to live, how to make bail.

I am finished with you.'' Well, within twenty-four hours he got himself into treatment. He's living in a halfway house where he follows the rules. He's no longer violent. He's clean and takes his meds. Mentally ill people are capable of *some* volition, some rational thinking. I can't tell you how much better I feel about him. I really look forward to seeing him now, because he's helping himself.

RENEGOTIATED FAMILY TIES: THE IMPERATIVE OF ACCOUNTABILITY

As these case histories make clear, no amount of parental pressure or guilt-giving can induce siblings and offspring to experience a sense of kinship they did not genuinely feel, even if they often go through the motions. When they are coerced into family involvement, rather than having a choice in the matter, they find it increasingly difficult to sustain that involvement.

If my study has taught me anything, it is the importance of resolving family ruptures and renegotiating family relationships so that each member—the sick and the well—can face the future with a measure of integrity, self-esteem, and hope.

The key variable in the outcomes of the family relationships in my study was not family rank, nor psychiatric diagnosis, nor even the availability of good psychiatric care and community support, although obviously these factors played an important part (these issues will be covered in chapter 14).

Rather, the strength of kinship ties depended upon the ability of each family member to hold themselves, *and one another*, accountable for their behavior. The more these individuals were able to take stock of themselves, and to do what they could to improve their own lives, the likelier they were to be able to count on one another for reciprocal love and support. This was true of parents, consumers, and siblings and offspring alike.

Parent Accountability. To some parents, the notion of ''account-ability'' as applied to their disturbed progeny, and to themselves, is anathema. Their ill children "can't help their behavior" because they're victims of their biochemistry. Therefore, parents are also exempt from accountability. In this view, the only people in the family who are "accountable" are well siblings and offspring, who are often held to a higher moral standard by virtue of their normalcy, and who may be judged harshly if they fail to do their "duty."

This double standard does little to promote family solidarity and sincere mutual support. When parents take such a hard line—however understandable their need to deflect a sense of utter failure—they do great harm to themselves and their kin. In denying or equivocating about their own part in family unhappiness, and in constantly covering for their ill children, they often bring about the very family ruptures they wish to avoid, which only adds to their burden.

Most of the adult offspring and siblings I interviewed would give a great deal to hear their parents say words to the effect of, "You were robbed. You were entitled to more. There may have been times when I neglected you, or didn't handle problems well, and I am truly sorry. Can we begin again? Let's not talk about the ill person. Let's talk about us." Such words validate the feelings of young family members and go a long way toward helping them address their sense of fragmentation, unworthiness, and guilt.

A fifty-two-year-old mother I interviewed was able to provide such validation for her well child. For years, she and her husband funneled the bulk of their time, attention, and finances into their schizophrenic daughter's care and medical treatment (today this daughter lives in a halfway house). They didn't notice that their *other* daughter, Nancy, now twenty-five, was slowly unraveling before their eyes. Says the mother:

> At fifteen, Nancy was a drug addict and and an alcoholic. I didn't even know it until she was nineteen, when, on her own, she joined AA. She has since told us that she always knew growing up that she was never the most important child. She remembers lying on her bed, listening to her sister raving, and wishing that somebody would come talk to her. In many ways I was unavailable to her. We've had a lot of family therapy over this, and I wish we had done it sooner. Part of the reason we didn't was that I couldn't bear to think there was anything wrong

with her. When we finally went for family counseling, we all just sobbed and sobbed. I told her I wished I could start over and show her how much I love her. I begged her forgiveness. I told her how proud I was of her and that she gives me so much joy. It helped us to heal as a family. It helped me heal about my other daughter. It made all the difference.

Such parental candor can help offspring to express their own sorrows or grievances and can permit parents themselves to adjust their expectations. Mothers and fathers do well to apply their considerable insights about their ill children to their other children. Parents might ask themselves, for example, whether or not a well child's distancing is due to emotional self-protection and defense, or because the child feels less important than the ill relative, or because of the child's innate temperament, or some combination of these factors.

When children feel accepted and appreciated by their parents, and are allowed to have different points of view, they are more likely to *want* to be involved, in keeping with their own emotional ''set points''—one's inherent way of responding to people. There are many ways offspring and siblings can help, as we shall see in part four, if given the opportunity to do so on their own terms and in their own way.

Consumer Accountability. Most of the mental health researchers and clinicians I interviewed, and most of the studies I read, assert that in all but the rarest cases, people with mental illness are capable of some measure of self-control. Even the most biologically oriented experts *simultaneously* argue that consumers—except for the most catastrophically ill—must be held accountable, if only to a limited degree, for their behavior. The consumers I interviewed also expressed this view. While the yardstick of accountability is lower for people with brain disorders than for the unimpaired, it is not altogether *absent*. Says Laurie Flynn of NAMI:

Consumers aren't saintly victims just because they have mental illness. You have nothing to work with if the person doesn't acknowledge that they have a disorder. It's an adult version of tough love. Relationships

are a two-way street, even if one person has to do 70 percent of the
work. There still has to be something coming from the other side.
There's no reason why individuals with a mental illness, if they have
any insight or any control at all, and most of them do, can't take some
responsibility. They need to understand that until they do, no one else
can really be of much help.

Consumers who are in total denial about their illnesses tend to do
poorly and often suffer repeated hospitalizations and even jail sentences. These people do not take their medications, do not monitor
their symptoms, do not reach out for counseling. Consequently, they
are frequently too ill or too disruptive to live either with their families,
or on their own, or in supervised housing. Some end up on the street.

Most consumers are capable of reversing at least some aspect of
this downward spiraling. Agnes B. Hatfield, Ph.D., in her book, *Family Education in Mental Illness*, argues that consumers do best when
they are allowed to suffer the consequences of their hostile or violent
behavior. Rescuing and eternally bailing them out, excusing and expecting nothing of them, underscores their victimhood. Whereas small
discomforts, such as being denied spending money, often prevent bigger ones, such as hospitalization, by motivating the person to adhere
to a reasonable level of acceptable behavior. They are then encouraged
to try harder, which builds their self-respect, confidence, and functioning. Writes Dr. Hatfield:

> Families should expect that their requirements will be tested and that
> more than likely they will have to apply predetermined sanctions. . . .
> [T]he only discussion . . . relates to the patient's understanding of what
> is expected of him or her. Families must prepare themselves to refuse
> to respond to anything else.

In his book, *Unstable Ideas: Temperament, Cognition, and Self*,
Dr. Jerome Kagan puts the matter more philosophically. He writes:

> [S]ome Americans have become too accepting of Darwin's view that
> "man still bears in his bodily frame the indelible stamp of his lowly

origin.'' An uncritical attitude toward that assumption could make it a self-fulfilling prophecy.

Matt, twenty-seven, whom we met in chapter 1, exemplifies the benefits of being held accountable for one's behavior. Currently he is serving a jail term for committing robbery during a manic episode (he has bipolar disorder). He says that taking responsibility for his criminal behavior and for managing his illness is essential to his recovery. As he puts it:

I can remember pointing the gun at the cashier and saying to myself, ''Wow, she'll have an exciting story to tell tomorrow.'' It scares me now to think how sick I had become. I was a boulder rolling down hill—I had to hit a wall to stop because I couldn't stop myself. It didn't sink in, what I had done and how far gone I was, until the cops called my parents after my arrest. My dad got on the phone and said, ''What happened to you, son?'' It just broke me, hearing the shock and disbelief in his voice. That was the hardest part, realizing how much I had hurt the people I love most, and how much I had screwed up their lives. I am determined not to hurt anyone, including myself, that much again.

Sibling and Offspring Accountability. The junior family members I interviewed who have been able to get beyond their early losses are those who have dug in and done something about their responses to those losses. As we have seen throughout this book, those who remain in the limbo of denial, blame, addictions, abusive relationships, or extreme defensiveness continue to lead shattered lives.

On the other hand, those who have joined support groups, or gone into therapy, and taken the necessary steps to remember—and to mourn—their past family histories are able to stop blaming others for their misfortunes. From this foundation of personal accountability they can then renegotiate their family ties and strengthen them, or at least relinquish their feelings of helplessness and rancor.

It is up to the siblings and offspring of the mentally ill to do something about their losses, and not wait for their families to change. By holding themselves accountable for their own behavior and self-repair, they are able to determine how best to help their ill relatives without sacrificing their own lives and identities.

PART FOUR

TURNING POINTS:
Coming into Your Own

CHAPTER 13

Awakenings:
Getting Help for Yourself

For a long time I had this overwhelming sense that everything in life was an illusion, that there was nothing you could count on. I think it's because in my family, no one ever put limits on my schizophrenic brother or discussed what was going on. At twenty-five, I realized I really needed to talk to somebody about this, and I went to see a therapist. When I told her my story, she looked at me with these big eyes and said, "Oh my God. What happened to you is terrible. How did you survive?" My first reaction was, Gee, was it really that bad? It was the first time anybody ever stood up for me or understood how I felt. It's so important to be able to shout the truth of your own experience.

—Jennifer, 34

The most painful legacy of having a parent or sibling with mental illness is the feeling of utter helplessness, the sense that no matter what you do, nothing will change and no one will listen. The most profound act of courage is to recognize and to engage in the hard work of overcoming that very despair.

Most siblings and offspring feel enormously ambivalent about acknowledging that their shattering experiences have damaged them. Accustomed in childhood to invisibility within their families, seldom encouraged to call attention to their bewilderment and unhappiness, in adulthood it feels faintly treasonous to admit that they might have serious problems of their own.

An undertow of fear tugs at these survivors. The very idea of coming out into the open and declaring their need for help sets off a backlash of self-doubt. Does this mean I'm a "head case" too? What will my parents say—haven't they been through enough? Who am I to complain, when my ill relative is so much more deserving of sympathy and attention?

Was it really that bad?

The tragedy for many family members is that they had been sending up silent cries for help, which went largely unheeded, all along. Says Karen Gail Lewis, Ed.D., coauthor of *Siblings in Therapy: Life Span and Clinical Issues*, who has treated families of the mentally ill in her private practice:

> When parents convey to their well children the message of, "Don't tell me you're sick, I can't handle it," their children often develop secret illnesses. These are indirect ways of saying, "I've got needs." Sometimes they do it through eating disorders, or alcoholism, or medical problems. Or they have business failures or get into lots of accidents. Or they get wound tighter and tighter until finally they just collapse. These people don't talk about their problems to their families or partners or therapists, because the expectation of parents and of society is that they *ought* to be able to cope. They think, I should be able to deal with all this stress. If I can't, I must be crazy.

To make matters worse, almost none of the people in my study were offered individual counseling when they were growing up. To the extent that they ever came in contact with mental health professionals, their experiences were uniformly frustrating. Often it was because their ill kin couldn't get treatment or because doctors wouldn't disclose the disturbed relatives' diagnoses.

What siblings and offspring resented most, however, was being psychological orphans, taken seriously by professionals only in terms of their usefulness to the family-as-treatment team. "Family therapy" was an especially sore subject, even though, as we shall see later in this chapter, it can be enormously beneficial.

Unfortunately, the people I interviewed who had been exposed to family therapy as youngsters—and they were few in number—reported it to have been at best unrewarding and at worst harmful. Either the sessions were always dominated by the parents' difficulties, or the afflicted relative made it seem as though everyone *else* in the family was deranged. The result was that the sufferings of young family members barely registered. Said a man whose brother has schizophrenia:

> My brother's psychiatrist thought he wasn't sick enough to be hospitalized, and that what was really needed was family therapy. So once a week my parents, my brother and I would all go to this guy's office and have these heated discussions about things we were "doing wrong" at home. For a long time I was silent. I didn't feel it was my place to talk about my problems, especially with my brother sitting right there. But I could see that the doctor just wasn't getting it, how this illness was tearing us all apart. So one day I just lost it. I yelled, "You have no idea what it's like! You see us once a week, and my brother can hold it together for one hour. You don't realize how often he gets crazy, running around with knives and trashing the house. I have to have my football buddies come over just to help us control him!" The doctor said, "Is it really that bad?" The next week, my brother was involuntarily hospitalized. That was the end of family therapy.

Despite such experiences with mental health workers, and their own efforts to ignore their pain, most of the siblings and offspring I talked to eventually had to face the reality that they themselves urgently needed help. As much as they wished to deny their own distress, the evidence was all around them—in their shaky relationships, their frayed family ties, their fragile emotions. The only variable was degree.

This awareness usually occurred at key turning points in their lives, when painful memories of the past were inexorably roused. For some, the turning point was a major event, such as leaving home for college; an impending marriage or divorce; the birth of a child; the loss of a job; a move to another city or state; a death in the family. For others the turning point was a medical emergency, such as a heart attack, or surgery, or the illness of a spouse or child. For still others the turning point was an "anniversary reaction" to the ill relative's first hospitalization or suicide.

Whatever the catalyst, these people had reached the end of their ropes. Attention had to be paid—to themselves. The challenge was to build a case *in their own minds* that their troubles were legitimate and worthy of outside intervention and support. Only by recognizing the detritus of their family experiences would they be able to come into their own.

Most of them scarcely knew where to begin.

NAMING THE PROBLEM: THE TRAUMA MODEL

The starting point of self-repair is to find an organizing principle for the survivor's psychological confusion. What follows should not be construed as a one-size-fits-all diagnosis. Nor is this a comment on all people with mental illness, who obviously differ widely in the severity of their impairments and responses to treatment. Rather, what follows is a working model that fits the emotional legacies of the majority of the siblings and offspring I interviewed.

In her book, *Trauma and Recovery*, Judith Lewis Herman, M.D., outlines a unique approach to picking through the tangled emotions that are the residue of prolonged, terrifying experience. Although her book is addressed primarily to survivors of inescapable political or domestic captivity and abuse, many of her findings also apply to siblings and offspring of the mentally ill.

The first order of business is to identify the problem and give it a name. Dr. Herman coined the term ''complex post-traumatic stress disorder'' to describe the painful psychological toll of entrapment. As she defines it, this disorder covers a range of reactions, from ''brief stress'' that clears up without treatment, to major ''personality deformations.''

Symptoms of the disorder can be physical, such as hyperarousal; psychological, such as irritability; or social, such as an inability to form loving attachments; or all three. It is the very range and heterogeneity of symptoms that qualifies the disorder for the adjective ''complex.''

The key concept of Dr. Herman's model is that these symptoms are *normal reactions to abnormal experience* rather than indications of inherent, pre-trauma pathology. As we have seen, most siblings and offspring have felt "entrapped" by a relative's mental illness. Thus, it is not surprising that many of them labor under the weight of innumerable symptoms of trauma, such as emotional numbing, substance abuse, suicidal thoughts, depression, and nervous breakdowns.

Of course, not all family members develop such symptoms. Countless studies have shown that living with madness "impinges" on some children more than others, depending on their own temperaments, sensitivities, sources of outside support, and family circumstances. Still, according to the people I talked to, no one emerges from the experience unscathed.

RESOLVING THE PROBLEM: A THREE-TIERED APPROACH

Recovery from traumatic experience, writes Dr. Herman, entails "a gradual shift from unpredictable danger to reliable safety, from dissociated trauma to acknowledged memory, and from stigmatized isolation to restored social connection."

Thus, getting beyond trauma involves three, not necessarily sequential, tasks, or "stages," which Dr. Herman calls:

- establishment of safety;
- remembrance and mourning;
- reconnection with ordinary life.

For siblings and offspring of the mentally ill, these tasks are eased immeasurably by various forms of intervention. What "works" for one person may not work for another; it depends on one's individual needs, readiness for change, and stage of recovery.

Establishment of Safety. The first task for survivors is to feel safe—unless they do, the other tasks simply cannot be accomplished.

The sense of being in peril is perhaps the most anguishing consequence of living with chronic and unpredictable madness. Many of the people in my study spoke of a persistent feeling of impending danger, of inevitable doom. Long after leaving their families to embark on their adult lives, they continued to feel unsafe in their own bodies, or their relationships, or their environments.

At the core of this anxiety is an inability to trust. In fact, it is this very sense of alienation—of being unmoored in an unfriendly universe—that propelled the overwhelming majority of the people I interviewed into psychotherapy.

Seventy-nine percent of the offspring in my sample, and 74 percent of the siblings, have been or are currently in therapy. Virtually all of them say that it has transformed them. Through therapy, they have restored their faith in themselves and in others, and have regained a sense of control over their lives.

Being able to trust is the single most important ingredient in recovering from the trauma of witnessing madness. Says psychiatrist Jane S. Ferber, M.D.:

> For people who lived in families with psychosis, where the ill person was out of control, the main problem is trust. How do you trust others to remain stable and consistent? These family members say to me, "I'll never trust anyone again as long as I live." That's why it's so humiliating for them to ask for help. If one of your defenses is denial, it's very difficult to admit that you, too, feel helpless. They're afraid that their thoughts and feelings will get so out of control that they'll just dissolve.

One caring person in the form of a seasoned, well-trained, compassionate mental health professional can provide the "safe zone" within which family members can gradually learn to trust, and to put the pieces of their shattered confidence together again. Although therapy is not the *only* way to accomplish this goal, as we shall see in a moment, it is often the most effective way to begin the process. For if you can learn to trust a therapist—whose job is to listen to your worst, most horrific feelings and fantasies and not reject you for them—you can come to trust others.

Building this sense of trust takes time. Young family members are terrified that they'll be judged, or abandoned, or in some way exploited. As Dr. Herman writes, "Trauma robs the victim of a sense of power and control; the guiding principle of recovery is to restore power and control to the survivor.'' Consequently, certain ground rules between the family member and the therapist may be appropriate in order for the family member to feel at ease.

For example, during the establishment of the safety stage, it should be understood that the therapist is the family member's advocate. While this professional "loyalty" may seem obvious, it is not always the case. As we saw earlier, survivors are used to coming last in the family and psychiatric scheme of things and to feeling trivialized.

But mental health workers also have their own legitimate problems. Chief among them is confidentiality. If, for instance, the professional is working with a mentally ill person, that consumer's thoughts and feelings cannot be disclosed to the family member. As an ethical matter, it may be a conflict of interest for these clinicians to give equal priority to consumers and their kin.

For these and other reasons, siblings and offspring may need a therapist of their own—someone in their corner to validate and bear witness to their devastating feelings of inadequacy, humiliation, and injustice. They need someone to stand up for them.

It should also be understood that survivors are not required to "forgive" their ill relatives. Some clinicians may confuse forgiveness with acceptance. The distinction between these two concepts is crucial. Unless therapists themselves have lived with an out-of-control mentally ill parent or sibling, it may be difficult for them to comprehend just how loaded the concept of forgiveness can be for survivors. Many family members told me that "the forgiveness piece" was the hardest to digest. They were having enough trouble just forgiving themselves for asking for help.

To forgive may be divine, but it obliges one to minimize or ignore one's own emotional or psychological wounds. Asking siblings and offspring to "forgive" when what they may need most is *protection* can be traumatic to them. Many parents put extraordinary pressure on their children to "forgive" and be unconditionally loyal to their disturbed, sometimes dangerous relatives. Clinicians may unwittingly add to this pressure in the initial stages of recovery.

For example, the therapist may prematurely offer elaborate scientific explanations for madness. Or the therapist may say of a relative's terrifying behavior, "It's the illness talking." To the vulnerable survivor, this information, however accurate and well-intended, misses the point and may be perceived as insensitivity. What the survivor seeks at this stage is *consolation*. If your ill relative ever held a knife to your throat, or assaulted you out of the blue, or invaded your bed, or never gave you a moment's peace—and no one protected you—it's hard to care *what* or *who* was "talking." You just wanted it to stop.

Countless siblings and offspring of the mentally ill know what it is to feel endangered every time they go home. They must be free of such dangers and attendant fears before they can begin to wrap their minds around anything so complex, and emotionally neutral, as the ill person's brain chemistry.

A more useful therapeutic strategy is to help these family members accept the reality that their relatives have incurable disorders for which survivors are neither to blame nor responsible. Acceptance makes it possible for siblings and offspring ultimately to reach a middle ground of understanding and even of compassion. In this regard, psychoeducation can be enormously beneficial. But not yet. These family members have first to collect themselves. They have a right to love their families provisionally, or from a distance, or not at all, if that's what it takes for them to establish a sense of safety.

Remembrance and Mourning. The second task of recovery follows from the first—feeling safe enough to stir up the memories of their experiences so that they can mourn their losses. These losses include:
- a "normal" childhood;
- a reliable, predictable, protective family haven;
- the well parents' time and attention;
- a fully reciprocal relationship with the ill person;
- a sense that they matter;
- the care and concern of friends and extended family.

The damage inflicted by such losses cannot be overstated. By remembering them and grieving, the harmful defenses of denial, blame, and emotional distancing can be retired.

What makes the task of mourning particularly daunting is that the people around whom the grieving process revolves—the disturbed relatives—are usually still alive. Their personality "death" is both ephemeral and piecemeal. People with mental illness "die" during episodes of hallucination or catatonia or deep depression. Yet in between episodes they are once again "alive" emotionally and intellectually, capable to one degree or another of returning one's love and engaging in stimulating conversation. Several family members spoke of this "Rip Van Winkle" phenomenon. As one survivor described it:

> My mother was in the hospital for months, not knowing me or anyone. She just sat there like a stone, not moving, not talking. She was simply gone. And then one day when I visited her, she looked up at me, smiled, and said, "Read any good books lately?" It blew my mind. I didn't know which version of her was real.

Contributing to this roller coaster of death-rebirth, sick-not-sick is the influence medications can have on the ill relative's personality. For instance, certain drugs have side effects that can cause extreme drowsiness or restlessness or an eerie, almost inhuman calm. They make it hard to figure out where the real person ends and the medicated person begins.

Another reason mourning is so difficult is that if in your mind the person is as good as dead, all hope for any kind of normal relationship, or closure, or reconciliation evaporates.

For these and other reasons, mourning the loss of the ill person's emotional and mental reliability *is not the same as mourning someone's actual physical death*. It is infinitely more complicated. As one survivor eloquently put it:

> You know, "mourning" is a catch-22. There's a way that my sister's illness feels raw all the time, and always will. If I ever felt okay about her condition, I would feel that was a betrayal. Resolution isn't about letting go. It's about staying connected with what's really happening

to her in her own mind. From my point of view it's not a done deal that she's sick. I want to stay connected to the part of her that's alive.

The task of mourning for siblings and offspring of the mentally ill is twofold. First is to accept what in all likelihood may never be, or may be only sometimes—an equal, steady relationship with the ill person. In this sense, mental illness is a lingering death because it is contingent upon the ill person's ups and downs. This aspect of mourning is an arduous, heartbreaking, necessary process. In ways, it never really ends. Grief, like the ill person who inspires it, may live on. In time, however, it will begin to yield its stranglehold.

The other purpose of mourning is for survivors to achieve their own psychological re-birth, contingent only upon themselves. By exhuming the feelings attached to their wrenching, repeated losses, they can then integrate these losses into their consciousness, lay their unhelpful defenses to rest, and begin to invest more fully in their lives, relationships, and futures.

Reconnection with Ordinary Life. The final task of working through one's traumatization is to rejoin the land of the living—to have healthy friendships and intimate attachments upon which to build a new sense of self. Says Jennifer, mentioned at the beginning of this chapter, "I'm tired of being a 'victim,' the eternal 'survivor.' I want some good stuff here."

This task is the "social" part of healing. Siblings and offspring need a support system of loving friends, relatives, and partners who understand their experiences and who can help them believe that they are worthwhile. As Dr. Herman writes:

> Recovery . . . is based upon the empowerment of the survivor and the creation of new connections. Recovery can take place only within the context of relationships; it cannot occur in isolation.

Reconnection is the stage at which survivors can best decide how involved they wish to be with a mentally ill sibling or parent. That involvement is determined both by one's emotional "set point" and by one's progress through the recovery process. For some, close involvement may feel comfortable. For others, a more discrete distance is in order.

With this approach to healing in mind—safety, remembrance, and reconnection—we now address the practical aspects of implementing the tasks of recovery.

PUTTING THEORY INTO PRACTICE: THE "HOW-TO" OF RECOVERY

As Dr. Herman's work suggests, there are many routes to self-repair. There is no magic bullet, no "correct" way to put oneself together again.

For some people, a one-on-one therapeutic relationship is enough to enable them to move on with their lives. For others, a purely "social" approach feels safer than the intimacy of psychotherapy; for them, a support group may be the answer. For still others, a combined approach of individual therapy and peer group support is useful. Moreover, one form of help might work in early adulthood, whereas another might be more suitable later on.

What follows, then, is a brief, and by no means complete, menu of the different kinds of help that are available. (See Appendix for phone numbers and addresses of these and other professional and self-help organizations.)

Choosing a Therapist. As we have seen, the primary purpose of psychotherapy is to give survivors the opportunity to express their own feelings of craziness, their ambivalances, their sorrow, their rage—especially their rage—within the safe harbor of the therapeutic relationship.

Thus, it is imperative that the survivor have a good "fit" with the therapist. Most siblings and offspring have extremely sensitive "antennae." They are adept at picking up on cues of stability and instability in others. This is the very skill upon which survivors can draw in selecting a therapist.

One way to begin the process, of course, is by word of mouth. If someone you respect has been successfully treated by a clinician, that recommendation is worth seeking a consultation with the clinician, who in all likelihood will refer you to a colleague. Another way to find a therapist is by asking your family doctor, or someone in the psychiatry department of a teaching hospital, for a referral.

During the initial visit, the clinician will want to know a great deal about you and your family history. The more details you can give, the better the person will be able to assess the scope of your difficulties.

Likewise, you need to find out certain things about the clinician. For instance, you should ascertain the therapist's professional training and experience, especially whether or not he or she has worked with siblings and offspring of the mentally ill. Such training is vital.

In a study of twenty siblings of chronically mentally ill people, social worker Joanne L. Riebschleger found that clinicians often are unaware of the specific issues of young family members. One such issue is that siblings want professionals to talk to them in *realspeak*, not in medical jargon or "diagnostic double-talk." Ms. Riebschleger writes:

> The social worker should . . . facilitate the healthy expression of grief and loss. A simple but important request of sibling respondents was that the worker openly use the words "crazy" and "mentally ill" to give the message that mental illness is not too shameful to talk about.

The clinician should also know about the biological aspects of mental illness. Many survivors may wonder if they are at risk for developing a severe and chronic brain disorder. Therapists who are not M.D.s can refer patients to psychiatrists to do a thorough workup with the survivor to rule out that possibility, or to spot it if it exists and perhaps recommend drug treatment.

It's helpful, too, if the clinician has special knowledge about the sibling relationship. As we saw in chapter 3, siblings have as much influence—sometimes, more—on one another as parents have on their children. For example, siblings who have distanced themselves from their disturbed brothers and sisters are often mired in guilt and feelings of estrangement. Unfortunately, many therapists lack training in the sibling attachment.

While specific forms of training are significant, most therapists have at least a working knowledge of these specialties and will honestly say when they feel their expertise does not fit their clients' needs. Clients have the right to reach the same conclusion and to consult with someone else.

The most important ingredient in choosing a therapist is a gut feeling about the person. One should not feel condescended to nor sense that the clinician is rigidly imposing his or her point of view. What matters is *the client's* point of view, and how he or she may wish to alter or improve it.

Schools of Therapeutic Thought. However, it's important to know the therapist's general philosophy about the goals of therapy because it will, in part, determine the length of time that will be devoted to the therapeutic process.

For most survivors who endured chronic neglect, abuse, and family chaos in childhood, there is no quick fix. Dr. Herman has found that just telling one's story, just getting out the words, can take months. She writes:

> Programs that promote the rapid uncovering of traumatic memories without providing an adequate context for integration are therapeutically irresponsible and potentially dangerous, for they leave the patient without the resources to cope with the memories uncovered.

Many of the survivors I interviewed were deeply, sometimes catastrophically, wounded by their family experiences. For these people, insight-oriented psychotherapy, in which the survivor delves into the past, may be appropriate. This can be a painful and seemingly endless business. It took time to feel helpless and disconsolate. It will take time to undo the damage.

As has been said, not all siblings and offspring have been psychologically ravaged by their relatives' illnesses. For these survivors, short-term or "brief" therapy can be extraordinarily productive. As we saw in chapter 8, one such approach is psychoeducation. According to psychiatrist Demitri Papolos, M.D., who conducts psychoeducation courses for families, this form of therapy can get results that often aren't possible in individual therapy, and in a shorter period of time. He says:

> There are underlying dynamics in families that can be improved in ten to fifteen sessions. One of the issues we deal with is denial on the parts of psychiatric patients and family members. Another issue is, who are the caretakers in the family? Some siblings were profoundly affected by their parents' always being involved with the ill person. When you can acknowledge these problems and talk about them openly, it helps people confront their conflicts in the family and learn to set limits. It reduces everyone's stress levels.

Clarice J. Kestenbaum, M.D., director of training in the division of child and adolescent psychiatry at Columbia University's College of Physicians and Surgeons, is another ardent advocate of family therapy. She says:

> When you're talking about children who stayed away from their mentally ill siblings, or who are afraid "it's catching," the best possible treatment is family therapy. Sometimes you can have family therapy where you work with each member alone and sometimes in groups of family members as well as all together. All of them get to talk about assessing what it was like living with the ill person and what their own problems were, such as being too young to handle the situation. The sibs get to work out their relationships in ways they can't by themselves.

Another form of brief therapy is called cognitive therapy, which can usually be accomplished in approximately twelve weeks. Cognitive therapists argue that psychological despair is a function not so much of our experiences but, rather, how we *think* about them.

According to Martin E. P. Seligman, Ph.D., the way we feel about events in our lives is governed by how we process information, which in turn determines our behavior. Dr. Seligman calls this phenomenon "explanatory style." For example, if you believe that bad things happen because of a flaw within yourself, you will tend to have low self-regard. Even if good things happen, you'll think it's because of luck rather than effort. Writes Dr. Seligman, "[P]essimistic habits of thinking can transform mere setbacks into disasters." But if you are a person who thinks that bad things occur because of some outside force, or that they are only temporary, you'll believe that your own efforts will produce positive results.

Cognitive therapy can alter how we think by teaching specific skills that enable us to "bounce back" from adversity. For instance, we can learn to recognize self-defeating thought patterns and beliefs and dispute them by marshalling evidence in our own lives of talent or success, and then think and behave more optimistically. Acting on positive beliefs is the process by which explanatory style is changed. Mastery of one problem leads to mastery in others.

Of course, beliefs are not easily dislodged, particularly if they are the result of painful, repeated traumatization. The facts of the lived experience can never be minimized.

Psychologist C. R. Snyder, Ph.D., who has researched the dynamics of hope, and his colleagues at the University of Kansas argue that the absence of negative thinking is not enough to produce optimism. One must also have a sense of "agency"—that is, that one's goals can be met. Thus one needs both the "will" and the "way," which together are the essence of hope.

One "way" to implement one's "will" is self-help groups—specifically those that are tailored to the mentally ill and their families. Neither interpersonal nor cognitive therapy can operate in a vacuum. It's one thing to hope that your therapist will understand you. It's another to know that other people have been in your metaphorical shoes, can identify with your problems, and can serve as true role models. Moving beyond loss requires the *opportunity* to implement the self-esteem acquired in therapy, with the encouragment of like-minded others. One way this goal can be accomplished is to join a support group.

Collective Courage: Support Groups. As increasing numbers of people with mental illness have been deinstitutionalized and sent back to the community to live, families have begun to organize on their behalf and to give one another support.

The largest of such organizations is the *National Alliance for the Mentally Ill* (NAMI), headquartered in Arlington, Virginia. NAMI is comprised of over 140,000 members in nearly 1,100 affliate AMI groups in all 50 states. The majority of members are families and friends of people with severe mental illness. Among NAMI's goals are self-help, public education, and advocacy at the federal, state, and local levels to lobby for increased funding for research and quality services.

In my study, 49 percent of the offspring, and 41 percent of the siblings, belong to NAMI. While most of them have also had therapy, some prefer NAMI to the psychotherapies because it provides the solace of therapy without the implications of I'm-okay-and-you're-not, as well as the comfort of common experience. Within NAMI, there are "special interest" support groups tailored to the individual needs of its members. The Sibling and Adult Children's Council, for example, addresses the conflicts and ambivalences that are specific to them. The purpose of SAC groups is to provide a forum within which to share one's experience; to help members overcome their survivor guilt; to give one another reality checks; to mourn the loss of a stable family; and to cope with the stigma of having a mentally ill relative.

The *National Depressive and Manic-Depressive Association* (NDMDA), whose main office is in Chicago, is the nation's largest patient-directed self-help organization, with approximately 275 affiliate chapters across the country. NDMDA provides education and support groups for patients and their families; dispenses information about treatments for affective disorders; and offers lists of recommended mental health professionals.

Other groups have formed to serve the needs of siblings of "special needs" children. These groups address many of the same practical and psychological issues that relatives of the mentally ill face. One such group is *Siblings for Significant Change*, which serves the New York City metropolitan region. This organization disseminates information about disabilities, conducts conferences and workshops, gives support to its members, and provides information about crisis intervention.

The *Sibling Support Project*, located at the Children's Hospital and Medical Center in Seattle, Washington, works with state-level agencies across the country to provide training seminars for family members and health care workers about the particular concerns of siblings of disabled children. The organization also teaches agency personnel how to create peer support, educational, and recreational programs, called "Sibshops," for school-age siblings ages eight to thirteen. In addition, it addresses the problem of what will happen to ill brothers and sisters when their parents age and die (the other organizations also address this problem).

Finally, there is the *Sibling Information Network*, located at the University of Connecticut. This group, in addition to providing educational material about and for brothers and sisters of disabled children, also serves as a clearinghouse of information about assorted sibling support groups across the country.

FAMILY INVOLVEMENT: FINDING YOUR EMOTIONAL "SET POINT"

I have reserved for the end of this chapter the question of how involved siblings and offspring can be, or ought to be, with their afflicted relatives and parents, both now and in the future. This issue is best confronted only after one no longer feels raw—that is, when one is well on the road to untangling and resolving the emotional damage of a relative's mental illness.

In reading through countless studies, the literature of self-help groups, and in interviewing dozens of young family members and mental health practitioners, it was impossible not to reach the conclusion that when it comes to involvement, the word "ought" needs to be replaced with the word "choice." Siblings and adult children must decide this issue for themselves, based on their personalities, needs, and the tenor of their family ties.

The most useful guidepost for family involvement is your own emotional "set point"—your intrinsic temperament and way of being in the world. A good indicator of this set point is how you respond generally to people in various situations, and not just with kin. For example, extroverted, physically demonstrative people are most themselves when they are on intimate or close terms with others. More circumspect, reserved types, on the other hand, are more comfortable only if people aren't too close, too invasive.

Just as there are many ways to *be*, there are many ways to *help*. There are innumerable means by which you can demonstrate your concern for your family without violating either your integrity or your comfort level. Indeed, your comfort level is the only barometer for involvement—not what others may say of it. Unless it is respected, siblings and offspring who severed all ties with their relatives may feel they have no alternative but to stay away.

Dr. Karen Gail Lewis summarized for me the various ways siblings and offspring of the mentally ill can help their families—*should they choose to do so*—based on their emotional set points and individual talents.

People always have very good reasons for keeping their distance from their families. But that doesn't mean they don't want to help. Siblings who want to remain uninvolved with the ill person can still be of important help to the others. I can imagine a scenario where one sibling might say to a caregiver, "I cannot be with the ill person. It's too threatening. But here's what I can do for *you*. I will support you if you need to ventilate and talk. I will be there for you." Or siblings can agree to divvy up responsibilities. One can volunteer to be the person who will call the doctor when the relative needs to be hospitalized. Another can offer to baby-sit for the caretaker. Another can send money to help the ill person financially. The point is that they all need to talk about it, and accept each other's way of helping.

Intriguingly, the siblings I interviewed who effected the most positive change in their afflicted kin were not always those who continually rescued and sacrificed their lives for them. Rather, it was the siblings who, by virtue of their distancing, greater objectivity, and candor, frequently inspired the best that their ill relatives had to give.

Among the people I interviewed, there were poignant reversals of family misfortune when they were finally able to create this therapeutic distance. This usually happened when the parents were too old to take care of the ill child or when the parents died.

Nancy, fifty-five, whose sister has schizophrenia, could well have been speaking for these family members when she told me,

My sister and I were never close, ever. But when our parents died, the relationship changed, not because of her illness but because of the emotional distance between us. Her illness was so traumatic for me that for a long time I just stayed away. Then she fell into my lap. I did everything I could to get her good medical treatment, but I could only keep it up if she did more to help herself, and she knew it. She listens when I tell her not to lay more on me than I can take. In a way, her illness has been a window of opportunity for both of us. The amazing thing is that we're closer than we've ever been. We're so open with each other now, and it was never like that in our family. You didn't talk about anything. Because of my sister, I have more of a sense of community with people. I've learned to reach out, and to be compassionate to others. And I have so much admiration for how hard my sister has worked to handle her illness. We're both better people for everything we've been through together.

CHAPTER 14

Transformed Lives:
Finding Meaning and Hope in
the Aftermath

Siblings and adult children of the mentally ill are the pioneers. We're not going to be silent and just stay in the closet. You can't ask us to be the future caregivers and expect us to keep secret what we have been through. We're tired of feeling guilty for being normal. We're tired of being ignored. We lived in such debilitating circumstances that those of us who made it out must *say how we did it. We must become advocates and help the next generation so they won't feel as alone as we did. Otherwise, our survival won't have any meaning, and we'll never be able to pull together on behalf of the mentally ill.*

—Emily, 45

The greatest antidote to despair is to glean a sense of purpose from one's suffering, to have something to fight for.

The people whose voices have been heard throughout this book all expressed a longing to make their devastating experiences count for something. They wanted to transform their sorrows into causes for hope. They wanted to make a difference.

Indeed, it was the keen desire to help others that motivated them to participate in my study in the first place, even though it was painful for them. They wanted to bear witness to the ravages of mental illness and its impact on families, and to offer suggestions as to what can be done about it. For they know better than anyone what happens when nothing is done.

At the end of all my interviews, I asked this question: "If you could gather all the mental health workers and policy makers of the world into one room and make them listen to you, what message would you give them?'' The question opened a floodgate of ideas— an agenda, if you will, for the future.

1. The Need for More Accessible and Improved Treatment for the Mentally Ill

Countless families of the mentally ill are on the brink of bankruptcy. Often it's because their ill relatives cannot get treatment due to cuts in state health care budgets and tight eligibility restrictions. More often it's because insurance for mental illness is not always available or has higher copayments than for physical illness. This inequity reverberates throughout the health care system despite the fact that mental illness has higher treatment success rates than many other serious medical disorders.

According to NIMH, each year an estimated 35 million adult Americans are afflicted by severe brain disorders. The amount of federal dollars spent per person to research these disorders is approximately $2.00 per year. By contrast, approximately 1 million Americans are diagnosed with cancer annually. The per-person amount of federal funding devoted to research this illness is $7.13.

Families have become their afflicted relatives' de facto treatment teams, usually because they have no choice. Asking them to ''treat'' mental illness, when what is needed is professional interventions such as medication, therapy, hospitalization, and rehabilitation, is like asking families to ''treat'' cancer or any other medical condition.

Mental illness can result in suicide, homelessness, violence, unemployment, substance abuse, and shattered families, and it costs the United States nearly $150 billion per year for treatment, social service and disability payments, and lost productivity. When you factor in costs to police, shelters, and the criminal justice system, the total bill is considerably higher.

Studies demonstrate that if brain disorders were appropriately diagnosed and treated with ongoing services, the amount now spent to hospitalize the mentally ill repeatedly on an emergency basis would be greatly reduced.

2. Safety: The Issue of Patients' Versus Society's "Rights"

Another concern expressed by the people I interviewed is the issue of personal and public safety.

A small percentage of the mentally ill, *when they are untreated,* become physically violent, often in response to voices in their heads that persuade them that their lives are in jeopardy. Others are extremely threatening and verbally abusive. Their families bear the physical and psychological scars.

It is a point of bitter irony that when these consumers are out of control, the first call their families usually make is to the police rather than to a doctor. That's because in many states it is virtually impossible to get a delusional or hallucinating individual into a hospital against his or her will unless the person is a "danger to himself or others."

This means that the person must actually have injured or killed someone—and not just threatened to do so—before he or she can be involuntarily committed. Even then, the person may be released prematurely, with no mandatory follow-up treatment. The result is that many families live in a state of prolonged terror that ends only when the ill person breaks the law and the police can be summoned.

"Our jails have . . . become surrogate mental hospitals." So concludes psychiatrist E. Fuller Torrey, M.D., and his colleagues in a 1992 report titled "Criminalizing the Seriously Mentally Ill: The Abuse of Jails as Mental Hospitals." An estimated 7.2 percent of jail inmates suffer from severe mental illness. The reason for this high percentage, say the authors, is the failure of state and local governments to provide necessary services for the deinstitutionalized mentally ill.

Civil libertarians, and many consumers, argue that the mentally ill have rights, among them *not* to be medically treated. But it seems to countless family members that their own right to safety is violated by this legal position.

It would also seem that the rights of the mentally ill *themselves* are violated by withholding treatment from them when they are too sick to made sound judgments. A humane approach would be to make judgments on their behalf until they are able to do so for themselves. Says a consumer I interviewed who has schizophrenia:

> The cultural expectation must be that people are responsible for their lives. You don't make an exception for the mentally ill. You do make an exception in terms of intent and consequence. Someone who beats his sister because he has schizophrenia does not have the same intent as a normal person who beats his sister. If a schizophrenic is a threat to society, he shouldn't be dealt with in the criminal justice system. He should be put away in a hospital. No exceptions.

If the laws of the land were rewritten to reflect society's rights to safety, some family members might not feel compelled to put as much distance as possible between themselves and their afflicted relatives.

3. Mining Untapped Resources: The Expertise of Family Members

Families of the mentally ill often wonder what the theories, diagnoses, and treatment recommendations of mental health professionals would be if they were required to spend a month in the constant company of someone who has severe schizophrenia, bipolar disorder, or depression. Unless you have lived with such a person—or have mental illness yourself—you simply cannot know what it's like, or what it does to families.

Siblings and offspring know what it's like. They know the whole person *behind* the illness—the best, the worst, the brilliant, the delusional, the loving, the frightening, the courageous, the irresponsible— who has been there all along. And they know what their parents are, or aren't, doing to help the ill person. Yet seldom are these family members consulted by professionals about the day-to-day behavior of their mentally ill relatives, let alone about the long-term treatment of those relatives.

Family members are a treasure trove of information, as thoughtful researchers have discovered. Family members are living laboratories in which the interactions between nurture and nature are played out.

For this reason, they must be included in studies and consulted in treatment plans.

4. Harvest of Shame: Combating Stigmatization

In 1995, *New York Times* columnist A. M. Rosenthal wrote,

> If a person breaks a leg on the street, civil help tends to him quickly—ambulance, doctors, police. Break your mind and you lie there. . . . Why are there so many mentally ill people cut off from help?

The answer is "stigma," defined in Merriam-Webster's Collegiate Dictionary, Tenth Edition, as "a mark of shame or discredit." People with brain disorders, and their families, often say that being stigmatized is harder to bear than the illnesses.

Stigma causes people to fear and to discriminate against the mentally ill. Stigma causes the mentally ill to refuse to acknowledge that they are sick. Stigma causes siblings and offspring to feel too ashamed to talk about their problems or ask for help. And stigma can cause some parents to deny that their seriously disturbed children have anything wrong with them, with horrifying results, as we have seen.

Stigma affects all levels of society, not only the uninformed public but also some mental health professionals, many lawmakers, and far too many policy makers.

With so many people suffering from mental illness, and with so many family members directly affected by it—an estimated 100 million Americans—it is astounding that it should be considered a rare and shameful condition.

The only way to combat stigma is massive public education. The warning signs of mental illnesses should be taught in every school health class, posted alongside those of other widespread illnesses.

Many siblings and adult children of the mentally ill are trying to combat stigma by telling others that they have mental illness in their families. Coming forward takes extraordinary courage because it can have distressing social repercussions—for example, the possible loss of friends and lovers who may know little about brain disorders. But simply telling one sympathetic friend helps to dispel the myths about mental illness.

Some survivors have taken a more public stance, giving speeches and writing books about mental illness in their families. The more information people have about psychiatric disorders, the greater the chance that stigma will disappear.

5. Wasted Talent: Educating Employers

In recent years, dozens of world-famous victims of mental illness have bravely discussed their conditions publicly. Such achievers as actors Patty Duke and Rod Steiger, Nobel laureate Salvador Luria, television newscaster Mike Wallace, Governor Lawton Chiles of Florida, and humorist Art Buchwald all have been treated for serious brain disorders and gone on the record about them.

Of course, these people "went public" about their disorders after they became successful, and would not be pauperized as a result of their disclosures. Unfortunately, many people with mental illness never get the chance to succeed, particularly if their conditions become known to unenlightened employers.

People with mental illness are everywhere, and most of those who receive treatment are as capable of performing their jobs as, say, people with diabetes. Depending on the severity of their illnesses, consumers may occasionally have to excuse themselves when their symptoms flare up. But so do people who have the flu or require kidney dialysis.

Under the 1990 Americans with Disabilities Act, people with mental illness must receive the same protection in the workplace as people with other disabilities. They cannot be fired or denied employment solely on the basis of having an illness unless the illness poses "undue hardship on the employer."

6. The Question of Biological Determinism

Although mental illness is considered by experts to be a disorder or a disease, there are perils in "medicalizing" all aberrant human behavior. Any discussion of the diagnosis and treatment of mental illness must also address the environmental and social ills that often trigger it. As Dr. Jerome Kagan has written, "[W]e should remain on guard against biological determinism that is so extreme it ignores the contributions of experience."

Some members of the scientific and psychological communities seem to be engaged in a kind of holy war, eager to prove themselves right and their ideological opponents wrong. The debate centers on whether or not brain disorders are caused by imperfect nature or flawed nurturing. Siblings and children of the mentally ill are caught in the ideological crossfire, as are consumers themselves.

The dangers of rigidly adhering either to the nature camp or the nurture camp are obvious. If mental illness is all in your biology, abusive parents are off the hook and prevention is moot. The purely biological viewpoint does not explain the nagging reality that an estimated 40 to 60 percent of psychiatric patients report that they were physically or sexually abused in their childhoods.

On the other hand, if mental illness is entirely a consequence of early childhood experience, that doesn't explain the equally nagging reality that innumerable loving, supportive parents, through no fault of their own, sometimes produce children with severe brain disorders.

Diagnoses and treatments may reflect these differing ideologies. People who desperately need biochemical intervention may be told instead to examine and talk about their family dynamics. People who desperately need psychotherapy may be told to take a pill. People who need both may be only half-treated.

Somewhere in the thickets of psychiatric specialization, the vulnerable human being—and his or her family—seems to have been lost. As Susanna Kayson writes in her book, *Girl, Interrupted*, which chronicles her struggles with mental illness:

> For nearly a century the psychoanalysts have been writing op-ed pieces about the workings of a country they've never traveled to, a place that . . . has been off-limits. Suddenly, the country has opened its borders and is crawling with foreign correspondents; neurobiologists are filing ten stories a week, filled with new data. These two groups of writers, however, don't seem to read each other's work. That's because the

analysts are writing about a country they call Mind and the neuroscientists are reporting from a country they call Brain.

William Styron, in his book, *Darkness Visible: A Memoir of Madness*, expresses the same view.

> The intense and sometimes comically strident factionalism that exists in present-day psychiatry—the schism between the believers in psychotherapy and the adherents of pharmacology—resembles the medical quarrels of the eighteenth century (to bleed or not to bleed) and almost defines in itself the inexplicable nature of depression and the difficulty of its treatment.

This lack of professional collaboration has tragic consequences for consumers and their families who can't seem to get straight answers that fit their individual circumstances. It is *essential* that researchers and clinicians pool their talents and findings. In this regard, psychologist Marvin R. Goldfried, Ph.D., fired a warning shot across the ideological bow in 1982 when he wrote:

> What may be needed to get us to mobilize our cooperative efforts is *an attack from outside the system itself.* . . . The pressure from governmental agencies and insurance companies—as well as the growing consumer movement—to have us demonstrate the efficacy of our intervention procedures may very well serve as the necessary impetus for the cooperative effort the field so sorely needs.

7. The Imperative of Prevention

Just as the needs of the mentally ill urgently require professional help, so, too, do their siblings and offspring. Attention *must* be paid to the prevention of mental illness, and not just to its treatment.

In a 1992 report by the National Mental Health Association called "America's Children Under Stress: Understanding and Preventing the Consequences," L. Patt Franciosi wrote:

We today need to . . . develop a systematic immunization process for the mental health needs of our children, to protect those children, to help them build and grow the antibodies that are desperately needed to buffer them against some of the stressors that have been identified in our society. There are between seven and nine million children in the United States who have been diagnosed with a severe emotional or mental disability. Just as with physical health, we will never prevent all of the mental illnesses that our children may develop. But we can begin to lessen the figures. As a society, we will never have enough dollars to treat all of the individuals who need mental health care. We must begin to focus on prevention efforts.

Some of the scientists I interviewed told me that severe mental illness cannot be prevented; it can only be managed. While this may be true of schizophrenia and bipolar disorder—both of which have robust genetic implications—the same cannot be said of *all* mental illnesses *all the time*. There is considerable scientific evidence that chaotic environments can induce severe manifestations of brain disorders, and in some cases may cause them.

The question of preventability is not about certainty but, rather, about odds. As professors of human development Robert Plomin, Ph.D., and Denise Daniels, Ph.D., have written:

The findings of greatest social significance to emerge from human behavioral-genetic research to date involve nurture, not nature. . . . In the rush to find neural causes of schizophrenia, who is now studying the major source of variability—the environment?

A profound sense of hopelessness can settle over even the most optimistic and resilient children when they are driven to the limits of their endurance by stressful environments and neglect.

But when we pay attention to the ways in which we raise our children—encouraging their strengths, reassuring them when they are afraid, respecting their individuality, recognizing and getting treatment for their ailments—we are, in fact, doing a great deal to prevent mental illness, or at least its most anguishing aspects.

8. *Hope in the Aftermath: The Importance of Advocacy*

Mental illness is not just a family matter. Because it affects so many people, and because good treatment is so hard to get, it has become a social and political matter as well.

Family members who have lived with madness are in the best possible position to do something about it by becoming advocates on behalf of the mentally ill and their families. Almost half the siblings and offspring I interviewed have taken up the banner of advocacy by joining the National Alliance for the Mentally Ill. They can be seen charging up Capitol Hill in Washington, D.C., or into their state and local legislatures, armed with sheets of "talking points" to persuade their government representatives to address the real needs of the millions of ordinary Americans who have extraordinary problems.

There are other less public but no less persuasive ways in which to change public opinion. In volunteering to be interviewed, the siblings and offspring I talked to have become advocates. Some worried that they might be recognizable to their ill and well relatives or friends—despite elaborate promises of journalistic disguisement—but did it anyhow. They felt it was vitally important to bear witness to their ill relatives' and their own struggles.

The very act of testifying, whether by anonymous interview or public disclosure and advocacy, can have transforming psychological effects on the testifier. In a University of Michigan study, psychologist Deborrah E. S. Frable discovered that people with culturally stigmatized and concealable characteristics are more inclined to feel unique—hence, alone—than people who are obviously and visibly "different." But when these "invisible" people come into contact with others who are like them, they feel less stigmatized.

Dr. Frable's study subjects were classified into three groups. The first had invisible characteristics or conditions which, if known to the general public, could lead to their cultural stigmatization—for example, gays, epileptics, juvenile delinquents, incest victims, and people with impaired hearing. The second group had obvious "marginalizing" conditions, such as being black or obese. The third group were "normals."

People with invisible, culturally devalued conditions felt like perpetual outsiders, and knew fewer people like themselves, than the people in the other groups. They also tended to form perceptions of themselves that reflected the stereotypes attached to their "conditions." But when they "came out" and found others like them, they felt less isolated and were able to correct their distorted self-perceptions. Writes Dr. Frable:

> [I]ndividuals in the process of becoming knowledgeable about their group—those who attend support functions, wear identification tags, act as activists—will meet similar peers, develop a more differentiated group view, and over time come to feel less unique.

Trudy L. Mason, introduced in chapter 11, put it more simply. Every time she gives a speech about being the sibling of someone with mental illness, at least one member of the audience comes up to her afterward and says, "Thank you. I thought I was the only one." The effect on Trudy is always the same. She says, "I know this sounds trite, but it makes everything I've gone through worth it."

FINAL THOUGHTS

For those of us who have lived with or witnessed a relative's mental disintegration, emotions can be dangerous territory. We sometimes need reminding that they are the essence of being human.

A couple of years ago, when I was still in the research stage of this book, an avalanche of events in my life caused me to feel that my mind was coming apart. My mother, to whom I had never been close, died. My husband and I moved to another community, where we knew no one. A close relative was diagnosed with terminal cancer.

There came a day—actually, many, many days—when, uncharacteristically, I couldn't stop crying. It scared the hell out of me. I couldn't understand why I was unable to shake it, this overwhelming, unbearable sadness. After all, I had finished therapy. Or so I thought.

Feeling desperate, I called my therapist, and fortunately, she was able to see me immediately. As I drove to her office, it suddenly occurred to me that this is what my sister, Deborah, had been struggling with all her life, this sense of being inches from cracking up. Maybe I had just been living on borrowed time. Maybe it was my turn to break down.

When I arrived for my appointment, for the first fifteen minutes I sat and sobbed uncontrollably. When at last I was able to catch my breath and tell the therapist my fears, she looked at me and gently said, "You do not have mental illness. This is called life. You are simply being human. How could you expect to have all these things happening at once and not feel terrible sorrow? If you *didn't* feel this way, I'd be worried."

We sat there for a while, neither of us speaking. Then she smiled and said, "You know, you're one of the lucky ones. You get to feel everything and still not lose your mind. You and your sister are not the same person. But perhaps now you understand her a little better."

I have thought about that day, and its parallels to all the days of my sister's life, a great deal. I have also thought about that day long ago when I visited Deborah in the hospital and she asked me, "Do you think I'm crazy?"

In researching and writing this book, I have been able to find the answers my sister was never able to give me. To the people with mental illness who generously allowed me to interview them—who told me what it's like to have a brain disorder and how it makes them think and feel—I am grateful beyond measure. Through them, I feel a connection to my sister.

To all the siblings and offspring who confirmed my own feelings of loss and alienation, I owe a debt I can never repay. Because of them, I no longer feel unmoored.

The worst thing in the world is not to be heard, not to be understood. My greatest wish is that this book will bring comfort to the siblings and offspring of the mentally ill—as it has to me—who feel that no one will listen, and that they have nowhere to turn. They are not, and need not be, alone.

APPENDIX

Sources for Information and Support

The National Alliance for the Mentally Ill (NAMI) has literature and support groups for siblings, offspring, parents, partners, other relatives and friends, as well as consumers. NAMI has chapters in all fifty states. To locate a group in your area, or to obtain information regarding starting either a Siblings and Adult Children or Spouses and Partners support group yourself, call or write to NAMI's national headquarters:

National Alliance for the Mentally Ill
200 North Glebe Road
Suite 1015
Arlington, VA 22203-3754
703-524-7600 FAX 703-524-9094
800-950-NAMI

The National Depressive and Manic-Depressive Association, or NDMDA, for consumers and their families, has chapters in most states. Call or write to the organization's national headquarters:

National Depressive and Manic-Depressive Association
730 North Franklin Street
Suite 501
Chicago, IL 60610-3526
312-642-0049 FAX 312-642-7243
800-82-NDMDA

Siblings of people with disabilities can get literature and information from the following sources:

Siblings for Significant Change
United Charities Building
105 East 22nd Street
New York, NY 10010
212-420-0776

Sibling Support Project
Children's Hospital & Medical Center
4800 Sand Point Way N.E.
P.O. Box 5371
Seattle, WA 98105-0371
206-368-4911
FAX 206-368-4816

Sibling Information Network
The University of Connecticut
A. J. Pappanikou Center
249 Glenbrook Road, U-64
Storrs, CT 06269-2064
203-486-4985

The National Institute of Mental Health publishes a variety of extremely useful pamphlets about various brain disorders. These publications, available at the addresses listed below, describe the symptoms, causes, and treatments, and are free. Three in particular are worthy of note: "Depressive Illnesses: Treatments Bring New Hope," "Schizophrenia: Questions and Answers," and "Understanding Panic Disorder."

For information about depression, NIMH has developed a public education program called D/ART (an acronym for Depression Awareness, Recognition and Treatment). Call or write to:

D/ART, NIMH
5600 Fishers Lane, Room 10-85
Rockville, MD 20857
301-443-4140
For a free brochure call 800-421-4211.

For information about schizophenia, write:

Public Inquiries Branch
National Institute of Mental of Mental Health
Room 15C-05
5600 Fishers Lane
Rockville, MD 20857

For information about panic disorders, call the NIMH Panic Disorder Education Program at 800-64-PANIC, or write to the above address.

The following organizations also provide information about mental illnesses:

American Psychiatric Association
1400 K Street, N.W.
Washington, DC 20005
202-682-6220

American Psychological Association
750 First Street, N.E.
Washington, DC 20002-4242
202-336-5500

The American Suicide Foundation
1045 Park Avenue
New York, NY 10028
800-531-4477

Anxiety Disorders Association of America
6000 Executive Boulevard
Suite 513
Rockville, MD 20852
301-231-9350

Center for Psychiatric Rehabilitation
Boston University
930 Commonwealth Avenue
Boston, MA 02215
617-353-3549

National Mental Health Association
1201 Prince Street
Alexandria, VA 22314-2917
800-969-NMHA

National Mental Health Consumers'
Self-Help Clearinghouse
311 South Juniper Street
Suite 1000
Philadelphia, PA 19107
800-553-4539

Obsessive Compulsive Foundation
P.O. Box 70
Milford, CT 06460
203-878-5669

NOTES

Unattributed quotations are from interviews conducted by the author.

INTRODUCTION: EXPERT WITNESSES: THE UNIQUE AUTHORITY AND TRAUMAS OF FAMILY MEMBERS

p. 2 "over five million" National Institute of Mental Health, "Prevalence & Costs of Mental Disorders," March 16, 1995.

p. 2 "An estimated ten percent" Ibid.

p. 3 "As to lifetime prevalence" "Lifetime and 12-Month Prevalence of *DSM-III-R* Psychiatric Disorders in the United States: Results from the National Comorbidity Survey," by Ronald C. Kessler, Ph.D., Katherine A. McGonagle, Ph.D., Shanyang Zhao, Ph.D., et al., *Archives of General Psychiatry*, Vol. 51, Jan. 1994, pp. 8–19.

CHAPTER 1: SHATTERED FAMILIES: WHEN LIGHTNING STRIKES

p. 20 "the age of onset . . . as young as five." *Diagnostic and Statistical Manual of Mental Disorders*, Fourth Edition, Washington, DC: American Psychiatric Association, 1994, p. 281.

p. 20 "Manic-depression can also" *Overcoming Depression*, Revised Edition, by Demitri F. Papolos, M.D., and Janice Papolos, NY: Harper-Perennial, 1992, p. 215.

p. 20 "as young as the age of five" Ibid, p. 219.

p. 25 "a higher treatment success rate" "Mental Illness," by Charles S. Clark, *CQ Researcher*, Congressional Quarterly Inc., Aug. 6, 1993, Vol. 3, No. 29, p. 675.

p. 25 " 'clubs to knock a man down with.' " *William James on Exceptional States: The 1896 Lowell Lectures*, reconstructed by Eugene Taylor, NY: Charles Scribner's Sons, 1982, p. 164.

p. 25 "only 20 to 40 percent" "Lifetime and 12-Month Prevalence of *DSM-III-R* Psychiatric Disorders in the United States: Results from the National Comorbidity Study," Ronald C. Kessler et al., *Archives of General Psychiatry*, Vol. 51, Jan. 1994, p. 8.

p. 25 " 'when you come right down to it' " *The Loony-Bin Trip*, by Kate Millet, NY: Simon & Schuster, 1990, p. 79.

p. 26 "In her disturbing book" *And They Call It Help: The Psychiatric Policing of America's Children*, by Louise Armstrong, Reading, MA: Addison-Wesley Publishing Co., 1993, p. 9, citing Schwartz, Ira M. and Butts, Jeffrey, "Preliminary Findings from a New Research Program on the Psychiatric Hospitalization of Adolescents," research brief, Center for the Study of Youth Policy, University of Michigan, Nov. 7, 1989.

p. 26 " 'It is a long way.' " Armstrong, *And They Call It Help*, pp. 10–11.

p. 26 "Psychiatrist Judith Lewis Herman" *Trauma and Recovery*, by Judith Lewis Herman, M.D., NY: BasicBooks, 1992.

p. 26 "crisis readiness" Ibid, p. 34.

p. 26 "wreak havoc on the brain" *Depression Runs in Families: The Social Context of Risk and Resilience in Children of Depressed Mothers*, by Constance Hammen, NY: Springer-Verlag, 1991, p. 120, citing Gold, P.W., Goodwin, F.K., and Chrousos, G.P. (1988), "Clinical and Biochemical Manifestations of Depression: Relation to the Neurobiology of Stress." *New England Journal of Medicine, 319*, pp. 413–420, and Post, R.M., Rubinow, D.R., and Ballenger, J.C. (1984), "Conditioning, Sensitization, and Kindling: Implications for the Course of Affective Illness." In Post, R. and Ballenger, J. (eds.), *Neurobiology of Mood Disorders* Baltimore, MD: Williams & Wilkins, 1984, pp. 432–466.

p. 26 " 'When and if a breakdown' " Herman, *Trauma and Recovery*, p. 114.

p. 26 " 'complex post-traumatic stress disorder' " Ibid, p. 119.

p. 27 "as Nancy C. Andreasen, M.D., Ph.D" *The Broken Brain: The Biological Revolution in Psychiatry*, by Nancy C. Andreasen, M.D., Ph.D., NY: Harper & Row, 1984, p. 160.

p. 27 "an estimated one in fourteen" "Criminalizing the Seriously Mentally Ill: The Abuse of Jails as Mental Hospitals," by Torrey E. Fuller, Stieber, Joan, Ezekiel, Jonathan, Wolffe, Sidney M., Sharfstein, Joshua,

Noble, John H., Flynn, Laurie M., A Joint Report of the National Alliance for the Mentally Ill and Public Citizen's Health Research Group, 1992, p. iv.

p. 27 "of the homeless, an estimated third" "Mental Illness," by Clark, Charles S., *CQ Researcher*, Aug. 6, 1993, Vol. 3, No. 29, p. 675.

p. 27 "Many disorders have similar symptoms" See "Diagnosis in Schizophrenia and Manic-Depressive Illness: A Reassessment of the Specificity of 'Schizophrenic' Symptoms in the Light of Current Research," by Pope, Harrison G., Jr., M.D., and Lipinski, Joseph F., Jr., M.D., *Archives of General Psychiatry*, Vol. 35, July 1978, pp. 811–828.

p. 28 "As Harrison G. Pope, Jr." Ibid.

p. 28 "These diseases include brain tumor" *Surviving Schizophrenia: A Manual for Families, Consumers and Providers*, Third Edition, by Torrey E. Fuller, M.D., NY: HarperPerennial, 1995, pp. 115–121.

p. 29 "The most important book" *Diagnostic and Statistical Manual of Mental Disorders*, Fourth Edition, Washington, DC: American Psychiatric Association, 1994.

p. 29 " 'a clinically significant' " Ibid, p. xxi.

p. 29 "have been divided into four general categories" Kessler et al., "Lifetime and 12-Month Prevalence of *DSM-III-R* Psychiatric Disorders in the United States: Results from the National Comorbidity Survey," pp. 8–19.

p. 29 "According to Demitri F. Papolos, M.D." *Overcoming Depression*, Revised Edition, by Papolos, Demitri F., M.D., and Papolos, Janice, NY: HarperPerennial, 1992.

p. 30 "15 percent of people" Ibid, p. 118.

p. 30 " 'veritable howling tempest' " *Darkness Visible: A Memoir of Madness*, by Styron, William, NY: Random House, 1990, p. 38.

p. 30 " 'an immense and aching' " Ibid, p. 46.

p. 30 " 'an unfocused dread' " Ibid, p. 45.

p. 30 "this disorder is not a 'dementing illness' " *Touched with Fire: Manic-Depressive Illness and the Artistic Temperament*, by Jamison, Kay Redfield, Ph.D., NY: The Free Press, 1993, p. 96.

p. 30 " '[B]etter to crawl away' " *On Human Nature*, by Wilson, Edward O., Cambridge, MA: Harvard University Press, 1978, p. 68.

p. 30 "surfeit of the 'fight or flight' " Andreasen, *The Broken Brain*, p. 65.

p. 31 "*84 percent* of these 'dually diagnosed' " "The Epidemiology of Co-occurring Mental Disability and Substance Abuse Disorders in the National Comorbidity Survey: Implications for Prevention and Service Utilization," by Kessler, Ronald C., Ph.D., Nelson, Christopher B., M.P.H., McGonagle, Katherine A., Ph.D., et al., *American Journal of Orthopsychiatry*, March 1995, p. 3.

p. 31 "10 to 13 percent of schizophrenics" Torrey, *Surviving Schizophrenia*,

p. 241, citing Caldwell, C.B. and Gottesman, I.I., "Schizophrenics Kill Themselves Too: A Review of Risk Factors for Suicide," *Schizophrenia Bulletin*, 16, 1990, pp. 571–589.

p. 31 "If you've ever seen a homeless" Andreasen, *The Broken Brain*, pp. 51–62.

p. 32 "Then there's schizoaffective disorder" Torrey, *Surviving Schizophrenia*, pp. 90–91.

p. 32 " 'a pervasive pattern of disregard' " American Psychiatric Association, *DSM-IV*, p. 645.

p. 32 "The majority of sociopaths" "Mental Illness: Should the Mentally Ill Get More Health Care Benefits?" by Clark, Charles S., *CQ Researcher*, p. 680, citing professor of psychiatry Linda A. Teplin, who studied Cook County (Chicago) inmates, quoted in *In Health*, Dec./Jan. 1991, p. 12.

p. 32 "Schizophrenia . . . is overdiagnosed" Papolos and Papolos, *Overcoming Depression*, p. 44.

pp. 32–33 "an estimated 56 percent" Kessler at al., "Lifetime and 12-Month Prevalence of *DSM-III-R* Disorders in the United States," p. 17.

p. 33 "an estimated 12.7 percent" Clark, "Mental Illness," p. 678, citing *American Psychologist*, April 1992.

p. 33 "But so are" Ibid.

p. 33 "According to a 1986 survey" *Family Education in Mental Illness*, by Hatfield, Agnes B., NY: The Guilford Press, 1990, p. 124.

p. 34 " 'changes in laws' " Torrey, *Surviving Schizophrenia*, p. 5.

p. 34 "a policy which provides $1 million" Clark, "Mental Illness," p. 676, citing Rosalynn Carter quoted in *The Washington Post*, June 24, 1993.

p. 35 "but not before as many as ten years" "Bipolar Disorder: Self-Portrait of an Illness," Executive Summary, Results of the National DMDA/APA First-Ever Survey of the Impact on People's Lives," presented at the American Psychiatric Association 146th annual meeting, May 24, 1993, p. 6.

p. 35 "the highest success rate" Papolos and Papolos, *Overcoming Depression*, pp. 173–175.

p. 35 "Repeated Transcranial Magnetic Stimulation" Dr. Robert Post of the biological psychiatry branch of the National Institute of Mental Health, describing RTMS at a panel presentation for the National Alliance for the Mentally Ill national convention at NIMH, Bethesda, MD, July 19, 1995.

p. 36 "these therapies can be as effective as drugs" "Psychotherapy Versus Medication for Depression: Challenging the Conventional Wisdom With Data," by Antonuccio, David O., Danton, William G., and DeNelsky, Garland Y., *Professional Psychology: Research and Practice*, 1995, Vol. 26, No. 6, pp. 574–585.

p. 37 "extreme environmental stress can also cause" Hammen, *Depression Runs in Families*, p. 106, citing Gold, P.W., et al. (1988), "Clinical and Biochemical Manifestations of Depression: Relation to the Neurobiology of Stress," *New England Journal of Medicine, 319*, pp. 413–420.

p. 39 "it is possible to carry a gene" "Beyond Diathesis: Toward an Understanding of High-Risk Environments," by Richters, John, and Weintraub, Sheldon, in *Risk and Protective Factors in the Development of Psychopathology*, Rolf, Jon, Masten, Ann S., Cicchetti, Dante, Neuchterlein, Keith H., and Weintraub, Sheldon, eds., Cambridge: Cambridge University Press, 1990, p. 70, citing Spring, B., and Coons, H., 1982, "Stress as a Precursor of Schizophrenia," in R.W.J. Neufeld, ed., *Psychological Stress and Psychopathology*, NY: McGraw-Hill, pp. 13–54.

p. 39 " 'You never know exactly when something begins' " *Brothers and Keepers*, by John Edgar Wideman, NY: Holt, Rinehart and Winston, 1984, p. 19.

CHAPTER 2: WHEN A PARENT IS MENTALLY ILL

p. 44 "According to London psychiatrist Michael Rutter" *Winning Life's Toughest Battles: Roots of Human Resilience*, by Segal, Dr. Julius, p. 7, citing Rutter, M., "Stress, Coping, and Development: Some Issues and Some Questions," in Garmezy, N. and Rutter, M., eds., *Stress, Coping and Development in Children*, NY: McGraw-Hill, 1983.

p. 44 "Schizophrenic mothers, for example" *The Limits of Family Influence: Genes, Experience, and Behavior*, by Rowe, David C., NY: The Guilford Press, 1994, pp. 74–75.

p. 44 "Depressed mothers tend to" *Depression Runs in Families: The Social Context of Risk and Resilience in Children of Depressed Mothers*, by Constance Hammen, NY: Springer-Verlag, 1991, p. 144, citing Weissman, M. M., Paykel, E.S., and Klerman, G. L. (1972), "The Depressed Woman As a Mother," *Social Psychiatry, 7*, pp. 98–108; and Davenport, Y. B., Zhan-Wexler, C., Adland, M.L., and Mayfield, A. (1984) "Early Childrearing Practices in Families with a Manic-Depressive Parent," *Journal of American Psychiatry, 141*, (2), pp. 230–235.

p. 45 " 'psychological death' " *No Voice Is Ever Wholly Lost*, by Kaplan, Louise J., NY: Simon & Schuster, 1995, p. 190.

p. 45 "more excrutiating to a child" Ibid, p. 106, citing Feigelson, Caroline,

1993, "Personality Death, Object Loss, and the Uncanny," *International Journal of Psychoanalysis*, 74: 331–346.

p. 45 "emotional conversation, or 'dialogue' " Ibid, p. 22, citing René Spitz, "The Evolution of Dialogue," *Drives, Affects, Behavior*, Vol. 2, edited by Schur, Max, NY: International Universities Press, 1965.

p. 45 "is 'derailed' " Ibid, p. 25, citing René Spitz, "The Derailment of Dialogue," *Journal of the American Psychoanalytic Association*, 12: 752–755.

p. 45 "more emotionally fluent caregiver" Hammen, *Depression Runs in Families*, p. 35.

p. 46 "Infants as young as two days" *The Interpersonal World of the Infant: A View from Psychoanalysis and Developmental Psychology*, by Stern, Daniel N., NY: BasicBooks, 1985, p. 50, citing Field, T.M., Woodson, R., Greenberg, R., and Cohen, D., 1982, "Discrimination and Imitation of Facial Expressions by Neonates," *Science, 218*, pp. 179–181.

p. 46 "sounds of their mothers' voices." Ibid., citing DeCasper, A.J., and Fifer, W.P., 1980, "Of Human Bonding: Newborns Prefer Their Mothers' Voices," *Science*, 208, pp. 1174–76.

p. 46 " 'perhaps the most exclusively social' " Ibid., Stern, p. 72.

p. 46 "If the mother is mentally ill" Kaplan, *No Voice Is Ever Wholly Lost*, p. 107, citing "Zur Psychologie des Unheimlichen [The Psychology of the Uncanny]" by Ernst Jentsch, *Psychiat. Neurol. Wschr.* 1906, 8: 219–21.

p. 46 " 'uncanny' " Kaplan, *No Voice Is Ever Wholly Lost*, citing Fiegelson (1993).

p. 46 "inviting or aversive activity" Stern, *The Interpersonal World of the Infant*, pp. 194–195.

p. 46 " 'no disappointment or hurt' " Kaplan, *No Voice Is Ever Wholly Lost*, p. 214.

p. 48 "because of divorce or death" "Early Life Precursors of Psychiatric Outcomes in Adulthood in Subjects at Risk for Schizophrenia or Affective Disorders," by L. Erlenmeyer-Kimling, L., Rock, Donald, Squires-Wheeler, Elizabeth et al., *Psychiatry Research*, 39, 1991, p. 249.

p. 48 "chronicity of abandonments" See "Beyond Diathesis: Toward an Understanding of High-Risk Environments," by Richters, John and Weibtraub, Sheldon, in Rolf, J. et al., eds., *Risk and Protective Factors in the Development of Psychopathology*, Cambridge: Cambridge University Press, 1990, pp. 67–91.

p. 48 "in young parents, these illnesses" Ibid, pp. 84–85.

p. 51 "the more 'pathological' the subsequent mourning" *Attachment and Loss, Vol. III: Loss: Sadness and Depression*, by Bowlby, John, NY: BasicBooks, 1980, pp. 216–217.

p. 51 "become extremely *self-involved*" Ibid, p. 68.

p. 51 "Others *displace*" Ibid.

p. 51 "*Denial* can be" Ibid, p. 69.

p. 51 "*defensive exclusion*" Ibid., pp. 45, 70.

p. 51 "*disavow*" Ibid, p. 70.

p. 52 "*splitting*" Ibid, p. 68.

p. 52 "*multiple personalities*" *Diagnosis and Treatment of Multiple Personality Disorder*, by Putnam, Frank W., M.D., NY: The Guilford Press, 1989, pp. 7–9.

p. 52 "three patterns of emotional transaction" Bowlby, *Attachment and Loss*, pp. 203, 206, 211.

p. 53 "the way they *perceive*" "How People Make Their Own Environments: A Theory of Genotype → Environment Effects," by Scarr, Sandra, and McCartney, Kathleen, *Child Development*, 1983, *54*, pp. 424–435.

p. 53 "hard-wired in the genes" "Individual and Maturational Differences in Infant Expressivity," by Tiffany Field, in Eisenberg, N., ed., *Empathy and Related Emotional Responses*, New Directions for Child Development, No. 44, San Francisco, CA: Jossey-Bass, Summer 1989, p. 15.

p. 53 "Even identical twins aren't always identical" Ibid..

p. 53 "Mary K. Rothbart, Ph.D., and her colleagues" "Temperament in the Development of Personality," by Rothbart, Mary K., and Ahadi, Stephen A., *Journal of Abnormal Psychology*, 1993, p. 5; see also "Temperament: A Developmental Framework," by Rothbart, Mary Klevjord, in Strelau, J., and Angleitner, Alois, eds., *Explorations in Temperament: International Perspectives on Theory and Measurement*, NY: Plenum Press, 1991, p. 61.

p. 54 " 'Children's perceptions of events' " *Separate Lives: Why Siblings Are So Different*, by Dunn, Judy, and Plomin, Robert, NY: BasicBooks, 1990, p. 162.

p. 54 "90 percent of the children of" *The Resilient Self: How Survivors of Troubled Families Rise Above Adversity*, by Wolin, Steven J., M.D., and Wolin, Sybil, Ph.D., NY: Villard Books, 1993, p. 68.

p. 54 "share certain abilities . . . sense of humor" Ibid, pp. 5–6.

p. 55 "at a safe distance" Ibid, pp. 79–89.

p. 55 "percentage of turned-on genes" "Nature, Nurture, and Psychopathology: A New Look at an Old Topic," by Rutter, Michael, *Development and Psychopathology*, 3, 1991, p. 132, citing Plomin, R., *Development, Genetics and Psychology*, Hillsdale, NJ: Erlbaum, 1986.

p. 55 "[E]nvironments children receive' " "Distinctive Environments Depend on Genotypes," by Scarr, Sandra, *Behavioral and Brain Sciences* (1987) 10:1, p. 38.

p. 55 " 'niche-picking' " Scarr and McCartney, "How People Make Their Own Environments," p. 427.

p. 56 "mental illness does *not* affect" *Schizophrenia and Manic-Depressive Disorder: The Biological Roots of Mental Illness as Revealed by the Landmark Study of Identical Twins*, by Torrey, E. Fuller, M.D., Bowler, Anne E., M.S., Taylor, Edward H., Ph.D., and Gottesman, Irving I., Ph.D., NY: BasicBooks, 1994, p. 149.

p. 56 "psychopaths tend to be extroverts" *Genes, Culture and Personality: An Empirical Approach* by Eaves, L. J., Eysenck, H. J., and Martin, N. H., NY: Academic Press, 1989, p. 13.

p. 56 " 'goodness of fit' " "Temperament and the Concept of Goodness of Fit," by Chess, Stella and Thomas, Alexander, in Strelau and Angleitner, eds., *Explorations in Temperament: International Perspectives on Theory and Measurement*, pp. 15–40.

p. 56 "An easygoing child" "Children of Depressed Parents: An Integrative Review" by Downey, Geraldine and Coyne, James C., *Psychological Bulletin*, 1990, Vol. 108, No. 1, p. 68.

p. 57 " 'misattunements' " Stern, *The Interpersonal World of the Infant*, p. 149.

p. 57 " '[U]p to a point, quality of experience' " *The Nature of the Child*, by Kagan, Jerome, NY: BasicBooks, 1984, p. 109.

p. 57 "Dr. Constance Hammen and her colleagues" Hammen, *Depression Runs in Families*.

p. 59 "The risk factors were" Ibid., p. 228.

p. 59 " 'A major logical error' " Ibid..

p. 60 "A significant finding" Ibid, p. 231.

CHAPTER 3: WHEN A SIBLING IS MENTALLY ILL

p. 65 "siblings can have as great an influence" "The Separate Worlds of Teenage Siblings: An Introduction to the Study of the Nonshared Environment and Adolescent Development," by Reiss, David, Plomin, Robert, Hetherington, E. M. et al., in Hetherington, E. M., Reiss, D., and Plomin, R., eds., *Separate Social Worlds of Siblings: The Impact of Nonshared Environment on Development*, Hillsdale, NJ: Erlbaum, 1993, p. 80.

p. 65 "As soon as siblings enter the picture" "Enchantment of Siblings: Effects of Birth Order and Trance on Family Myth," by Permuttter, Morton S., in *Siblings in Therapy: Life Span and Clinical Issues*, by Kahn, Michael D., and Lewis, Karen Gail, eds., NY: W.W. Norton & Co., 1988, p. 28.

p. 66 "a 'parental vacuum' " *The Sibling Bond*, by Bank, Stephen P., Ph.D., and Kahn, Michael D., Ph.D., NY: BasicBooks, 1982, p. 123.

p. 66 "In their study of intensely loyal" "Intense Sibling Loyalties" by Bank, Stephen P., and Kahn, Michael D., in Lamb, Michael E. and Sutton-Smith, Brian, eds., *Sibling Relationships: Their Nature and Significance Across the Lifespan*, Hillsdale, NJ: Erlbaum, 1982, p. 264.

p. 66 "teaching the value of justice" Bank and Kahn, *The Sibling Bond*, p. 102.

p. 67 "this scrutiny of self and other" *Separate Lives: Why Siblings Are So Different*, by Dunn, Judy and Plomin, Robert, NY: BasicBooks, 1990, p. 112.

p. 67 " 'social comparison' " "Sibling Deidentification and Split-Parent Identification: A Family Tetrad," by Schacter, Frances Fuchs, in Lamb and Sutton-Smith, eds., *Sibling Relationships*, p. 124, citing Festinger, Leon, "A Theory of Social Comparison Processes," *Human Relations*, 1954, 7, pp. 117–140.

p. 67 " 'Being *singled out*' " Reiss et al., "The Separate Worlds of Teenage Siblings," p. 96.

p. 68 "siblings can confirm for one another" Bank and Kahn, *The Sibling Bond*, p. 115.

p. 68 "Victor G. Cicirelli of Purdue University" "Sibling Influence Across the Lifespan," by Cicirelli, Victor G., in Lamb and Sutton-Smith, eds., *Sibling Relationships*, p. 273, citing Cicirelli, V. G., "A Comparison of College Women's Feelings Toward Their Siblings and Parents," *Journal of Marriage and the Family*, 1980, *42*, pp. 95–102.

p. 68 "opposite sex siblings" Schacter, "Sibling Deidentification and Split-Parent Identification: A Family Tetrad," p. 129.

p. 68 "In a study of 40 pairs" "Siblings in Dyads: Relationships Among Perceptions and Behaviors," by Graham-Bermann, Sandra A., *The Journal of Genetic Psychology*, *152* (2), June 1991, pp. 211–214.

p. 69 "The only siblings who feel 'obliged' " Cicirelli, "Sibling Influence Throughout the Lifespan," p. 274.

p. 69 "Identification: The 'Mortar' of Sibling Ties," Bank and Kahn, *The Sibling Bond*, pp. 84–109.

p. 69 "children are more likely to pay attention" "Sibling Relationships in Middle Childhood," by Bryant, Brenda K., in Lamb and Sutton-Smith, eds., *Sibling Relationships*, p. 109, citing Greenbaum, M., "Joint Sibling Interview As a Diagnostic Procedure," *Journal of Child Psychology and Psychiatry*, 1965, *6*, pp. 1696–1703.

p. 70 " 'Parents sometimes embrace' " "Psychotherapy With Siblings of Disabled Children," by Seligman, Milton, in Kahn and Lewis, eds., *Siblings in Therapy*, NY: W.W. Norton & Company, 1988, p. 180.

p. 71 " 'Even when they were small toddlers' " Rappaport, Judith L., M.D.,

NIMH panel for the national NAMI convention, NIMH, Bethesda, MD, July 19, 1995.

p. 71 "an estimated 25 to 40 percent" *Schizophrenia and Manic-Depressive Disorder: The Biological Roots of Mental Illness as Revealed by the Landmark Study of Identical Twins*, by Torrey, E. Fuller, M.D., Bowler, Ann E., M.S., Taylor, Edward H., Ph.D., Gottesman, Irving I., Ph.D., NY: BasicBooks, 1994, p. 85.

pp. 71–72 "In a survey of people with bipolar" "Bipolar Disorder: Self-Portrait of an Illness," Executive Summary, Results of the National DMDA/APA First-Ever Survey of the Impact on People's Lives," presented at the American Psychiatric Association Annual Meeting, May 24, 1993, p. 6.

p. 72 " 'Children with severe depression' " Rappaport, NIMH panel for NAMI.

p. 72 "people who kill themselves . . . third leading cause of death" "Suicide Facts, 1994," NIMH fact sheet.

p. 72 "One researcher has found" Seligman, "Psychotherapy with Siblings of Disabled Children," p. 168, citing Wasserman, R., "Identifying the Counseling Needs of the Siblings of Mentally Retarded Children," *Personnel and Guidance Journal*, pp. 622–627.

p. 75 "*Close identification*," "*Partial identification*," "*Distant identification*" Bank and Kahn, *The Sibling Bond*, pp. 84–111.

p. 78 "The ill child is treated by parents as younger" "The Influence of the Family Environment on Personality: Accounting for Sibling Differences," by Hoffman, Lois Wladis, *Psychological Bulletin*, 1991, Vol. 110., No. 2, p. 197, citing Hagen, J.W., Myers, J.T., and Allswede, J.S., "The Psychological Impact of Children's Chronic Illness," in D.L. Featherman, D.L., Lerner, R.M., and Perlmutter, M., eds., *Life Span Development and Behavior* (Vol. II), Hillsdale, NJ: Erlbaum 1984.

CHAPTER 4: WHEN A PARTNER IS MENTALLY ILL

p. 87 "People with affective disorders" "The Relationship of Personality to Affective Disorders: A Clinical Review," by Akiskal, Hagop S., M.D., Hirschfeld, Robert H.A., M.D., Yerevanian, Bognos I., M.D., *Archives of General Psychiatry*, Vol. 40, July 1983, citing Weissman, M., and Paykel, E.S., *The Depressed Woman: A Study of Social Relationships*, Chicago: University of Chicago Press, 1974.

p. 87 "People with schizophrenia" "Children of Depressed Parents: An Integrative Review," by Downey, Geraldine and Coyne, James C., *Psycho-

logical Bulletin, 1990, Vol. 108, No. 1, p. 64, citing Goodman, S.H., and Brumley, H.E., 1990, "Schizophrenic and Depressed Mothers: Relationship Deficits in Parenting, *Developmental Psychology, 26,* pp. 31–39.

p. 88 "Many well partners" "Depression and Families," by Anderson, Carol, in *Chronic Disorders and the Family,* Walsh, Froma, Ph.D., and Anderson, Carol, Ph.D., eds., NY: The Haworth Press, 1988, pp. 35–37, citing McCranie, E.J., "Depression, Anxiety and Hostility," *Psychiatric Quarterly,* 45, 1971, pp. 117–133, and Merikangas, K.R., "Divorce and Assortative Mating Among Depressed Patients," *American Journal of Psychiatry,* 141, 1, 1984, pp. 74–76.

p. 88 "people with bipolar illness relapse" "Family Factors and the Course of Bipolar Affective Disorder," Miklowitz, D. J., Goldstein, M. J., Neuchterlein, K. H., et al., *Archives of General Psychiatry,* Vol. 45, March 1988, pp. 228–231.

p. 88 "High relapse rates" Ibid.

p. 89 "According to psychiatry professor Silvano Arieti" "The Family of the Schizophrenic and Its Participation in the Therapeutic Task," by Arieti, Silvano, in *American Handbook of Psychiatry* (2nd edition), Arieti, Silvano and Brodie, H. Keith, eds., NY: BasicBooks, 1981, p. 280.

p. 89 "Some medications blunt" Ibid, p. 281.

p. 89 "The ill person's shaky self-esteem" Ibid.

p. 89 "spouses who are informed" *Working with Families of the Mentally Ill,* by Bernheim, Kayla F., Ph.D., and Lehman, Anthony F., M.D., NY: W.W. Norton & Co., 1985, p. 19.

p. 89 "In a survey of people with bipolar disorder" "Bipolar Disorder: Self-Portrait of an Illness," Executive Summary, Results of the NDMDA/APA Survey, presented at the American Psychiatric Association, May 24, 1993, p. 4.

p. 90 "An estimated 40 percent" Downey and Coyne, "Children of Depressed Parents: An Integrative Review," p. 67, citing Coyne, J.C., Kessler, R.C., Tal, M., et al., 1987, "Living with a Depressed Person: Burden and Psychological Distress," *Journal of Consulting and Clinical Psychology, 55,* pp. 347–352.

p. 90 "when wives are ill" "Culture and Mental Illness: The Family Role," by Lefly, Harriet P., in *Families of the Mentally Ill: Coping and Adaptation,* Hatfield, Agnes B. and Lefly, Harriet P., eds., citing Parsons, T., and Fox, R.C. (1952) "Illness, Therapy, and the Modern Urban American Family," *Journal of Social Issues,* 8, pp. 31–44.

p. 90 "nearly 60 percent" NDMDA/APA, "Bipolar Disorder: Self Portrait of an Illness," p. 6.

p. 90 "nine times more likely" "A Review and Evaluation of Marital and Family Therapies for Affective Disorders," by Prince, Stacey E., and Jacobson, Neil S., *Journal of Marital and Family Therapy*, 1995, Vol. 21, No. 4, p. 382, citing Merikangas (1984), "Divorce and Assortative Mating Among Depressed Patients."

p. 94 "Researchers at the Clarke Institute" pamphlet entitled "Schizophrenia: Courses and Outcome," by Thornton, John F., M.B., Seeman, Mary V., M.D., Plummer, Elizabeth D., R.N., Clarke Institute of Psychiatry, University of Toronto, p. 12.

p. 95 " 'I need to tell you' " "Twelve Aspects of Coping for Persons with Schizophrenia," by Frese, Frederick J., *Innovations and Research*, Vol. 2, No. 3, 1993, p. 43.

p. 95 " 'premorbid functioning' " "Beyond Diathesis: Toward an Understanding of High-Risk Environments," by Richters, John, and Weintraub, Sheldon, in *Risk and Protective Factors in the Development of Psychopathology*, Jon Rolf et al., eds., Cambridge: Cambridge University Press, 1992, p. 85.

p. 96 " 'subjective burden' " Arieti, "The Family of the Schizophrenic and Its Participation in the Therapeutic Task," pp. 281–282.

p. 96 " 'the symptom controllability hypothesis' " Richters and Weintraub, "Beyond Diathesis: Toward an Understanding of High-Risk Environments," p. 88.

p. 97 " 'Of course the mentally ill have responsibilities' " *The Broken Brain: The Biological Revolution in Psychiatry,* by Andreasen, Nancy C., M.D., Ph.D., NY: Harper & Row, 1984, p. 249.

p. 99 "Longitudinal studies" commentary by McFarland, Bentson H., M.D., Ph.D., in *The Family Face of Schizophrenia: Practical Counsel from America's Leading Experts* by Backlar, Patricia, NY: A Jeremy P. Tarcher/Putnam Book, G.P. Putnam's Sons, 1994, p. 58.

CHAPTER 5: ALTERED LIVES:
LIVING WITH MENTAL ILLNESS

p. 115 " 'Months and years go by' " *The Sibling Bond*, by Bank, Stephen P., Ph.D., and Kahn, Michael D., Ph.D., NY: BasicBooks, 1982, p. 235.

p. 115 " 'To some extent' " "The Impact of Mental and Physical Illness on Family Life," by Anthony, E. James, M.D., *American Journal of Psychiatry, 127: 2*, August 1970, p. 141.

p. 115 "Dr. Anthony and his colleagues" Ibid..

p. 117 "An estimated 65 percent" "Families As Caregivers: A Historical Perspective" by Hatfield, Agnes B., in *Families of the Mentally Ill: Coping and Adaptation*, Hatfield, Agnes B. and Lefly, Harriet P., eds., NY:

The Guilford Press, 1987, p. 8, citing Minkoff, K. (1978) "A Map of the Chronic Mental Patient" in Talbott, J.A., ed., *The Chronic Mental Patient*, Washington, DC: American Psychiatric Association, pp. 11–37.

p. 117 "In their study of siblings and parents" "Ethnic Differences in Caregiving Duties and Burdens Among Parents and Siblings of Persons with Severe Mental Illnesses," by Horwitz, Allan V., and Reinhard, Susan C., *Journal of Health and Social Behavior*, Vol. 36, No. 2, June 1995, pp. 138–150.

p. 118 "An estimated 15 to 20 percent" "Short-Term, Subchronic, and Chronic Sequelae of Affective Disorders," by Cassano, Giovanni B., M.D., Ph.D., Maggini, Carlo, M.D., and Akiskal, Hagop S., M.D., in *The Psychiatric Clinics of North America*, Vol. 6, No. 1, March 1983, Philadelphia, PA: W.B. Saunders and Co., Hagop S. Akiskal, M.D., guest ed., p. 55, citing Beck, A.I., *Depression*, NY: Harper & Row, 1967.

p. 118 "People with bipolar disorder" "Graphic Representations of the Life Course of Illness in Patients with Affective Disorder" by Post, Robert M., M.D., Roy-Byrne, Peter P., M.D., and Uhde, Thomas W., M.D., *American Journal of Psychiatry*, 145: 7, July 1988, p. 846.

p. 118 "an estimated one third eventually recover" *Welcome Silence: My Triumph over Schizophrenia*, by North, Carol S., M.D., NY: Simon & Schuster, 1987, p. 315.

p. 118 "by the ten-year, post-onset" *Surviving Schizophrenia: A Manual for Families, Consumers and Providers*, Third Edition, by Torrey, E. Fuller, M.D., NY: HarperPerennial, 1995, p. 131, citing Stephens, J. H., "Long Term Prognosis and Follow-up in Schizophrenia," *Schizophrenia Bulletin*, 4 (1978): pp. 25–47.

p. 118 " 'Some neurons may in a sense' " *The Broken Brain: The Biological Revolution in Psychiatry*, by Andreasen, Nancy C., M.D., Ph.D., NY: Harper & Row, 1984, p. 219.

p. 119 "The following do's and don'ts" "Journey of Hope Family Education Course," compiled and written by Burland, Joyce, Ph.D., Louisiana Alliance for the Mentally Ill, Chapter 8, pp. 22–25, citing a talk by Amenson, Christopher, Ph.D., to the San Luis Obispo chapter of the California Alliance for the Mentally Ill, and The Training and Education Center Network, Mental Health Association of Southern Pennsylvania, Philadephia, PA.

p. 119 " 'expressed emotion' (EE)" Hatfield, "Families as Caregivers: A Historical Perspective," p. 14, citing Vaughn, C.E., and Leff, J.P., 1981, "Patterns of Emotional Response in Relatives of Schizophrenic Patients," *Schizophrenia Bulletin*, 7, pp. 43–44.

p. 119 "One study found that nine months" Lefley, "Culture and Mental Illness: The Family Role," by Lefley, Harriet P., in Hatfield and Lefley, eds., *Families of the Mentally Ill*, p. 36, citing Brown, G.W., Birley, J.L.T., and Wing, J.K., "Influence of Family Life on the Course of Schizophrenic Disorders: A Replication," *British Journal of Psychiatry*, *121*, 1972, pp. 241–258.

p. 120 "A survey of 125 white and non-white families" "Family Coping with the Mentally Ill: An Unanticipated Problem of Deinstitutionalization," by Doll, W., *Hospital and Community Psychiatry*, *27*, 1976, pp. 183–185.

p. 120 "In one study, the strain of coping" Hatfield, "Families as Caregivers: A Historical Perspective," p. 18, citing Holden, D.R., and Lewine, R.R.J., 1982, "How Families Evaluate Mental Health Professionals, Resources, and Effects of Illness," *Schizophrenia Bulletin*, *8*, pp. 626–633.

p. 120 " 'interruption theory' of stress" "Identity Processes and Social Stress," by Burke, Peter J., *American Sociological Review*, December 1991, Vol. 56, pp. 836–837, citing Mandler, George, "Stress and Thought Processes," pp. 88–104, in *Handbook of Stress: Theoretical and Clinical Aspects*, Goldberger, L., and Breznitz, S., eds., NY: The Free Press, 1982.

p. 121 "According to a study of NAMI families" "At Issue: Should the Severely Mentally Ill Be Given Highest Priority in Treatment?" by Flynn, Laurie, *CQ Researcher*, Aug. 6, 1993, Vol. 3, No. 29, p. 689.

p. 122 "One study of family members' perceptions" "New Perspectives on Schizophrenia and Families," by Walsh, Froma, in *Chronic Disorders and the Family*, Walsh, Froma and Anderson, Carol, eds., NY: The Haworth Press, 1988, p. 25, citing Summers, F., and Walsh, F. (1977), "The Nature of the Symbiotic Bond Between Mother and Schizophrenic," *American Journal of Orthopsychiatry*, *47*, pp. 484–494.

p. 122 "Studies demonstrate that fathers" *Women and Their Fathers: The Sexual and Romantic Impact of the First Man in Your Life*, by Secunda, Victoria, NY: Delta, 1993, pp. 1–23.

p. 123 "This reluctance of fathers" *Of Human Bonding: Parent-Child Relations Across the Life Course*, by Rossi, Alice S., Ph.D., and Rossi, Peter H., NY: Aldine de Gruyter, 1990, p. 279.

p. 123 " 'topic avoiders' " Ibid.

p. 123 "In the Rossi study, mothers" Ibid., p. 278.

p. 126 " '[A]ssuming blame in the face of misfortune' " *Winning Life's Toughest Battles: Roots of Human Resilience*, by Segal, Dr. Julius, NY: McGraw-Hill, 1986, p. 79.

p. 127 " 'the law of disruption and reintegration' " *Resilience: Discovering a New Strength at Times of Stress*, by Flach, Frederic, M.D., NY: Fawcett Columbina, 1988, p. 12.

p. 127 " 'I . . . see falling apart' " Ibid., p. 14.

CHAPTER 6: DOUBLE LIVES:
ROLES INSIDE AND OUTSIDE THE FAMILY

p. 132 "children fall into roles that reflect" *The Sibling Bond*, by Bank, Stephen P., Ph.D., and Kahn, Michael D., Ph.D., NY: Basic Books, 1982, p. 238.

p. 132 " 'de-identify' " Ibid., p. 234.

p. 132 "may become enmeshed with that sibling" Ibid., pp. 246, 248.

p. 132 "Most siblings, say the researchers" Ibid., p. 234.

p. 134 "As Drs. Bank and Kahn point out" Ibid., p. 126.

p. 134 "occupied by firstborn girls" Ibid, pp. 113, 137.

p. 134 "younger siblings tend to turn" "Sibling Relationships in Middle Childhood," by Bryant, Brenda K., in *Sibling Relationships: Their Nature and Significance Across the Lifespan*, Lamb, Michael E., and Sutton-Smith, Brian, eds., Hillsdale, NJ: Erlbaum, 1982, p. 113, citing Bryant, B., and Crockenberg, S., "Correlates and Dimensions of Prosocial Behavior: A Study of Female Siblings with Their Mothers," *Child Development*, 1980, *51*, pp. 529–544.

p. 134 "In families with only boys" Bank and Kahn, *The Sibling Bond*, p. 120.

p. 134 "older siblings are likely to" Bryant, "Sibling Relationships in Middle Childhood," p. 110.

p. 135 " 'caregiving' and 'caretaking' " Bank and Kahn, *The Sibling Bond*, p. 114.

p. 135 "less vulnerable to . . . breakdown" Ibid., p. 128.

p. 135 " 'a deprived person' " Ibid.

p. 135 "only children, who may be in danger" Ibid.

p. 135 "In a study of offspring" "Invisible People: Children of Parents with Mental Illness," by Riebschleger, Joanne, A.C.S.W., Freddolino, Paul, Ph.D., Kanage, Barbara, M.S.W., and Miller, Jennifer, B.S.W., Oct. 5, 1993, submitted as part of a plenary presentation, "People with Mental Illness As Parents: A Neglected Research and Policy Issue," 1993 National Conference on State Mental Health Agency Services, Annapolis, MD, p. 9.

p. 135 "This role often goes to middle-borns" For a discussion of birth rank, see Bryant, "Sibling Relationships in Middle Childhood," p. 102, citing Miller, N., and Maruyama, G., "Ordinal Position and Peer Popularity," *Journal of Personality and Social Psychology*, 1976, *33*, pp. 123–131.

p. 136 "They act as 'lightning rods' " Bank and Kahn, *The Sibling Bond*, p. 321.

p. 136 "promotes family solidarity" Ibid, pp. 204–205.

p. 137 "a national study of adolescent" *Separate Lives: Why Siblings Are So Different*, by Dunn, Judy, and Plomin, Robert, p. 81, citing Daniels, D., Dunn, J., Furstenberg, F., and Plomin, R., 1985, "Environmental Differences Within the Family and Adjustment Differences Within Pairs of Adolescent Siblings," *Child Development*, 56: pp. 764–74.

p. 137 "Another study found that" Dunn and Plomin, *Separate Lives*, p. 81, citing Dunn, J., Stocker, C., and Beardsall, L., "Sibling Differences in Self-Esteem," paper presented at biennial meeting of the Society for Research in Child Development, Kansas City, April 1989.

p. 138 "you could easily fall *out* of favor" For a discussion of the effect of parental favoritism, see "The Separate Worlds of Teenage Siblings: An Introduction to the Study of The Nonshared Environment and Adolescent Development," by Reiss, David, Plomin, Robert, Hetherington, E. Mavis, et al., in *Separate Social Worlds of Siblings: The Impact of Non-Shared Environments on Development*, Hetherington, E.M. et al., eds. Hillsdale, NJ: Erlbaum, 1993, p. 96.

p. 139 "Big Five traits" *The Limits of Family Influence: Genes, Experience, and Behavior*, by Rowe, David C., NY: The Guilford Press, 1994, p. 63.

p. 139 "University of Minnesota Twin Study" "Personality Similarity in Twins Reared Apart and Together," by Tellegen, Auke, Lykken, David T., Bouchard, Thomas J., Jr., et al., *Journal of Personality and Social Psychology*, Vol. 54, No. 6, 1988, pp. 1031–1039.

p. 140 "Texas Adoption Project" Rowe, *The Limits of Family Influence*, pp. 108–109, citing Horn, J.M., Loehlin, J.C., and Willerman, L. (1982), "Aspects of the Inheritance of Intellectual Abilities," *Behavior Genetics*, *12*, pp. 479–516.

p. 140 " 'thinking twice' " "Predictive Validity," by Hettema, Joop, in *Personality and Environment: Assessment of Human Adaptation*, Hettema, P.J., ed., Chichester, England: John Wiley & Sons, 1989, p. 191.

p. 140 "Situations that allow you to 'be yourself' " "Towards a Two-Process Conception of Human Adaptation," by Hettema, Joop, in Hettema, ed., *Personality and Environment*, p. 206.

p. 141 *"The more powerful the situation"* Ibid, pp. 209–210.

p. 141 "Strategies tailored to survive" For a discussion of the role of motivation in children's behavior, see Thomas, Alexander and Chess, Stella, in "Roundtable: What Is Temperament? Four Approaches," by Goldsmith, H. Hill, Buss, Arnold H., Plomin, Robert, Rothbart, Mary Klevjord, Thomas, Alexander, and Chess, Stella, et al., *Child Development*, 1987, *58*, p. 508.

p. 141 "responsiveness to the environment" "Personality Development: A Life-Span Perspective," by Lerner, Richard M., in Hetherington, E.M. et al., eds., *Child Development in Life-Span Perspective*, 1988, p. 21.

p. 141 "As situations . . . change" "Child Psychology and Life-Span Development," by Hetherington, E. Mavis, and Baltes, Paul B., in Hetherington et al., eds., *Child Development in Life-Span Development*, pp. 11–12.

p. 142 "Putting some emotional distance" See "Children at High Risk for Psychosis Growing Up Successfully," by Anthony, E. James, in *The Invulnerable Child*, Anthony, E. James, M.D., and Cohler, Bertram J., Ph.D., eds., NY: The Guilford Press, 1987, p. 157.

p. 143 "researchers took a group of college students" *Positive Illusions: Creative Self-Deception and the Healthy Mind*, by Taylor, Shelley E., Ph.D., NY: Basic Books, 1989, p. 31, citing Geer, J.H., Davison, G.C., and Gatchel, R.I., 1970, "Reduction of Stress in Humans Through Nonveridical Perceived Control of Aversive Stimulation," *Journal of Personality and Social Psychology*, *16*, pp. 731–738.

p. 143 " 'the state of affairs' " *Learned Optimism: How to Change Your Mind and Your Life*, by Seligman, Martin E.P., NY: Pocket Books, 1992, p. 5.

p. 144 " 'possible selves' " Taylor, *Positive Illusions*, p. 84, citing "Possible Selves," by Marcus, H. and Nurius, P., *American Psychologist*, *41*, 1986, pp. 954–969.

p. 144 " 'positive illusions' and 'creative self-deceptions' " Taylor, *Positive Illusions: Creative Self-Deception and The Healthy Mind*.

p. 147 "When you can't 'read' or be 'read by'" "Identity Processes and Social Stress," by Burke, Peter J., *American Sociological Review*, 1991, Vol. 56, p. 842.

p. 148 "In a study of children of psychotic mothers" "Growing Up with a Psychotic Mother: A Retrospective Study," by Dunn, Bonnie, M.S.W., *American Journal of Orthopsychiatry*, *62*(2), April 1993, p. 184.

p. 148 "So, interestingly, is an attachment to animals" Bryant, "Sibling Relationships in Middle Childhood," in Lamb and Sutton-Smith, eds., *Sibling Relationships*, p. 116.

CHAPTER 7: WHEN FAMILIES CAN'T COPE

p. 152 "troubles that unite families are 'nonemotional' " *Of Human Bonding: Parent-Child Relations Across the Life Course*, by Rossi, Alice S., and Rossi, Peter H., NY: Aldine de Gruyter, 1990, p. 235.

p. 152 "parents' 'emotional troubles' " Ibid, p. 232.

p. 153 "most researchers must rely instead on" *Mood Disorders: Toward a New Psychobiology* by Whybrow, Peter C., M.D., Akiskal, Hagop S.,

M.D., and McKinney, William T., Jr., M.D., NY: Plenum Press, 1984, p. 185.

p. 155 " 'disengaged' . . . 'hostile' . . . 'multiple patient' . . . 'high denial' . . . 'dependent on the patient's illness' " *Working with Families of the Mentally Ill*, by Bernheim, Kayla F., Ph.D., and Lehman, Anthony F., M.D., NY: W.W. Norton & Co., 1985, pp. 175–183.

p. 156 " '[B]ehavior disorders can develop' " *The Dynamics of Psychological Development*, by Thomas, Alexander, M.D., and Chess, Stella, M.D., NY: Brunner/Mazel, 1980, p. 74.

p. 156 "And Dr. Jerome Kagan and his colleagues" "Temperamental Factors in Human Development," by Kagan, Jerome, and Snidman, Nancy, Aug. 1991, *American Psychologist*, Vol. 46, No. 8, pp. 856, 861–862.

p. 161 "what Dr. Judith Lewis Herman calls 'captivity' " *Trauma and Recovery*, NY: BasicBooks, 1992, p. 74.

p. 161 "American parents tend to have a 'template' " *The Nature of the Child*, by Kagan, Jerome, NY: BasicBooks, 1984, p. 247.

p. 161 " 'malevolent intention' " Ibid.

p. 162 " 'Generally, parents who are secure' " Ibid.

p. 162 "In a study of fourteen adult siblings" "Sibling Perspectives on Schizophrenia and the Family," by Gerace, Laina M., Camilleri, Dorothy, and Ayres, Lioness, *Schizophrenia Bulletin*, Vol. 19, No. 3, 1993, pp. 637–647.

p. 166 " 'Silence breaks the heart' " "A Choice of Weapons," by McGinley, Phyllis, *Times Three*, NY: Viking, 1960, p. 159.

p. 166 "Dr. Julis Segal, an authority" *Winning Life's Toughest Battles: Roots of Human Resilience*, by Segal, Dr. Julius, NY: McGraw-Hill, 1986, pp. 12–13.

p. 166 "American prisoners of war" Ibid.

p. 166 "By one estimate" Ibid., p. 19, citing Caplan, Gerald, "Mastery of Stress: Psychosocial Aspects," *The American Journal of Psychiatry*, 138, April 1981, pp. 413–420.

p. 167 " 'I have only just discovered' " *Searching for Mercy Street: My Journey Back to My Mother, Anne Sexton*, by Sexton, Linda Gray, Boston, MA: Little, Brown and Co., 1994 pp. 21–22.

p. 167 "core sense of self" For a discussion of the dynamic nature of identity, see *The Interpersonal World of the Infant: A View from Psychoanalysis and Developmental Psychology*, by Stern, Daniel N., NY: Basic Books, 1985, p. 200.

p. 169 " 'When neither resistance nor escape' " Herman, *Trauma and Recovery*, p. 34.

p. 169 " '[T]he victim of chronic trauma' " Ibid., p. 86.

p. 169 " 'invisible barriers' " Ibid., p. 74.

p. 169 " *'Hyperarousal'* " Ibid., p. 35.

p. 169 " *'Intrusion'* " Ibid., p. 37.

p. 170 " *'Constriction'* " Ibid., pp. 42–43.

p. 170 "Those who cannot summon" Ibid., p. 44.

p. 170 "a function of 'kindling' " "Conditioning and Sensitization in the Longitudinal Course of Affective Illness," by Post, R.M., Rubinow, D.R., Ballard, J.C., *British Journal of Psychiatry*, 149, pp. 191–201.

p. 171 " 'spontaneous attacks of anxiety' " *Unstable Ideas: Temperament, Cognition, and Self*, by Kagan, Jerome, Cambridge, MA: Harvard University Press, 1989, p. 173.

p. 171 " [F]rightening environmental event[s]' " Ibid, p. 172.

p. 171 "Numerous studies have shown" See "Accumulation of Environmental Risk and Child Mental Health," by Sameroff, Arnold J., and Siefer, Ronald, in *Children of Poverty: Research, Health, and Policy Issues*, Fitzgerald, Hiram E., Lester, Barry M., Zuckerman, Barry, eds., NY & London: Garland Publishers, 1985, p. 245.

CHAPTER 8: WHEN FAMILIES CAN COPE

p. 177 " 'those efforts persons make to master' " "Coping and Adaptation: A Conceptual Framework for Understanding Families," Hatfield, Agnes B., and Lefley, Harriet P., eds., NY: The Guilford Press, 1987, p. 63.

p. 177 "black families tend to extend help" "Ethnic Differences in Caregiving Duties and Burdens Among Parents and Siblings of Persons with Severe Mental Illness," by Horwitz, Allan V. and Reinhard, Susan C., *Journal of Health and Social Behavior*, Vol. 36, No. 2, June 1995.

p. 177 "According to a recent national survey" "Lifetime and 12-Month Prevalence of *DSM-III-R* Psychiatric Disorders in the United States: Results from the National Comorbidity Survey," by Kessler, Ronald C., Ph.D., McGonagle, Katherine A., Ph.D., et al., *Archives of General Psychiatry*, Vol. 51, Jan. 1993, p. 13.

p. 178 "Whereas rich people can afford" "The Family of the Schizophrenic and Its Participation in the Therapeutic Task," by Arieti, Silvano, in *American Handbook of Psychiatry* (2nd Edition), vol. 7, *Advances and New Directions*, Arieti, Silvano and Brodie, H. Keith, eds., NY: Basic-Books, 1981, p. 280.

p. 178 "Studies demonstrate that resilient children" "Psychosocial Resilience and Protective Mechanisms," by Rutter, Michael, in *Risk and Protective Factors in the Development of Psychopathology*, Rolf et al., eds., Cambridge: Cambridge University Press, 1992, p. 182, citing Garmezy,

N. (1985) "Stress Resistant Children: The Search for Protective Factors," in Stevenson, J. (Ed.), *Recent Research in Developmental Psychopathology*, Oxford: Pergamon Press, 1985.

p. 178 "But resilience . . . is a *process*" Rutter, "Psychosocial Resilience and Protective Mechanisms," p. 209.

p. 181 "a new 'homeostasis' " *Resilience: Discovering a New Strength at Times of Stress*, by Flach, Frederic, M.D., NY: Fawcett Columbine, 1988, p. 8.

p. 181 "Survivors of adversity who do best" Ibid., p. 22.

p. 181 "Resilience . . . 'depends on our ability to recognize' " Ibid, p. 29.

p. 183 "Picking up on that signal" "New Perspectives on Schizophrenia and Families," by Walsh, Froma, in *Chronic Disorders and the Family*, Walsh, Froma and Anderson, Carol, eds., NY: The Haworth Press, 1988, p. 21.

p. 186 "The psychoeducation model was developed" Ibid., pp. 20–29, citing "Family Treatment of Adult Schizophrenic Patients: A Psychoeducational Approach," by Anderson, C.M., Hogarty, G., and Reiss, D.J., *Schizophrenia Bulletin*, 6, 1980, pp. 490–505.

p. 191 " 'The well-being of other family members' " *Family Education in Mental Illness*, by Hatfield, Agnes B., NY: The Guilford Press, 1990, p. 64.

CHAPTER 9: RISKS: AM I NEXT?

p. 201 "fashion a 'false self' " For a discussion of the "false-self personality," see *The Maturational Processes and the Facilitating Environment* by Winnicott, D.W., NY: International Universities Press, 1965.

p. 201 "In a classic paper" "Fear of Breadown," by Winnicott, D.W., *The International Review of Psycho-Analysis*, Vol. 1, 1974, pp. 103–107.

p. 202 " 'primitive agonies' " Ibid, p. 104.

p. 202 " 'the death that happened but was not experienced' " Ibid, p. 106.

p. 202 "the first family study of schizophrenia" "The New York High-Risk Project: Psychoses and Cluster A Personality Disorders in Offspring of Schizophrenic Parents at 23 Years of Follow-up," by Erlenmeyer-Kimling, L., Ph.D., Squires-Wheeler, Elizabeth, Ph.D., Adamo, Ulla Hildoff, M.A., et al., *Archives of General Psychiatry*, Vol. 52, Oct. 1995, p. 857, citing Rudin, E., *Zur Vererbung und Neuentstehung der Dementia Praecox*, NY: Springer-Verlag, 1916.

p. 203 "But even that trait is subject." "Nature, Nurture, and Psychopathology: A New Look at an Old Topic," by Rutter, Michael, *Developmental Psychopathology, 3,* 1991, p. 127.

p. 204 "an estimated 0.7 percent" "Lifetime and 12-Month Prevalence of *DSM-III-R* Psychiatric Disorders in the United States: Results from the National Comorbidity Survey," by Kessler, Ronald C., Ph.D., et al., *Archives of General Psychiatry,* Vol. 51, Jan. 1994, p. 10.

p. 204 "According to Irving I. Gottesman" *Surviving Schizophrenia: A Manual for Families, Consumers, and Providers,* 3rd edition, by Torrey, E. Fuller, M.D., NY: HarperPerennial, 1995, p. 314, citing Gottesman, I.I., "Schizophrenia and Genetic Risks," Arlington, VA: NAMI, 1984.

p. 205 "Some scientists" Torrey, *Surviving Schizophrenia,* p. 314.

p. 205 "in the general population, the lifetime risk" Kessler et al., "Lifetime and 12-Month Prevalence of *DSM-III-R* Psychiatric Disorders in the United States," p. 12.

p. 205 "Dr. Nancy C. Andreasen reports" *The Broken Brain: The Biological Revolution in Psychiatry,* by Andreasen, Nancy C., M.D., Ph.D., NY: Harper & Row, 1984, p. 237.

p. 205 "Adoption studies have found" "The Family Psychoeducational Approach: Rationale for a Multigenerational Treatment Modality for the Major Affective Disorders," by Papolos, Demitri F., in *Genetic Studies in Affective Disorders: Overview of Basic Methods, Current Directions, and Critical Research Issues,* Papolos, Demitri F., and Lachman, Herbert M., eds., NY: John Wiley & Sons, p. 120, citing Mendlewicz, J., and Ranier, J. (1977) "Adoption Study Supporting Genetic Transmission in Manic-Depressive Illness," *Nature, 268,* pp. 327–329.

p. 205 "Dr. Constance Hammen and her colleagues" Papolos, "The Family Psychoeducational Approach," p. 121, citing "Longitudinal Study of Diagnoses in Children of Women with Unipolar and Bipolar Affective Disorder," by Hammen, C. et al., *Archives of General Psychiatry, 47,* 1990, pp. 1112–1117.

p. 205 "for bipolar disorder is 'almost incontrovertible' " *Touched with Fire: Manic-Depressive Illness and the Artistic Temperament,* by Jamison, Kay Redfield, NY: The Free Press, 1993, p. 193.

p. 205 "If one identical twin" Ibid, citing Bertelson, A., "A Danish Twin Study of Manic-Depressive Disorders," in Schou, M., and Stramgren, E., eds., *Origin, Prevention and Treatment of Affective Disorders,* London: Academic Press, 1979, pp. 227–239.

p. 205 "an unexpressed gene" *The Limits of Family Influence: Genes, Experience, and Behavior,* by Rowe, David C., NY: The Guilford Press, 1994, p. 76.

p. 206 "As of 1995, the 'lifetime prevalence' rates" Erlenmeyer-Kimling, et al., "The New York High-Risk Project," pp. 857–865.

p. 206 "highest risk period for schizophrenia" *Diagnostic and Statistical Manual of Mental Disorders*, Fourth Edition, Washington, DC: American Psychiatric Association, 1994, p. 281.

p. 209 " 'an individual's chances of succumbing' " "Beyond Diathesis: Toward an Understanding of High-Risk Environments," by Richters, John and Weintraub, Sheldon, in Rolf, Jon, et. al, eds., *Risk and Protective Factors in the Development of Psychopathology*, Cambridge: Cambridge University Press, 1992, p. 77.

p. 209 "Among the characteristics of mentally ill mothers" "Accumulation of Environmental Risk and Child Mental Health," by Sameroff, Arnold J., and Seifer, Ronald, in *Children of Poverty: Research, Health, and Policy Issues*, Fitzgerald, Hiram E., Lester, Barry M., and Zuckerman, Barry, eds., NY & London: Garland Publishing Inc., 1995, pp. 238–239.

p. 210 "in the case of IQ, thirty points" Ibid, pp. 239–257.

p. 210 "the greatest danger to these children" "Early Indicators of Developmental Risk: Rochester Longitudinal Study," by Sameroff, Arnold J., Seifer, Ronald, Zax, Melvin, and Barocas, Ralph, *Schizophrenia Bulletin*, Vol. 13, No. 2, 1987, pp. 383–394.

p. 210 " 'If environments change' " Rutter, "Nurture, Nature, and Psychopathology," p. 128.

p. 210 "In a fascinating 1995 *National Geographic*" "Quiet Miracles of the Brain," by Swerdlow, Joel L., *National Geographic*, June 1995, pp. 2–41.

pp. 211–212 "psychological trauma can cause memories" *Self-Destruction in the Promised Land: A Psychocultural Biology of American Suicide*, by Kushner, Howard I., New Brunswick, NJ: Rutgers University Press, 1989, pp. 167–168, citing Mishkin, Mortimer, and Appenzeller, Tim, "The Anatomy of Memory," *Scientific American*, 256, June 1987, pp. 80–89.

CHAPTER 10: EFFECT ON RELATIONSHIPS

p. 216 "in the general population, 61.2 percent" "Marital Status and Living Arrangements: March 1993," Current Population Reports, P20-482, U.S. Bureau of the Census.

p. 216 "22.6 of all Americans" Ibid.

p. 216 "42 percent of women" "Fertility of American Women: June 1994," P20-482 ER, U.S. Bureau of the Census.

p. 218 "Such wise, well-planned" "Psychosocial Resilience and Protective Mechanisms," by Rutter, Michael, in Rolf, Jon, et al. eds., *Risk and Protective Factors in the Development of Psychopathology*, Cambridge: Cambridge University Press, 1992, p. 195. See also *Separate Lives: Why*

Siblings Are So Different, by Dunn, Judy, and Plomin, Robert, pp. 126–127, citing Quinton, D., and Rutter, M., 1988, *Parenting Breakdown: The Making and Breaking of Intergenerational Links*, Aldershot, England: Gower, 1988.

p. 226 "this is a shockingly common phenomenon" "The Family Psychoeducational Approach: Rationale for a Multigenerational Treatment Modality for the Major Affective Disorders," by Papolos, Demitri. F, in *Genetic Studies in Affective Disorders: Overview of Basic Methods, Current Directions, and Critical Research Issues*, Papolos, Demitri. F, and Lachman, Herbert M., eds., NY: John Wiley & Sons, 1994, p. 128. Unreported survey by Dr. Papolos of eighty psychiatric patients admitted consecutively to an inpatient New York municipal hospital: 90 percent of the patients and 98 percent of the family members did not know the patients' diagnosis.

p. 228 "According to Judith Lewis Herman" *Trauma and Recovery*, by Herman, Judith Lewis, M.D., NY: BasicBooks, 1992, pp. 110–111.

p. 229 " '[T]here is not the slightest suggestion' " *Genes, Culture and Personality: An Empirical Approach*, by Eaves, L.J., Eysenck, H.J., and Martin, N.G., NY: Academic Press, 1989, p. 125.

p. 229 "ethnicity, gender, and social status" "The Social Context of Development," by Sameroff, Arnold J., in *Contemporary Topics in Developmental Psychology*, Eisenberg, N., ed., NY: Wiley, 1987, p. 277.

p. 229 "A groundbreaking study of older identical" "Neuroticism, Extroversion, and Related Traits in Adult Twins Reared Apart and Reared Together," by Pedersen, Nancy L., Plomin, Robert, McClearn, G.E., and Friberg, Lars, *Journal of Personality and Social Psychology*, 1988, Vol. 55, No. 6, pp. 950–957. See also "Explanatory Style Across the Life Span: Achievement and Health," by Seligman, Martin E.P., Kamen, Leslie P., and Nolen-Hoeksema, Susan, in *Child Development in Life-Span Perspective*, Hetherington, E. Mavis et al., eds., Hillsdale, NJ: Erlbaum, 1988, p. 97.

CHAPTER 11: EFFECT ON ACHIEVEMENT

p. 238 " 'We of the craft are all crazy' " *Touched with Fire: Manic-Depressive Illness and the Artistic Temperament*, by Jamison, Kay Redfield, Ph.D., NY: The Free Press, 1993, p. 2.

p. 238 " 'find a home for [their] tears' " *No Voice Is Ever Wholly Lost*, by Kaplan, Louise J., NY: Simon & Schuster, 1995, p. 203.

p. 239 "Having 'lost' and been 'lost by' " Ibid, p. 205.

p. 239 " 'Art would become the solution' " Ibid, p. 205.

p. 239 "In a seminal fifteen-year investigation" "Creativity and Mental Illness: Prevalence Rates in Writers and Their First-Degree Relatives," by Andreasen, Nancy C., M.D., Ph.D., *American Journal of Psychiatry, 144: 10*, October 1987, pp. 1288–1292.

p. 240 "In a follow-up paper" "Bipolar Affective Disorder and Creativity: Implications and Clinical Management," by Andreasen, Nancy C., and Glick, Ira D., *Comprehensive Psychiatry*, Vol. 29, No. 3, May/June 1988, pp. 207–217.

p. 242 "The Soul's Welfare" *The Undiscovered Self*, by Jung, C.G., translated from the German by Hull, R.F.C., Boston, MA: Little, Brown & Co., 1958, p. 112.

p. 243 " 'It may be . . . that two basically different' " "Current Status and Future Directions in Psychotherapy," by Goldfried, Marvin R., and Padower, Wendy, in *Converging Themes in Psychotherapy*, Goldfried, Marvin R., Ph.D., ed., NY: Springer Publishing Co., 1982, p. 28.

p. 245 "a certain 'hostility to peers' " *Unstable Ideas: Temperament, Cognition, and Self* by Kagan, Jerome, Cambridge, MA: Harvard University Press, 1989, p. 208.

p. 245 " 'psychological power' " Ibid..

p. 246 " 'replace established beliefs' " Ibid., p. 209.

p. 246 "A degree of 'uncertainty' " Ibid, p. 211.

p. 249 " 'success in accomplishing tasks' " "Psychosocial Resilience and Protective Mechanisms," by Rutter, Michael, in Rolf, et al., *Risk and Protective Factors in the Development of Psychopathology*, Cambridge: Cambridge University Press, 1992, p. 206.

p. 249 "can compensate for and 'neutralize' " Ibid., p. 197, citing Tennant, C., Bebbington, P., and Hurry, J., "The Short-Term Outcome of Neurotic Disorders in the Community: The Relation of Remission to Clinical Factors to 'Neutralizing' Life Events," *British Journal of Psychiatry, 139*, 1981, pp. 213–220.

p. 251 "In their examination of explosive children" "Moving Against the World: Life-Course Patterns of Explosive Children," by Caspi, Avshalom, Elder, Glen H., Jr., and Bem, Daryl N., 1987, *Developmental Psychology*, Vol. 23, No. 2, p. 308–313.

p. 251 "Family dysfunction . . . can create and *sustain*" Ibid., citing Patterson, G.R., *Coercive Family Processes*, Eugene, OR: Castilla, 1982.

p. 251 " 'cumulative continuity' " Ibid., "Moving Against the World," p. 308.

p. 251 "As for the shy children" "Moving Away from the World: Life-Course Patterns of Shy Children," by Caspi, Avshalom, Elder, Glen H., Jr., and Bem, Daryl, *Developmental Psychology*, 1988, Vol. 24, No. 6, pp. 842–831.

CHAPTER 12: FAMILY TIES: RESPONSIBILITY, OBLIGATION, AND ACCOUNTABILITY

p. 265 "In general, 'kinship obligation' " *Of Human Bonding: Parent-Child Relations Across the Life Course*, by Rossi, Alice S., and Rossi, Peter H., NY: Aldine de Gruyter, 1990, p. 158.

p. 265 " 'secondary kin' " Ibid., p. 213.

p. 265 "tends to favor younger relatives" Ibid., pp. 181–182.

p. 265 "it peaks between the ages of nineteen and thirty" Ibid., p. 223.

p. 265 "the more difficult or hostile" Ibid., pp. 230–231.

p. 265 " 'For them . . . the past colors' " Ibid., p. 359.

p. 266 "Victor G. Cicirelli of Purdue" "Sibling Influence Throughout the Lifespan," by Cicirelli, Victor G., in *Sibling Relationships: Their Nature and Significance Across the Lifespan*, Lamb, Michael E. and Sutton-Smith, Brian, eds., Hillsdale, NJ: Erlbaum, 1982, pp. 267–283.

p. 266 " 'collaborative' . . . 'crisis-oriented' . . . 'detached' " "Sibling Perspectives on Schizophrenia and the Family," by Gerace, Laina M., Camilleri, Dorothy, and Ayers, Lioness, *Schizophrenia Bulletin*, Vol. 19, No. 3, 1993, pp. 641–643.

p. 272 " 'Families should expect that their requirements' " *Family Education in Mental Illness*, by Hatfield, Agnes B., NY: The Guilford Press, 1990, p. 172.

p. 272 " '[S]ome Americans have become too accepting' " *Unstable Ideas: Temperament, Cognition, and Self*, Cambridge, MA: Harvard University Press, 1989, p. 12.

CHAPTER 13: AWAKENINGS: GETTING HELP FOR YOURSELF

p. 280 " 'complex post-traumatic stress disorder' " *Trauma and Recovery*, by Lewis, Judith Herman, M.D., NY: BasicBooks, 1992, p. 119.

p. 280 " 'brief stress' " Ibid.

p. 280 " 'personality deformations' " Ibid., p. 158.

p. 280 "Symptoms of the disorder can be physical . . . or all three" Ibid., pp. 156–157.

p. 280 "*normal reactions to abnormal experience*" Ibid., p. 158.

p. 281 " 'a gradual shift from unpredictable danger' " Ibid., p. 158.

p. 281 "establishment of safety . . . remembrance and mourning . . . reconnection with ordinary life" Ibid., p. 155.

pp. 282–283 " 'Trauma robs the victim of a sense of power' " Ibid., p. 159.

p. 286 " 'Recovery . . . is based upon the empowerment' " Ibid., p. 133.

p. 288 " 'diagnostic doubletalk' " "Families of Chronically Mentally Ill People: Siblings Speak to Social Workers," by Riebschleger, Joanne L., *Health and Social Work*, Vol. 16, No. 2, May 1991, p. 101.

p. 288 " 'The social worker should . . . facilitate' " Ibid.

p. 288 "special knowledge about the sibling relationship" See *The Sibling Bond*, by Bank, Stephen P., M.D., and Kahn, Michael D., Ph.D., NY: BasicBooks, 1982, p. 232.

p. 289 " 'Programs that promote the rapid uncovering' " Herman, *Trauma and Recovery*, p. 184.

p. 291 " 'explanatory style' " *Learned Optimism: How to Change Your Mind and Your Life*, by Seligman, Martin E.P., Ph.D., NY: Pocket Books, 1992, p. 79.

p. 291 " [P]essimistic habits of thinking' " Ibid., p. 8.

p. 291 "we can learn to recognize self-defeating" Ibid., pp. 89–90.

p. 291 "One must also have a sense of 'agency' " "The Will and the Ways: Development and Validation of an Individual-Differences Measure of Hope," by Snyder, C.R., Harris, Cheri, Anderson, John R., et al., *Journal of Personality and Social Psychology*, 1991, Vol. 60, No. 4, pp. 570.

p. 291 "Thus one needs both the 'will' and the 'way' " Ibid., pp. 570–585.

CHAPTER 14: TRANSFORMED LIVES: FINDING MEANING AND HOPE IN THE AFTERMATH

p. 297 "According to NIMH" NIMH handout, based on budget and population figures as of Jan. 1, 1993.

p. 297 "nearly $150 billion per year" Ibid.

p. 298 " 'Our jails have . . . become surrogate mental hospitals' " "Criminalizing the Seriously Mentally Ill: The Abuse of Jails as Mental Hospitals," by Torrey, E. Fuller, et al., A Joint Report of the National Alliance for the Mentally Ill and Public Citizens' Health Research Group, 1992, p. iv.

p. 298 "An estimated 7.2 percent" Ibid.

p. 300 " 'If a person breaks a leg' " *The New York Times*, Jan. 17, 1995, p. A15.

p. 302 " [W]e should remain on guard' " *Unstable Ideas: Temperament, Cognition, and Self*, by Kagan, Jerome, Cambridge, MA: Cambridge University Press, 1989, p. 6.

p. 302 "an estimated 40 to 60 percent" Herman, *Trauma and Recovery*, p.

122, citing, among other studies, Bryer, J. B., Nelson, B. A., Miller, J. B., and Krol, P. A., "Childhood Sexual and Physical Abuse as Factors in Adult Psychiatric Illness," *American Journal of Psychiatry, 44* (1987): 1426–30.

p. 302 " 'For nearly a century the psychoanalysts' " *Girl, Interrupted,* by Kayson, Susanna, NY: Turtle Bay Books, 1993, pp. 142–143.

p. 303 " 'The intense and sometimes comically strident' " *Darkness Visible: A Memoir of Madness,* by Styron, William, NY: Random House, 1990, p. 11.

p. 303 " 'What may be needed to get us to mobilize' " "Toward the Delineation of Therapeutic Change Principles," by Goldfried, Marvin R., in *Converging Themes in Psychotherapy,* Goldfried, Marvin R., Ph.D., ed., NY: Springer Publishing Co., 1982, pp. 387–388.

p. 304 " 'We today need to . . . develop' " Preface, by Franciosi, L. Patt, "America's Children Under Stress: Understanding and Preventing the Consequences," National Mental Health Association, May 23, 1992, p. 1.

p. 304 " 'The findings of greatest social significance' " "Why Are Children in the Same Family So Different from One Another?" by Plomin, Robert, and Daniels, Denise, *Behavioral and Brain Sciences* (1987), *10,* p. 1.

p. 305 "In a University of Michigan study" "Being and Feeling Unique: Statistical Deviance and Psychological Marginality," by Frable, Deborrah S., *Journal of Personality* 61:1, March 1993, pp. 85–110.

p. 306 " '[I]ndividuals in the process of becoming' " Ibid., p. 106.

BIBLIOGRAPHY

BOOKS

American Psychiatric Association, *Diagnostic and Statistical Manual of Mental Disorders*, Fourth Edition, Washington, DC: American Psychiatric Association, 1994.

Andreasen, Nancy C., *The Broken Brain: The Biological Revolution in Psychiatry*, NY: Harper & Row, Publishers, 1984.

Anthony, E. James, M.D., and Bertram J. Cohler, Ph.D., *The Invulnerable Child*, NY: The Guilford Press, 1987.

Antonovsky, Aaron, *Health, Stress, and Coping: New Perspectives on Mental and Physical Well-Being*, San Francisco, CA: Jossey-Bass Publishers, 1979.

Arieti, Silvano, "The Family of the Schizophrenic and Its Participation in the Therapeutic Task," in *American Handbook of Psychiatry*, 2nd edition, Silvano Arieti, editor-in-chief, Vol. 7, *Advances and New Directions*, Silvano Arieti and H. Keith Brodie, editors, NY: BasicBooks, 1981.

Armstrong, Louise, *And They Call It Help: The Psychiatric Policing of America's Children*, Reading, MA: Addison-Wesley Publishing Co., 1993.

Backlar, Patricia, *The Family Face of Schizophrenia: Practical Counsel from America's Leading Experts*, NY: A Jeremy P. Tarcher/Putnam Book, G.P. Putnam's Sons, 1994.

Bank, Stephen P., and Michael D. Kahn, *The Sibling Bond*, NY: BasicBooks, Inc. 1982.

Berger, Diane, and Lisa Berger, *We Heard the Angels of Madness: One Family's Struggle with Manic Depression*, NY: William Morrow and Company, Inc., 1991.

Bernheim, Kayla F., Ph.D., and Anthony F. Lehman, M.D., *Working with Families of the Mentally Ill*, NY: W.W. Norton & Co., 1985.

Bowlby, John, *Attachment and Loss, Vol. III, Loss: Sadness and Depression*, NY: BasicBooks, Inc., 1980.

Carlisle, Wendy, *Siblings of the Mentally Ill*, Saratoga, CA: R&E Publishers, 1984.

Cauwels, Janice M., *Imbroglio: Rising to the Challenges of Borderline Personality Disorder*, NY: W.W. Norton & Company, 1992.

Chesler, Phyllis, *Women and Madness*, NY: A Harvest/HBJ Book, Harcourt Brace Jovanovich, Publishers, 1989.

Chodorow, Nancy J., *The Reproduction of Mothering: Psychoanalysis and the Sociology of Gender*, Berkeley, CA: University of California Press, 1978.

————, *Feminism and Psychoanalytic Theory*, New Haven and London: Yale University Press, 1989.

Coles, Robert, *The Moral Life of Children*, Boston, MA: The Atlantic Monthly Press, 1986.

Daniels, Norman, *Am I My Parents' Keeper? An Essay on Justice Between the Young and the Old*, NY: Oxford University Press, 1988.

Diener, Ed, Ed Sandvik, and William Pavot, "Happiness Is the Frequency, Not the Intensity, of Positive Versus Negative Affect," in *Subjective Well-Being: An Interdisciplinary Perspective*, Fritz Strack, Michael Argyle, and Norbert Schwartz, eds., NY: Pergamon Press, 1991.

Dugan, Timothy F., M.D., and Robert Coles, M.D., eds., *The Child in Our Times: Studies in the Development of Resiliency*, NY: Brunner/Mazel, Publishers, 1989.

Duke, Patty, and Gloria Hochman, *A Brilliant Madness: Living with Manic-Depressive Illness*, NY: Bantam Books, 1992.

Dunn, Judy, and Robert Plomin, *Separate Lives: Why Siblings Are So Different*, NY: BasicBooks, 1990.

Eaves, L. J., H. J. Eysenck, and N. G. Martin, *Genes, Culture and Personality: An Empirical Approach*, London: Academic Press, 1989.

Erlenmeyer-Kimling, L., Barbara Cornblatt, David Friedman, Yvonne Marcuse, Jacques Rutschmann, Samuel Simmens, and Sarala Devi, "Neurological Electrophysiological, and Attentional Deviations in Children at Risk for Schizophrenia," in *Schizophrenia as a Brain Disease*, Henry A. Nasrallah and Fritz A. Henn, eds., NY: Oxford University Press, 1982, pp. 61–98.

Flach, Frederic, M.D., *Resilience: Discovering a New Strength at Times of Stress*, NY: Fawcett Columbine, 1988.

Garbarino, James, Edna Guttman, Janis Wilson Seeley, *The Psychologically Battered Child: Strategies for Identification, Assessment, and Intervention*, San Francisco, CA: Jossey-Bass, Inc., 1986.

Goldfried, Marvin R., Ph.D., ed., *Converging Themes in Psychotherapy*, NY: Springer Publishing Company, 1982.

Hammen, Constance, *Depression Runs in Families: The Social Context of Risk and Resilience in Children of Depressed Mothers*, NY: Springer-Verlag, 1991.

Hatfield, Agnes B., *Family Education in Mental Illness*, NY: The Guilford Press, 1990.

Hatfield, Agnes B., and Harriet P. Lefley, eds., *Families of the Mentally Ill: Coping and Adaptation*, NY: The Guilford Press, 1987.

Herman, Judith Lewis, M.D., *Trauma and Recovery*, NY: BasicBooks, 1992.

Hetherington, E. M., D. Reiss, and R. Plomin, eds., *Separate Social Worlds of Siblings: The Impact of Non-Shared Environment on Development*, Hillsdale, NJ: Lawrence Erlbaum Associates, 1993.

Hetherington, E. Mavis, Richard M. Lerner, and Marion Perlmutter, eds., *Child Development in Life-Span Perspective*, Hillsdale, NJ: Lawrence Erlbaum Associates, 1988.

Hetherington, E. Mavis, "The Role of Individual Differences and Family Relationships in Children's Coping with Divorce and Remarriage," in Cowan, Philip A., and E.M. Hetherington, eds., *Advances in Family Research: Volume II, Family Transitions*, Hillsdale, NJ: Lawrence Erlbaum Associates, 1993, pp. 165–194.

Hettema, P. J., ed., *Personality and Environment: Assessment of Human Adaptation*, Chichester: John Wiley & Sons, 1989.

James, William, *William James on Exceptional States: The 1896 Lowell Lectures*, reconstructed by Eugene Taylor, NY: Charles Scribner's Sons, 1982.

———, *Psychology*, Cleveland and New York: The World Publishing Company, 1948.

Jamison, Kay Redfield, *An Unquiet Mind: A Memoir of Moods and Madness*, NY: Alfred A. Knopf, 1995.

———, *Touched with Fire: Manic-Depressive Illness and the Artistic Temperament*, NY: The Free Press, a division of Macmillan, Inc., 1993.

Johnson, Julie, *Hidden Victims: An Eight-Stage Healing Process for Families and Friends of the Mentally Ill*, NY: Doubleday, 1988.

Jung, C. G., *Psychological Types*, a revision by R.F.C. Hull of the translation by H. G. Baynes, Bollingen Series XX, *The Collected Works of C. G. Jung*, Vol. 6, Sir Herbert Read, Michael Fordham, Gerhard Adler, William McGuire, eds., Princeton, NJ: Princeton University Press, 1971.

———, *The Undiscovered Self* by C. G. Jung, translated from the German by R.F.C. Hull, An Atlantic Monthly Press Book, Boston, MA: Little, Brown and Company, 1958.

———, *The Development of Personality: Papers on Child Psychology, Education, and Related Subjects* by C. G. Jung, Vol. 17 of *The Collected*

Works of C.G. Jung, Bollingen Series XX, translated by R.F.C. Hull, Pantheon Books, 1954.

Kahn, Michael D., and Karen Gail Lewis, eds., *Siblings in Therapy: Life Span and Clinical Issues*, NY: W.W. Norton & Company, 1988.

Kagan, Jerome, *Unstable Ideas: Temperament, Cognition, and Self*, Cambridge, MA: Harvard University Press, 1989.

————, *The Nature of the Child*, NY: BasicBooks, 1984.

Kaplan, Louise J., Ph.D., *No Voice Is Ever Wholly Lost*, NY: Simon & Schuster, 1995.

————, *Oneness and Separateness: From Infant to Individual*, NY: Simon & Schuster/Touchstone, 1978.

————, *Adolescence: The Farewell to Childhood*, NY: Simon & Schuster/Touchstone, 1985.

Kaysen, Susanna, *Girl, Interrupted*, NY: Turtle Bay Books, a division of Random House, 1993.

Kerr, Michael E., M.D., and Murray Bowen, M.D., *Family Evaluation: An Approach Based on Bowen Theory*, NY: W.W. Norton & Company, 1988.

Kestenbaum, Clarice J., "Childhood Psychosis: Psychotherapy," in *Handbook of Treatment of Mental Disorders in Childhood and Adolescents*, Benjamin R. Wolman, ed., NJ: Prentice Hall, Inc., 1978, pp. 354–384.

Kestenbaum, Clarice J., M.D., Ian A. Canino, M.D., and Richard R. Pleak, M.D., "Schizophrenic Disorders of Childhood and Adolescence," in *Child and Adolescent Disorders Annual Review*, Vol. 13, Washington, DC: American Psychiatric Association, 1989, pp. 242–261.

Klagsbrun, Francine, *Mixed Feelings: Love, Hate, Rivalry, and Reconciliation Among Brothers and Sisters*, NY: Bantam Books, 1992.

Konner, Melvin, *Why the Reckless Survive . . . And Other Secrets of Human Nature*, NY: Viking Penguin, 1990.

Kron, Leo, and Clarice J. Kestenbaum, "Children at Risk for Psychotic Disorder in Adult Life," in *Handbook of Clinical Assessment of Children and Adolescents*, C. J. Kestenbaum and D. T. Williams, eds., NY: New York University Press, 1988, pp. 650–672.

Kron, Leo, Paolo Decina, Clarice J. Kestenbaum, Susan Farber, Margaret Gargan, and Ronald Fieve, "The Offspring of Bipolar Manic-Depressives: Clinical Features," in *Adolescent Psychiatry*, Vol. 10, , S. C. Feinstein, J. G. Looney, A. Z. Schwartzbery, et al., eds., Chicago, IL: University of Chicago Press, 1982, pp. 273–291.

Kushner, Howard I., *Self-Destruction in the Promised Land: A Psychocultural Biology of American Suicide*, New Brunswick, NJ: Rutgers University Press, 1989.

Lamb, Michael E., and Brian Sutton-Smith, eds., *Sibling Relationships: Their*

Nature and Significance Across the Lifespan, Hillsdale, NJ: Lawrence Erlbaum Associates, Publishers, 1982.

Meyer, Donald J., M.Ed. and Patricia F. Vadasy, M.P.H., *Sibshops: Workshops for Siblings of Children with Special Needs*, Baltimore, MD: Paul H. Brookes Publishing Co., 1994.

Miller, Alice, *For Your Own Good: Hidden Cruelty in Childrearing and the Roots of Violence*, NY: Farrar Straus & Giroux, 1984.

––––––, *The Drama of the Gifted Child*, NY: BasicBooks, 1981.

Millet, Kate, *The Loony-Bin Trip*, NY: Simon & Schuster, 1990.

Moorman, Margaret, *My Sister's Keeper: Learning to Cope with a Sibling's Mental Illness*, NY: W.W. Norton & Co., 1992.

Myrtek, Michael, *Constitutional Psychophysiology: Research in Review*, Psychophysiology Research Group, Institute of Psychology, University of Freiburg, Freiburg, West Germany, London: Academic Press, Inc., 1984.

North, Carol S., M.D., *Welcome Silence: My Triumph over Schizophrenia*, NY: Simon & Schuster, 1987.

Papolos, Demitri F., M.D., "The Family Psychoeducational Approach: Rationale for a Multigenerational Treatment Modality for the Major Affective Disorders," in *Genetic Studies in Affective Disorders: Overview of Basic Methods, Current Directions, and Critical Research Issues*, Demitri F. Papolos and Herbert M. Lachman, eds., NY: A Wiley-Interscience Publication, John Wiley & Sons, Inc., 1994, pp. 119–145.

Papolos, Demitri, M.D., and Janice Papolos, *Overcoming Depression*, Revised Edition, NY: HarperPerennial, 1992.

Piaget, Jean, *The Mechanisms of Perception*, translated by G. N. Seagrim, NY: BasicBooks, 1969.

Putnam, Frank W., M.D., *Diagnosis and Treatment of Multiple Personality Disorder*, NY: The Guilford Press, 1989.

Rolf, Jon, Ann S. Masten, Dante Cicchetti, Keith H. Neuchterlein, and Sheldon Weintraub, eds., *Risk and Protective Factors in the Development of Psychopathology*, Cambridge: Cambridge University Press, 1992.

Rossi, Alice S. and Peter H. Rossi, *Of Human Bonding: Parent-Child Relations Across the Life Course*, NY: Aldine de Gruyter, 1990.

Rothbart, Mary Klevjord, "Temperament: A Developmental Framework," in A. Angleitner and J. Strelau, eds., *Explorations in Temperament: International Perspectives on Theory and Measurement*, NY: Plenum, 1991, pp. 61–74.

––––––, "Biological Processes in Temperament," in *Temperament in Childhood*, G. A. Kohnstamm, J. E. Bates, and M. K. Rothbart, eds., NY: John Wiley & Sons, 1989, pp. 77–110.

––––––, "Temperament and Development," Ibid., pp. 187–248.

Rowe, David C., *The Limits of Family Influence: Genes, Experience, and Behavior*, NY: The Guilford Press 1994.

Sameroff, Arnold J., "The Social Context of Development," in N. Eisenberg, ed., *Contemporary Topics in Developmental Psychology*, NY: Wylie 1987, pp. 273–291.

Sameroff, Arnold J., and Ronald Seifer, "Accumulation of Environmental Risk and Child Mental Health," in *Children of Poverty: Research, Health, and Policy Issues*, Hiram E. Fitzgerald, Barry M. Lester, Barry Zuckerman, eds., NY and London: Garland Publishing, Inc., 1995.

Sanford, Linda T., *Strong at the Broken Places: Overcoming the Trauma of Childhood Abuse*, NY: Random House, 1990.

Schaeffer, Susan Fromberg, *The Madness of a Seduced Woman*, NY: E.P. Dutton, 1983.

Segal, Dr. Julius, *Winning Life's Toughest Battles: Roots of Human Resilience*, NY: McGraw-Hill Book Company, 1986.

Seligman, Martin E. P., Ph.D., *Learned Optimism: How to Change Your Mind and Your Life*, NY: Pocket Books, 1992.

Sexton, Linda Gray, *Searching for Mercy Street: My Journey Back to My Mother, Ann Sexton*, Boston, MA: Little, Brown and Company, 1994.

Sheehan, Susan, *Is There No Place on Earth for Me?*, Boston, MA: Houghton Mifflin, 1982.

Snyder, C. R., Lori M. Irving, and John R. Anderson, "Hope and Health," in *Handbook of Social and Clinical Psychology: The Health Perspective*, C. R. Synder and D. R. Forsyth, eds., Elmsford, NY: Pergamon Press, 1991.

Sorensen, Aage B., Franz E. Weinert, Lonnie R. Sherrod, eds., *Human Development and the Life Course: Multidisciplinary Perspectives*, Hillsdale, NJ: Lawrence Erlbaum Associates, 1986.

Steinem, Gloria, *Outrageous Acts And Everyday Rebellions*, NY: Holt, Rinehart and Winston, 1983.

Stern, Daniel N., *The Interpersonal World of the Infant: A View from Psychoanalysis and Developmental Psychology*, NY: Basic Books, 1985.

Storr, Anthony, *The Integrity of the Personality*, NY: Ballantine Books, 1992.

———, *Solitude: A Return to the Self*, NY: The Free Press, 1988.

Strelau, Jan, and Alois Angleitner, eds., *Explorations in Temperament: International Perspectives on Theory and Measurement*, London and NY: Plenum Press, 1991.

Strelau, Jan, *Temperament, Personality, Activity*, London: Academic Press, 1983.

Styron, William, *Darkness Visible: A Memoir of Madness*, NY: Random House, 1990.

Sullivan, Harry Stack, M.D., *The Interpersonal Theory of Psychiatry*, NY: W.W. Norton & Company, 1953.

Swados, Elizabeth, *The Four of Us: The Story of a Family*, NY: Farrar, Straus & Giroux, 1991.

Taylor, Shelley E., Ph.D., *Positive Illusions: Creative Self-Deception and the Healthy Mind*, NY: BasicBooks, 1989.

Thomas, Alexander, M.D., and Stella Chess, M.D., *The Dynamics of Psychological Development*, NY: Brunner/Mazel, 1980.

Toman, Walter, *Family Constellation: Its Effects on Personality and Social Behavior*, 3rd edition, NY: Springer Publishing Company, Inc., 1976.

Torrey, E. Fuller, M.D., *Surviving Schizophrenia: A Manual for Families, Consumers and Providers*, 3rd edition, NY: HarperPerennial, 1995.

————, *Nowhere to Go: The Tragic Odyssey of the Homeless Mentally Ill*, NY: Harper & Row, 1988.

Torrey, E. Fuller, M.D., Ann E. Bowler, M.S., Edward H. Taylor, Ph.D., Irving I. Gottesman, Ph.D., *Schizophrenia and Manic-Depressive Disorder: The Biological Roots of Mental Illness as Revealed by the Landmark Study of Identical Twins*, NY: BasicBooks, 1994.

Torrey, E. Fuller, Joan Stieber, Jonathan Ezekiel, Sidney M. Wolfe, Joshua Sharfstein, John H. Noble, Laurie M. Flynn, *Criminalizing the Seriously Mentally Ill: The Abuse of Jails As Mental Hospitals*, A Joint Report of the National Alliance for the Mentally Ill and Public Citizen's Health Research Group, 1992.

Tuma, A. Hussain, and Jack D. Maser, eds., *Anxiety and the Anxiety Disorders*, Hillsdale, NJ: Lawrence Erlbaum Associates, 1985.

Turecki, Stanley, M.D., and Leslie Tonner, *The Difficult Child*, NY: Bantam Books, 1985.

Walsh, Froma, and Carol Anderson, eds., *Chronic Disorders and the Family*, NY: The Haworth Press, 1988.

Walsh, Maryellen, *Schizophrenia: Straight Talk for Families and Friends*, NY: William Morrow & Company, 1985.

Whybrow, Peter C., M.D., Hagop S. Akiskal, M.D., and William T. McKinney, Jr., M.D., *Mood Disorders: Toward a New Psychobiology*, NY: Plenum Press, 1984.

Wideman, John Edgar, *Brothers and Keepers*, NY: Holt, Rinehart and Winston, 1984.

Wilson, Edward O., *On Human Nature*, Cambridge, MA: Harvard University Press, 1978.

Wolin, Steven J., M.D. and Sybil Wolin, Ph.D., *The Resilient Self: How Survivors of Troubled Families Rise Above Adversity*, NY: Villard Books, 1993.

STUDIES AND PAPERS

Akiskal, Hagop S., guest editor, "Recent Advances in the Diagnosis and Treatment of Affective Disorders," *Psychiatric Clinics of North America*, Vol. 6, No. 1, Philadelphia, PA: W.B. Saunders & Co., March 1983.

Akiskal, Hagop S., M.D., John Downs, M.D., Patti Jordan, Pharm.D., et al., "Affective Disorders in Referred Children and Younger Siblings of Manic-Depressives: Mode of Onset and Prospective Course," *Archives of General Psychiatry*, Vol. 42, Oct. 1985, pp. 996–1003.

Akiskal, Hagop S., M.D., Robert M. A. Hirschfeld, M.D., and Boghos I. Yerevanian, M.D., "The Relationship of Personality to Affective Disorders: A Critical Review," *Archives of General Psychiatry*, Vol. 40, July 1983, pp. 801–810.

Andreasen, Nancy C., M.D., Ph.D., "Creativity and Mental Illness: Prevalence Rates in Writers and Their First-Degree Relatives," *American Journal of Psychiatry*, Vol. 144, No. 10, October 1987, pp. 1288–1292.

Andreasen, Nancy C., and Ira D. Glick, "Bipolar Affective Disorder and Creativity: Implications and Clinical Management," *Comprehensive Psychiatry*, Vol. 29, No. 3, May/June 1988, pp. 207–217.

Anthony, E. James, M.D., "The Impact of Mental and Physical Illness on Family Life," *American Journal of Psychiatry*, 127:2, August 1970, pp. 138–146.

Antonuccio, David O., William G. Danton, Garland Y. DeNelsky, "Psychotherapy Versus Medication for Depression: Challenging the Conventional Wisdom with Data," *Professional Psychology: Research and Practice*, 1995, Vol. 26, No. 6, pp. 574–585.

Beard, John H., Rudyard N. Propst, and Thomas J. Malamud, "The Fountain House Model of Psychiatric Rehabilitation," *Psychosocial Rehabilitation Journal*, Vol. V, No. 1: January 1982, pp. 47–53.

Bouchard, Thomas J., Jr., and Matthew McGue, "Genetic and Rearing Environmental Influences on Adult Personality: An Analysis of Adopted Twins Reared Apart," *Journal of Personality*, 58:1, March 1990, pp. 263–292.

Burke, Peter J., "Identity Processes and Social Stress," *American Sociological Review*, Vol. 56, December 1991, pp. 836–849.

Caspi, Avshalom, Glen H. Elder, Jr., and Daryl J. Bem, "Moving Away From the World: Life-Course Patterns of Shy Children," *Developmental Psychology*, Vol. 24, No. 6, 1988, pp. 824–831.

———, "Moving Against the World: Life-Course Patterns of Explosive Children," *Developmental Psychology*, Vol. 23, No. 2, 1987, pp. 308–313.

Clark, Charles S., "Mental Illness: Should the Mentally Ill Get More Health-

Care Benefits?'' *CQ Researcher*, Vol. 3, No. 29, August 6, 1993, pp. 673–699.

Crits-Christoph, Paul, Kathryn Baranackie, Julie S. Kurcias, Aaron T. Beck, et al., "Meta-Analysis of Therapist Effects in Psychotherapy Outcome Studies," *Psychotherapy Research*, I(2), 1991, pp. 81–91.

Dickens, Rex M., and Diane T. Marsh, eds., "Anguished Voices: Siblings and Adult Children of Persons with Psychiatric Disabilities," *1994 Psychiatric Rehabilitation & Community Support Monograph*, Vol. 2, No. 1, Center for Psychiatric Rehabilitation, Sargent College of Allied Health Professions, Boston University.

Doll, William, Ph.D., "Family Coping with the Mentally Ill: An Unanticipated Problem of Deinstitutionalization," *Hospital & Community Psychiatry*, Vol. 27, No. 3, March 1976, pp. 183–185.

Downey, Geraldine, and James C. Coyne, "Children of Depressed Parents: An Integrative Review," *Psychological Bulletin*, Vol. 108, No. 1, 1990, pp. 50–76.

Dunn, Bonnie, M.S.W., "Growing Up with a Psychotic Mother: A Retrospective Study," *American Journal of Orthopsychiatry, 63 (2)*, April 1993, pp. 177–189.

Erlenmeyer-Kimling, E., Ph.D.; Elizabeth Squires-Wheeler, Ph.D.; Ulla Hilldoff Adamo, MA; Anne S. Bassett, MD, et al., "The New York High-Risk Project: Psychoses and Cluster A Personality Disorders in Offspring of Schizophrenic Parents at 23 Years of Follow-up," *Archives of General Psychiatry*, Vol. 52, Oct. 1995, pp. 857–865.

Erlenmeyer-Kimling, L., Barbara A. Cornblatt, Donald Rock, Simone Roberts, Marietta Bell, and Ann West, "The New York High-Risk Project: Anhedonia, Attentional Deviance, and Psychopathology," *Schizophrenia Bulletin* Vol. 19, No. 1, 1993, pp. 141–153.

Erlenmeyer-Kimling, L., Donald Rock, Elizabeth Squires-Wheeler, Simone Roberts, and Jack Yang, "Early Life Precursors of Psychiatric Outcomes in Adulthood in Subjects at Risk for Schizophrenia or Affective Disorders," *Psychiatry Research*, 39, 1991, pp. 239–256.

Feigelson, Carolyn, "Personality Death, Object Loss, and the Uncanny," *International Journal of Psycho-Analysis*, 74, 1993, pp. 331–345.

Field, Tiffany, "Individual and Maturational Differences in Infant Expressivity," in N. Eisenberg, ed., *Empathy and Related Emotional Responses*, New Directions for Child Development, No. 44, San Francisco, CA: Jossey-Bass, Summer 1989, pp. 9–23.

Frable, Deborrah E.S., "Being and Feeling Unique: Statistical Deviance and Psychological Marginality," *Journal of Personality*, 61:1, March 1993, pp. 85–110.

Frese, Frederick J., "Twelve Aspects of Coping for Persons with Schizophrenia," *Innovations and Research*, Vol. 2, No. 3, 1993, pp. 39–46.

Furman, Wyndol, and Duane Buhrmester, "Children's Perceptions of the Qualities of Sibling Relationships," *Child Development*, Vol. 56, No. 1, 1985, pp. 448–461.

Gardner, Russell, Jr., M.D., "Mechanisms in Manic-Depressive Disorder: An Evolutionary Model," *Archives of General Psychiatry*, Vol. 39, Dec. 1982, pp. 1436–1441.

Gerace, Laina M., Dorothy Camilleri, and Lioness Ayers, "Sibling Perspectives on Schizophrenia and the Family," *Schizophrenia Bulletin*, Vol. 19, No. 3, 1993, pp. 637–647.

Goldsmith, H. Hill, Arnold H. Buss, Robert Plomin, Mary Klevjord Rothbart, Alexander Thomas, Stella Chess, Robert A. Hinde, and Robert B. McCall, "Roundtable: What Is Temperament? Four Approaches, *Child Development*, 1987, *58*, pp. 505–529.

Graham-Bermann, Sandra A., "Siblings in Dyads: Relationships Among Perceptions and Behavior," *The Journal of Genetic Psychology*, 152(2), June 1991, pp. 207–216.

Hoffman, Lois Wladis, "The Influence of the Family Environment on Personality: Accounting for Sibling Differences," *Psychological Bulletin*, Vol. 110, No. 2, September 1991, pp. 187–203.

Holmes, Thomas H., and Richard H. Rahe, "The Social Readjustment Rating Scale," *Journal of Psychosomatic Research*, Vol. 11, 1967, pp. 213–218.

Horwitz, Allan V., and Susan C. Reinhard, "Ethnic Differences in Caregiving Duties and Burdens Among Parents and Siblings of Persons with Severe Mental Illness," *Journal of Health and Social Behavior*, Vol, 36, No. 2, June 1995, pp. 138–150.

House, James S., Karl R. Landis, and Debra Umberson, "Social Relationships and Health," *Science*, 29 July 1988, Vol. 241, pp. 540–545.

Kagan, Jerome, and Nancy Snidman, "Temperamental Factors in Human Development," *American Psychologist*, Vol. 46, No. 8, August 1991, pp. 856–862.

Kendall, Philip C., David Kipnis, and Laura Otto-Salaj, "When Clients Don't Progress: Influences on and Explanations for Lack of Therapeutic Progress," *Cognitive Therapy and Research*, Vol. 16, No. 3, 1992, pp. 269–281.

Kessler, Ronald C., Ph.D., Christopher B. Nelson, M.P.H., Katherine A. McGonagle, Ph.D., Mark J. Edlund, B.S., et al., "The Epidemiology of Co-Occurring Mental Disorders and Substance Use Disorders in the National Comorbidity Survey: Implications for Prevention and Service Utilization," in press *American Journal of Orthopsychiatry*, March 1995.

Kessler, Ronald C., Ph.D., Katherine A. McGonagle, Ph.D., Shanyang Zhao,

Ph.D., et al., "Lifetime and 12-Month Prevalence of *DSM-III-R* Psychiatric Disorders in the United States: Results from the National Comorbidity Survey," *Archives of General Psychiatry*, Vol. 51, January 1994, pp. 8–19.

Kestenbaum, C. J., "Children at Risk for Manic-Depressive Illness: Possible Predictors," *American Journal of Psychiatry*, 136, Sept. 9, 1979, pp. 1206–1208.

Kochanska, Grazyna, "Socialization and Temperament in the Development of Guilt and Conscience," *Child Development*, 62, 1991, pp. 1379–1392.

Lively, Sonya, M.A., R.N., Rose Marie Friedrich, M.A., R.N., Kathleen C. Buckwalter, Ph.D., R.N., "Sibling Perception of Schizophrenia: Impact on Relationships, Roles, and Health," *Issues in Mental Health Nursing*, 16, 1995, pp. 225–238.

Marsh, Diane T., Rex M. Dickens, Randi D. Koeske, et al., "Troubled Journey: Siblings and Children of People with Mental Illness," *Innovations & Research*, Vol. 2, No. 2, 1993, pp. 13–23.

McCartney, Kathleen, Monica J. Harris, and Frank Bernieri, "Growing Up and Growing Apart: A Developmental Meta-Analysis of Twin Studies," *Psychological Bulletin*, Vol. 107, No. 2, 1990, pp. 226–237.

Miklowitz, D. J., M. J. Goldstein, K. H. Neuchterlein, K. S. Snyder, and J. Mintz, "Family Factors and the Course of Bipolar Affective Disorder," *Archives of General Psychiatry*, Vol. 45, March 1988, pp. 225–231.

Murphy, James P., and Gary G. Galbraith, "Effects of Personal and Universal Helplessness upon Self-Esteem," *Psychological Reports*, 67, 1990, pp. 963–972.

National Depressive and Manic-Depressive Association/American Psychiatric Association, "Bipolar Disorder: Self Portrait of an Illness," results of the National DMDA/APA survey, presented at the American Psychiatric Association scientific symposium, "The Experience of Bipolar Disorder," May 24, 1993.

National Mental Health Association, Conference Proceedings, "America's Children Under Stress: Understanding and Preventing the Consequences," May 23, 1992, Washington, DC.

Pedersen, Nancy L., Robert Plomin, G. D. McClearn, and Lars Friberg, "Neuroticism, Extraversion, and Related Traits in Adult Twins Reared Apart and Reared Together," *Journal of Personality and Social Psychology*, Vol. 55, No. 6, 1988, pp. 950–957.

Plomin, Robert, Hilary Coon, Gregory Carey, J. C. DeFries, and David W. Fulker, "Parent-Offspring and Sibling Adoption Analyses of Parental Ratings of Temperament in Infancy and Childhood," *Journal of Personality*, 59:4, December 1991, pp. 705–732.

Plomin, Robert, "The Role of Inheritance in Behavior," *Science*, Vol. 248, April 1990, pp. 183–188.

Plomin, Robert, and Danise Daniels, "Why Are Children in the Same Family So Different from One Another?" *Behavioral and Brain Sciences*, *10*, 1987, pp. 1–60.

Plomin, Robert, and John R. Nesselroade, "Behavioral Genetics and Personality Change," *Journal of Personality* 58:1, March 1990, pp. 191–219.

Pope, Harrison G., Jr., M.D., Joseph F. Lipinski, Jr., M.D., "Diagnosis in Schizophrenia and Manic-Depressive Illness: A Reassessment of the Specificity of 'Schizophrenic' Symptoms in the Light of Current Research," *Archives of General Psychiatry*, Vol. 35, July 1978, pp. 811–828.

Posner, Michael I., Mary K. Rothbart, and Catherine Harman, "Cognitive Science Contributions to Culture and Emotion," paper presented to the conference on Culture and Emotion, Eugene, OR, June 1992 (in press, in S. Kitayama and H. Markus, eds. *Culture and Emotion*, Washington, DC: American Psychological Association).

Post, Robert M., M.D., Peter P. Roy-Byrne, M.D., and Thomas W. Uhde, M.D., "Graphic Representation of the Life Course of Illness in Patients with Affective Disorder," *American Journal of Psychiatry*, 145:7, July 1988, pp. 844–848.

Post, Robert M., D. R. Rubinow, and J. C. Ballenger, "Conditioning and Sensitization in the Longitudinal Course of Affective Illness, *British Journal of Psychiatry*, 1986, 149, pp. 191–201.

Prince, Stacey E., and Neil S. Jacobson, "A Review of Marital and Family Therapies for Affective Disorders," *Journal of Marital and Family Therapy*, Vol. 21, No. 4, pp. 377–401.

Riebschleger, Joanne L., "Families of Chronically Mentally Ill People: Siblings Speak to Social Workers," *Health and Social Work*, Vol. 16, No. 2, May 1991, pp. 94–103.

Riebschleger, Joanne, A.C.S.W., Paul Freddolino, Ph.D., Barbara Kanaga, M.S.W., Jennifer Miller, B.S.W., "Invisible People: Children of Parents with Mental Illness," Oct. 5, 1993, submitted in part of a plenary presentation: "People with Mental Illness as Parents: A Neglected Research and Policy Issue," 1993 National Conference on State Mental Health Agency Services Research and Program Evaluation, The National Association of State Mental Health Program Directors Research Institute, Inc., Annapolis, MD. The Children of Parents with Mental Illness Project, Michigan State University.

Rose, Richard J., Markku Koskenvuo, Jaakko Kaprio, Seppo Sarna, and Heimo Langinvainio, "Shared Genes, Shared Experiences, and Similarity of Personality: Data from 14,288 Adult Finnish Co-Twins," *Journal of Personality and Social Psychology*, Vol. 54, No. 1, 1988, pp. 161–171.

Rosenkrantz, Judith, and Thomas L. Morrison, "Psychotherapist Personality Characteristics and the Perception of Self and Patients in the Treatment of

Borderline Personality Disorder,'' *Journal of Clinical Psychology*, Vol. 48, July 1992, pp. 544–553.

Rowe, David C., ''Genetic and Environmental Components of Antisocial Behavior: A Study of 265 Twin Pairs,'' *Criminology*, Vol. 24, No. 3, 1986, pp. 513–531.

Rutter, Michael, ''Nature, Nurture, and Psychopathology: A New Look at an Old Topic,'' *Development and Psychopathology*, 3, 1991, pp. 125–136.

Ryff, Carol D., Young Hyun Lee, Marilyn J. Essex, and Pamela S. Schmutte, ''My Children and Me: Midlife Evaluations of Grown Children and of Self,'' *Psychology and Aging*, 1994, Vol. 9, No. 2, pp. 195–205.

Sameroff, Arnold, Ronald Seifer, Melvin Zax, and Ralph Barocas, ''Early Indicators of Developmental Risk: Rochester Longitudinal Study,'' *Schizophrenia Bulletin*, Vol. 13, No. 3, 1987, pp. 383–394.

Scarr, Sandra, ''Distinctive Environments Depend on Genotypes,'' *Behavioral and Brain Sciences*, 10:1, 1987, pp. 38–39.

Scarr, Sandra, and Kathleen MacCartney, ''How People Make Their Own Environments: A Theory of Genotype → Environment Effects,'' *Child Development*, *54*, 1983, pp. 424–435.

Schmutte, Pamela S., and Carol D. Ryff, ''Success, Social Comparison, and Self-Assessment: Parents' Midlife Evaluations of Sons, Daughters, and Self,'' *Journal of Adult Development*, Vol. 1, No. 2, 1994, pp. 109–126.

Silver, Roxanne L., Cheryl Boon, and Mary H. Stones, ''Searching for Meaning in Misfortune: Making Sense of Incest,'' *Journal of Social Issues*, Vol., 39, No. 2, 1983, pp. 81–102.

Snyder, C. Rick, ''Hope for the Journey,'' paper presented at the Conference on Cognitive Coping in Families Who Have a Member with a Developmental Disability: Theoretical and Empirical Implications and Directions, June 5–6, 1991, the University of Kansas.

Snyder, R.C., ''The Negotiation of Self Realities: Psychic Shootout at the 'I'm Okay' Corral,'' paper presented at the annual meeting of the American Association for the Advancement of Science, Washington, DC, Feb. 16, 1991.

Snyder, C.R., Chari Harris, John R. Anderson, Sharon A. Holleran, et al., ''The Will and the Ways: Development and Validation of an Individual-Differences Measure of Hope,'' *Journal of Personality and Social Psychology*, Vol. 60, No. 4, 1991, pp. 570–585.

Snyder, R.C., and Raymond L. Higgins, ''Excuses: Their Effective Role in the Negotiation of Reality,'' *Psychological Bulletin*, Vol. 104, No. 1, 1988, pp. 23–35.

Squires-Wheeler, Elizabeth, Andrew E. Skodol, Ulla Hilldoff Adamo, Anne S. Bassett, George R. Gerwirtz, William G. Honer, Barbara A. Cornblatt, Simone A. Roberts, and L. Erlenmeyer-Kimling, ''Personality Features and

Disorder in the Subjects in the New York High-Risk Project," *Journal of Psychiatric Research*, Vol. 27, No. 4, 1993, pp. 379–393.

Stocker, Clare, Judy Dunn, and Robert Plomin, "Sibling Relationships: Links with Child Temperament, Maternal Behavior, and Family Structure," *Child Development*, 60, 1989, pp. 715–727.

Tellegen, Auke, David T. Lykken, Thomas J. Bouchard, Jr., Kimerly J. Wilcox, Nancy L. Segal, and Stephen Rich, "Personality Similarity in Twins Reared Apart and Together," *Journal of Personality and Social Psychology*, Vol. 54, No. 6., 1988, pp. 1031–1039.

Weissman, Myrna M., Ph.D., Elliot S. Gershon, M.D., Kenneth K. Kidd, Ph.D., et al., "Psychiatric Disorders in the Relatives of Probands with Affective Disorders: The Yale University-National Institute of Mental Health Collaborative Study," *Archives of General Psychiatry*, Vol. 41, Jan 1984, pp. 13–21.

Winnicott, D. W., "Fear of Breakdown," *International Review of Psycho-Analysis*, Vol. 1, 1974, pp. 103–107.

Wortman, Camille B., and Roxanne Cohen Silver, "The Myths of Coping with Loss," *Journal of Consulting and Clinical Psychology*, Vol. 57, No. 3, 1989, pp. 349–357.

INDEX